Sweet
chum KAY
2

118390

12.70

dianesonau

12.70

CURRICULUM

CURRICULUM
A Comprehensive Introduction

SECOND EDITION

John D. McNeil
University of California, Los Angeles

LITTLE, BROWN AND COMPANY
Boston   Toronto

Library of Congress Catalog Card No. 80-81742

ISBN 0-316-563080

9 8 7 6 5 4 3 2 1

MV

Published simultaneously in Canada
by Little, Brown & Company (Canada) Limited

Printed in the United States of America

PREFACE

This book is designed as a tool for the study of curriculum. Although it is intended primarily for use in college and university courses in curriculum, it may also prove of interest to practicing teachers, administrators, parents, and concerned citizens who wish to engage in serious reflections about curriculum. You are not expected to bring to the reading of this book a knowledge of the technical skills of curriculum making. The necessary curriculum concepts and methods are explained and developed as required.

This book has several distinctive features. First, it is comprehensive. Several perspectives of curriculum are treated in some detail. There is no intention of narrowing the field of curriculum into a study of history, sociology, or any other specialization. Instead, the outlooks from many disciplines are sought for their contributions to our understanding of curriculum. This approach is in contrast to one in which individual scholars find the curriculum problem too complex and, therefore, try to redefine the problem narrowly in terms of their own disciplines.

This is a textbook. It is not a monograph dealing in depth with a small corner of the curriculum field. As a result of reading this book, responding to the discussion questions at the end of chapters, engaging in the suggested supplementary reading, and questioning and adapting the ideas and prescriptions presented in the chapters, students of curriculum will, I hope, be drawn into new paths for determining why certain procedures are superior to others. Although I have striven for a realistic conception of what constitutes curriculum and have suggested ways to do better the things that are now necessary, much has been intentionally left to the reader and instructor. Everything that ought to be known about curriculum has not been put into the book. My aim was brevity and simplicity of treatment.

Second, the presentation is not rhetorical. Curriculum, like so many other fields has had in recent years its share of books advocating particular conceptions and solutions. My purpose is not to argue the case for one favored view but rather to demonstrate that many factors need to be considered in any reflective analysis of curriculum questions. I seek to evoke a quality of response and make a deliberate attempt to show the strengths and weaknesses of competing points of view. Indeed, each of the views presented here has merit; it would be a loss for any one of them to dominate. A straightforward analysis of the different positions is given in every chapter. Usually, my options are reserved for a concluding comment.

A third feature of the book is its topical division and order. Each topic has been given a certain degree of independence, as a separable unit of study appropriate for one or more class sessions. The order in which the topics are sequenced may be changed. For example, it is possible to start with the last part of the book, preferring to have the curriculum field defined before embarking on its study.

Part One examines four prevailing conceptions of curriculum. The assumptions underlying these different orientations with respect to curriculum purpose, method, organization, and evaluation provide a framework for relating many subsequent topics. Part Two features the technical skills of curriculum development. The chapters in this part help answer questions like "*what* should be taught," "*how* should it be taught," and "*how* can curriculum be most effectively implemented and evaluated." By examining various curriculum models, techniques, and practices we can gain important insights into the task of making curriculum decisions. Part Three continues with the art and techniques of curriculum making by focusing on the important problems of how best to organize the curriculum. The first chapter in this part is a treatment of what has been thought about curriculum organization and the second chapter is a description and appraisal of the different organizational structures found in practice.

Part Four examines curriculum in a wider context and from a broader point of view. One chapter deals with curriculum issues of importance to citizens and curriculum specialists alike. Another reveals trends in the teaching of the subject fields, and a third presents a realistic picture of curriculum policy making.

Finally, Part Five is devoted to curriculum as a field of study. The first chapter in this part brings a historical perspective to the field, showing our inherited ways of thinking about curriculum problems. A second chapter describes the work of the growing edge of scholars in the field of curriculum. The content of this chapter indicates the kind of studies which will explain the nature of "the curriculum" and stakes out the domains and processes of curriculum inquiry.

This revised edition contains the same major principles and concepts that were featured in the first edition. The content, however, is different in that it includes fresh descriptions of recent developments in curriculum practice, particularly those found in areas of rapid change—evaluation, current issues, directions in the subject fields, politics, and research. I believe that the text has been strengthened by adding material that clarifies basic ideas. A differentiation between curriculum as social reconstruction and curriculum as social adaptation, for example, has been made.

Appreciation for helpful suggestions in revising the text is gratefully expressed to the following reviewers: John W. McLure, University of Iowa, C. M. Clarke, North Texas State University, and Daniel Purdom, University of South Florida.

The guidance of Mylan Jaixen, Senior Editor, has been invaluable.

CONTENTS

V / Research
Theory and
Curriculum   317

14 / A Historical Perspective of Curriculum-Making   319

15 / The Promise of Theory and Research in Curriculum   346

CURRICULUM

1 / CONCEPTIONS OF CURRICULUM

Prevailing conceptions of the curriculum can be classified usefully into four major categories: humanistic, social reconstructionist, technological, and academic. Holders of these viewpoints have different ideas about what should be taught, to whom, when, and how.

Those with a humanistic orientation hold that the curriculum should provide personally satisfying experiences for each individual. The new humanists are self-actualizers, who see curriculum as a liberating process that can meet the need for growth and personal integrity. They should not be confused with those persons in a liberal arts tradition who regard the humanities as separate disciplines, such as art, music, or literature, and who attempt to deal with the human being through cultural creations.

Social reconstructionists stress societal needs over individual interests. They place primary responsibility on the curriculum to effect social reform and to derive a better future for society. They emphasize the development of social values and how to use these in the process of critical thought.

The technologists view curriculum making as a technological process for producing whatever ends policymakers demand. They conceive of themselves as agents of their clients. Accordingly, they hold themselves accountable by producing evidence indicating that their curriculum attains intended objectives. This is not a neutral orientation, because holders have a commitment to method that in turn has consequences for curriculum goals and content.

Persons with an academic orientation see curriculum as the vehicle by which learners are introduced to subject matter disciplines and organized fields of study. They view the organized content of subjects as a curriculum to be pursued rather than as a source of information for dealing with social problems. Those within this orientation assume that an academic curriculum is the best way to develop the mind—that mastery of the kind of knowledge commonly found in such a curriculum contributes to rational thinking.

In the chapters that follow, each of these four orientations will be described, analyzed, and evaluated. Readers who understand these four positions will be better able to formulate their own ideas regarding purpose, content, method, organization, and evaluation of curriculum. The question of the extent to which one or more of the conceptions applies at a given time and place is a unifying thread in the organization of this text.

1 / THE HUMANISTIC CURRICULUM

The humanistic curriculum is viewed by some educators as a gimmick or turn-on; others see it as a way to cut vandalism and to boost learning of school subjects. Still others see it as the basis for a truly liberating education. In order to bring the reader a little closer to the truth, in this chapter we will describe different versions of the humanistic curriculum, define common humanistic assumptions, and outline the strengths and weaknesses of this important curriculum conception.

A new humanism is promoting new ways of knowing, and is shifting curriculum emphasis from subject matter to the individual. Its goals include increased personal awareness and decreased self-estrangement. Specifically, humanism is a matter of "consulting oneself and supposedly enjoying one's capacity to discriminate and sense the world."[1]

Participants in this movement include confluent educators, new mystics, and the radical critics. Confluent educators want to engender in students a total life orientation. They believe that one should respond as a whole person (including feelings, ideas, and emotions) to the totality of all things. The new mystics are those persons who have found value in sensitivity training, meditation, yoga, or other transpersonal techniques. Radical critics are naturalists who prefer to see education as a joyful unfolding of native capacities rather than as an artificial attempt to shape the individual to the institutions of a dehumanized society.

This chapter is about these different versions of the humanistic curriculum, and about their practices and assumptions. Questions will be raised about both the conceptualizations and the consequences of this curriculum orientation.

[1]Carl Weinberg, "Social Science and Humanistic Education," NSSE Yearbook, *Uses of the Sociology of Education* (Chicago: The National Society for the Study of Education, 1974).

CHARACTERISTICS OF THE HUMANISTIC CURRICULUM

Purpose

Humanists believe that the function of the curriculum is to provide each learner with intrinsically rewarding experiences that contribute to personal liberation and development. To them the goals of education are dynamic personal processes related to the ideals of personal growth, integrity, and autonomy. Healthier attitudes toward self, peers, and learning are among their expectations. The ideal of the self-actualizing person is at the heart of the humanistic curriculum. Such a person is not only coolly cognitive, but also developed in aesthetic and moral ways; one who does good works and has good character.

The humanist views actualization growth as a basic need. Each learner has a self that is not necessarily conscious. It has to be uncovered, built up, taught. Humanists believe that the self is hidden or distorted; the curriculum must help people find out what they are already rather than shape themselves into a form that someone else has designated in advance.

Third force psychology is closely associated with the humanistic curriculum. This psychology is largely a reaction to the inadequacies of behaviorism and Freudian psychologies. The third force psychologist believes that behaviorism is mechanistic and that behaviorists view the learner as a detached intellect, ignoring affective responses and higher order aspects of the personality such as altruism. Freudian psychologies, he or she says, are overly cynical about the motives of persons and emphasize humankind's pathological and unconscious emotional forces.

The late Abraham Maslow was a key figure in the development of third force psychology. Maslow viewed self-actualization as having several dimensions. He saw it as a life achievement, a momentary state, and the normal process of growth when a person's deficiency motives are satisfied and his or her defenses are not mobilized by threat. Maslow assumed that humankind is a specieshood; that is, the human being has a biological essence. Hence, the search for self means attending to impulses from within that hint at a species, that indicate that an individual is a part of nature as well as being unique.[2]

It follows that the humanistic curriculum must encourage self-

[2]Abraham H. Maslow, "Some Educational Implications of the Humanistic Psychology," *Harvard Educational Review* 38 (Fall 1968): 685–96.

actualization, whereby learners are permitted to express, act out, experiment, make mistakes, be seen, get feedback, and discover what they are. Maslow thought we learn more about ourselves through examining responses to *peak experiences*, those experiences which give rise to love, hate, anxiety, depression, and joy. For him, the peak experiences of awe, mystery, and wonder are both the end and the beginning of learning. Thus a humanistic curriculum should value and try to provide for such experiences as moments in which cognitive and personal growth take place simultaneously.

Method

A humanistic curriculum demands the context of an emotional relationship between pupils and teacher. The teacher must provide warmth and emotional nurturance while functioning as a resource center. He or she should present materials imaginatively and create challenging situations to facilitate learning. Humanistic teachers motivate their children through mutual trust. They encourage their students to identify with them by teaching out of their own interests and commitments while believing that each child can learn. Those who assume a leadership role in affective approaches to learning must get in touch with themselves; they must know what the teaching role does to the teacher as well as the pupil. Manipulative methods are out. The humanistic teacher does not coerce students to do anything they do not want to do. Although there are numerous techniques associated with humanistic teaching, not all who use these techniques are humanistic teachers. Only those who are committed to the ideas underlying the techniques are viewed as being truly humanistic. Also, teachers who are kind and humane to students are not necessarily implementing a humanistic curriculum. Kindness may be associated with any curriculum conception.

BASIS FOR SELECTING LEARNING ACTIVITIES

Today there are many resources offering exercises, techniques, and activities for advancing the humanistic goal of psychological growth. Some attention has been given to ways of selecting from among these resources. One way is to identify a concern, theme, or topic, such as self-judgment, and then to select procedures or exercises that appear to be related. Another way is to leave the content open-ended and let themes and issues arise spontaneously from the procedures and instructional materials. When you are following the latter mode, your procedures and materials should match the learners' willingness to risk self-disclosure and to give up privacy. Such willingness in turn can be increased when the procedures used create trust in the group situation, helping individuals view comfortably their own discomfort. Weinstein has also stressed the importance of activities and materials that will teach one to use the language necessary for communicating in self-awareness programs (for example, "Right now I am aware that . . .").[3]

Self-awareness is believed best attained when one can observe one's feelings. As one reveals one's feelings, one should indicate where and how intensive they are. Examination of one's thoughts— sentences, dialogs, and fantasies—also increases self-awareness. So, too, does study of personal actions, movements, and physical expressions.

The humanistic curriculum must allow learners to seek typical personal patterns in their own responses to a series of activities. Acceptance rather than denial of one's patterns is necessary in order to change an aspect of self. The learner often is taught to distinguish ends from means. An activity might reveal that a silent member wants to be viewed as intelligent. This is an end or a goal. If this silence is seen as reflecting intimidation rather than intelligence, the silent one may be willing to learn a different means. The teacher should at this point provide activities that permit learners to experience alternative ways of behaving, and to evaluate these behaviors in terms of their consequences, such as the reactions of friends. These consequences, in turn, will enable them to decide whether to keep all, some, or none of the new responses.

Organization

One great strength of the humanistic curriculum appears to lie in its stress on *integration.* Integration refers to the learner's increased unity of behavior. In helping the learners integrate emotions, thoughts, and actions, humanists achieve an effective organization. Their schemes do much to resolve the weakness of the traditional curriculum in which the logical organization of subject matter, as defined by an expert, fails to connect with the learners' psychological organization. Also, the humanist's concerns for wholeness and

[3]Gerald Weinstein, "The Trumpet: A Guide to Humanistic Psychological Curriculum," *Theory Into Practice* 13, no. 5 (December 1974): 335-42.

process vs product ✱

Gestalt lead to a curriculum that encourages comprehensiveness of experience, counteracting the prevailing practice of fragmenting curricula.

It is true, however, that the humanistic curriculum may lack sequence; students may have little chance to broaden and deepen a single aspect of their development. Glatthorn has written of schools that offer a smorgasbord curriculum of minicourses such as The Jazz Age, Sexism in America, Writing Poetry, and Zen and the Western World, in which the total program seems to be just an unsystematic collection of bits and pieces.[4] Models of promise for sequence are, however, being tried within courses. For example, some teachers are dealing with preconceptual feelings before symbolization; others try to foster wonder before awe; still others try to stimulate conflict before confrontation. Many think that persistence should be emphasized before resolution, and a few believe that action should take place before understanding.

A particularly interesting scheme for sequencing dimensions of affective experiences has been proposed by Shiplett.[5] His strategy is to order experiences as follows: (1) Arrange activities to reveal concerns and blockages. Use experiences that help children deal with fears and unmet needs like security and self-worth. (2) Introduce materials with orientation loadings; that is, arrange for activities that treat topics, subject matter, and learning tasks likely to help make pupils want to learn. Activities that stimulate curiosity are cases in point. (3) Present engagement loadings (activities that are rewarding in themselves). The student should be given pleasurable experiences, such as movement and novelty. (4) Finally, introduce accomplishment loadings (the effects of completing a learning task). Mastery and satisfaction are accomplishment loadings.

Evaluation

Unlike the conventional curriculum, which is objectively defined and in which there are criteria for achievement, the humanistic curriculum stresses growth regardless of how it is measured or defined. The humanist as evaluator emphasizes process rather than product. It is true, however, that humanistic evaluators of a confluent cur-

[4]Allan A. Glatthorn, _Alternatives in Education Schools and Programs_ (New York: Dodd, Mead, 1975).

[5]John M. Shiplett, "Beyond Vibration Teaching: Research and Curriculum Development in Confluent Education," in _The Live Classroom_, George I. Brown, ed. (New York: The Viking Press, 1975), pp. 121–31.

riculum ask whether activities are helping students become more open, independent human beings. They view activities as something worthwhile in themselves and as a possible contribution to future values. They value classrooms that provide experiences to help pupils become more aware of themselves and others and develop their own unique potential. Humanistic teachers pride themselves on knowing how students are responding to activities, either by observing pupils' actions or by seeking feedback after the exercises provided.

When asked to judge the effectiveness of their curriculum, humanists usually rely on subjective assessments by teachers and pupils. They also may present outcome measures, such as students' paintings or poems, or talk of marked improvement in pupil behavior and attitudes. Carl Rogers has summarized many of the research results showing positive association between affective classrooms and growth, interest, cognition, productivity, self-confidence, and trust.

A CONFLUENT CURRICULUM

Rationale for Confluence

The essence of confluent education is the integration of the affective domain (emotions, attitudes, values) with the cognitive domain (intellectual knowledge and abilities). It is an *add on* curriculum, whereby emotional dimensions are added to conventional subject matter so that there is personal meaning to what is learned. Confluentists do not downplay objective knowledge, such as scientific information, in favor of subjective or intuitive (that is, direct and immediate) knowledge. The confluent teacher of English, for example, links affective exercises to paragraphing, organization, and argumentative and other discursive forms of writing. By beginning with the student's personal, imaginative, and emotional responses and working out from these, the confluentist helps learners both to acquire language skills and to discover themselves.

Confluentists do not believe that the curriculum should teach people what to feel or what attitudes to have. Their goal is to provide persons with more alternatives to choose from in terms of their own lives, to take responsibility for seeing these choices, and to realize that they, the learners, can make these choices.

Essential Features of Confluent Education

In order to clarify the concept of confluent education, Shapiro and others analyzed examples and nonexamples of confluence.[6] Their conclusion was that a confluent curriculum is composed of the following elements:

1. *Participation.* There is consent, power sharing, negotiation, and joint responsibility by coparticipants. It is essentially nonauthoritarian and not unilateral.
2. *Integration.* There is interaction, interpenetration, and integration of thinking, feelings, and action.
3. *Relevance.* The subject matter is closely related to the basic needs and lives of the participants and is significant to them, both emotionally and intellectually.
4. *Self.* The self is a legitimate object of learning.
5. *Goal.* The social goal or purpose is to develop the whole person within a human society.

Gestalt psychology is one of the bases for confluent education. The theory behind it is existentially based; that is, it focuses on what is happening here and now rather than interpreting one's history. With respect to the curriculum decision of what to teach, the Gestalt theory forces one to question goals, and to ask about our heritage questions such as: "Is it of value to us now? Does it make us more alive or does it deaden us and tend to keep us hung up on the outmoded ways of thinking and perceiving? Does it tie us to old models and goals for ourselves and for our children that are passé and counterproductive to a society without NDD [neurosis, disease, discontent]?"[7]

The principles of Gestalt therapy are openness, uniqueness, awareness, and personal responsibility, which are seen as essential to human growth and potential. Programs consistent with the theory do not emphasize competition but personal responsibility; there are no right or wrong answers. Awareness training affirms that healthy growth can occur only as individuals become aware of their existence and the possibility of personal change.

According to Gestalt psychology, discrete elements of a whole are

[6]Stewart B. Shapiro, "Developing Models by 'Unpacking' Confluent Education," Occasional Paper No. 12, *Development and Research in Confluent Education* (Santa Barbara, Calif.: University of California, 1972).

[7]Geri Metz, "Gestalt and the Transformation," *The Live Classroom* (New York: The Viking Press, 1975), p. 21.

meaningful only in relation to that whole. Hence, in confluent education, there is effort to unify. The confluent teacher helps learners
attend to both how they learn and how they keep themselves from
learning. The confluent curriculum combines subjective and objective knowledge and is aimed at merging the suffering of doubt and
frustration with the warmth of sharing. Content is related to the
student's life, selected on the basis that it will meet both individual
and social concerns.

Activities within the Confluent Curriculum

Confluent curricula have been prepared by teachers at various
levels and in most fields. These curricula include goals, topics,
materials, and texts. Confluent lessons, units, and course plans have
been field-tested and are available for inspection.[8]
Many of these materials utilize *affective* techniques. George I.
Brown has given us forty examples of such affective techniques
including the following:

Dyads. As an exercise in communication, two persons—new
friends—sit back to back and try to communicate without
turning their heads. Next, they face each other and, without
talking, try to communicate using only their eyes. They are to
be aware of how they feel as they do this (for example, silly,
embarrassed, fascinated). Later, they close their eyes and
communicate by only touching hands; and, finally, they
communicate any way they wish. The pedagogy of the exercise
is to move participants from little risk to more. That is, one
reveals more of oneself and becomes more vulnerable as the
exercise proceeds.

Fantasy body trip. Members of a group are asked to close their
eyes, be comfortable, move into themselves. Each person is
asked to concentrate on different body parts, beginning with
toes, moving up to the head, experiencing any sensations felt
emanating from the separate parts of the body. After this
fantasy trip, the group shares their experiences. Applications of
this technique can be used in discussing such concepts as: "What
is a person?" and "Who am I?" Students begin with rediscovering
their bodies. Other exercises concentrate on other parts of the
person or on the experience of being a whole.

[8]George I. Brown, "Examples of Lessons, Units, and Course Outlines in Confluent
Education," *The Live Classroom* (New York: The Viking Press, 1975), pp. 231–95.

Rituals. A large group is divided into five subgroups and asked to create a new ritual. A ritual is a custom or practice—such as shaking hands. The idea is to invent a ritual either to replace one we already have or for a situation in which no ritual at present exists.

Gestalt "I have available" technique. This technique is to help persons get in touch with their own strengths or resources. Each participant completes a sentence beginning with "I have available . . ." and gains understanding by being aware of whatever emerges. For example, one may recognize personal characteristics, other persons, and things that can help one cope with the world.[9]

Unlike most curriculum writers, the authors of confluent materials do not expect others to carry out the suggested plans exactly or even roughly as described. Whoever uses the confluent materials should make them a part of their own philosophy; they should not just regard them as techniques. Ideally, teachers will create new approaches for their own classrooms. To design such approaches, however, one should understand and accept the rationale underlying the techniques.

Weinstein and Fantini offer a "curriculum of concern," a type of confluent education in which students' basic concerns determine what concepts will be studied. They carefully distinguish between *interests* and *concerns*. Interests are the activities that attract students. Concerns are the basic physiological and sociological drives of students. Weinstein and Fantini point out, for instance, that a student might be *interested* in cars because he is *concerned* with feelings of powerlessness. Thus, the proper approach to the student is not necessarily *Hot Rod* magazine but some way to help the student explore an understanding of power.[10]

Borton has written about his experience in applying the Weinstein-Fantini model. His curriculum featured the major concerns of self-identity and allowed students to explore the disparity between what they thought about in school, what they were concerned about in their own lives, and the way they acted. The curriculum outline consisted of a series of questions designed to lead the student to a personal sense of identity and finally to an examination of the actions that would express that sense of self. Some of the questions

[9]George I. Brown, *Human Teaching for Human Learning* (New York: The Viking Press, 1971).
[10]Gerald Weinstein and Mario Fantini, *Toward Humanistic Education: A Curriculum of Affect* (New York: Praeger Press, 1970).

were: What is human about human? Who am I? How can we find actions to express our thoughts and feelings?

There were plentiful activities, such as a trip to the zoo to contrast humans with animals, improvisational drama to imitate the movement of animals, discussion of animal metaphors in the characterization of humans, and debates about animal and human groups. Note that such activities can be undertaken without changing the orientation of the school in any major way. They can supplement the commitment to teaching reading, writing, and arithmetic.

Students draw generalizations as a result of these experiences. For example, students conclude that self-consciousness allows persons to use their own diversity for their own benefit. Thus, "If a consciousness of self is one of the major differences between animals and humans, then one of the most effective ways to make persons more human, or more humane, would be to help them explore the significance of their own diversity."[11]

MYSTICISM IN THE HUMANISTIC CURRICULUM

Although humanistic psychologists typically emphasize the affective and cognitive domains, some humanists are interested in treating higher domains of consciousness as well. One of the means they use is _transcendental meditation_ (TM). Transcendental meditation is concerned with altering states of consciousness, voluntary control of inner states, and growth beyond the ego. It has been tried as an adjunct to the high school curriculum partly because it is seen as a way to diminish drug abuse among students. Essentially, TM is a simple technique for turning attention "inwards toward the subtler levels of thought until mind transcends the experience of the subtlest state of thought and arrives at the source of thought. This expands the conscious mind and at the same time brings it in contact with the creative intelligence that gives rise to every thought."[12] TM has been used to reach some very commonplace curriculum goals, such as reduction of social tension, increased learning ability, and improved athletic performance. It has also inspired

[11]Terry Borton, "What Turns Kids On?" _Saturday Review_ 50, no. 15 (April 15, 1967): 72–74.
[12]Maharishi Mahesh Yogi, _Maharishi Mahesh Yogi on the Bhagavad-Gita, A New Translation and Commentary_ (Baltimore: Penguin Books, 1969), p. 470.

more novel goals, such as growth in consciousness and in other ways of knowing.

One caution concerning transcendental meditation, practiced in such courses as The Science of Creative Intelligence, is that its inclusion in the curriculum may violate legal precedents opposed to sectarian indoctrination. The "science" of TM is held by some to be essentially a religious philosophy. Its presupposition about the source of life and energy reflect monistic Hinduism with pantheistic consciousness.[13]

Other transpersonal techniques with curricular implications are biofeedback for controlling brain waves, deep hypnosis, yoga, and the use of dreams. In English, for example, dreams may be used as a basis for creative writing, because they contain the emotional impact of messages from the unconscious. Physical education, too, may use aspects of the transpersonal. Thomas Roberts, for instance, has argued that "If physical education means learning to control one's body for optimum health and physical fitness, then biofeedback and yoga have important places in the curriculum of the future."[14]

Roberts also cites the use of such techniques as relaxation and imaginary journeys: "A high school shop teacher relaxed his class and had them imagine they were electrons being pulled and pushed by the fields around induction coils." He reports: "The next day the students read the chapter in the book dealing with induction coils. The students said they had no trouble visualizing the forces described in the book, and the quality of their lab work seemed to bear this out. It is quite evident to me that the trip was worth taking since I have taught this subject matter before but not with this much success.[15]

Philip Phenix has a very different understanding of transcendence (that is, the experience of going beyond any given state or realization of being). He has taken theological views regarding transcendence and indicated their implications for curriculum.[16] Phenix, in his curriculum of transcendence, states that the curriculum should be multidisciplinary; it should offer opportunities for understanding

[13]David Haddon, "Transcendental Meditation—A K-8 Curriculum Option," *Learning* 4, no. 1 (August-September 1975): 71–72.
[14]Thomas Roberts, "Transpersonal: The New Educational Psychology," *Phi Delta Kappan* 56, no. 3 (November 1974): 191.
[15]Ibid., p. 192.
[16]Philip H. Phenix, "Transcendence and the Curriculum," *Teachers College Record* 73 (December 1971): 271–83.

diverse areas of human experience, like the theoretical, the practical, and the affective. In this regard, Phenix meets the humanistic criterion of wholeness. He would allow for specialized inquiry but would show how particular specialized modes of investigation relate to other specializations. He believes, however, that no set of disciplines provides the full and final disclosure of the nature of things. The curriculum should encourage hope because the impulse to learn presupposes confidence in the possibility of improving one's existence. The curriculum should also foster creativity in all persons and encourage awareness. Awareness for Phenix is centered less on one's self than on others; it means having sympathetic predispositions toward all other persons, cultures, groups, and objects of nature. A curriculum of transcendence should foster a constructive spirit of criticism toward existing practices and encourage wonder (the attraction of unrealized potentialities), awe (a sense that life and the cosmos are of capital importance), and reverence (recognition that one's existence is a surprising and renewable gift, not a secure possession and an autonomous achievement).

THE RADICAL CRITICS

A litany of despair was heard in the early 1970s. Paul Goodman, Edgar Friedenberg, John Holt, Herbert Kohl, Jonathan Kozol, and Charles Silberman were among those who wrote of the evils in our schools, denouncing the "mutilation of spontaneity, of joy in learning, of pleasure in creating, of sense of self."

Some of these writers were social critics who said that both school and society were sick and that symptoms of this sickness included competitiveness, vulgarity, racism, manipulation, and inhumanity. Others, including Kohl, Holt, and Kozol, presented their case studies of what it takes to make school interesting and exciting. They introduced content that was emotionally arousing. Children responded to the content because it was intrinsically motivating and not because it related to some extrinsic reinforcement such as grades, praise, or bribes. Most radical critics admonished the teacher to encounter the children without preconceptions and to explore with them what is meaningful to learn.

SELF-DIRECTED LEARNING AS A RESPONSE TO "BACK TO THE BASICS"

The late 1970s saw a mighty wind of change away from the radical critics' call for a child-centered curriculum based on interests, natural mode of growth, and impulses for action. Instead pressures were strong in the direction of a competency-based curriculum emphasizing the teaching of the basic skills of reading, writing, and arithmetic. Humanists responded by saying that the basics should include a sense of ability, clarity of values, positive self-concept, capacity for innovation, and openness—characteristics of the self-directed learner. There is more to be learned than facts or skills. The development of joy in learning, and the motivation to move on to new, stimulating tasks are essential.[17]

An illustration of a curriculum emphasizing self-directed learning is found in Evan Keislar's model for a curriculum with development as the goal.[18] He draws ideas from many sources: *achievement motivation*—those persons who are motivated by hope of success have an incentive to learn when the task is not too easy and when there is an expectation of success. Persons motivated by fear of failure, on the other hand, tend to select tasks that are either so easy that they cannot fail or so difficult that no embarrassment results from failure; *attributive theory*—achievement-oriented individuals are more likely to see themselves as a cause of their success; *children's interests*—when children find schoolwork distasteful and yet are driven to engage in more of the distasteful work, they acquire learned helplessness, having no interests related to learning. Freedom to undertake a self-directed study of something that concerns the learner seems to be an important condition for developing channeled effort; *locus of control*—locus of control is the extent to which persons feel they have control over their own destiny. Internal control is highly correlated with achievement.

The goal of Keislar's program is to optimize future growth and development of the individual. In this curriculum, learners are helped to mediate key decisions by reflecting on their level of cognitive development and by testing proposed courses of action. Resources

[17]Annie L. Butler, "Humanistic Early Childhood Education—A Challenge Now and in the Future," *Viewpoints in Teaching and Learning* 55, no. 3 (Summer 1979): 83–89.

[18]Evan R. Keislar, "A Developmental Model for a Curriculum in the Primary Grades," unpublished paper, UCLA Graduate School of Education, Los Angeles, 1979.

are provided for helping learners deal with uncertainty, take risks, try out ideas, and profit from mistakes. The teacher's role is to make sure that the child is facing situations that arouse questions and lead to exploration. Challenges are matched to the child's pattern of development. Although the teacher is available to help the child find needed resources, the teacher does not do so when information is readily available. Since growth proceeds through encounters with conflict and tension, this curriculum promotes an optimum level of uncertainty.

As with other humanistic curricula, the self-directed curriculum aims at development in several areas: _cognitive_—children respond to the requirements of problematic situations, not simply to external directions. By anticipating consequences, they learn to make wise choices about goals. Allowances are made for those children whose thinking is tied to immediate perceptions and for those who are ready for inferential thought; _affective_—children learn to deal, at an emotional level, with such uncertainties as social conflicts, evaluation, and challenge. They learn to view failure as a learning experience; _social_—assertiveness training, role training, experimenting with competitive and cooperative groups are among the activities provided; _moral_—moral development is fostered through consideration of moral conflicts that arise from the social activities of the class and the wider community; _ego development_—the development of self-respect and self-confidence occur through a social climate in which a person's world does not depend on ability or level of maturity. Each individual has an opportunity to attain success for their is no scarcity of rewards.

In many ways this new self-directed curriculum is consistent with what John Dewey suggested more than sixty years ago—a curriculum that poses problems rooted within the present experience and capacity of learners, problems that arouse an active quest for information and invite the production of new ideas.[19]

CRITICISMS OF THE HUMANISTIC CURRICULUM

Four charges are commonly made against the humanists. First, critics charge that they prize their methods, techniques, and experiences instead of appraising them in terms of conse-

[19]John Dewey, _Experience and Education_ (New York: The Macmillan Company, 1939.)

quences for learners. They have been lax in seeing the long-term effects of their programs. If they appraised their system more thoroughly, they might see that their use of emotionally charged practices such as sensitivity training and encounter groups can be psychologically or emotionally harmful to some students. The self-awareness they develop is not always a happy experience and a change in self concept is not always a change for the better. Thus, a second criticism is that the humanist is not concerned enough about the experience of the individual. Although humanists say that their curriculum is individualistic, most students in a given classroom are actually exposed to the same stimuli. For example, everyone may have taken part in group fantasy, hostility games, and awareness exercises. A third criticism, however, is that humanists give undue emphasis to the individual. Critics would like the humanists to be more responsive to the needs of society. Fourth, critics charge that the theory on which the humanistic curriculum rests is deficient. Instead of advancing unity and relatedness among the psychological principles from different schools of psychology, the theory increases the disconnectedness of scientific knowledge. Third force psychology does not bring together the knowledge from behaviorism and psychiatry.

Rebuttals to these attacks take varied forms. A leading humanistic educator, George I. Brown, admits that the techniques of confluent education can be misused. He argues, however, that teachers who would abuse their teaching role would do so whether or not they had affective techniques available. Further, he says, because his approach helps teachers learn more about themselves, those teachers will show less negative and destructive behavior. Brown would not require all students to participate in the confluent curriculum because he believes that it may not be appropriate for everyone at the curriculum's present stage of development. Also, he views this curriculum as promising a fuller realization of the democratic potential of our society. The goals of the confluent curriculum call for students who can perceive clearly, act rationally, make choices, and take responsibility both for their private lives and for their social milieu.

The "in house" differences of opinion regarding underlying theories of humanistic education testify to its intellectual vitality. Efforts to revise Maslow's writings are one indicator that the field is not moribund. Chiefly, these efforts center on difficulties with the concept of self-actualization on which the whole personal growth movement is based. Humanists must realize that vice and evil are as much in the range of human potentiality as virtue: "Our biology cannot be made to carry our ethics as Maslow would have it."[20] Self-actualization may not always lead to the common good.

Shortly before his death, Maslow addressed the question of whether we can teach for personal growth and at the same time educate for competence in academic and professional fields.[21] He thought it was possible, although difficult, to integrate the two goals. (The teacher's role of judge and evaluator in competency education is often seen as incompatible with the humanistic role.) In his last article, Maslow expressed uneasiness over some practices in curricula of the ESALEN type, especially trends toward antiintellectualism and against science, discipline, and hard work. He worried about those who considered competence and training irrelevant. For Maslow, the learning of content need not be the denial of growth. He thought subject matter could be taught humanistically with a view to enlightenment of the person. Study in a subject field could be a help toward seeing the world as it really is, a training in sensory awareness, and a defense against despair. To believe that real knowledge is possible and that weak, foolish human beings can band together and move verified knowledge forward toward some small measure of certainty encourages us to count upon ourselves and our own powers.

Among the friendly critics of the humanistic orientation to curriculum is Mario Fantini. He is not putting down the movement nor the people in it. He is trying to improve its direction. Fantini is concerned because too many Americans view the humanistic approach negatively. Although most people would support increased human potential and self-worth as ends, they are suspicious of what appear to be bizarre procedures, such as exploring the senses through touch/feel exercises and emphasizing the sensual, if not the sexual. "In certain professional circles, the movement is facetiously referred to as the 'touchy-feely' crowd, connoting an almost illegitimate status among the established disciplines."[22]

Fantini is concerned that there may be too much focus on self. He believes a humanist should be someone who is more involved with the welfare of others—one should not seek personal pleasure while other people slave. If thought, feeling, and action cannot be

[20]Norman Leer, "On Self Actualization: A Transambivalent Examination of Focal Theme in Maslow's Psychology," *Journal of Humanistic Psychology* 12, no. 2 (Spring 1973): 17–33.

[21]Abraham H. Maslow, "Humanistic Education," *Journal of Humanistic Psychology* 19, no. 3 (Summer 1979): 13–27.

[22]Mario Fantini, "Humanizing the Humanism Movement," *Phi Delta Kappan* 15, no. 1106 (February 1974): 400–402.

separated, then neither should feelings be separated from injustices faced by one's fellows. Rather than *feel* the "joy" of a "blind walk," Fantini would *feel* the "repulsion" and "outrage" of hungry children.

Critics of the humanistic curriculum reveal their own bias as social reconstructionists by demanding that the humanists do more than strengthen present courses. New teaching techniques that involve learners and their feelings in each lesson are not enough. They want to broaden the boundaries of the humanistic curriculum from self-study to political socialization; they would like it to include such problem areas as medicine, parental care, and journalism. Fantini and others want the humanistic curriculum to deal with the exposure of injustice so that the learner's growth would be less restricted. To do so, however, would require a blending of humanism and social reconstructionism.

CONCLUDING COMMENTS

Listening, self-evaluation, and goal setting are important curriculum goal areas. Learners have a real concern about the meaning of life, and curriculum developers should be responsive to their concern. Putting feelings and facts together makes good sense. We should also help our learners acquire different ways of knowing. Still, few persons would want the humanistic curriculum to be the dominant one or to be mandated for all. We have much to learn before we can develop curricula that will help pupils become self-directed.

A fruitful approach for improving humanistic curriculum has begun. It includes focusing on physical and emotional needs of learners and attempting to design learning experiences that will help fulfill these needs. The idea that curriculum objectives and activities should match emotional issues that are salient at particular stages of life is powerful. Curriculum developers should ask how particular subject matters might be structured in order to help pupils with developmental crises. Adolescents, for example, who are experiencing an identity crisis and trying to reconcile conflicts with parents might study history to illuminate the origins of parents' attitudes and beliefs, considering the present validity of these origins. They might use the sciences to reinterpret long-standing conflicts with parents. Or they might use the arts to express their feelings and their natural desire to be themselves.

QUESTIONS

1. Should schools use transcendental meditation or spiritual resources as aids in providing discipline and motivation in the lives of students? If so, how can they best be undertaken without violating legal precedents?
2. What is your response to those who believe that schools should not undertake the complicated responsibilities that an affective curriculum implies and that such programs may infringe on the civil liberties of children?
3. What are the expected outcomes from a classroom in which there is a "sad corner"; an "I feel" wheel with an arrow that points to "fine," "tired," "sick," scared"; and a plant that is ignored while another is loved so that pupils can see that "if we love it more, it will grow more, like people"?
4. Designers of affective programs have been accused of equating good mental health with conformity. They are said to promote compliance with school routines and instruction and to discourage the kind of initiative, individuality, and creativity that demands changes, "rocks the boat," and gives learners control over the institution in which they must exist. To what extent are these accusations true?
5. Reflect on some of the ideas, concerns, and activities associated with humanistic education. Which of these are likely to prove fruitful and have a continuing effect on what is taught in the curriculum? You may wish to consider (a) psychological assumptions about the importance of freedom, learning by doing, and risk taking, (b) views of knowledge such as those stressing subjective or intuitive knowledge and the idea that the subject that matters is one in which the learner finds self-fulfillment, and (c) instructional techniques (value clarification, cooperative games, use of dreams, etc.).

SELECTED REFERENCES

Borton, Terry. *Reach, Touch and Teach: Student Concerns and Process Education.* New York: McGraw-Hill, 1970.

Brown, George Isaac, ed. *The Live Classroom.* New York: The Viking Press, 1975.

Della-Dora, Delmo and Blanchard, Lois Jerry, eds. *Moving Toward Self-Directed Learning: Highlights of Relevant Research and Promising Practices.* Alexandria, Va.: ASCD, 1979.

Gross, Beatrice and Ronald, eds. *Radical School Reform.* New York: Simon and Schuster, 1971.

Moustakas, Clark and Perry, Cereta. *Learning to be Free.* Englewood Cliffs, N.J.: Prentice-Hall, 1973.

Newberg, Norman A. *Affective Education in Philadelphia*. Bloomington, Ind.: Phi Delta Kappa Ed. Foundation, 1977.

Ringness, Thomas A. *The Affective Domain in Education*. Boston: Little Brown, 1975.

Rubin, Louis J. *Facts and Feelings in the Classroom*. New York: The Viking Press, 1974.

Sprinthall, Norman A. and Mosher, Ralph L. *Value Development as the Aim of Education*. Schenectady, N.Y.: Character Research Press, 1978.

2 / THE SOCIAL RECONSTRUCTIONIST CURRICULUM

Social reconstructionists are opposed to the notion that the curriculum should help students adjust or fit into the existing society. Instead, they conceive of curriculum as a vehicle for fostering critical discontent and for equipping learners with the skills needed for conceiving new goals and effecting social change.

After reading this chapter, one should understand the common premises of social reconstruction, as well as the divisions within the movement as voiced by the radical consensus and the futurologists.

Aspects of reconstructionism appeared in American curriculum thought in the 1920s and 1930s. Harold Rugg was concerned about the values for which the school should work. He tried to awaken his peers to the "lag" between the curriculum, a "lazy giant," and the culture, a torrential current of change with its resultant staggering social cleavage. Rugg's textbooks, teaching, and professional leadership had one overriding quality: the spirit of social criticism. He wanted learners to use newly emerging concepts from the social sciences and aesthetics to identify and solve current social issues. Rugg and his colleague, George Counts, author of *Dare the School Build a New Social Order?*, were among the frontier thinkers who called on the school to begin creating a "new" and "more equitable" society.[1]

In the early 1950s, Theodore Brameld outlined the distinctive features of social reconstructionism.[2] First was a commitment to building a new culture. Brameld was infused with the conviction that we are in the midst of a revolutionary period, from which will emerge nothing less than control by the common people of the industrial system, of public services, and of cultural and natural resources. Thus, Brameld's second point was that the working people should control all principal institutions and resources if the world is to become genuinely democratic. Teachers should ally with the organized working people. A way should be found to enlist the majority of people of all races and religions into a great democratic body with power to enforce its policies. The structure, goals, and policies of the new order must be approved at the bar of public opinion and enacted with popular support.

Brameld also believed that the school should help the individual, not only to develop socially, but to learn how to participate in social planning as well. The social reconstructionist wants no overstating of the case for individual freedom. Instead, the learners must see how society makes a people what they are and find ways to satisfy personal needs through social consensus. Lastly, said Brameld, learners must be convinced of the validity and urgency of change. But they must also have a regard for democratic procedures. Ideally, reconstructionists are opposed to the use of intimidation, fear, distortion, and mere compromise in the attempt to get a "community of persuasion." However, the reconstructionists take sides and encourage all to acquire common knowledge about crucial problems, to make up their minds about the most promising situations, and then to act in concert to achieve those solutions. The social reconstructionists believe they are representing values already cherished by the majority whether consciously or not. Most people are not now able to act responsibly, they say, because they have been persuaded and stunted by a dominating minority—those who largely control the instruments of power. Hence most persons do not exercise their citizenship in behalf of their own interests—their cherished values—but in behalf of scarcity, frustration, and war.

[1]George Counts, *Dare the School Build a New Social Order?* (Yonkers, N.Y.: World Book, 1932).

[2]Theodore Brameld, *Toward a Reconstructed Philosophy of Education* (New York: The Dryden Press, 1956).

A SOCIAL RECONSTRUCTIONIST
CURRICULUM DESIGN

Brameld has presented a detailed but largely conjectural design that is meant as a standard by which to measure alternative curricula. It is a curriculum design in that purposes, organizing questions and patterns, instructional objectives, concepts, and methods are related. Acquaintance with certain features of this design is helpful as a basis for analyzing the nature of the social reconstructionist conception of curriculum.[3]

1. *Assumptions.* The prime purpose of the curriculum is to confront the learner with the array of severe, ominous disturbances that humankind faces. The social reconstructionist believes that these disturbances are not the exclusive concern of "social studies" but pervade every aspect of life, including economics, aesthetics, chemistry, and mathematics. Thus, he says, we are now in a critical period. The crisis is universal, and this universality must be dramatized in the curriculum.

2. *Some Crucial Problems.* A social reconstructionist might organize learning activities around questions such as these: Can the ordinary human being fulfill his or her own capabilities in the face of depersonalized forces? Can neighborhoods learn to work together in attacking their own difficulties? Can economic and accompanying political establishments be rebuilt so that people in every part of the earth have access to physical and human resources? Such questions are intended to invite explorations into learning, not only by means of books and laboratories, but firsthand involvement in the experiences of people in communities.

3. *Organizational Patterns.* At the secondary level, there is a plan likened to a wheel. The "hub" consists of a general assembly engaged in studying one of the central critical questions. There are also "spokes," which are courses composed of discussion groups, content and skill studies, vocational training, and recreation. These courses are to support the matter treated in the hub. Less concrete but clearly delineated in the curriculum plans is a "rim," or unifying theme for the enterprise. The theme might be a principle, predicament, or aspiration for all humankind. The rim synthesizes the questions treated in the general assemblies, binding the whole.

[3]Theodore Brameld, "A Cross-Cutting Approach to the Curriculum: The Moving Wheel," *Phi Delta Kappan* 51, no. 7 (March 1970): 346–48.

Objectives and Content

Social reconstructionist curriculum has no universal objectives and content. The first year of such a curriculum might be concerned with formulating reasons for goals in the sphere of politico-economic reconstruction, for example. Activities related to this objective might include any or all of the following: (1) a critical survey of the community (for example, one might collect information on local patterns of savings and expenditures); (2) a study relating the local economy to national and worldwide situations; (3) a study treating the historic causes and trends as they relate to the local economic situation; (4) examination of political practices in relation to economic factors; (5) consideration of proposals for change in political practices; (6) evaluation of all proposals in terms of the degree to which each maximizes the wants of most people.

Objectives in other years might call for identifying problems, methods, needs, and goals in science and art; evaluating the interconnection between education and human relations; and identifying aggressive attitudes and strategies for effecting change.

Methods

Inasmuch as the faculty must help students discover their own particular interests, the curriculum maker relates national and world purposes to the students' goals. Students thus use their interests to help find solutions to the social problems being emphasized in the assemblies or hub. A community may, for example, want to encourage participation of multiethnic groups in public meetings. A foreign language class could use their second language skills to effect such participation. There is opportunity for interplay between discussion groups, general assemblies, and skills and content of special interest.

Cooperation with the community and its resources is stressed. Students may, for example, spend extended recesses or absences from the school participating in community health projects (science) or community acting, writing, or dance programs. It should be clear that even the study of subjects like art must be integrated with other concerns in the program. The interconnection between art and science and art and economics, for example, might be strengthened as the art student looks at art in home and city planning and contrasts unhealthy communities with "ideal garden cities" and tries to see how the quality of life is affected by the desire for business profits.

With respect to the primary school, Brameld stresses group experiences. He believes that projects should demand interdependence and social consensus. Children of different ages should join in community surveys and other integrative activities. The curriculum of an upper elementary school keeps the Utopian faith by giving generous exercises in social imagination. It might allow children to create rough models of future institutions, such as hospitals, and thus stimulate the children's awareness of our grave problems.

Evaluation

Students help to select, administer, and evaluate examinations. Tests are examined critically for their bias and adequacy of content, and for their ability to reflect the qualitative goals of the social reconstructionists. Comprehensive examinations during the last year of school have the aim of synthesizing and evaluating the student interpretation of prior work.

But evaluation must deal with more than the students and their learning. A social reconstructionist is also interested in the effect of schooling on the community. Factors to be weighed include the growth of community consensus, increased political power of the working classes, and an improved quality of life.

SOCIAL RECONSTRUCTION IN PRACTICE

Few schools have tried to develop a curriculum completely within the framework of social reconstructionism. Within the United States, such efforts have chiefly been in poor communities. Similarly, worldwide, the Peace Corps and the Third World countries have attended to the concept and tried to apply it, chiefly in rural areas. Recent trends toward involving the community in establishing goals for their neighborhood schools and participating in the conduct of learning opportunities in pursuit of these goals are consistent with social reconstructionism.

Some features of social reconstructionism were found in the 1940s. For example, the school program at Holtville, Alabama, a consolidated rural high school located in a poor area, had as its ideal better living conditions for all in the community.[4] In Holtville, the students were challenged to study their community situation, and

[4]*The Story of Holtville: A Southern Association Study School* (Nashville, Tenn.: Cullum and Ghertner, 1944).

they found heavy meat spoilage, the outside purchase of canned fruits and vegetables when these same fruits and vegetables were grown in the community, and overemphasis on production of a single crop.

With the cooperation of local farmers, the students secured a loan from a governmental agency to construct a slaughterhouse and refrigeration plant. Guided by a teacher, the students began processing meat and renting lockers to the farmers. Soon, they had paid off the loan. Then they did more. They started a hatchery and arranged to sell chicks to the farmers and buy back eggs below the market price, making money on the enterprise. Subsequently, they undertook to manage a cannery at the school; installed a water supply; helped homes install modern facilities; restored homes; purchased modern machinery, which they rented or used in working for the farmers; planted over 65,000 trees to prevent erosion; planted, sprayed, and pruned 50,000 peach trees for farmers; and set up woodwork and machine shops, a beauty shop, a local newspaper, a movie theatre, a game library, a bowling alley, and a cooperative store in which many of their own products were sold, including toothpaste made in their chemistry department.

Descriptions of current student activities conducted along social reconstructionist principles can be found in *Synergist*, a journal published three times a year by ACTION/National Student Volunteer Program. Reports in *Synergist* relate the efforts of students in solving local poverty problems and poverty-related problems. Typical activities involve students organizing community resources to solve consumer problems, helping foreign-born nursing home residents survive, correcting discriminatory employment practices, determining community needs, establishing facilities for mental patients, and reforming state utility laws.

Paulo Freire's Practice of Social Reconstructionism in the Third World

Today, the leading social reconstructionist in both theory and practice is Paulo Freire.[5] Although Freire has concentrated on the challenges facing Latin America and one African country in this time of change, he believes that other areas of the Third World differ only in small details and that they must follow his "cultural action for conscientization" if they are to be liberated.

[5]Paulo Freire, *Pedagogy of the Oppressed* (New York: Herder and Herder, 1970).

Conscientization is the process by which persons, not as recipients but as active learners, achieve a deep awareness both of the sociocultural reality that shapes their lives and of their ability to transform that reality.[6] It means enlightening people about the obstacles that prevent them from having a clear perception of reality. One of these obstacles is a standardized way of thinking—acting, for example, according to the prescriptions received daily from the communications media rather than recognizing one's own problems. Other obstacles are dehumanizing structures that control learning from the outside, educational systems whose schools are an instrument for maintaining the status quo, and political leaders who mediate between the masses and the elite while keeping the masses in a dependent state. Conscientization means helping persons apprehend the origins of facts and problems in their situations rather than attributing them to a superior power or to their own "natural" incapacity. Unless people see these facts objectively, they will accept the situation apathetically, believing themselves incapable of affecting their destiny.

Freire has put his philosophy into action. His plan and materials for teaching reading to adult illiterates show how to put the reconstructionist's theory into practice.[7] Table 1 shows the contrast between Freire's approach and the conventional approach to teaching reading in adult literacy campaigns.

Freire contends that oppression comes from within the individual as well as from without. Hence, the felt needs of individuals must be challenged if they are to be freed from blind adherence to their own world views as well as to the uncritically examined views of others. If farmers come to Freire demanding a course in use of pesticides in order to increase yields of their crops, for example, Freire assists them by examining the causes of their felt need for such instruction, thereby rediagnosing their need for the course. Probing into causes might lead the participants to conclude that a course in use of pesticides, as initially perceived, is not needed as much as a course on marketing practice.

The aim of education in Freire's approach is not to accommodate or adjust learners to the social system, but to free them from slavish adherence to it.

A recent report on efforts to eradicate illiteracy in the United States

[6]Paulo Freire, "Cultural Action and Conscientization," *Harvard Educational Review* 40, no. 3 (May 1970): 452–77.
[7]Paulo Freire, "The Adult Literary Process as Cultural Action for Freedom," *Harvard Educational Review* 40, no. 3 (May 1970): 205–25.

attests to the inadequacy of curricula that are not immediately relevant to people's lives.[8] The authors of this report advocate that participants help design a literacy program based on their own needs. The creation of a network of community-based literacy programs in the neighborhoods of the poor supposedly has the potential to win the confidence of people who would otherwise be suspicious of solutions that they perceive as imposed upon them from the outside.

TABLE 1

Conventional Approach	Freire Approach
The teacher chooses words to read and proposes them to the learner.	Poor people create texts that express their own thought-language and their perceptions of the world.
Primers feature word selections that have little to do with the students' sociocultural reality. (For example, "The dog barks." "Mary likes the animals.")	Words are chosen for (1) their pragmatic value in communicating with one's group (for example, the word *soul* has special meaning for blacks); (2) phonetic reasons; (3) generative features, such as syllabic elements by which learners can compare and read new words of importance to themselves.
The teacher implies that there is a relationship between knowing how to read and getting a good job.	The teacher stresses that merely teaching persons to read and write does not work miracles. If there are not enough jobs, teaching reading will not create them.
Learning to read is viewed as a matter of memorizing and repeating given syllables, words, and phrases.	Learning to read is viewed as reflecting critically on the process of learning to read and on the profound significance of language.

[8]Carmen St. John Hunter and David Marman, "Adult Illiteracy in the United States," *A Report to the Ford Foundation* (New York: McGraw-Hill, 1979).

✳THE RADICAL CONSENSUS

A new left has evolved that seeks social reforms, using the schools and colleges to awaken allies in labor, civil rights, and other groups with the need for control and power. John S. Mann applies Marxist techniques to social reconstructionism and criticizes the traditional social reconstructionists. He accuses older social reconstructionists of being naive for believing that they could transform society using a "new wave of students who have been nurtured in the practice of democracy in the school." He says, "Social reconstructionists fail to recognize that oppression and exploitation are a fundamental characteristic of class structure in the United States and cannot be altered by tinkering with the schools."[9]

Perhaps Mann is too hard on these forerunners. They did not speak of the school as remaking society in any total sense, but believed that the school might shape some of the perspectives that could influence behavior in the face of social problems. They realized very well that attitudes and beliefs would not be sustained unless supported by actual change in the structure of society. They held that the primary task of the school was moral and intellectual reconstruction and that it should precede sociological reconstruction if the latter was not to be automatic and blind. Unlike Mann, they did not believe that the school should be an instrument of subversion and revolution. Instead they would use the school to extend the ideals to which the people were already committed. The early social reconstructionists' curriculum called for study, not indoctrination.

Mann follows traditional social reconstructionist thought in advocating the following procedures for students:

1. Analyze concrete contradictions of democracy in the school and community.
2. Devise specific actions through which students, teachers, and others can combat antidemocratic aspects of their situations.
3. Plan to implement those actions in ways consistent with the following procedures.
   a. Dialectical action whereby actions produce new events to be incorporated into the study.
   b. A collective method of discussion, analysis, and criticism, in

---

[9]John Mann and Alex Molnar, "On Student Rights," *Educational Leadership* 31, no. 8 (May 1974): 670.

which the purpose is to use everyone as a resource in order to get fullest knowledge and most successful action.
c. Decision making by consensus rather than by vote.

Mann has envisioned a curriculum in which angry radical students criticize and analyze current school practices and formulate alternatives to these practices, are involved in learning about their own political and legal powers and rights of power in the school system, and engage in direct political action over specific issues, some of which are educational and some more broadly political. Students are encouraged to hold public meetings, solicit support from other groups, and otherwise engage in the political process.[10]

Mann and five other members of the 1975 ASCD Yearbook Committee presented a call to action aimed at the development of a curriculum to reveal to students the nature of dominant socioeconomic structures. These writers have urged educators to:

1. Protect their own living standards and their democratic rights, and, in order to do this, they must distinguish between the struggle based on analysis of class on the one hand and liberal reformism on the other. Further, they must unite as broadly as possible with other educators, with students, and with working-class and liberation-oriented organizations on the basis of the principles of class analysis.
2. In order to carry forward their professional work, educators must raise the demand for:
   a. Democracy for students in the schools;
   b. A curriculum that is designed to serve the interests of the dominated—the broad working class;
   c. The right to link directly and concretely the education of students with the education and the democratic struggle of the wage-earning and salaried working class.

While the details of action will vary from situation to situation, the following general categories of action are probably appropriate for any "public" school educator:

1. Develop in your school a core of three or four of the most progressive teachers, initially for the purpose of studying your school from the point of view of whose interests are expressed in the program. For example, begin to examine such data as the relative

[10]John Mann, "High School Student Protest and the New Curriculum Worker: A Radical Alliance," ASCD Yearbook 1972, *A New Look at Progressive Education* (Washington, D.C.: Association for Supervision and Curriculum Development, 1975), pp. 325–44.

variance in achievement of lower class and other children. Ask in whose interests the testing program operates. Examine materials, methods, and school policies for differential group bias in relation to the interest structure. Look at educational reform and research projects and reports to reveal the interest base embedded in the implicit assumptions of the proposals and conclusions.

2. Encourage the most progressive students you know to form a group to study and prepare a report upon the presence and/or absence of democracy for students in the school. Involve yourself in the student rights movement and serve as a resource person for examining the concrete mechanisms in school which abridge student rights. Encourage students to ask and answer "In whose interest?" are these policies or procedures.

3. As the study on dominant class interests progresses, bring your findings to the most progressive parents, and expand your core group to include these parents. Focus discussion both on the school and the broad parallels to these circumstances found in society at large.

4. Bring your work to the attention of educators in other schools through the teachers' union and other professional organizations. Encourage the formation of groups like yours in other schools. Plan to meet to compare findings.

5. When investigation at several schools in the area is sufficiently advanced to do so confidently, begin to expose the class content and context of your school program publicly—for example, at PTA and teachers' union meetings. Form a group in the union or teacher organization to carry the study forward.

6. Through parents, enlist the help of both community people and members of working-class organizations and establish curriculum committees specifically to develop curriculum based on the interest of the broad community of the working class. This must not be some currently typical "career education" package, but must include as minimal demands:

   a. The teaching of modern history focused upon the struggles of Western-dominated "third world" countries, the working class, the oppressed national minorities, and women against exploitation.

   b. Full equality for the language and culture of oppressed national minorities.

   c. Concrete investigation of the social class relations in the area of the school's population.

   d. Instruction in the fundamentals of socioeconomic analysis of social relations.

   e. Development of cultural activities specifically aimed at the acceptance and validation of traditional working-class culture.

7. Establish close links between your organization and the developing student organization, including joint meetings and joint presentations at PTA, school board, and other public meetings.

8. Develop close links between your organization and working-class and community organizations to which parents in your school area belong. This also should include joint presentations, as well as the planning of ways for students, as part of their regular school work, to participate in community action against attacks on living standards and democratic rights.

9. Establish an areawide committee of teachers to investigate and report upon the wage structure of teachers and the situation with regard to their democratic rights. Formulate demands on the basis of this report.

10. Establish an areawide committee, composed of teachers, students, parents, and representatives of progressive community, working class, national minority, and women's organizations to coordinate:

   a. Plans for putting forward demands for democracy for staff and students in the schools; for a curriculum based on the interests of the dominated groups in society; for the linking of students' education directly and practically to the struggle for liberation; and for protection of the living standards and democratic rights of teachers.

   b. A plan for the broadest possible dissemination, through leaflets, newsletters, and meetings, of information and analysis showing the relations among these demands, the relation of these demands to the demands of various sectors of the community, the relation of all of these demands to the basic class structure of society, and the necessity to form a united front among all dominated groups against the increasingly apparent move toward more centralized and rigid control by the power structure.[11]

The radical consensus with its direct appeal to the labor movement and its use of Marxist language should not be regarded as dominating the social reconstructionist movement. Indeed *reconstruction* is not destruction requiring a rejection of all traditional views and values. Many social reconstructionists are interested not in political revolution but in conceptualizing an ideal society as a basis for curriculum

[11]From ASCD Yearbook, *Schools in Search of Meaning*, pp. 158–161. Reprinted with permission of the Association for Supervision and Curriculum Development. Copyright © 1975 by the Association for Supervision and Curriculum Development. All rights reserved.

development. Thus they try to separate defensible aspects of society from less rational elements and to take into account advances in knowledge and changing circumstances.

A critique of the radical attack on schools has been made by Diane Ravitch.[12] She seeks to weaken what she believes are the harmful effects of radical criticism. She challenges the view that American schools have been oppressive; not liberating, and that they were *intended* to be oppressive by those who developed them. In particular, she attempts to show the fallacy of believing (1) that school life is mechanistically determined by economic life in the large society; (2) that purposes of schooling can be disclosed through a portrait of the school's organization or structure; and (3) that the effects of schooling indicate the intents of schooling.

How individuals and groups attempt to use for their own ends schools established for a particular purpose is an issue currently gaining attention. Under the rubric of *cultural reproduction*, for example, there is increasing interest in how the form and content of school knowledge is related to advanced corporate societies and to the stratification of social class.[13]

FUTUROLOGISTS

Curriculum futurologists advocate making deliberate choices regarding the world of the future (Utopia). They would study trend data, estimate the social consequences of future development foreshadowed by the trends, and then try to facilitate probable futures seen as "good" and divert or prevent those seen as "bad."

There are many futurologists in society at large. The World Future Society, a nonprofit, nonpolitical organization, alone has 16,000 members ranging from economists and philosophers to Venus watchers. Generally, they are not attempting to predict what is going to happen in ten or fifteen years but are trying to get a better feel of what they want to happen so they can then make their choices a little more intelligently.

Harold G. Shane, professor at Indiana University, represents those

[12]Diane Ravitch, *The Revisionists Revised: A Critique of the Radical Attack on the Schools* (New York: Basic Books, 1978).

[13]Michael W. Apple, review of Madeline MacDonald, *The Curriculum and Cultural Reproduction* (Milton Keynes, England: Open University Press, 1977), in *School Review* 87, no. 3 (May 1979): 333–35.

who would use future planning as a basis for curriculum making.[14] He urges planning the future, not planning for the future. As with other social reconstructionists, he stresses the power of persons to shape their own destiny and to believe that they are not bound to an inescapable future to which they must conform.

Shane would obligate curriculum developers to study trends first. Trends may be technological developments that have been identified with the help of specialists in academic disciplines. Such trends include reduction of hereditary defects, three dimensional philosophy, increase in life expectancy, chemical methods for improving memory, and home education via video. Trends also may be inventoried problems such as are found in the literature of disaster (for example, famine, dwindling resources, pollution). Shane would have educators, after they had studied trends, engage with a wide number of participants in analyzing the consequences of the trends. Such consequences might be mandatory foster homes for children whose natural homes are harmful to their physical or mental health; psychological prerequisites for candidates seeking public office; use of biochemical therapy for improving mood, memory, or concentration; reversal of counterecological trends; controlled growth; and concern for equity rather than equalitarianism. Professional specialists—those with expert knowledge—would decide whether the promised consequences would humanize or dehumanize. Final judgment about desirability, however, must rest with the people concerned.

Most social reconstructionists are very clear about the role of the professional expert in the determination of social policy. Although they use experts in analyzing complicated social problems, they do not entirely relegate the solution of these problems to the experts. "In the realm of social policy, the decisions of the whole people, when they have full access to the facts, are in the long run typically wiser than those made by any single class or group. The cult of the expert is but the prelude to some form of authoritarian society."[15] Reconstructionists favor pressing society for decisions and for developing a clearer social consensus as to what the "good life" is. In achieving this consensus, the ideas of children, parents, administrators, and teachers should be considered. Those ideas that are seen by the group as

[14]Harold G. Shane, "Future Planning as a Means of Shaping Educational Change," NSSE Seventieth Yearbook, *The Curriculum: Retrospect and Prospect* (Chicago: University of Chicago Press, 1971), pp. 185–217.

[15]B. Othanel Smith et al., *Fundamentals of Curriculum Development* (Yonkers, N.Y.: World Books, 1950), p. 638.

having merit must become the basis for "mutual coercion"—control for a socially worthy purpose.

Typical recommendations for future-oriented curriculum content focus on the exploitation of resources, pollution, warfare, and water; the effect of population increase; the unequal use of natural resources; propaganda, especially in press and screen; or self-control in the interests of one's fellows.

SOCIAL ADAPTION

Both social adaption and social reconstruction derive aims and content from an analysis of the society the school is to serve. Curriculum development in response to social needs—career education, sex education, ecological studies, parenting programs, energy conservation—are often more adaptive than reconstructive. Such curriculum represents a mechanism for adjusting students to what some groups believe to be an appropriate response to critical needs within society. Social adaption differs from social reconstruction in that usually no attempt is made to develop a critical consciousness of social problems and to do something about them. Under adaption, students instead are given information and prescriptions for dealing with situations as defined. No attempt is made to seek a fundamental change in the basic structure of society. While those with a social adaption bent look at society to find out what students need to achieve in the real world—to fit into society as it is—social reconstructionists look at society with the intent of building a curriculum by which students can improve the real world.

CRITICISMS OF SOCIAL RECONSTRUCTIONISM

Reconstructionism is appealing because of its faith in the ability of humankind to form a more perfect world. Further, it claims to use the best of science in determining status and possibilities. Among the reconstructionists' difficulties, however, is the fact that scientific findings permit varied interpretations. Established empirical conclusions are scant. Even the futurologists have been grouped into the "bleak sheiks" (pessimists) and the "think-tank utopians" (optimists). Further, there are no direct implications for curriculum. What one sociologist or economist holds as true may be refuted by another. Few agree about what conduct is best for a planned society.

The reconstructionist commitment to particular social ideas determined by "social consensus" may have tough sledding in an individualistic United States. Americans have so many competing interests and different views regarding moral, religious, aesthetic, and social issues that it would be difficult indeed to reach agreement on an ideal. There is also concern about the reconstructionists' efforts to change our political structure. Their ideological bent is in the direction of totalitarianism, a collective society, in which meaning is attained by a problem-solving approach through social consensus.

CONCLUDING COMMENTS

Social reconstructionists are concerned with the relation of the curriculum to society as it *should* be as opposed to society as it *is*. Many of the tenets of this group are consistent with our highest ideals, such as the right of those with a minority viewpoint to persuade a majority, and faith in the intelligence of common people and in their ability to shape their own destiny in desired directions. The radical consensus within the social reconstructionist ranks would pit class against class and advocate a biased socioeconomic analysis. The futurists in the movement are far less ideologically oriented and would be quite happy if the curriculum would help learners "want well"—that is, conceive of a desirable future after taking into account crucial social trends.

We can expect accelerated curriculum development along reconstructionist lines, especially whenever there is a need for resolving a value conflict. Such need often exists in multicultural neighborhoods. Cultural groups frequently have different interpretations of history, different ideas regarding nature, different levels of aspiration, and different views regarding social conduct. The prediction also applies whenever there is a breakdown in the barriers that isolate the school from the community. Accelerated curriculum development should thus occur when parents and community members become involved in teaching and social service roles, when students and adults participate in effecting changes outside the school building, when needs assessment techniques are used by community members to asess local social and economic needs or deficiencies and to decide how the institutions in the community can contribute to the improvement of the selected priority needs.

The close tie of the radical consensus with professional teacher organizations makes it likely that these reconstructionists will clash with reconstructionists representing local community groups and parents. Rivalry between teacher and parent power movements regarding *what* should be taught and *how* has already surfaced. The challenge, therefore, will be to apply the principle that calls for a "community of persuasion," probably by including teachers in the decision-making process but giving the community—parents and others—more of a controlling voice.

QUESTIONS

1. What do members of the radical consensus mean by "public" schools? Do they mean schools that are open to all, schools that are financed by taxes, or schools that are to serve the interests of a particular class?
2. What circumstances would most likely give rise to a curriculum along social reconstructionist lines?
3. How are textbooks by scholars used in a social reconstruction curriculum? Are they criticized, "raided," or accepted as authoritative?
4. Paulo Freire speaks of curriculum obstacles preventing a clear perception of reality (for example, control of learning from the outside, content and method that fosters learner dependency, and standardized ways of thinking). Can you provide specific examples of these obstacles as found in schools you have known?
5. Consider the home economics, career education, and other social studies courses known to you. Were they adaptive or social reconstructionist?

SELECTED REFERENCES

Brameld, Theodore. *Toward a Reconstructed Philosophy of Education.* New York: The Dryden Press, 1956.

Freire, Paulo. *Pedagogy in Process—The Letters to Guinea-Bissau.* New York: Seabury Press, 1978.

MacDonald, James B. and Zaret, Esther, eds. *Schools in Search of Meaning,* ASCD 1975 Yearbook. Washington, D.C.: National Education Association, 1975.

Schiro, Michael. "Social Reconstruction Ideology," in *Curriculum for Better Schools: The Great Ideological Debate.* Englewood Cliffs, N.J.: Educational Technology Publications, 1978.

Shane, Harold G. *Curriculum Changes Toward the 21st Century.* Washington, D.C.: National Education Association, 1977.

Van Til, William. *Curriculum: Quest for Relevance.* Boston: Houghton Mifflin, 1974.

*3 / TECHNOLOGY AND THE CURRICULUM

Educational consumers are familiar with technology in the form of teaching tools like computer-based instruction, self-instructional modules, individualized learning systems, and video and audio cassettes. They are less aware that technology is also a process for analyzing problems and devising, implementing, evaluating, and managing solutions. Technology as a curriculum perspective aims at effectiveness of programs, methods, and materials in reaching prespecified ends or purposes. This perspective has been expressed in many forms—needs assessment, systems approaches to educational design, programmed instruction, validated instructional sequences, mastery learning, and diagnostic-prescriptive teaching. Currently, the technological perspective has reemerged in the competency testing movement and other responses to public demands for school accountability.

This chapter includes both a description of technology as applied in classrooms and an analysis of the technology of curriculum development. The reader should become better able both to understand the characteristics of and to discern the strengths and weaknesses in the technological conception of curriculum. *Learner User as not good a God.*

Technology is applied to curriculum in two ways. First, it comes as a plan for the systematic use of various devices and media, and as a contrived sequence of instruction based on principles from behavioral science. Computed-assisted instruction, systems approaches using objectives, programmed materials, tutors using predetermined learning sequences aimed at a specific skill, and criterion-referenced tests applied in an organized way are examples of technology. A defining element of technology is that its systems and products can be replicated. The same results can be attained on repeated occasions and the system itself is exportable—useful in many situations.

Second, technology is found in models and procedures for the construction or development and evaluation of curriculum materials and instructional systems. The developmental process can be stated as rules which, if followed, will result in more predictable products.

Technology at first glance appears to be concerned with *how* to teach rather than *what* to teach. Technologists themselves view their curricular function as finding efficient and effective means to predetermined ends. A second glance shows that technology—the means produced—has a lot to do with what is or is not learned. The more successfully a learning sequence effects a meaningful specific consequence, the less successful it is in generating multiple meanings.

ILLUSTRATIONS OF TECHNOLOGY AS A LEARNING SYSTEM

Technology in Higher Education

Over 90 percent of the nation's colleges and universities use highly sophisticated electronic devices to transmit some portion of their curriculum to students. As the use of educational technology has become more widespread, the teacher tends to relinquish the role of imparter of knowledge for that of manager. The content of instruction and its applications are set in advance. In contrast to traditional higher education, the boundaries of knowledge are not fluid, and the results obtained are more important than the process. When course content is viewed as finite, it can be packaged in advance, duplicated, and transmitted. This view also allows students to work at their own pace. One popular use of technology as a solution to more effective instruction is known as the personalized system of instruction (PSI). This system is a soft technology involving persons, content, materials, and organizations as opposed to a hard technology, which involves only devices such as television, projectors, and computers. PSI utilizes the behavioral science principles that call for frequent active responses from students, immediate knowledge of results, and a clear statement of objectives. It also allows for individualization; different students may use different

PSI—personalized system of instruction

amounts of time and different approaches for attaining mastery of the instructional tasks.

With PSI a course or subject is broken into small units of learning, and at the end of each unit learners take tests to determine whether they are to go ahead to new material or receive additional instruction. Whenever students believe they are ready, they go to a "proctoring room" staffed by advanced students who administer the test, score it, and give feedback to the students. If less than "unit perfection" performance is shown, the proctor becomes a tutor, explaining the missing points and guiding the student in restudy. There is no penalty for failing a unit, but one must study further and try again. Frequent interaction with proctors often develops affect and contributes to understanding.

PSI permits one instructor to serve as many as 1,000 students, or possibly more. Instructors are responsible for conducting one- or two-hour weekly large group sessions for motivating and clarifying. They also have overall responsibility for planning the course, including the procedures and procurement or development of materials and examinations.

IPI—individually prescribed instruction

Technology in Elementary and Secondary Schools

Individually prescribed instruction (IPI) is an example of the technology found in elementary schools. Instructional objectives, arranged in an assumed hierarchy of tasks, are the keystone to the system, and lesson materials are built around that arrangement. The objectives are the intended outcomes of instruction. Each pupil must master them before going on to the next step in the learning hierarchy. Objectives in the teaching of mathematics, for example, are grouped by topics such as numeration, place value, and subtraction.

IPI lesson materials are matched with the objectives and allow the pupil to proceed independently with a minimum of teacher direction. The pattern for involving the pupil with the system has three parts.

1. Finding out what the pupil already knows about the subject. Usually a general placement test is administered to reveal the pupil's general level of achievement. The pupil is also given a pretest to reveal specific deficiencies.
2. Giving the pupil self-instructional materials or other carefully designed learning activities. Such activities are aimed at teaching a task that will overcome one of the specific deficiencies previously identified.

3. Giving the pupil evaluative measures to determine his or her progress. Such measures will help you decide whether to move the pupil ahead to a new task or to provide additional materials or tutoring.

Materials include placement tests, pre- and posttests, skill booklets, response booklets, a record system, games and manipulatives, and cassettes and filmstrips. Paid aides and volunteers, such as parents, assist pupils, check response sheets, and help to keep the materials organized.

At the secondary level, technology is a frequent answer to how best to remedy skill deficiencies found through mandated competency or proficiency testing. Accordingly, students who have been identified as lacking particular math, writing, or reading skills are given self-instructional booklets and student study guides. The booklets offer opportunity to practice both the enroute skills and the terminal performance of separate skills; the study guides describe in simple language each basic skill and include practice test items and their answers as well as a brief exposition of the skill and a set of selected textbook references for student use. The secondary school teacher, too, is given a skill-focused guide including a thorough explanation of what the skill calls for, a test item format, content delineation, and an accounting of the requisite types of intellectual operations. A set of appropriate instructional tactics is also indicated.

GENERAL CHARACTERISTICS OF CLASSROOM TECHNOLOGICAL SYSTEMS

Objectives

Objectives have a behavioral or empirical emphasis. They specify learning products or processes in forms that can be observed or measured. There is no inherent reason why technological systems cannot employ affective as well as psychomotor and cognitive objectives. Indeed, some technological systems do feature affective objectives. Typically, however, the objectives are detailed, specific, and skill-oriented. Commerically available materials feature objectives that are likely to be appropriate for most children in this country. Those skills which most curriculum developers believe useful in learning to read and in solving mathematical problems, for example, are featured. The instructional objectives of technological systems thus tend to reinforce the importance of conventional goals and the traditional divisions of academic subject matter. With the exception of locally designed materials, such as Unipacs, objectives more appropriate for meeting particular local social conditions are seldom treated. Neither are there many opportunities for pupils to generate their own objectives.

Methods

Learning is viewed as a process of reacting to stimuli—attending to relevant cues—rather than as a transactional process in which the learner might influence the stimuli. The learner is directed to attend to significant features and is reinforced for appropriate behavior. Goals of instruction are predetermined rather than emergent.

Individualism is restricted to pacing and to the number of tasks to be learned. Some children can make their responses more quickly and require fewer exercises in order to learn a generalization. Individual children need not spend time on tasks leading to behaviors already in their repertoire.

Typically, learners work alone, although there may be occasional periods of small group work. There is a set of common expectations. All pupils are to master the objectives of the program. The paradigm of instruction follows these principles:

1. *Perceived purpose.* Learners are told why it is important to learn a certain objective or at least are given a clear explanation of what they are to learn.
2. *Appropriate practice.* Learners have opportunities to practice both the prerequisite skills not already attained and the behavior specified by the objective. The desired response is frequently obtained by prompting. Eventually, however, the prompts are removed and the child responds to the problem using the concept or principles taught.
3. *Knowledge of results.* Pupils are given feedback indicating whether their responses are adequate and are helped to make them more appropriate, if necessary.

Organization

The technologist's curriculum is usually related to subject disciplines such as mathematics, sciences, reading and other language arts, arts, and to applied technical fields. Usually only a few aspects of these fields are selected for treatment at any one time. Decimals in math, for example, are treated in a separate program, not as mathematics in general. The objectives of instruction are arranged in a fixed continuum or hierarchy of skills—an end-of-program objective such as ability to multiply would follow enroute objectives of addition and subtraction. End-of-program objectives are precisely and operationally stated, and these objectives are the basis for organizing instruction. The objectives are analyzed in terms of prerequisites; each prerequisite in turn is then stated as an enroute objective, and these enroute objectives are arranged in an assumed hierarchical order. A learner may follow a series of activities or tasks such as the following:

1. Define a given concept.
2. Recognize instances and noninstances of the concept.
3. Combine two given concepts into a principle.
4. Combine given principles into a strategy for solving new problems.

Complex subject matter, in short, is sequenced by the simple components. A particular sequence may vary in length from a single lesson to a year's course of instruction.

Evaluation

Unique to the technologist is the assumption that if the intended learner (the kind of person for whom the program was designed) does not master the specified objectives, the program maker is at fault. Learners are not responsible for their own success or failure. Programs are developed, tried out on a sample of the intended population of learners, and revised according to the findings until the program attains intended results.

Until recently, technologists usually evaluated their programs only in terms of their own objectives. Unanticipated side effects were seldom sought. Neither was the validity or justification for end-of-program objectives established by considering the full range of criteria that various consumers might apply to both process and product. Technologists examined achievement but sometimes did not consider whether attaining the objective produced desirable or undesirable effects on the community or whether the individualized techniques inadvertently impaired learners' social skills. Thus, the technologist, as such, is concerned more with the effectiveness of the process than with the validity of the objectives.

process — vs validity
of the objectives

Generally, the technological approach is most effective for conventional, easily measurable tasks. Pupils achieve more with these techniques than they would otherwise. "The tightly structured programmed approach including frequent and immediate feedback to the pupil, combined with a tutorial relationship, individual pacing, and somewhat individualized programming are positively associated with accelerated pupil achievement."[1] Again, however, it must be remembered that such positive evaluation rests on achievement defined either by scores on standardized tests or by program-specific tests treating aspects of traditional school subjects.

TECHNOLOGY IN THE DEVELOPMENT OF CURRICULUM

Older practice in the development of textbooks, courses, lessons, and other curriculum materials involved art and politics more than technology. Curriculum development has been a search for some general value—an important idea, problem, or skill—around which content and activities could be organized. Newer criteria for technological curriculum making have only recently been accepted as guides to practice.[2] These criteria are: (1) the developmental procedures used should be reviewed and validated by other developers; they should be able to be replicated; (2) products developed in accordance with models that can be replicated should produce similar results.

The heart of the technological revolution in curriculum is, however, the belief that curriculum materials themselves, when used by those learners for whom the materials are developed, should produce specified learner competencies. This belief is a great advance over the belief that curriculum materials are mere resources that may or may not be useful or influential in a given situation. The change in concept can be seen in two different ways for judging curriculum materials (see Table 2, next page).

[1]Edmund W. Gordon, "Utilizing Available Information from Compensatory Education and Surveys," *Final Report* (Washington, D.C.: Office of Education, 1971), p. 24.

[2]*Recommendations for Reporting the Effectiveness of Programmed Instruction Material*, prepared by the Joint Committee on Programmed Instruction and Teaching Machines, Division of Audio Instructional Service, National Education Association, Washington, D.C., 1966, was one of the first sets of criteria for judging materials by demonstrated merit.

TABLE 2

Old Criteria	New Criteria
Do authors have professional reputations?	Where and how extensively have materials been tried out?
Are materials based on sound pedagogical principles? Are they consistent with established suggestions for instruction and practice? Will the content broaden the children's view of the world?	Is information available about the number of students who started and completed the materials? Does the information say how much time learners of different ability spent on portions of the material and give differential results?
Are selections arranged by level to satisfy the needs and interests of children as they mature? Is the art imaginative and appealing?	Do the materials specify intended-learner characteristics including enumeration of prerequisites?
Are type faces and sizes, lengths of lines, and space between lines appropriate for the maturity of the children at each level?	Are materials being revised to reflect trial results? How are student responses used in revising the material?
Do materials use high quality paper, clear print, and sturdy binding?	How effectively do students learn specified skills? Do appropriate criterion-referenced tests show student gains?

Responses to the Demands of the Technologists

A major force in the production of curriculum materials, the publishers, usually agree that teachers need help in deciding which new and unfamiliar materials are most appropriate for their particular needs. Further, they recognize the vague feeling that education needs to be protected from big government and big business, since either one could foist ideas and products on the educational community before they are properly tested.

Textbook publishers admit that their materials are designed and evaluated intuitively rather than systematically. Publisher Lee C. Deighton, for example, has recounted the pragmatic mode he uses to evaluate materials.

> We do our best intuitively to prepare materials that will be productive in the classroom. Then we listen attentively to what the users of these materials have to say about them, and modify succeeding revisions to take this experience into account. Sometimes the revision is better; sometimes it is merely different.[3]

Although they agree with technologists that there is a need for better evaluations and more consistent results, publishers still have many questions. *Who* would do the field testing—developers or outside agencies? What constitutes a reasonable sample? Will the schools pay for the higher costs incurred for the more expensive trials and revisions? Will producers publish complete data or only positive findings?

A nonprofit corporation, Educational Products Information Exchange Institute (EPIE) has attempted to make impartial studies of the availability, use, and effectiveness of educational materials, equipment, and systems. EPIE reports tend to be descriptive. They indicate the effects of the materials on teacher time, costs, and staffing, and state the underlying assumptions or philosophy of the materials. They also reveal the extent to which there has been learner verification of the materials. A National Center for the Evaluation of Educational Materials has also been established at the University of Miami. This center provides guidance and evaluates the effectiveness of curriculum materials.

Federal funds have supported technological curriculum development at a number of places. For example, individually prescribed instruction was developed at the Learning Research and Development Center of the University of Pittsburgh, and Project Plan was developed by the American Institute for Research of Palo Alto, California. Typical of the developmental process used by such institutions is that of the Southwest Regional Laboratory for Educational Research and Development. Eva Baker has given an account of this federally funded activity.[4] She indicates that more extrinsic efforts were made at formulating a product, that is, a communication skills program, than in formulating the goals and program thrust. The decision to emphasize reading was a policy matter, and once it was made the following kinds of developmental activities were undertaken:

[3]Remarks made at American Educational Research Association, Chicago, February 8, 1968.

[4]Eva L. Baker, "The Technology of Instructional Development," in *Second Handbook of Research on Teaching*, Robert M.W. Travers, ed. (Chicago: Rand McNally, 1973).

1. Decisions about content were made (for example, linguistic requirements were specified and initial word lists were established).
2. There were general decisions about the nature of the materials (for example, it was decided to feature story books in order to provide opportunities to practice the skills of reading).
3. Brief trials of segments, modifications in selection of words, book format, and typography were undertaken.
4. Instructional support materials like games, practice sequences, and lesson plans were developed. During this phase, specific objectives were stated. Materials were tried out on small groups of learners and reviewed by experts and teachers.
5. Field trials were initiated with modest teacher training, followed by observations of classroom procedures and use of techniques for obtaining teacher comments.
6. Both teacher comments and results from interim criterion tests provided a base for revision.

Concurrent with the above steps, another division of SWRL completed an analytic research in psycholinguistics to determine what improvement could be made in the words and language structure content. Studies were made to determine the effects of different response modes and illustrations.

Common Elements in Technologists' Models for Curriculum Development

There are five common elements in the technologist's process of curriculum development:

Formulation. The foundation of an idea for a product rests on the decision that that product is needed. Need may be based on a presumed market. Court and legislative action, for example, may demand a changed emphasis. Bilingual materials were formulated in response to court decisions giving impetus to teaching non-English-speaking pupils in their own language.

Specification. Specification of outcomes is undertaken both to guide the development of the product and to provide a basis for product evaluation. Delineation of the measures to be used in determining the effectiveness of the program is helpful in planning for evaluation. Specification includes a description of the situation (stimuli) to which the learner will be expected to respond (the domain). Standards for determining the adequacy of a response are also stipulated. Specifications describing component skills requisite for the achievement of the objectives are usually stated and ordered. The characteristics of the intended learners are also specified. Learners' entry skills and other attributes that may bear on the development and use of the product should be listed. The models should also tell whether the product will be self-instructional or require the use of tutor, parent, or teacher; and they should indicate the extent of involvement of instructors.

Prototype. Variations in learning sequences are produced and tried out with a few learners. Decisions about composite formats, media, and organization are made during this phase.

Initial Trials. Segments of instruction are tried out with a sample of learners to determine whether the component achieves its objectives and to reveal weaknesses. The use of data to improve the product is essential to the technologist. Data include not only performance on end-of-sequence tests but errors made while responding to the material. Modest revisions of a component usually increase overall performance of the system.

Trial of Product. The product is put into use with existing school instruction. Data are collected about training, special problems in implementation (such as the need for teacher training or unanticipated side effects), and results achieved.

ISSUES IN A TECHNOLOGICAL APPROACH TO CURRICULUM DEVELOPMENT

On the one hand, many claim that the technological approach leads to products that are consistent with the learner's predispositions because the developer must be attentive to the learner and not rely on armchair planning. The approach is also said to provide procedures for curriculum making that can be replicated and manipulated, helping us learn what works and what does not.

On the other hand, people are concerned about the technological approach's costliness, which has resulted in a greater need for government financing. Such funding is automatically suspect when people fear governmental influence on what their children learn and view federal influences as antagonistic to local development of the curriculum. Also, the technologist's logical approach, which aims at helping the learner achieve mastery of specified objectives, has been faulted for excluding more potential influences on learning outcomes than it includes.In many ways, the older notion of providing rich environments without specific preplanned objectives may have encouraged the development of richer and more important outcomes for learners.

Special Problems

Technologists have not fully succeeded in defining essential prerequisites and learning hierarchies for complex subject matter. Neither have they been able to determine the degree of mastery required for programs. Attempts to determine mastery or competency through statistical or psychological means have not been satisfactory. In fact, Gene Glass and Mary Lee Smith have argued that the attempt to set standards of performance for promotion is futile except as a political endeavor.[5] Organizational plans of the technologists' curriculum sometimes make no real contribution to the problem of helping learners transfer what they learn to new subject matters and to a real world.

Individualization in the technological curriculum seldom, if ever, allows the learners to generate their own objectives. Also, technologists have not given sufficient attention to learners' predispositions toward specific methods. Low aptitude students, for example, may respond differently to some technological features than do high aptitude students. Technologists might take their responses into consideration by developing alternative programs rather than expecting all to learn from the same materials. Tightly structured programs may be more effective for those with lower aptitude. Provisions for learners who overgeneralize, for example, might be considered. There are indications that technology may move beyond individual instruction to individualized instruction based upon cognitive styles.[6] based upon cognitive styles.[6]

A final criticism of technology is that it has been tied to the achievement of traditional or static goals, to those things which schools have long been attempting to do. Its main contribution is to allow schools to do these things more effectively.

    [5]Gene V. Glass and Mary Lee Smith, "The Technology and Politics of Standards," *Educational Technology* 18, no. 5 (May 1978): 12–18.
    [6]Lynna J. Ausburn and Floyd B. Ausburn, "Cognitive Styles: Some Information and Implications for Instructional Design," *Educational Communication and Technology* 26, no. 4 (Winter 1978): 337–54.

CONCLUDING COMMENTS

Technology has greatly improved curriculum. Its emphasis on objectives has led curriculum makers to ask what kinds of objectives are most valuable. Some people question the tendency of the technologists' curriculum to maintain objectives consistent with conventional fragmented or compartmentalized subject matter areas. We are likely to have more warranted objectives as a result of this questioning.

The technologists' influence on curriculum developers has been great. Without the technologists' prodding for evidence of results, most developers would have been satisfied to provide what they thought were valid educational environments, never taking responsibility for the consequences. More clearly to be seen is the technologists' contribution to instructional effectiveness, the ordering of instructional sequences, and the monitoring of pupil progress. It is reasonable to suppose that more persons can now produce an effective curriculum by following the technologists' model. Many of these persons may not, however, do any better or as well as the rare creative developer following his or her own intuition.

People who make decisions about how to develop curriculum, such as publishers and school officials, will have to weigh the value of the technologists' model against its heavier development costs (often a threefold time increase over traditional approaches to curriculum development). They may find that the higher costs are balanced by increased learning for more pupils when the model is implemented.

One weakness in the technologists' model for curriculum development is that it does not give sufficient attention to implementation of the products and the dynamics of innovation. Just developing a more effective product is often not enough. Unless attention is given to changing the wider environment (school organization, teachers' attitudes, community views), the good product may not be used or at least not in a way that will fulfill its promise. Efforts to improve the conditions of implementation, however, are likely to draw resources away from efforts to improve the product itself.

Lest this chapter present technology in too grim a light, a reviewer reminds us that there are affective aspects "of keeping the pupil's nose against the content grindstone," citing the computer program "The Dove" that is an aesthetic experience and the computer versions of "Dungeons and Dragons" and the "Star Trek" games as fantasy adventures.

QUESTIONS

1. How might school environments have to change in order to take maximum advantage of microcomputers, hand calculators, video discs,
   computer-assisted instruction, televised sequences of instruction, and
   other technological materials?
2. What possible side effects or indirect consequences might follow the use
   of technologists' products that elicit and confirm particular responses
   from the learner?
3. How does a technologist show that a teaching method, procedure, or
   product works? How do the technologist's criteria differ from criteria
   traditionally used in judging material?
4. The personalized system of instruction (PSI) is often associated with
   large numbers of students, continuous monitoring of student progress,
   and constructive feedback for remediation. In what situations would
   you expect this kind of technology to be highly acceptable?
5. Technologists speak as if their focus were on *how* learning should take
   place rather than *what* is to be learned. They conceptualize the curriculum function as finding effective means to predetermined ends. In
   what ways, however, might this commitment to procedure have consequences for goals and content as well?

SELECTED REFERENCES

Alkin, Marvin. *The Evaluation of Educational Technology.* Philadelphia:
   Research for Better Schools, 1975.
Baggalay, J.P. and others, eds. *Aspects of Educational Technology,* Proceed-
   ings of the 1974 Annual Conference of the Association for Programmed
   Learning and Educational Technology, no. 8. London: Pitman, 1975.
Briggs, Leslie and associates. *Instructional Design: Principles and Applica-
   tions.* Englewood Cliffs, N.J.: Educational Technology Publications,
   Inc., 1977.
Meyrowitz, Joshua. "Instructional Technology and the Multiversity,"
   Educational Forum XLIII, no. 3 (March 1979): 279–89.
Northwest Regional Educational Laboratory. *Stages of Product Develop-
   ment and Installation.* Portland, Ore.: Northwest Regional Educational
   Laboratory, undated.
Professional Development and Educational Technology. Washington,
   D.C.: Association for Educational Communications and Technology,
   1980.
Task Force on Definition and Terminology. *Educational Technology:
   Definition and Glossary of Terms.* Washington, D.C.: Association for
   Educational Communications and Technology, 1979.

4 / THE ACADEMIC SUBJECT CURRICULUM

Academic subject matter dominated American schooling during the 1960s. Scholars selected the goals and the content, and recommended activities to appear in programs and materials. Suddenly in the 1970s there was a decline in federal funding for scholars preparing national curricula in their fields. Government policymakers changed their priorities. The crises of domestic, economic, and social strife became more important than scientific rivalry with the Soviets. Consequently, monies were shifted to projects that aimed at new social concerns such as multicultural education, career education, and the teaching of functional literacy, and to curriculum makers who were outside traditional disciplines. Humanists also weakened the academicians' hold on the curriculum by encouraging subjective and personal knowledge as an alternative to the academicians' objective knowledge that can be tested through reasoning and empirical evidence. The conception of an academic curriculum did not die, however, with the rise in emphasis on social and personal relevancy. Indeed, there are now three discernible trends in the subject matter approach to curriculum. In this chapter, the reader will learn about these trends and gain understanding of the ways local curriculum developers are strengthening academic curriculum models.

KNOWLEDGE AND THE CURRICULUM

Just as the heart of schooling is curriculum, the irreducible element of curriculum is knowledge. The nucleus of knowledge and the chief content or subject matter of instruction are found in academic subjects that are primarily intellectual, such as

53

language and literature, mathematics, the natural sciences, history, social sciences, and the fine arts.

These disciplines represent a range of approaches to truth and knowledge. Academicians define knowledge as *justified belief*, as opposed to ignorance, mere opinions, or guesses. Paul H. Hirst is an example of a curriculum theorist who represents a current academic orientation.[1] As with other academicians, he believes that the curriculum must develop the mind. His message is that the development of a rational mind is best achieved by mastering the fundamental rational structure of knowledge, meaning, logical relations, and criteria for judging claims to truth. In answer to the classical curriculum question, "What knowledge is of most worth?" Hirst proposes seven or eight forms of cognitive knowledge for understanding the world. Each of these forms is said to meet four criteria: (1) certain concepts are peculiar to the form (for example, gravity, acceleration, and hydrogen are concepts unique to the physical science form); (2) each form has a distinct logical structure by which the concepts can be related; (3) the form, by virtue of its terms and logic, has statements or conclusions that are testable; and (4) the form has methods for exploring experience and testing its statements (for example, in mathematics the "truth" of any proposition is established by its logical consistency with other propositions within a given system, while in physical science, knowledge—generalizations, laws, and theories—is validated by data from observation). The forms of knowledge discerned by these criteria are: mathematics, physical sciences, knowledge of persons, literature and the fine arts, morals, religion, and philosophy. This range in forms allows for many different kinds of meaning.

In proposing forms of knowledge rather than stipulating a particular fixed substance of subject matter (particular facts and operations), such as is inferred in "back to the basics" programs, Hirst argues for a dynamic curriculum. His forms do not, however, encourage a subjective or relative view of knowledge. To him, knowledge consists of ways to structure experience so that it can be public, shared, and instrumental or useful in daily living.

Criticisms of Hirst's views of knowledge and the curriculum center on whether he has indeed discovered distinct forms and whether he has slighted the idea of subject matter as substance. Robin Barrow, for instance, thinks that Hirst's forms overlap in that several of them

---

[1]Paul H. Hirst, *Knowledge and the Curriculum* (London: Routledge & Kegan Paul, Ltd., 1974).

rely on logical consistency and compatibility with observable facts in validating conclusions or claims to truth.[2] On the other hand, Jonas Soltis worries that a focus on the forms of knowledge will result in an absence of attention to specific knowledge of what has been learned about the world.[3] Soltis believes that learning a form should include learning the substance within it, not just acquiring knowledge of concepts, rules, and criteria for claims to truth. Hirst admits that there is no complete agreement on the descriptions of the forms of knowledge and that mastery of the formal features of a discipline should not be mistaken for mastery of a particular area of knowledge itself.[4] He therefore wants pupils to acquire both substantive knowledge that has significance for them and knowledge of the general principles and ways of thinking that are the inherent features of the forms by which knowledge is won.

Curriculum developers working within the academic orientation have two choices with respect to theories of knowledge. They may accept recent theories explaining the tentative nature of knowledge—that it is subject to change, modification, and evolution—or they may favor a traditional view that knowledge is not created but that it already exists, independent of persons. The latter view leads to the belief that certain truths or principles that have been discovered through intuitive reason are fixed and eternal. According to the traditional view, the curriculum content consists of principles and ideas that have always been true and in all essential matters will always be true.

As is true of Hirst, most curriculum theorists today reject this fixed view of knowledge and instead hold that knowledge can be constructed. The creation of knowledge—valid statements, conclusions, or truths—occurs by following the inquiry systems of particular disciplines or cognitive forms. The acquiring of disciplinary forms for creating knowledge constitutes the most valid aspect of the modern academic curriculum; the recitation of given conclusions apart from the methods and theories by which they are established is less defensible in a period characterized by both expansion and revision of knowledge—new truths departing from older principles.

Those with humanistic conceptions of curriculum and those with a

[2]Robin Barrow, *Commonsense and the Curriculum* (Hamden, Conn.: Linnet Books, 1976).

[3]Jonas A. Soltis, "A Review of Knowledge and the Curriculum," *Teachers College Record* 80, no. 4 (May 1979): 785–89.

[4]Paul H. Hirst, "A Reply to Jonas Soltis," *Teachers College Record* 80, no. 4 (May 1979): 785–89.

social reconstructionist orientation reject the traditional view of knowledge and the view that knowledge is best won through cognitive forms. Instead, humanists claim that all knowledge is personal and subjective. For them, knowledge is the result of an individual's unique perceptions of the world. Social reconstructionists, on the other hand, see knowledge not only as a human product, but as a product of particular social groups. They think socially constructed knowledge is ideology. Hence, they regard attempts to impose a particular content on students in the same way as they regard imposing a particular ideology—a form of social control.

RECENT HISTORY OF THE ACADEMIC CURRICULUM

Academic Curriculum Reform in the 1960s

The so-called curriculum reform movement of the 1960s was identified with the shock that came with the Russians' first satellite launching. In the cold war climate, fear moved government to emphasize the teaching of science and mathematics. Scholars in colleges and universities prepared materials focused on single subjects. These programs reached from kindergarten up and were designed on the assumption that all pupils should understand the methods of science and the basic properties of mathematics. This was in contrast to the prevailing practice of teaching scientific facts and a style of treatment in mathematics best characterized as rote and applied. Algebra, in the "reform" course, was treated as a branch of mathematics dealing with the properties of various number systems rather than as a collection of manipulative tricks.

The Structure of Knowledge Approach to Curriculum Development

In his celebrated book, *The Process of Education*, Jerome Bruner proposed that curriculum design be based on the structure of the academic disciplines. He proposed that the curriculum of a subject should be determined by the most fundamental understanding that can be achieved of the underlying principles that give structure to a discipline. The basis for his argument was economy. Such learning permits generalizations, makes knowledge usable in contexts other than that in which it is learned, and facilitates memory by allowing the learner to relate what would otherwise be easily forgotten, unconnected facts. "The school boy learning physics is a physicist, and it is easier for him to learn physics behaving like a physicist than doing something else."[5] (Incidentally, ten years later, Bruner, caught up in the social movements of the day, urged a deemphasis on the structure of history, physics, math, and the like and instead called for an emphasis on subject matter as it related to the social needs and problems of the American people.[6])

The concept of *structure in the disciplines* was widely heralded as a basis for curriculum content. This concept refers to rules for pursuing inquiry and for establishing truth in particular disciplines. Three kinds of structure are posited: (1) *organizational structure*—definitions of how one discipline differs in a fundamental way from another. A discipline's organizational structure also indicates the borders of inquiry for that discipline; (2) *substantive structure*—the kinds of questions to ask in inquiry, the data needed, and ideas (concepts, principles, theories) to use in interpreting data; and (3) *syntactical structure*—the manner in which those in the respective disciplines gather data, test assertions, and generalize findings. The particular method used in performing such tasks makes up the syntax of a discipline. Sociologists, for example, generally observe in naturalistic settings, identify indicators believed to correspond to the theoretical framework guiding the inquiry, and often rely on correlational data to show relations among factors observed. Experimental psychologists, on the other hand, manipulate their treatment variables in an effort to produce desired consequences. Experimentalists believe they have found knowledge when they are able to produce a predicted result.

The structure of the disciplines concept was widely used in designing curriculum whereby students were to learn how specialists in a number of disciplines discover knowledge. An intellectual emphasis was the basis for most nationwide curriculum development projects of the 1960s. Curriculum builders of this period were primarily subject matter specialists who organized their materials around the primary structural elements of their respective disciplines: problems or concerns, key concepts, principles, and modes of inquiry.

[5]Jerome S. Bruner, *The Process of Education* (Cambridge, Mass.: Harvard University Press, 1960), p. 31.
[6]Jerome S. Bruner, "The Process of Education Revisited," *Phi Delta Kappan* LIII, no. 1 (September 1971): 18–22.

What little debate there was regarding the "new programs" centered on the argument that what was being taught would be needed only by students who were to become professional scientists and mathematicians. The rebuttal offered these arguments:

1. There is need for appreciation from the popular culture for well-trained scientists and their fields.
2. It is better to develop a deeper comprehension of the fundamentals than to touch on many facts that are often the outdated conclusions of science. A discipline approach, for example, can help the learner deal with the "knowledge explosion."
3. True understanding of the facts in more fields of learning comes only from an appreciation of various interpretations, and a continuing investigation is far more interesting to the student than a set piece. There is a growing realization that the process of inquiry itself is a form of knowledge to be acquired.
4. A discipline is an internal organization, a subject matter suitable for efficient learning.

In virtually every field—English, social studies, art, health education—there was an updating of content, a reorganization of subject matter, and fresh approaches to method. Typically, the stress was on a separate entity: not science, but biology, chemistry, or physics; not social studies, but history, geography, or economics; not English, but literature, grammar, or composition.

Reaction Against a Structure of Knowledge Approach in the 1970s

Not all went as well as hoped. Teachers who themselves had never produced knowledge—who had not made an original scientific finding or historical interpretation—had difficulty leading students in the ways of discovery. The validity of the concept of structure as a basis for curriculum development was questioned—that the concept was only an after-the-fact description of the way knowledge can be organized by mature scholars and not the way it was really won, and that such structure is not necessarily the best way to organize knowledge for instructional purposes or start and direct significant inquiry and reflection. Enrollments in advanced physics courses declined. Many students, in both high and low ability groups, did not achieve as intended. The public was dissatisfied with the decline in mathematical skills. A National Assessment Educational Progress Report in 1975 revealed that only 35 percent of the nation's seventeen-year-olds could solve a simple multiplication problem with decimals, and 40 percent could not do basic work in addition, subtraction, multiplication, and division.[7] Separate assessments of students' academic achievement indicated that United States public school students were learning less than they did a decade ago. The College Entrance Examination Board decided that a decade-long decline in scores on the Scholastic Aptitude Test was "real" and caused by a decline in student reasoning ability. The National Assessment of Educational Progress reported that students knew less about science than similar students in 1969 to 1970.[8]

No causal relation was shown, however, between reform projects and lower student interest or achievement. Other factors, such as students' changing social attitudes in an era of social discontent, might have been more influential.

The availability of numerous programs created problems of maintaining balance and organization. By 1971, there were, for example, more than 100 curriculum projects in the social studies alone. Many subjects had to be omitted from a school's offerings. Further, the subject specializations were so narrowly focused that it was difficult to combine their concepts into broader fields.

The 1970s saw a decline in the academic approach to curriculum making. The popularity of a disciplined approach to the science curriculum, for example, waned with a growing distrust of science. It was argued that scientists should be doing more to solve humanity's problems. Also, those with nonacademic curriculum bents attacked the structure of knowledge approach to curriculum development through an attack on a well-publicized exemplar of this approach: MACOS.

MACOS, the acronym for *Man: A Course of Study*,[9] was to have been the primer for curriculum in the 1970s. Bruner himself established the initial guide for this curriculum and directed much of its development, which was supported by the National Science Foundation (NSF) and the United States Office of Education in order to "reform" the teaching of social sciences and humanities. MACOS is a curriculum designed for students in the elementary school, and consists of books, films, posters, records, games, and other classroom

---

[7]*National Assessment of Educational Progress.* Education Commission of the States, Second Report on Knowledge of Science and Math Skills (Denver, Colo., 1975).

[8]*Phi Delta Kappan* 61, no. 9 (May 1975): 652.

[9]*Man: A Course of Study* (Washington, D.C.: Curriculum Development Associates, 1970).

material. More important, it sets forth assumptions about humans. Three central questions define the intellectual concerns and reveal the assumptions of MACOS: What is human about human beings? How did they get that way? How can they be made more human? The developers of the course wanted children to explore the major forces that have shaped and continue to shape humanity; language, tool use, social organization, mythology, and prolonged immaturity. Through contrast with other animals, including the baboons, children examine the biological nature of humans. By comparing American society with that of a traditional Eskimo group, they explore the universal aspects of human culture.

The intellectual models used to get ideas across to children are disciplinary. Children are given examples of field notes and encouraged to construct their ideas about animals and humans in the ways ethnologists and anthropologists do. The principal aims of MACOS are intellectual: to give children respect for and confidence in the powers of their own minds and to provide them with a set of workable models that make it simpler to analyze the nature of the social world. Its values include the scientific mode of observation, speculation, hypothesis making and testing; understanding of particular social science disciplines; and the joy of discovery.

Attacks on MACOS came from those with different curricular concerns. Richard Jones, a humanist, in *Fantasy and Feeling in Education*, criticized Bruner for failing to recognize MACOS' potential for fostering emotional growth.[10] Social reconstructionists opposed MACOS on the ground that it was created by a scholarly elite. A ruling class should not foster ideas in teachers and students, they said. The topics that children are asked to study are not related to improving the social life of the community in which they live. Congressman John B. Conlan blasted the course on the House floor as depicting "abhorrent and revolting behavior by a nearly extinct Eskimo tribe." Conlan said the material was full of references to adultery, cannibalism, killing of female babies and old people, trial marriage, wife-swapping, and violent murders. Many congressmen and others began to view the National Science Foundation as indoctrinating children and showing preference for certain scientists and curriculum makers. The controversies surrounding MACOS led to restricted NSF funding for educational research and greater surveillance of NSF by Congress. In 1979, a suit in federal court asked that

---

[10]Richard M. Jones, *Fantasy and Feeling in Education* (New York: Harper and Row, 1968).

the state be enjoined from compelling children to participate in MACOS. The plaintiffs charged that this curriculum espoused secular humanism and that the United States Supreme Court had defined this as a religion. They argued that this course violated the First Amendment.

TRENDS IN THE ACADEMIC SUBJECT CURRICULUM

Revival of the Academic Curriculum in the 1980s

A revival of the academic curriculum is now occurring. For example, in 1979-1980, Harvard University introduced a new undergraduate *core curriculum* designed to bring purpose and coherence to courses of study. This curriculum requires students to meet academic requirements in five areas: literature and the arts, history, social analysis and moral reasoning, science, and foreign cultures. The new curriculum replaces a list of eighty to 100 highly specific courses—ranging from the historical origins of inequality to lectures on law and social order. It requires also that students show proficiency in writing, mathematics, and the use of computers.

Harvard curriculum reform is partly a response to a laissez faire curriculum policy in the 1970s that encouraged an educational smorgasbord with a student's tastes alone determining choice. This reform aims at helping the student to see how the various parts of education fit together and at presenting important legacies for a citizen of the world—the knowledge of the past that illuminates the present. Knowledge is not to be conveyed by rattling off facts but by helping students understand the modes of thought employed by a range of disciplines in a spectrum of fields.

Similarly, secondary schools are retreating from the practice of permitting a wide choice of content for the curriculum. Centralized structured and required curriculum emphasizing such subjects as English, science, social science, math, practical and fine arts are replacing the large number of courses formerly available. This trend implies that certain areas of knowledge are of more value than others.

Currently at least three trends are discernible in the academic subject curriculum. One of these continues the forms and structure of knowledge approach by which pupils learn how to acquire or justify facts rather than merely recall them. It is estimated that 20 percent of the nation's school districts, for example, are using materials for teaching a "new history," in which each student compiles his or her own version. This is an inquiry approach that seeks to teach pupils to judge evidence. Students are taught how to judge conflicting evidence and draw their own conclusions; and each student's position is valid if researched, reasoned, and articulated. New history minimizes the importance of chronology and memorization. Advocates stress that they do not want students to reach absolute conclusions but to learn how to judge, weigh evidence, see the other side, and recognize the biases of other interpreters. Secondary school students are questioning interpretations of Jefferson, Jackson, and Lincoln. They are comparing capitalism with socialism. They are examining the United States treatment of the Indians and the historical records of the Spanish-American War as well as Vietnam and other recent events. The approach is not without criticism. Some scholars fret about the loss of chronology and absence of traditional historical content. Others believe the approach develops cynics; they say that students need belief in heroism and virtues to build clear ideals and confidence.

The second trend marks a renaissance of ideas prominent in curriculum proposals of the 1930s—integrated studies. *Integrated studies* is a generic term applied to any curriculum development effort in which two or more previously separate subjects are combined. It is a response to the changes in society and the need for more comprehensive models of knowledge. Science educators, for example, have identified 170 unified science programs in which boundaries between the specialized sciences are dissolved in favor of pervasive ideas and characteristics. Organizing themes for instruction are major concepts, scientific processes, natural phenomena, and persistent problems. Most of these science programs have been developed locally and are designed to be conducted over a period of more than one year.

Among persons committed to the new patterns of subject matter and reduced redundancy are members of the Federation for Unified Science Education (FUSE), the International Council of Scientific Unions (ICSU), and the Science Teaching Division of UNESCO. These groups use the following approach in developing an integrated curriculum:

Choosing a unifying theme. The unifying theme is generally either a big idea (concept) that permeates all sciences, or a process of science, a natural phenomenon, or a social problem inviting scientific interpretations.

Incorporating learning activities from several specialized sciences. Activities that involve content and process from one or more of the behavioral or social sciences and related to the theme are offered.

Incorporating a variety of learning modes. Concrete experiences that reflect the interests and needs of learners in the particular area and deal with local phenomena are to be used.

One such program is found at the Laboratory School, University of Florida, where high school students over a three-year period acquire interdisciplinary concepts and abilities to investigate scientific questions of social concern. Concepts like order, change, equilibrium, models, and quantification are important in all sciences. These concepts have become the basis for the selection and organization of subject matter. The older system of studying separate subjects has been replaced by one in which chemistry, physics, biology, and technology are combined in trying to understand a complex question.

In order to understand equilibrium, for example, the student should study how the body maintains internal balance. In studying the processes and phenomena occurring in the human body, students will draw on content from different fields. They may use Newton's Laws (balance); center of gravity, rotational and linear equilibrium, forces, and torques; biomechanics (explanation of vertigo); body structure; anatomy; roles of body systems in maintaining homeostasis; and "feedback systems models" as applied to their own body functions. Students are led to consider the role of body chemicals in maintaining a stable body and to explore the meaning of chemical equilibrium and acid-base regulation processes in the body. The knowledge needed to teach such a course normally requires team teaching, and teachers learn from one another. Student response is positive, with dramatic rises in course enrollments, successful advanced work in science, and increased ability to see relationships.

A third trend in the academic curriculum can be found in the "back to basics" movement and in the increasing number of *fundamental* offerings. Accordingly, school subjects are taught *directly*, with an emphasis on learning to read, write, and solve mathematical problems. Grammar is part of the English curriculum. Latin, French, mathematics, and science are presented without attempts at relevance or interesting project designs. Fundamentalists disapprove of both courses that emphasize methods and concepts of inquiry without imparting facts, and courses that encourage pupils' expression of opinions and value preferences. They oppose what they see as a nihilistic tendency, the offering of a curriculum whereby good and bad are merely subjective opinions and all ideas are equal.

Few schools offer a curriculum based on the proposition that there is a body of eternal and absolute truth, valid under all conditions, or that reason can be enhanced by familiarity with the most profound and grandest of humankind's intellectual works. St. John's College in Maryland is an exception. When students take biology at St. John's College, they are handed a stiff frog and an Aristotelian treatise. In this school an older view of academic education—including science, mathematics, Greek, French, music, and the Great Books seminars— is maintained. In preceptorals, similar to electives, seven or eight students and a tutor work intensively on one of the Great Books or on a limited subject like Freud. In the all-required curriculum, third- and fourth-year students study physics, measurement theory, and chemistry in their science course. Sophomore biology emphasizes anatomy, embryology, and genetics in the framework of evolution. When they dissect their frogs, students read Aristotle's book *On the Parts of Animals* and ponder his notion of aliveness. They also read Galen, the second-century physician whose works were definitive for more than a thousand years, while they dissect rabbits. When they progress to the rabbit's circulatory system, they discuss William Harvey's treatise, "On the Motion of the Heart and Blood in Animals," published in 1628. Rather than presenting only the most current research to students to memorize and repeat in exams, tutors encourage students to practice scientific inquiry. To do that, they believe, students must confront the great minds. Almost half of the biology sessions are spent in laboratory dissections and experiments that demonstrate genetics and embryological theory. Although students read from a half-dozen contemporary books, they also read and discuss the works of such trailblazers as Claude Bernard, Gregor Johann Mendel, and Karl Ernst Von Baer.

CHARACTERISTICS OF CURRICULUM AS ACADEMIC SUBJECT MATTER

Whether it is presented as forms of knowledge, compartmentalized disciplines, integrated subjects, or Great Books, the academic curriculum has certain attributes. These attributes are related to purpose, method, organization, and evaluation.

Purpose and Function

The purposes of the academic curriculum are to develop rational minds and to train students in the use of the most beneficial ideas and processes for investigating the problems of specialized research. There are those who would separate cognitive development from mastery of academic disciplines. Elliot Eisner and Elizabeth Vallance, for instance, refer to a cognitive conception of curriculum whereby intellectual skills are developed independently of any academic subject matter.[11] In my opinion, there is little present evidence to warrant employment of such a conception. Efforts to measure cognitive processes without regard to content have been unsuccessful. Persons do not think thoughts, they think subject matter. Those who favor the academic curriculum believe that students who become knowledgeable in the forms of knowledge and the methods for continued growth after school years in the wider society should learn to cultivate reason and perhaps even to control their appetites. The school should allow pupils to realize the finest achievements of their cultural heritage and, when possible, to add to these achievements through their own efforts.

Methods

Exposition and inquiry are two techniques commonly used in the academic curriculum. Ideas are stated and elaborated so that they may be understood. Main ideas are ordered, illustrated, and explored. Problems that fall within given disciplines are formulated and pursued. Appropriate methods for winning and validating truths in the different disciplines are taught. Students discover that reason and sense perception are used to win knowledge in the sciences, logic in math, individual form and feeling in art, and coherence in history (a fact must be consistent with other known facts). They examine statements to ascertain their meaning, their logical grounding, and their factual support. They read the greatest works in order to stretch their minds, to keep in touch with the past and with other people in their own age. Books that have most influenced great lives are not neglected.

[11]Elliot W. Eisner and Elizabeth Vallance, *Conflicting Conceptions of Curriculum* (Berkeley, Calif.: McCutchan, 1974).

Organization

Alternative organizational patterns for improving the academic curriculum are many. A few are listed here:

Unified or concentrated. Major themes serve to organize the subject matter from various disciplines. The concept of energy, for example, can be studied from biological, physical, chemical, and geological perspectives.

Integrated. Skills learned in one subject are used as tools in another field. Mathematics, for instance, is taught for the solving of scientific problems.

Correlated. Disciplines retain their separate identities, but students learn how concepts in one discipline are related to those in another. For example, history, geography, and English may be taught so as to reinforce one another.

Comprehensive problem solving. Problems may be drawn from current social interests such as consumer research, recreation, and transportation. Students must draw on skills and knowledge from the sciences, social sciences, mathematics, and art in the attempt to optimize a solution.

Within a course, academic subject matter is typically organized in a linear fashion based on some provision for a progressive development of a concept or a method. Organizational principles that guide this development include: simple to complex (one-celled animals before many-celled animals); whole to part (allowing for topographical study showing the overall scheme of the course before studying detailed topics); chronological narration (events are arranged in a time sequence); learning hierarchies (learning to place cells in empty matrices comes before learning to infer the characteristics of the object needed to fill an empty cell).

With respect to sequence within total school programs, it is interesting to recall John Dewey's views that the learner should be reintroduced to certain forms of subject matter at different school levels. He stressed the continuity of subject matter and illustrated how subject matter can be adapted in light of the learner's maturation (see Table 3).

Evaluation

At the classroom level, the means of evaluation vary according to the objectives of the different subject matters. In humanities, essays are preferred over multiple-choice tests, and answers that reflect

TABLE 3

School Level	Subject Matter Emphasis
Primary	Varied subject matter through concrete experiences.
Upper elementary	Mastery of fundamental tools of inquiry and communication— reading, writing, arithmetic, observation, investigation.
Secondary	Differentiation of subject matter— systematic instruction in separate fields.
	Views of how each subject is related to another (encyclopedic survey).
Higher education	Subject matter in accordance with individual capacity and interest.

logic, coherence, and comprehensiveness rather than a single right or wrong choice. In the arts, the expression is judged by faithfulness to personal subjectivity and to standards for beauty and taste, such as adherence to the principles of unity and balanced contrast. The highest grades in mathematics are given to the students who learn to appreciate the formal axiomatic nature of the field. In science, numerous criteria are used. Value is placed on the learner's use of given processes and modes of thought as well as knowledge of facts and themes. Logical rigor and experimental adequacy are highly prized.

Academic specialists are often ambivalent toward evaluation of their curriculum. They see evaluation as valuable, providing useful information, yet they often worry that it will interfere with the realization of broad teaching objectives. They also believe that evaluation may antagonize the teacher and students, take time that can be spent in other ways, and demand a compulsive attitude toward record-keeping, which is not compatible with a spirit of enthusiasm. Further, they share the fear that short-run evaluation may focus on simple skills rather than the complex skills of inductive reasoning. Ideally, the academician would survey not a term, but five or ten years of work. They want the child to change, not for a weekly examination, but for life.

ISSUES IN THE CURRICULUM AS ACADEMIC SUBJECT MATTER

Selecting among Disciplines

There is a problem in selecting from among the more than 1,000 disciplines those that could become part of the school curriculum. The problem is not new:

> Good Lord! how long is Art,
> And life, how it goes flying!
> . . . .
> It is so hard to gain the means whereby
> Up to the source one may ascend.
> And ere a man gets half-way to the end,
> Poor devil! he's almost sure to die![12]

It is impossible for an individual to delve very deeply into many disciplines. How shall those administering the curriculum decide which disciplines to offer? A number of measuring rods are proposed: (1) comprehensiveness with respect to ways at arriving at or justifying truth or knowledge; (2) social utility—the usefulness of the discipline for all citizens; (3) prerequisite knowledge—the importance of certain disciplines as a basis for others or for subsequent education.

In the interest of comprehensiveness, it would be well to sample disciplines that emphasize different avenues for justifying knowledge. This is the intent of Hirst in offering forms of knowledge. Philip Phenix has illustrated how to achieve comprehensiveness in the fundamental disciplines. His *Realms of Meaning* describes and analyzes six basic types of meaning, each of which has a distinctive logical structure.[13] Art, with its concern for subjective validation, can balance a discipline like science, which uses objective observations to confirm an expected occurrence. History can be used to illustrate the criteria of coherence and verifiability—to show that ideas have to fit together and that new conclusions can be checked

---

[12]Goethe's *Faust*, translated and edited by J.F.L. Raschen (Ithaca, N.Y.: The Thrift Press, 1803), pp. 29–31.
[13]Philip H. Phenix, *Realms of Meaning* (New York: McGraw-Hill, 1964).

out in terms of past events. Mathematics can prepare learners to gain knowledge through reason and logic. It may be possible to find a form that will help students recognize that some forms of knowledge can be validated by intuition and divine revelation. Such a curriculum would preclude the exclusivity of today's schools, which tend to emphasize the scientific mode of learning.

Few people contend that a discipline is an end in itself. Specialists in each field believe that knowledge in the field will be relevant to some aspect of a better life. The phrase "knowledge for knowledge's sake" is not taken seriously. However, not all disciplines will serve equally well the educational needs of persons in a given social context. Some very narrow specialties have little to contribute to problems that directly touch all lives. Newer disciplines claim to be more relevant than older ones. Psychology, for instance, is challenging literature for the honor of interpreting human nature. Anthropology begs admission on the ground that it can do a better job of helping pupils gain a valid world view than can history, a field known for reflecting parochial interests.

Including certain subjects as prerequisites is sometimes defended on the ground that there is a logical dependency between fields of knowledge, which supersedes learner interest or relevancy to social problems. There are scientists, for example, who would not make biology the first course in the secondary school curriculum in science; they believe that to learn biology one needs to understand the principles of chemistry and that to understand chemistry, one must, in turn, know the basic concepts of physics. Others believe that a prerequisite discipline should help the learner know what posture to assume, what sources to consult, and what to admit as relevant for a point at issue. Because philosophy leads to an understanding of all fields of knowledge, it has been suggested as the initial course in the academic curriculum to prepare learners to see similarities and differences among the disciplines they will meet.

A less defensible use of the prerequisite criterion is associated with requirements for college admission. These requirements have set the standard for the high school curriculum for many years. Many schools gear their curriculum to the subject matters demanded by the College Board's Admission Testing Program—four years of English, mathematics, science, and foreign language, and three to four years of social studies. Similarly, academic disciplines have been chosen because of the manpower requirements of government or industry. Both knowledge and students are considered by some policymakers as resources or instruments to serve their goals and programs.

How to Make Subject Matter More Appealing
to Growing Minds

The academic curriculum has been indicted for putting the logic and orderliness that appeals to the academic mind over the psychological logic of the learner. The failure of the subject organization to inspire learners is a common challenge. The fact that teachers often are not willing or able to carry out the curriculum plans of the academic scholars with the intended enthusiasm and insight is related to this criticism. Academicians are also said to be guilty of two curriculum fallacies: the fallacy of content and the fallacy of universalism.

Those who commit the *fallacy of content* are preoccupied with the importance of *what* students study rather than *how* they study. They overemphasize content that they believe to be intellectually rigorous and difficult and that they presume will make the necessary demands on students. As indicated in the following quotation, processes are as important as concepts, principles, and generalizations.

> The fallacy of content has attractive features. All ideas are not created equal, and some concepts and generalizations, some ideas and products of past inquiry are more useful and profound than others. To deny students access to the very best intellectual and aesthetic products that civilization has created is to deny them the core of what education can provide. But the products of science and art do not speak for themselves. Ideas become instrumental and works of art become aesthetic only when they are approached through appropriate modes of inquiry and perception.[14]

The *fallacy of universalism* rests on the belief that some content areas have universal value regardless of the characteristics of particular learners. One extreme of this view has been given by one of America's best known educators, the late Robert Maynard Hutchins, who said that "Education implies teaching. Teaching implies knowledge as truth. The truth is everywhere the same. Hence education should be everywhere the same."[15] Another instance of universalism is the presumption that academicians can package the disciplinary mode of university scholarship for wide use in elementary and secondary schools by pupils who are anything but budding knowledge specialists.

[14]From *Conflicting Conceptions of Curriculum*, by Elliot W. Eisner and Elizabeth Vallance on page 15, © 1974 by McCutchan Publishing Corporation. Reprinted with permission of the publisher.

[15]Robert Maynard Hutchins, *Higher Learning in America* (New Haven, Conn.: Yale University Press, 1936), p. 66.

Partly in response to these criticisms, efforts are being undertaken to improve the academic subject matter curriculum. Curriculum in newer academic subject matter encourages intuition—clever guessing—as a handmaiden to the recognized analytical thinking of the disciplines. School people are supplementing, adapting, and developing the scholars' curriculum materials, not regarding them as panaceas for given local educational needs. For example, teachers are preparing extra resources for less able pupils, as well as additional ways to stimulate the gifted child. Local facilities are being organized for introducing more creative elements into programs and for alternative studies illustrating the disciplines' techniques in a different environment than that intended by the original planners. Instead of studying biology solely from a textbook, students learn the nature of biology from studies of tidepools and animal husbandry. Homegrown academic programs are flourishing. Indeed, they may survive better than the national transplants.

The achievement of the primary school in challenging the conception and organization of subject matter has not gone unnoticed.

> What the best traditions of early education have done amounts to a major reorganization of subject matter into a common and coherent framework. The sand and water and clay, the painting and writing and reading, the cooking and building and calculation, the observing and nurture of plants and animals are woven together into a complex social pattern which sustains romance as it extends a concern for detail and for generalization. The organized discourse and text do not disappear but they do not dominate. . . . Teachers of the young are not regarded by themselves or by others as "intellectual." Yet the skillful among them are able to see order and number, geography and history, moral testing grounds, and aesthetic qualities in all the encounters of young children with the furniture of a rich environment.[16]

In short, some teachers seem able to see how certain learning opportunities that are appealing and well within the learners' capacities can serve as the starting point for organizing subject matter intellectually as the specialist does. They are able to differentiate between those activities that lead to growth and those that do not. These teachers have taken a long look ahead. They know the academic forms—the facts, principles, and laws—to which the children's present activities belong. These teachers are giving children opportunities for intelligent activity—for seeing how things interact with one another to produce definite effects—instead of aimless activity or the following of whims.

[16]*Forum* 17, no. 2 (Spring 1975): 40.

CONCLUDING COMMENTS

Academic specialists have attempted to develop a curriculum that will equip learners to enter the world of knowledge with the basic concepts and methods for observing, noting relationships, analyzing data, and drawing conclusions. They intend learners to act like physicists, biologists, or historians so that as citizens they will follow developments in disciplines with understanding and support and, if they continue their studies, become specialists themselves. One weakness in the approach is the failure to give sufficient attention to integrative objectives. Learners are thus unable to relate one discipline to another and to see how the content of a discipline can be brought to bear on the complex problems of modern life not answerable by a single discipline. Two current movements to overcome this weakness are (1) "integrated" studies in which content from several fields is applied to important social problems, and (2) the teaching of a manageable number of knowledge forms so that learners acquire a range of perspectives for understanding experience.

A second weakness in the academic conception of curriculum has been a tendency to impose adult views of the subject matter. Academic specialists have often given insufficient attention to the present interests and backgrounds of particular learners. They might have used those interests as sources for problems and activities by which learners might acquire the intellectual organization that constitutes academic subject matter. There are signs that this weakness is being corrected in some schools, too.

Academic subject matter will remain a prevailing curriculum conception. The search for sensation will not replace the quest for reason. We can expect to see knowledge and imagination entering the school as partners. More appropriate subject matter objectives will be derived, and academic instructional strategies will be revised. Already a few teachers are moving from an emphasis on transmitting of knowledge to an emphasis on the winning of knowledge. Some students in science classrooms, for example, are asked to criticize existing scientific assertions and to help design tests for refuting them. When the theories are refuted, these teachers give students the opportunity to create new ones; hence the students are learning to advance knowledge.

QUESTIONS

1. In the past few years people have become disenchanted with science and scholarship. Academic promises to enrich everyone's life and solve the tragic situations in society have gone sour. Instead, many people believe that science has done as much harm as good; academics once perceived as giants are now perceived as "pygmies," and scholars are seen as ideologists rather than objective seekers of truth. What are the implications of this disenchantment for an academic curriculum? Should the curriculum encourage the learner to view those in the academic disciplines as saviors? Should the curriculum illuminate disciplines as patient, unhurried searches for data, principles, and laws that may enlarge our understanding of the world?

2. The following two paragraphs contain different viewpoints on curriculum goals. What is your position?

    The right to an academic education means that the curriculum should be concerned with the permanent and enduring, not with the ephemeral. The curriculum should be concerned with order and rigor, not with uncertainties and incoherence.

    The daily lives of most people are going to be messy and constantly changing. They will be assailed by new laws, new traffic schemes, and new sex-roles; and these will loom larger in their lives than the works of Shakespeare or the Third Law of Thermodynamics. They will not be able to find the "right" answers to their daily problems. Neither will they be able to categorize the problems into subjects like history or physics. So more value should be placed on education for ordinary life than on academic education.

3. Judge each of the following definitions of the academic curriculum in terms of feasibility (ease of learning and teaching), utility (extent to which it contributes to learners' basic needs for survival, independence, and respect), and idealism (degree to which it is consistent with the highest ideals about human nature).

    a. Academic subject matter consists of the intellectual tools—the questions, methods, concepts, processes, and attitudes—by which knowledge is currently acquired.

    b. Academic subject matter consists of conclusions—the facts, principles, and laws—carefully chosen from those derived by specialists on the basis of their relevancy to the conduct of daily living.

    c. Academic subject matter consists of the finest achievements of our cultural heritage, the works of those great minds that have had an effect on civilization.

4. Both John Dewey and the new developmentalists have held that it is important both (a) to bring subject matter to bear on the interests,

problems, and progress of the child and (b) to attend to activities like drawing, performing music, nature walks, and manual construction so that they lead or lure the learner to the abstract, systematic, and theoretical ideas of which these activities are a part. What competence in subject matter would a teacher need in order to achieve both?

5. Under what circumstances might you favor one or more of the following organizational patterns in the academic curriculum:
   a. *Unified or concentrated.* Courses are organized by themes or concepts common to many fields.
   b. *Integrated subject matter.* One subject serves as a tool to another.
   c. *Correlated subject matter.* Separate subjects and courses reinforce each other.
   d. *Comprehensive problems.* Solutions require knowledge from many fields.
6. Does correlation reinforce two subjects equally? Does correlation serve English as well as it does history, for example?

SELECTED REFERENCES

Barrow, Robin. *Common Sense and the Curriculum.* Hamden, Conn.: Linnet Books, 1976.

Diorio, Joseph A. "Knowledge, Truth and Power in the Curriculum," *Educational Theory* 27, no. 2 (Spring 1977): 103–11.

Ford, G.W. and Pugno, Lawrence, eds. *The Structure of Knowledge and the Curriculum.* Chicago: Rand McNally, 1964.

Hirst, Paul H. *Knowledge and the Curriculum.* London: Routledge & Kegan Paul, Ltd., 1974.

Hullett, James. "Which Structure?" *Educational Theory* 24, no. 1 (Winter 1974): 60–72.

Kuhn, Alfred. *Unified Social Science: A System-Based Approach.* Homewood, Ill.: Dorsey Press, 1975.

Phenix, Philip H. *Realms of Meaning.* New York: McGraw Hill, 1964.

Robinson, Donald W., ed. "What Is Liberal Education?" A special feature in which six authors give their views. *Phi Delta Kappan* 60, no. 9 (May 1979): 639–48.

II / TECHNICAL SKILLS IN CURRICULUM DEVELOPMENT

The metaphor of the *game* has been suggested for curriculum development. In one way, it is a bad metaphor because curriculum building is, unlike most games, a serious business with many consequences. In other ways, however, the metaphor is appropriate. As a challenging game, curriculum making calls for imagination within a framework of ordering principles and constraints. It has rules to follow and pieces to play. Purposes, goals, objectives, learning activities, subject matter content, social contexts, anticipated learners, and philosophical and legal constraints are among the more important pieces to be considered and related.

Also, game strategies vary. We believe, however, that participants can be helped to become more skillful. To this end, in the next four chapters there is an orientation to the task, a sense of what is expected in curriculum development and a description of available options.

The chapters convey a sense of what is involved in the technical procedures for curriculum development and indicate the degrees of freedom that participants have. Although the rules, processes, and limitations are not firmly fixed, there is every reason to believe that the following concerns are most important: how to derive defensible educational outcomes, how to plan learning activities that are both valuable in themselves and a means for the learner to achieve desired goals, how to have curriculum plans implemented by teachers and others, and how to assess and revise plans through evaluation.

5 / DETERMINING CURRICULUM ENDS

The determining of curriculum ends—purposes, functions, goals, and objectives—is the subject of this chapter. After indicating the different contexts in which curriculum ends are set, we will describe and appraise four models and one nonmodel for deciding what should be taught. The discerning reader will see the association among certain models, curriculum conceptions, and kinds of schools. No curriculum task is more important than determining warranted ends. It is therefore crucial to reflect on ways to derive educational goals and objectives. In this chapter we depart from most curriculum texts by describing several basic approaches for deciding what to teach, instead of presenting a single procedure for formulating ends. We also indicate why one or another of these approaches is more appropriate in given situations. By learning about various models for formulating curriculum ends, the reader should become more effective in a range of situations. The reader may wish to compare these models with the way purposes often are derived in practice. As gaps between the model and practice are identified, improvements can be made.

ARENAS FOR DEVELOPING ENDS

Levels of Decision Making

Curriculum planning, including decisions about what to teach and to what purpose, occurs at different levels of remoteness from intended learners. John Goodlad classifies these levels as *societal*, *institutional*, and *instructional*.[1] Participants at the societal level include boards of education (local or state), state departments

---

[1] John I. Goodlad with Maurice N. Richter, Jr., *The Development of a Conceptual System for Dealing with Problems of Curriculum and Instruction* (Los Angeles: Cooperative Research Program, USOE Project 454, University of California, 1966).

of education, federal agencies, publishers, and national blue ribbon curriculum reform committees. At the institutional level, administrators, and faculty groups are the prominent actors. Parents and students, too, are playing an increasing role in institutional decision making with respect to curriculum. The instructional level refers to decisions made primarily by a teacher or teams of teachers guiding specific groups of learners. Recently the personal or experiential has been proposed as a fourth decision level in curriculum making. This level is consistent with the view that learners are potential generators and not merely passive recipients of curriculum ends and means.[2]

Different techniques and personnel are involved in curriculum making at the different levels. Curriculum making at the national societal level includes development of goals and objectives as well as textbooks and other instructional materials for wide use; for example, federally financed curriculum projects in universities and educational regional laboratories, the curriculum work of nonprofit organizations funded by the federal government and private foundations, and the objectives that accompany school materials produced by publishing houses in cooperation with professional educators. Often curriculum designers at this level do not focus on a wide range of educational goals such as social adjustment, self-expression, manual dexterity, and general social attributes. Instead they center on domains and objectives that are specific to a single subject area, grade level, or course. In this arena, specialized personnel—subject specialists, curriculum specialists, and editors—make most of the decisions about *what* should be taught and *how*. These specialists do, however, attend to professional and public opinion as reflected in the yearbooks published by national subject matter organizations such as the National Council for Social Studies (NCSS), professional journals, and popular media. They also seek the advice of representative teachers, textbook salespeople, and other consultants. Results from marketing efforts and trials of preliminary versions also bring about changes in both the ends and means of their curriculum.

Curriculum development at the state level involves the production of curriculum guides and frameworks. These materials are prepared by professional staffs in state departments of education assisted by representative teachers, college and university personnnel, and curriculum specialists. The purposes and goals set forth in these mate-

[2]John I. Goodlad and associates, *Curriculum Inquiry: The Study of Curriculum Practice* (New York: McGraw-Hill, 1979).

rials are usually formulated by advisory committees composed of professional educators, representatives from educational agencies, and selected laypersons. State department personnel also engage in curriculum making in response to state laws pertaining to the teaching of such topics as narcotics, health, and physical education.

Beginning in 1977 and continuing into 1980, legislation in most states mandated minimum competency testing for elementary and secondary students. These mandates concentrated on skill areas to be tested, grade levels to be covered, and elaborate procedures for test selection. State departments of education were given responsibility for implementing competency-based education programs. These statewide actions and similar testing programs initiated independently in many local school districts have had an implicit but inevitable effect on curriculum. An increasing public insistence on "accountability," focusing on the "basic skills," has forced widespread adjustment in curriculum emphasis.

The most common arena for curriculum planning is the school district, although there are signs that curriculum decision making at individual schools is increasing. Districts usually involve specialized personnel in curriculum as well as curriculum generalists, subject matter specialists, consultants, representative teachers, and some laypersons. Ideally, these persons should be concerned with adapting and designing curriculum to be relevant to local phenomena and problems. They should consider the implications of regional economy, history, and arts for learners in the local schools. Curriculum making at the individual school level should involve all classroom teachers and administrators, and representative parents and students. Their activities should focus on goals, materials, organization, and instructional strategies. Within the self-contained or nongraded classroom, the individual teacher or teaching team should develop the curriculum objectives and activities that are most appropriate for particular pupils, keeping in mind the general goals of the school. Although many teachers rely on an outside source, such as a textbook or course of study, to determine the concepts to be taught, they frequently expand on this curriculum, reflecting on pupil responses. A teacher may ask, "What questions have my pupils asked that will serve as a means for developing the concepts?"

The relative importance of the levels of decision making varies from country to country, state to state, and school to school. Centralized educational systems such as those in Japan and France give the ministry of education more authority over curriculum ends. Less

centralized educational systems such as are found in the United
Kingdom have established local organizations to explore aspects of
the curriculum and to develop new schemes or projects intended to
improve the quality and relevance of what is offered to pupils. In the
United States, local authority for curriculum decisions has been
greatest in New England and among the states of the Midwest. State
control has always been more evident in such states as Texas,
Florida, New York, and California. Now, however, the central role
of the teacher in curriculum planning and development is increasing
everywhere, partly because of a growing belief that no curriculum
derived from outside agencies would be successful without teacher
commitment.

Different Curriculum at Different Levels. Casual readers about
curriculum get inconsistent messages. On one hand, they read that
the curriculum is rapidly changing—a new program in mathematics,
health education, more appropriate content for the gifted, and
mastery learning for the slow. On the other hand, there are reports
indicating that schools are teaching the same thing in the same way as
always—reading, writing, arithmetic in the elementary school and
vocational and college preparatory programs in the secondary
school.

One explanation for the conflicting reports of change versus per-
manence is that the reports do not all refer to the same curriculum. A
curriculum formulated at one level is not necessarily adopted and implemented at another. John Goodlad and his associates, for example,
have proposed five different curricula, each operating at a different
level.[3]

Ideal Curriculum. From time to time foundations, governments,
and special interest groups set up committees to look into aspects of
the curriculum and to advise on changes that should be made. Curriculum recommendations proposed by these committees might treat
multicultural curriculum, a curriculum for the talented, early childhood curriculum, career education curriculum, and the like. These
proposals might represent ideals or describe desired directions in curriculum as seen by those with a particular value system or special interest. The proponents of such ideal curricula are competing for
power within the society. It should be clear, however, that the im-

[3]John I. Goodlad and associates, *Curriculum Inquiry* (New York: McGraw-Hill, 1979).

pact of an ideal curriculum depends on whether the recommendations are adopted and implemented.

2. *Formal Curriculum*. Formal curriculum includes those proposals that are approved by state and local boards. Such a curriculum may be a collection of ideal curricula, a modification of the ideal, or other curriculum policies, guides, syllabi, texts sanctioned by the board as the legal authority for deciding what shall be taught and to what ends.

3. *Perceived Curriculum*. The perceived curriculum is what the teachers perceive the curriculum to be. Teachers interpret the formal curriculum in many ways. Often there is poor linkage (decoupling) between the formally adopted curriculum and the teachers' perception of what the curriculum means or should mean in practice.

4. *Operational Curriculum*. This curriculum is what actually goes on within the classroom. Observations by researchers and others who make records of classroom interaction often reveal discrepancies between what teachers say the curriculum is and what teachers actually do.

5. *Experiential Curriculum*. The experiential curriculum consists of what students derive from and think about the operational curriculum—that which they have experienced. This curriculum is identified through student questionnaires, interviews, inferences from observations of students, and other ways of eliciting the personal meanings obtained by students from their classroom experiences.

RANGE OF ACTIVITY IN CURRICULUM DEVELOPMENT

Curriculum developers' efforts are directed at producing programs of study, catalogs of goals and objectives, curriculum guides, course outlines, and lesson plans. They also produce more specific instructional materials: textbooks, taped and filmed programs, and instructional sequences. These materials often require the curriculum developer to detail steps for the teacher or child to follow and to prepare tests and record-keeping systems, as well as procedures for training the teacher on how to use the materials.

Before undertaking the production of any materials, the curriculum developer will consider time and the intended learners. Will the material serve an hour's lesson, a year's work, a six-year program? What are the ages, mental and physical characteristics, and experiential backgrounds of the future users of the materials?

In determining what the individual or target population should learn, curriculum developers take either a restricted or unrestricted approach. In the restricted approach, the developer looks for possible objectives from within a domain of knowledge and practice. Mathematics, health, intellectual development, and vocational education are typical domains. In an unrestricted approach, the curriculum developer is willing to regard any problem, idea, or situation as having possible implications for what should be taught. The curriculum maker's task of conceiving possible and desirable outcomes does not mean that all proposed ends will be accepted and acted upon. Boards of education, principals, teachers, and pupils all have ways of rejecting the best conceived purposes. However, persons who propose outcomes should be able to justify them. Later in this chapter, we will describe the ways in which developers justify ends.

INSTITUTIONAL PURPOSES AND FUNCTIONS INFLUENCE CURRICULUM OBJECTIVES AND PROCEDURES FOR DEVELOPING CURRICULUM

Those who plan to develop curriculum within a given institution must attend to the nature of that school, especially to the school's manifest purposes. Why? One reason is that the selection of an appropriate model or set of procedures for formulating objectives depends on the central purpose of that school. Vocational and other training schools, for example, are expected to prepare students for specific jobs. Hence, the use of *job analysis*, a technique for deriving objectives that directly contributes to helping students find jobs and keep them, is warranted. This technique seeks to ensure a match between what the student learns and what he or she will do on the job. The method can be amplified, of course, with procedures for collecting data that will help one anticipate likely job requirements. Job analysis would, however, be a less appropriate tool to use in formulating objectives within an institution whose mission is perceived as furthering humanistic goals. Such an institution should use a different technical tool in formulating objectives, one more consistent with actualizing learners as individuals.

Illustrations of how institutional purposes should match procedures for curriculum development can be seen in the familiar practices of the community college. There is more freedom for formulating new expected outcomes in a community college than in a traditional school devoted to the liberal arts. Community colleges frequently have a very broad goal—community services, an invitation to meet the educational needs of the community. Because of this goal and the state legislature's practice of funding community colleges solely on the basis of student enrollment, the curriculum problem becomes a search for courses that will attract students. Anything that appeals to the aged, young mothers, veterans, immigrants, and the like must be considered. The appropriate technical tool for formulating objectives in this case is needs assessment, defined both as a procedure for uncovering local deficiencies and trends with implications for what might be taught, and as a way to sample and stimulate interests in various kinds of learnings.

Changes in Institutional Purposes

Some curriculum leaders do not want curriculum objectives to be shackled to institutional purposes. Indeed, some people believe that curriculum specialists should be trying to change the purposes of institutions. Bruce Joyce, who is opposed to the idea of accepting all present institutional definitions of purpose, has advanced the interesting thesis that curriculum developers have been shaped by the bureaucratic nature of the schools. He believes that objectives have been formulated to serve an industrial model of education with an emphasis on efficiency. He would rather see curriculum workers advance both futuristic and humanistic ends; institutions should focus on helping people to define problems that were not perceived before and to make contact with one another in new and stronger ways.[4]

Joyce is opposed to having the role of the curriculum worker determined by the constraints of educational institutions. One of his recommendations is that curriculum workers create new institutional forms and environments. The introduction of forms such as non-

[4]Bruce R. Joyce, "The Curricular Worker of the School," NSSE Yearbook, *The Curriculum: Retrospect and Prospect* (Chicago: University of Chicago Press, 1971), pp. 307–55.

directive teaching roles, pupil goal setting, technological self-instructional systems, and therapeutic modes of working might make possible the addition of humanistic goals within a traditional school.

Identifying Functions of the Curriculum

Before preparing any curriculum plan, whether for a textbook, lesson, course of study, document, product, or program, one should be clear about the functions the proposed curriculum will serve. Those persons responsible for a school's total curriculum offerings will also find a functional concept useful in bringing balance to their programs of study. Typically, four functions have been recognized:

1. *Integration or General Education.* This function is met through curriculum that addresses the learner as a responsible human being and citizen, not as a specialist or one with unique gifts or interests. It means, for instance, including as content the ground rules—Bill of Rights—for participating in the civic affairs of the community and developing those minimal competencies essential for the health, welfare, and protection of all. Successful general education enables everyone to support and share in the culture; hence, a curriculum worker must decide what the individual needs in order to communicate with others. The planner must consider what outcomes and experiences all should have in common.

2. *Supplementation.* Individuality is the key to understanding supplementation. Objectives consistent with it deal with both personal lacks and unique potentials. To serve this function, a curriculum might be designed for those whose talents and interests enable them to go much further than the majority or those whose defects and deficiencies are severe enough to require special attention. Such a curriculum is personal and individual, not common or general.

3. *Exploration.* Opportunities for learners to discover and develop personal interests capture the meaning of exploration. When well executed, it enables learners to find out that they do or do not have either the talent or zeal for certain kinds of activities. Exploring experiences should *not* be organized and taught as if their purpose were to train specialists. Neither should they be conceived as shoddy and superficial. Exploration demands a wide range of contacts within a field, realization of the possiblities for further pursuit, and revelation of one's own aptitudes and interests.

4. *Specialization*. A specializing function is rendered by a curriculum in which the current standards of a trade, profession, or academic discipline prevail. Students are expected to emulate those who are successfully performing as skilled workers or scholars. Entry into such a curriculum requires that students already have · considerable expertise and drive.

The balance among the different functions varies every few years. Within secondary schools, for example, academic specialization was in the ascendancy in the 1960s. In the 1970s, there was a weakening of general education in favor of exploration; minicourses, optional modules, alternative curriculum, and other electives were used. Currently, the "back to basics" demand by parents and some educators is moving the curriculum in the direction of general education. Vocational specialization, too, is getting more attention. It is often carried on outside the school itself through job entry plans.

In higher education too newer curriculum policy favors general education—often said to be an unwelcome chore. Opposition to general education comes from humanists and academic specialists who (albeit for different reasons) believe it best for teachers and students to select their own areas of interest for study. As a counter to the charge of narrowness, the academic specialist says that by understanding one field in depth, the student will learn to appreciate a wider array of intellectual tools and artistic achievement. This notion has not gone unchallenged. Elliot Eisner, for instance, views it with skepticism.

> I am not convinced by the thesis that specialization breeds general understanding, or that it cultivates an appreciation of the variety of ways in which meaning can be secured. . . . If attention to a wide range of problems and fields of study is necessary for the type of personal and intellectual range one wished to develop in students, how then can one cultivate, in depth, those idiosyncratic interests and aptitudes which almost all students have?[5]

The return to general education is spearheaded by Harvard University's Dean Henry Rosovsky, who bemoans the absence of a core of general studies—a missing common denominator—and the lack of a broad perspective for sense of purpose. His recognition of

[5]Elliot W. Eisner, "Persistent Dilemmas in Curriculum Decision Making," *Confronting Curriculum Reform* (Boston: Little, Brown, 1971), pp. 168–69.

the problem is a clear signal to the nation's higher schools that it is time once again for essential reexamination of function.

The curriculum also performs less recognized or hidden functions. They include *consummation* (whetting the student demand for material things such as a car or the latest washing machine), the *custodial* function (keeping students from job markets and entertaining them), and variants of the *socializing* function (allowing students to meet members of the opposite sex).

MODELS FOR DETERMINING CURRICULUM ENDS

Needs Assessment Model

The power to frame educational purposes is central in the curriculum field. Those who are not sensitive to the need for this power—who merely accept ends that others have proposed—are in one sense instruments. The paragraphs to follow describe the ways individuals and groups generate and select curriculum ends—aims, goals, and objectives. These ends indicate the purposes for which our programs and lessons are undertaken. They give direction to what would otherwise be blind activities and enable us to prepare plans of action. A curriculum end-in-view is more than a whim or desire. Its formulation is a complex intellectual operation involving observation, study of conditions, collection of relevant information and, most of all, judgment. There can be no true curriculum end without an intellectual anticipation and valuing of consequences.

Needs assessment is the process by which educational needs are defined and priorities are set. In the context of curriculum, a need is defined as a condition in which there is a discrepancy between an *acceptable* state of learner behavior or attitude and an *observed* learner state.

Needs assessment is one of the most frequently used ways for determining justified curriculum goals and objectives. Several reasons underlie the recent popularity of needs assessment as a tool for formulating desired outcomes. Some people are motivated by efficiency. They want to identify and resolve the most critical needs so that resources can be employed in the most cost-efficient manner. They want to avoid the practice of trying to do a little bit in many problem areas and solving none of them. Other people are concerned about social disorganization, the lack of consensus among the school community. They see needs assessment as a way to effect shared values and mutual support. Discussion of alternative ends by parents, students, teachers, and other citizens is an educational activity in itself. Finally, there are people who want new value orientations to be reflected in the curriculum and who see needs assessment as a vehicle for influence. Cultural pluralists, for example, use needs assessment to elicit the values of subcultures such as those of Mexican-Americans, blacks, or the Chinese. They also try to have the dominant society accept these values as worthy goals to be advanced through the curriculum.

Steps in Needs Assessment

A. *Formulating a Set of Tentative Goals Statements.* Comprehensive sets of goals that reflect the dominant culture are readily available.[6] Such goals statements are collected from curriculum guides, textbooks, evaluation studies, and basic research studies by psychologists and educators. These goals refer to the conventionally sought outcomes in most schools: fundamental competencies for reading, writing, mathematics, health, citizenship, aesthetics. The goals statements also include attributes of character such as friendliness, respect, activeness, and independence.

Goals that reflect subculture values are more difficult to obtain. Cross-cultural investigations such as those by Luis Laosa reveal fundamental differences among the values of different cultural groups.[7] Many Mexican-American parents, for example, believe that learners should make their choices in terms of family interests rather than personal wants. Some Mexican-Americans do not want their children to express personal feelings in the presence of an adult. These goals often contrast sharply with those of many in the dominant culture and with goals of other subcultures. Sometimes, goals statements from minority group members reflect a desire to gain better treatment for their children in majority-dominated schools. Such a goal might be that learners should see school as a friendly place and as helpful in fulfilling their purposes.

[6]Center for the Study of Evaluation, *Elementary School Evaluation Kit: Needs Assessment* (Boston: Allyn and Bacon, 1972).

[7]Luis M. Laosa, "Cross Cultural and Subcultural Research in Psychology and Education," *Inter-American Journal of Psychology* 7 (1973): 241–48.

Goals statements reflecting a community's own values must also be obtained. Those conducting needs assessments must consider more than the conventional "canned" goals available from lists of commercially prepared statements. They must focus on their own perception of what they want their learners to think, feel, or be able to do as a result of school instruction.

Typical techniques for eliciting data for needs assessment are *concerns conferences* and *sponsor speakups*. Concerns conferences, organized by school administrators and curriculum specialists, are attempts to identify problems in the community as perceived by a great number of people. At a large convocation, community members are oriented to the tasks of identifying community problems, and later, in small discussion groups, problems are articulated and suggestions made for their solution. Frequently, new educational goals are proposed in order to contribute to the solution of the identified problem. In sponsor speakups students are organized into groups so that they work cooperatively to identify the most pressing needs of their school situation. Efforts are made to encourage uninhibited student expression. Although many of these needs may be met by actions that are not curricular in nature, it is important to consider the curriculum goals that might contribute to resolving the perceived difficulties.

Assigning Priority to Goal Areas. The second phase consists of accumulating preference data, typically from parents, staff, students, and community members. Members of these groups are given goal statements and asked to rank them in terms of importance. Opportunities are provided for the respondents to augment the set of goals presented. Usually they rate the goals on a five-point scale (a rating rather than a ranking allows more goals to be considered). Samples of goals can be given to different individuals to effect average group estimates. Later, the combined ratings of all the people sampled will reveal those goals considered very important, important, average, unimportant, and very unimportant.

Determining the Acceptability of Learner Performance in Each of the Preferred Goal Areas. In the third phase either a subjective or an objective approach can be taken. A subjective approach calls for a group of judges to rate the acceptability of present learner status on each goal. No direct measure of the learners with respect to the goals is undertaken; judges estimate the present status of learners with respect to each goal. Their impression might be gained by whatever they have observed or been led to believe by the media and reports from the children and other neighbors. Judges' ratings become indices of need. The objective approach requires actually measuring the status of students relative to each goal. Measures must be congruent with the goals, of course. To this end, instructional objectives within each goal area are selected. Matching assessment devices are chosen and administered to representative samples of pupils. If the students' level of performance on a measure is less than the acceptable level, a need is indicated. Levels obtained on each measure are compared. Those showing the widest gap indicate a greater priority. However, one must also consider the relative importance of the goal as indicated by preference data.

Translating High Priority Goals into Plans. In the fourth phase, goals that are preferred and for which a need has been identified become the bases for new curriculum instructional plans. The selection of new target outcomes, goals, and objectives has implications for course offerings and for instructional materials and arrangements because the realization of new goals requires new facilitating means. Learning activities, teaching strategies, and evaluation techniques must be changed. For example, having once identified a need for pupils to learn to read and write in Spanish and acquire minority cultural values as well as positive attitudes toward school, the school may need to develop a bilingual program. Consequently, the staff must acquire new materials in the Spanish language and offer activities consistent with minority values—group cooperation and family involvement. Further, teachers must be helped to use culture-matching teaching strategies, like learning how to indicate nonverbal acceptance through touching.

Problems in the Needs Assessment Technique

Technical and philosophical problems need to be resolved before needs assessment can fulfill its promise. One technical problem is that of communicating the meaning of goals so that those indicating their preferences are responding to the same referent. A vague goal, such as citizenship, creative fluency, or application of scientific methods, indicates only a general direction. On the other hand, making a vague goal specific often results in numerous objectives, so many in fact that no one person could rank them according to their value. More than fifty years ago, Boyd H. Bode commented on Franklin Bobbitt's claim that some 1200 high school teachers in Los Angeles had given an almost unanimous judgment on a long list of objectives. Bode said, "If the list really represents common judgment, we are bound to conclude that men and women are more amenable to reason in Los Angeles than anywhere else on the globe. . . . One almost wonders whether the teachers of Los Angeles did not mistake Bobbitt's list of abilities for a petition to be signed."[8] One answer to the problem of how to discriminate among objectives is to rely on precise and observable objectives that represent significant competencies rather than to stipulate the many objectives that contribute to the general competency. Another answer is to engage in sampling whereby different individuals rate different goals and objectives, no one person having to evaluate carefully more than seven, a "digestible" number.

It is helpful to ask all who are to rate goals to engage first in common discussion and to ascertain that particular goals or objectives satisfy these three criteria: (1) that the goal is needed for future learning and contributes to fundamental needs, such as making a living and gaining the respect of others; (2) that the goal is teachable; and (3) that it is not likely to be acquired outside the school.

Needs assessment is frequently used by those with adaptive conceptions of curriculum who see it as a way to ensure that the curriculum is responsive to changing social conditions. It can also be used by social reconstructionists who want not so much to prepare students for changing conditions as to alter the social institutions that are creating undesirable social conditions. Group deliberation and judgment thus become factors in needs assessment. There must be opportunity for sharing facts and logical persuasion—facts and ideas brought by the participants themselves, not by total outsiders—and there must be deliberation involving normative philosophical considerations. That something exists does not mean it is desirable. The reflective curriculum worker inquires about not only what is desired but also whether it is worthwhile, right, and good. Those who regard needs assessment as nothing more than a scientific information gathering procedure see it as a way to avoid ethical issues by justifying the curriculum merely on the basis of the popularity of certain goals and the magnitude of the discrepancy between where learners

[8]Boyd H. Bode, "On Curriculum Construction," *Curriculum Theory* 5 (1975): 43, reprinted from *Modern Educational Theories* (New York: Macmillan, 1927), p. 43.

are and where learners *should* be with respect to these popular goals. Needs assessment has been opposed when it is regarded solely as an information gathering procedure on the grounds that "No scientifically derived information can yield a judgment about 'what should be' because science deals not with normative considerations but with facts."[9]

It remains to be seen whether the dominant groups in schools will attend to the goal priorities of minority groups. Can the curriculum reflect the priorities of all groups within the community or must a consensus be reached? If there is group conflict, how will the conflict be resolved?

THE FUTURIST MODEL

There is a growing realization that the world of the future is going to be very different from the present, that it will demand new kinds of people, and that the time is short to prepare the citizens of the future. Hence, efforts have been made to develop educational objectives consistent with this realization and specific enough to imply action.

Although there are slight differences among authors' conceptions of the model, the following techniques and phases are regarded as important:

1. *The multidisciplinary seminar.* Professional educators and specialists from outside education—political scientists, economists, medical psychologists—meet for several days to discuss possible future developments that would affect curriculum planning. Members of this seminar prepare papers examining the research frontiers in their field. The results of literature searches on educational innovations and goals are also presented.

2. *Judgment of projected trends.* Major anticipated changes are ordered according to their importance to society and probability of occurrence. The difficulty of bringing about these changes in terms of time, money, and energy is considered. A period of occurrence is estimated. The potential social effects of these changes are classified as good or bad on the basis of carefully examined opinions on which there is a consensus. Participants

---

[9]Maurice L. Monette, "Need Assessment: A Critique of Philosophical Assumptions," *Adult Education* 29, no. 2 (1979): 83–95.

rate each change from "very desirable" to "very undesirable."[10]
3. *Educational acceptance for creating the future.* After the social consequences of trends have been established and rated, school persons and others suggest how they think the schools should respond. In deciding the educational responsibility to be taken, consideration is given to the certainty of a future occurrence, the social consequences of that occurrence, and the possibility that educators can effect it or can prepare students for it. Educational objectives, thus formed, should be stated to support "good" futures and to resist "bad" ones. The educators also decide what items in the present curriculum are unlikely to prepare students for the future world and suggest that these items no longer be supported.
4. *Scenario writing.* A group of writers prepares at least two descriptions. One is a description of what learners will be like if action is taken on the decision in Phase 3 and implemented by the school. The second is a description of the necessary related changes in subject matter, learning activities, curriculum organization, and methods. Attention is also paid to institutional arrangements that will bear on the new curriculum.

The Delphi method is used by curriculum workers as a way to obtain consensus on generalized goals and objectives for the future. By this method one tries to obtain the relevant intuitive insights of experts and then uses these judgments systematically. Gary Reeves and Lawrence R. Jauch have reported on the method as applied in designing a curriculum for higher education.[11] Their case study involved the choice of content for an undergraduate business school curriculum in light of what is likely to be useful to future graduates of the school. Fifty-eight members of a business advisory council to the school were sent a series of questionnaires. The first questionnaire indicated present content offerings and asked participants to indicate their recommended course subject areas and amount of time to be spent on each. In an attempt to gain consensus, a second questionnaire was sent, providing information about how all participants responded to the first. Participants were asked to reconsider their first recommendations and to give their reasons. Results indicated a movement toward consensus among survey participants.

[10]Harold G. Shane, "Future Planning as a Means of Shaping Educational Change," NSSE *Seventieth Yearbook* (Chicago, Ill.: University of Chicago Press, 1971), pp. 185–217.
[11]Gary Reeves and Lawrence R. Jauch, "Curriculum Development Through Delphi," *Research in Higher Edcation* 8, no. 2 (1978): 157–68.

Problems with the Futurist Model

The difficulty any group of people faces in trying to predict or invent the future is problem enough. There are also difficulties associated with getting a broad enough base of participation within and outside school systems and with understanding the complex factors that affect school curriculum. Different community contexts and different views of the school's role delay consensus. There is no consensus about what different educational institutions should be trying to achieve. A related aspect of the problem is that many people do not like to make choices, and many find it difficult to make even hypothetical choices. Even when groups arrive at a consensus on some preferred alternatives, many dissensions remain unresolved. Educational objectives frequently are not internally consistent or single-valued even for one person. One objective may call for the learner to show initiative; a second objective may call for the learner to follow directions. Respondents experience tension in deciding between creativity on the one hand and order and tradition on the other.

THE RATIONAL MODEL

Ralph Tyler's rationale is the best-known rational model for answering questions about formulating educational purposes, selecting and organizing educational experiences, and determining the extent to which purposes are being attained.[12] It is called an ends-means approach because the setting of purposes or objectives as ends influences the kinds of activity and organization most likely to assist in reaching the goal. Evaluation, too, according to this model, is undertaken to see how the learning experience as developed and organized produces the desired results.

Tyler's assumption is that objectives will be more defensible—will have greater significance and greater validity—if certain kinds of facts are taken into account. One source of facts consists of studies of the intended learners. A second source is found in studies of contemporary life outside the school, and a third source is made up of suggestions about objectives from subject matter specialists regarding what knowledge is of most worth for citizens. The following will

[12]Ralph W. Tyler, *Basic Principles of Curriculum and Instruction* (Chicago, Ill.: University of Chicago Press, 1950).

elaborate how objectives are derived from data provided by the different sources.

Learners. In order to derive objectives from this source, one would study learners in terms of their deficiencies with respect to knowledge and application of a broad range of values in daily living; their psychological needs for affection, belonging, recognition, and a sense of purpose; and their interests. Essentially, the process of deriving an objective from studies of the learner demands that an inference be drawn about what to teach after looking at the data. Making inferences also involves value judgments. If the data show that learners are chiefly interested in reading comic books, one still must decide whether this is a desirable interest to be extended or a deficiency to be overcome.

Let us assume that the curriculum worker has discovered this fact: "During adolescence, learners are likely to have the cognitive skills of intuition, generalization, and insight; and their sensibilities toward justice are awakened." The curriculum planner can use this information to infer what to teach, perhaps deciding that learners should acquire knowledge of Utopian thought and the methods for effecting a more perfect social order. The curriculum planner might also infer that students should suppress the tendency to believe that wars, tyrannies, and the like are caused by human nature and believe instead that changes in social structure may preclude injustices.

Social Conditions. Facts about the community—local, national, or world—must be known and taken into account if what is to be taught is to be made relevant to contemporary life. Again, one needs to make a value judgment in deciding what kinds of facts to collect. Comprehensiveness is sometimes sought: one might collect data on health, economics, politics, religion, family, and conservation. The educational responses to these facts often provoke controversy. After discovering from health data that venereal disease is at an epidemic level, the curriculum worker might make inferences that range from: (1) learners should be taught the causes and means for preventing communicable diseases; to (2) learners should be taught those moral principles governing sexual conduct which uphold the sanctity of marriage. One can easily see that a curriculum worker's responses in such a case could be controversial.

Subject Matter Specialists. In rational curriculum making, scientists and scholars, the discoverers and creators of knowledge, are consulted in order to find out what the specialist's subject can contribute to the education of the intended learners. Suppose you asked this question: "What in your field might best contribute to the aim that learners generate new questions and that they conceptualize alternatives and their consequences?" You would receive different kinds of answers from specialists in different fields. A historian might reply: "You should teach the principles for interpreting historical events. Help students to comprehend such schemes as the great-man theory, cultural movements, and economic determinism as explaining factors." A linguist's response might be: "You should teach concepts that show the unitary and meaning-bearing sequences of language structures, such as intonation patterns." An anthropologist might want you to stress the processes of inquiry that illuminate culture or might say, "Be sure learners understand the symbolic devices, institutions, and things constructed by people."

Selecting from Among Proposed Educational Objectives

After formulating tentative objectives, the rationalist applies the following criteria to them before accepting them as suitable for the selection of learning activities:

Congruency with function. Objectives must relate to the functions adopted by the controlling agency. If authorities for the institution value general education, objectives must further common understanding; if they value specialization, then objectives must be related to the development of specialists in a field.

Comprehensiveness. Objectives that are more encompassing, that do not deal with a minuscule sort of learner behavior, are more highly valued. Often many such objectives can be coalesced into a single powerful objective.

Consistency. Objectives should be consistent with one another. One should not have objectives stressing both openness or inquiry and dogmatism or unconditional acceptance.

Attainability. Objectives should be achievable by the intended learners.

Feasibility. Objectives should be capable of being reached without great strain. The curriculum maker should consider teacher and community concurrence, costs, and availability of materials.

As guides to instructional planning, educational objectives are then stated in a form that makes clear the content that the learner must use, the *domain* or situation in which the knowledge is to apply, and the kind of *behavior* to be exhibited by the learner. The following objective is an illustration: "Given various kinds of writing samples (domain), the learner will be able to recognize (behavior) unstated assumptions (content)."

Learning activities must allow the learner to work with the defined substantive element at a level of behavior consistent with that called for in the objective. Activities designed to teach prerequisites to that terminal task can also be provided, of course.

Problems with the Rational Model

The Tyler model represents conciliatory eclecticism. In recommending the three sources to use in formulating objectives, Tyler confronts the decision maker with three warring conceptions of the curriculum. The learner as a source is consistent with the humanistic conception—especially when data regarding the learners' own psyche needs and interests are considered. Society as a source is in keeping with social adaptive and some reconstruction orientations, while the subject matter specialist as a source tends to recognize the academic conception of curriculum.

Little help is given in the way of assigning weight to each source when one must take precedence over another. On the other hand, the model offers the possibility of treating learners, society, and subject matter as part of a comprehensive process rather than seeing them in their separateness.

The philosophical screen by which one excludes some objectives is not stipulated by the model. Users of the model must identify their own set of philosophical axioms for screening objectives. The fact that objectives must be consistent with one another does not in itself indicate the value of the objectives formulated.

The role of values and bias is not highlighted in the model. Values and bias operate at all points in the rationale—in the selection of particular data within the sources, in drawing inferences from the data, in formulating the objectives, in selecting from among the objectives, and the like.

Three other criticisms remain. The model tends to lock curriculum making into the "top to bottom" tradition, with those at the top setting the purposes and functions that narrow the school's objectives; the objectives, in turn, control classroom instruction. Those who favor teacher or learner autonomy in the selection of ends and learning opportunities oppose the model. They charge that the predetermined objectives which guide all other aspects, such as learning experiences, are like a production model with its input (students), processes (learning experiences), and output (prespecified objectives). The second criticism, that the model takes time to implement, is related to the third: the resolving of disagreement over values. The practical difficulties of getting the "right" data sources and being able to infer appropriate implications for schools require imaginative thinkers. The model does not resolve the political conflict in curriculum policymaking even if common values are accepted. Even those characterized as devout members of the same value persuasion may have their disagreement over methods:

> Those who agree that the truths honored in our tradition should be the primary curriculum elements may still disagree over whether certain classics should be taught in English translation, Latin translation, or the original Greek. They may argue whether to include Virgil together with Tacitus and Julius Caesar in a fixed time of study. They may differ over the amounts of time to be allotted to the Bible and other more strictly oriented texts. The resolution of such problems requires a decision procedure in addition to a value base.[13]

THE VOCATIONAL OR TRAINING MODEL

Training implies narrower purposes than educating. Educating allows for objectives dealing with the wholeness of a student's life as a responsible human being and a citizen. Training looks to the student's competence in some occupation. Although these two sides of life are not altogether separable, different procedures are needed for deriving training objectives than are needed for educational objectives. The training model for formulating proposed outcomes has essentially two functions: One is to reveal particular manpower needs or occupations, which the institutions or programs should serve. A second purpose is to determine the specific competencies that must be taught in order for learners (trainees) to take their place within the target occupations.

Determining Occupational Targets

Procedures for determining needed occupations rely initially on existing studies and plans. Most states release detailed area manpower

---

[13]Michael W. Kirst and Decker F. Walker, "An Analysis of Curriculum Policy Making," *Review of Educational Research* 41, no. 5 (December 1971): 485. Copyright 1971, American Educational Research Association, Washington, D.C. Reprinted by permission.

requirements for more than 400 key occupational categories, reflecting for each category current employment, anticipated industry growth, and personnel replacement. The annual *Manpower Report of the President* issued by the United States Department of Labor gives an overall picture of the employment problems facing the nation. Specific organizations such as the military, large industries, and business have projected their own manpower needs, which indicate the types of training that will be necessary. State and regional planners attempt to estimate future employment opportunities and to foresee fluctuations in mobility within the area and in mobility likely to result as firms enter or leave an area. These planners try to coordinate the programs that determine vocational services with those aimed at developing jobs. They take into account job market analysis, program reviews, curriculum resources, and state, local, and national priorities.

It is customary to use advisory councils in connection with planning vocational programs. These councils are composed of parents, students, representatives from labor, and potential consumers of the training "product." (The term *product* as used to describe a person is not seen as demeaning by trainers who regard an individual's occupational efficiency as but one important dimension of total personal worth and development.) Members of these councils help supply more information on both what will happen in a community and what kinds of employees employers are seeking. Further, they help inform the community of the forces that are affecting the job economy.

Determining the Objectives
for Training Programs or Courses

Job descriptions and task analysis procedures are used to enhance the relevancy of the training program to the job to be performed. A job description is a paragraph or two listing the tasks involved and any unusual conditions under which those tasks are carried out. All classes of tasks are listed. The task analysis begins with a study of the particular job or jobs. The curriculum developer tries to answer these questions: What tasks are required on this job? How frequently are they required? What skills and information is the graduate of the training program expected to bring to each task?

Task identification occurs through interviews, questionnaires, reports of critical incidents, and hardware analysis. Observation shows what the employees *do* while being observed; questionnaires and interviews reveal what they *say* they do. Critical incident techniques also indicate what people say they do. A critical incident report may describe a specific work assignment which an employee carried out very effectively or very ineffectively. Such reports are especially valuable in identifying contingencies, difficult tasks, and interpersonal aspects of a job. Reports are sorted into topics such as equipment, problems, or groups of incidents that go together. The features common to these incidents are categorized. Each incident is judged effective or ineffective and characterized by the presence or absence of some "skill or knowledge." The records may be further classified by such dimensions as "work habit," "management effectiveness or ineffectiveness," and "method problem." From these data one derives new training objectives for courses. Critical incident reports are completed by representative samples of job holders and of persons who interact with job holders.

Robert F. Mager and Kenneth M. Beach define a task as a logically related set of actions required by a job objective.[14] They see the first step in the task analysis as listing all tasks that might be included in the job. Next, for each of these tasks an estimate is made of the frequency of performance, relative importance, and relative ease of learning. A third step is to detail the task by listing what the person does when performing each of the tasks. Note that what is done is not necessarily the same as what is known. Each of the actions on this list, too, is rated for learning difficulty (easy, moderately difficult, difficult).

The job analysis and a knowledge of the characteristics of the intended learners are all that one needs for the blueprint of expected student performance. By subtracting what the student is already able to do from what he or she must be able to do one can obtain the course objectives. Course objectives are not the same as task analyses. They describe the abilities that a specific learner must have to do the job; task analyses describe the job as performed by a highly skilled person. Subtracting what students are already able to do from what they must be able to do helps one to decide the course objectives. However, one cannot go directly from a task analysis to the formulation of objectives for a course. It is necessary to decide which of the skills demanded by the occupation may be better taught on the job or in the course.

[14]Robert F. Mager and Kenneth M. Beach, Jr., *Developing Vocational Instruction* (Palo Alto, Calif.: Fearon Publishers, 1967).

Problems with the Vocational Training Model

There are several criticisms of the training model. First, the objectives derived from it usually prepare a learner for work as it *is* rather than as it *should* be. Related to this criticism is the charge that the model is associated with *presentism*, a focus on today's situation rather than on a likely future condition. Hence, the objectives derived are potentially obsolete as well as narrow. Most critics admit, however, that the model is ahead of the prevailing curriculum practice of deriving objectives only from tradition, convention, and the curriculum maker's personal experiences.

DISJOINTED INCREMENTALISM

Disjointed incrementalism is not really a model; we will call it a nonmodel. It means allowing curriculum decisions to be made without following a systematic procedure. In the nonmodel, decisions about what will be taught occur through a political process. Advocates of a particular curriculum try to justify the ends they already have in mind. Advocates of great works and fundamental skills appeal to tradition; advocates of cognitive skills appeal to psychological and educational research; advocates of relevant vocational skills appeal to community; advocates of self-improvement appeal to personal judgment. Those who must resolve the conflicting pressures—school boards, advisory councils, textbook publishers, professional educators—tend to use informal methods of decision making. Michael Kirst and Decker Walker called their methods *disjointed incrementalism*. Disjointed incrementalism, they said, is a strategy, and it has these rules:

1. Contemplate making only marginal changes in the existing situation.
2. Avoid making radical changes and consider only a few policy alternatives.
3. Consider only a few of the possible consequences for any proposed change.
4. Feel free to introduce objectives consistent with policy as well as to change policy in accord with objectives.
5. Be willing to look for problems *after* data are available from implementation.
6. Tinker with piecemeal changes rather than making a single comprehensive attack.[15]

Decisions made under disjointed incrementalism are not based on much objective data. Hence, political processes are used to resolve conflicts. In chapter 13, we shall describe this process in detail.

Problems with Disjointed Incrementalism in Curriculum Making

Disjointed incrementalism in making curriculum decisions about what to teach is not too different from what occurs in other political areas of government and industry. It tends to result in a fragmented curriculum that lacks continuity. Many, however, prefer such an irrational model over a more logical and effective model that might be more appropriate in a totalitarian society. A main defect in the procedure is one associated with the democratic process: the lack of well-informed citizens who will exercise wide participation, assume responsibility for starting social improvements, and show competency in the skills of political action.

Disjointed incrementalism is probably the approach used in most educational institutions for determining curriculum ends. It represents a realization that conflict over what to teach is not just a conflict of ideas but of persons, groups, and factions. Under disjointed incrementalism, conflicts over goals and objectives are not resolved on the basis of principles but by political power.

A COMMENT ON MODELS FOR CURRICULUM BUILDING

Alan Purves has been building curriculum for over twenty years. When asked to think about the processes by which he developed and arranged materials to effect people's learning, he realized that existing models are a fine way to look at curriculum but that they don't tell one how to proceed any more than a blueprint tells where to begin building a house. Purves realizes that curriculum reflects the maker's view of the society, the people who are to be affected, and the nature of what is to be learned. However, he thinks the metaphor of a game is the best way to describe the process by which one builds curriculum.

Rules for playing the curriculum game center on these pieces: legal constraints and administrative structure. Who is the decision maker

[15]Kirst and Walker, "An Analysis of Curriculum Policy Making," p. 485.

in the school—the principal, the teachers, or some more remote body? How does the proposed curriculum fit with other curricula? Other pieces include teacher attitude and capacity, student interests, principles for sequencing activities, activities themselves, and the constraints of time and resources. Obviously, formulating objectives and anticipating possible outcomes are important pieces. Purves believes that the formulating of objectives and outcomes might take place at the same time as the selection and arrangement of materials, just as evaluation can take place during the course of devising the curriculum.

Curriculum is, however, a game board. Just having the pieces does not mean one knows how to play the game. Some start with a sense of what the classroom should look like, structured or open. Others begin with a view of how society should be. Purves says, "A number have started with evaluation and built a dog to fit the tail."[16] Some begin with behavioral objectives and others with a set of materials. Others start with a theory about subject matter.

Purves's rules indicate that a player may start with any piece, just as long as all the pieces are picked up. His next rule is that all pieces must be perceived in some relationship to one another. Activities should relate to objectives and theories of learning. A final rule is that there are several ways to win the game. One way is to have the pieces all placed in some relation to one another. Another way is to have the finished board approximate a model of rationality with objectives determining learning activities, organization, and evaluation. One can also win by showing that the intended outcomes were achieved by the learner. If the learner achieves the stated purposes, no matter what else is learned, it is a winning curriculum. It is even possible to have a winning curriculum by virtue of the attractiveness of the materials or their intellectual modernity. Conflicting views of winning make curriculum one of the most controversial games in town.

CONCLUDING COMMENTS

The needs assessment model for determining curriculum is growing in popularity. It is seen as one way to restore community confidence in the school and to advance the interests of

[16]Alan C. Purves, "The Thought Fox and Curriculum Building," in *Strategies for Curriculum Development*, Jon Schaffarzick and David Hampson, eds. (Berkeley, Calif.: McCutchan, 1975), p. 120.

previously ignored groups. It is closely associated with the adaptive and social reconstructionists' conceptions of curriculum.

As the name implies, the futuristic model emphasizes future conditions more than present status. It is a form of needs assessment in that future needs are anticipated. For this model, one decides what students should be like in light of some desirable future.

Few models are as idealistic and comprehensive as the rational model. It is appealing because it gives attention to the interests of learner, society, and the fields of knowledge. In practice, however, curriculum makers often fail to respond equally to these interests. Once specialization is accepted as the overriding function of a school program or course, the outlooks of subject matter specialists carry the most weight. Similarly, when those in an institution prize the general function—wanting to develop shared values and to make schooling relevant to social needs—they tend to respond to generalizations about society to the exclusion of other considerations.

The vocational training model is most appropriate in institutions claiming to prepare students for jobs. Those using this model must be aware, however, that its use may tend to perpetuate the status quo.

Curriculum ends should not be narrowly conceived. Objectives that are relevant to present and likely future conditions, to the concerns of the learners, and to a wide span of cultural resources are better than those that rely solely on tradition. The final acceptance of educational ends is a value judgment. The decision to accept, however, should be influenced by evidence that shows that the end—the goal or objective—will be of value to the learner, that it is attainable, and that it probably will not be achieved without deliberate instruction.

To keep curriculum workers in touch with reality, let us admit that disagreement on the proper base for assessing the worth of the curriculum is likely. Hence, political processes are used for dealing with the value conflicts.

QUESTIONS

1. Consider the mission of an institution known to you—a training center, junior college, or elementary school. Which model for formulating goals and objectives is most appropriate for that institution? Why?
2. In using the needs assessment model, would you prefer the preferences of special groups—parents, teachers, students—to be given equal or weighted importance? Why or why not?

3. State an educational aim of importance to you, such as health, conservation of resources, self-worth, vocational skill. Then refine this aim
into an educational objective by indicating what one might know or do
in order to progress toward the aim.
4. Read the following generalizations and then infer what should be taught
in light of each generalization.
    a. Secondary school students construe moral issues in terms of power
    relationships and physical consequences. They see morality as
    something outside their control.
    b. Adults are strangers who grant neither substance nor interest to one
    another and do not see a society larger than their private world.
    c. The cry for law and order is a fundamental demand for cognitive
    order, for normative clarity, and for predictability in human affairs.
    d. Within humans are powerful forces leading toward diversity, variety,
    and heterogeneity rather than uniformity.
5. What do you believe is the function of the school? Is there something the
school can do better than any other agency? Indicate how your answer
might be used in deciding what and what not to teach.

SELECTED REFERENCES

Goodlad, John I. and associates. *Curriculum Inquiry.* New York: McGraw-
Hill Book Company, 1979.
Hegarty, Elizabeth H. "The Public Identification Phase of Curriculum
Deliberation," *Journal of Curriculum Studies* 9, no. 1 (1977): 31–41.
Kaufman, Roger and English, Fenwick. *Needs Assessment: Concept and
Application.* Englewood Cliffs, N.J.: Educational Technology Publica-
tion, 1979.
Kingston, Richard D. and Stockton, William P. "Needs Assessment: A
Problem of Priorities," *Educational Technology* 19, no. 6 (June 1979):
16–21.
Mager, Robert F. and Beach, Kenneth M., Jr. *Developing Vocational
Education.* Palo Alto, Calif.: Fearon Publishers, 1967.
McNeil, John D. "Deriving Objectives" and "Selecting Among Educational
Objectives—Defensible Choices," in *Designing Curriculum: Self-
Instructional Modules.* Boston: Little, Brown, 1976.
Schaffarzick, Jon and Hampson, David, eds. *Strategies for Curriculum
Development.* Berkeley, Calif.: McCutchan, 1975.
Shevach, Eden. "The Translation of General Educational Aims Into Func-
tional Objectives: A Needs Assessment Study," *Studies in Educational
Evaluation* 1, no. 1 (Spring 1975): 5–11.
Short, Jerry, ed. "Special Issues on Task Analysis," *Improving Human
Performance* 2, no. 1 (Spring 1973).

6 / DEVELOPING CURRICULUM MEANS

This chapter has two general purposes. One is to show the different considerations involved in deciding on learning opportunities—books, materials, experiences, activities, programs, and the like. In order to do this, we will contrast the nature of instructional decisions at societal and institutional levels with decisions at classroom levels. The conflict between those who see learning opportunities as having inherent worth and those who see them as means to be appraised is also treated. The reader should gain a sense of the strengths and weaknesses of some arguments used in justifying learning opportunities.

A second purpose is to analyze and compare the procedures used by technologists, humanists, social reconstructionists, academicians, and teachers in developing instructional materials and programs. The description given should serve as a heuristic device for criticism and discussion.

A CURRICULUM CONFLICT: LEARNING ACTIVITIES AS MEANS OR ENDS?

In the curriculum field, as in travel, some people find their joy in the journey—in movement—and others prize the destination and value the opportunities involved in getting there only to the extent that they contribute to goal attainment.

Theorists such as Mauritz Johnson, James Popham, and Marvin Alkin define curriculum as the destination—the intended outcomes of instructional activity.[1] They regard the planning and implementation of strategies for achieving ends as instruction or means. Further, they see the instructional component as consisting of both planning and interactive phases. Planning involves formulating intended objectives and instructional activities and stipulating the characteristics of instructional materials to be used. Interaction refers to the actual carrying out of plans, such as a teacher presenting a lesson.

Other theorists such as James MacDonald, James Raths, and Bernice Wolfson tend to prize learning opportunities—sometimes called learning experiences, learning activities, interventions, or contacts—as valuable in themselves.[2] These theorists value a rich environment. They define worthwhile opportunities as those that are relevant to the students' purposes, that give students opportunities to make informed choices, that provide a moral quality, that offer aesthetic satisfaction, and that display other indicators of quality of life.

IMPLICATIONS OF CONFLICT

Those who view learning opportunities as instrumental select and design activities that are most likely to have prespecified consequences. *Instrumentalists* are oriented to product or outcome rather than to process; they appraise activities by results, not by inherent attributes alone. Their distinction between planning and teaching allows them to assess the effects of the plan separately from the way the plan is carried out. A plan might be quite effective with one teacher who follows it carefully. It may still be a good plan even if poorly executed by another teacher.

In contrast, those who view activities as ends are the *expressives* or humanists; they see learning activities as expressions of individuality, significant as such. They tend to be process-oriented and believe that

[1]Mauritz Johnson, Jr., "Definitions and Models in Curriculum Theory," *Educational Theory* 17, no. 2 (April 1967): 127–40; W. James Popham, "Objectives and Instruction," AERA Monograph Series on Curriculum Evaluation, vol. 3, *Instructional Objectives* (Chicago: Rand McNally, 1969); Marvin C. Alkin, "Evaluation 'Curriculum' and 'Instruction,'" *Curriculum Theory Network* 4, no. 1 (1973–74): 43–51.

[2]James B. MacDonald, "Responsible Curriculum Development," in *Confronting Curriculum Reform*, Elliot W. Eisner, ed. (Boston: Little, Brown, 1971), 120–34; James D. Raths, "Teaching Without Specific Objectives," in *Emerging Educational Issues*, Julius Menacker and Erwin Pollack, eds. (Boston: Little, Brown, 1974), 370–78; Bernice J. Wolfson, "A Phenomenological Perspective on Curriculum and Learning," *Curriculum Theory*, Alex Molnar and John A. Zahorik, eds. (Washington, D.C.: ASCD, 1977).

the curriculum person can accept responsibility only for offering the best of conditions, not for controlling the behavior of others or effecting outcomes that are likely to be unpredictable. The expressives do not try to control what students are to become but only what they are to undergo.

Much strife occurs because of this difference between instrumentalists and expressives. Communities have fought bitterly over whether a particular work, such as Shakespeare's plays or Langston Hughes's poetry, shall be included in the school's offerings. Expressives view such works on their face value; instrumentalists want to withhold judgment until they see what happens to learners as a result of studying a work and its concomitant activity.

Once it is decided that certain things are to be learned, an instrumentalist selects or designs activities on the basis of their likely contribution to a desired objective. An activity is justified on the basis of results produced. An expressive, on the other hand, prizes particular experiences or opportunities which reflect the values of the designers, tending to assume that desirable experiences have desirable consequences rather than to appraise systematically the learning that follows. Measurement of results in terms of predetermined objectives is incompatible with the view of the expressives.

INSTRUCTIONAL PLANNING AT MACRO LEVELS

The range of learning activities is infinite, which is why curriculum making and teaching are creative fields. We can, however, distinguish types of learning opportunities that are common at different levels of instructional planning. Those responsible for curriculum development at the macro level—for an entire school system or an institution—select general categories of opportunity that are called domains or areas of study. Domains indicate what kinds of programs will be offered students and suggest what is likely to be learned. They can be considered planned activities although they are general. Breadth and variety of classroom activities are somewhat limited once the domains are established. Examples of sets of domains are: (1) symbolic studies, basic sciences, developmental studies, and aesthetic studies;[3] (2) academic disciplines—English,

[3]Harry S. Broudy, B. Othanel Smith, and Joe R. Burnett, *Democracy and Excellence in American Secondary Education* (Chicago: Rand McNally, 1979).

mathematics, science, social science, the arts; and applied fields—agriculture, business education, industrial arts, vocational education; (3) the personal, the social, and the academic;[4] and as was mentioned in chapter 5, domains that correspond to functions of the school, general education, exploratory and enrichment studies, specialization studies, and remedial studies.

Other categories of instructional opportunities selected at the macro level are: (1) programs of study, such as a foreign language program or a program in physical education, and (2) course offerings, such as introductory Spanish or advanced German. Note that a program indicates continuities over a longer period of time—two or three years or more; while a course may be of shorter duration—a quarter, semester, or year. The teacher's selection of classroom activities is sometimes further constrained by the problems, projects, themes, centers of interest, and topics selected at macro levels as important for a course. In a curriculum developed by a rational model, categories of activity are consistent with the school's goals or functions. In a curriculum developed in accordance with humanistic tenets, the offerings must elicit the enthusiasm of students as well as serve the major goal of individual self-realization.

INSTRUCTIONAL PLANNING
AT THE MICRO LEVEL

At the classroom or micro level, planned learning opportunities become more specific, and in the case of a rational curriculum allow learners to practice what is called for in predetermined instructional objectives. An instrumentalist defines a learning activity as a specification or product delineating content or method intended to influence or shape the learner in given ways. To the expressive or humanist, it is a situation that gives learners the opportunity to have valued experiences. Particular books, films, games, and manipulative and other instructional products are selected as the means for instruction. Field trips, debates, projects, demonstrations, and the like are common activities at this level. Interestingly, although learning opportunities at macro and micro levels differ considerably in form, the criteria used in justifying their selections are the same. Values such as inquiry and personal or social relevancy can

---

[4]J. Galen Saylor and William Alexander, *Planning Curriculum for Schools* (New York: Holt, Rinehart and Winston, 1974), p. 169.

serve in the justification of domains, programs, and course offerings at the macro level as well as in the justification of texts, lessons, and excursions at the micro level. Individuals making decisions at any level, however, often do not employ the same criteria. One person may, for example, put more value on practicality whereas another may give greater weight to tradition.

CRITERIA FOR SELECTING
LEARNING ACTIVITIES

Five kinds of criteria are used in guiding and justifying the selection of learning activities: philosophical, psychological, technological, political, and practical. Those with a particular curriculum orientation tend to place priority on certain of these criteria. Humanists, for example, are more interested in the inherent qualities of a learning activity than in data indicating that the activity has had an effect in some specific but limited way. Learning activities are judged as good or bad when they meet our value expectations or philosophical assumptions. If one holds human variability, for instance, to be of great worth, then one will favor activities that advance learner variability rather than activities that stress common outlooks and capacities. Learning activities are also judged in accordance with psychological criteria. Those who differ on whether learning should be painful or pleasant will differ on their assessments of learning opportunities. The technologists' studies of learning and instruction have resulted in a number of new criteria to use in designing and evaluating learning activities. Technologists claim that their criteria are empirically based principles for effective learning rather than canons established by philosophical beliefs.

Philosophical Criteria

Values are the chief basis for judging proposed learning activities. Typically, these value positions appear as options as indicated in the following curriculum maker's dilemma.

Psychological Criteria

Psychological beliefs about how learning best takes place often determine whether a learning activity is acceptable or not. Not all people agree, however, on the particular learning principles to

TABLE 4

Learning Activities Should:	But They Also Should:
Be immediately enjoyable.	Lead to desirable future experiences.
Show the ideal: the just, beautiful, and honorable.	Show life as it is, including corruption, violence, and the profane.
Treat the thinking, feeling, and acting of the group to which the learner belongs.	Treat the thinking, feeling, and acting of the groups other than those to which the learner belongs.
Minimize human variability by stressing common outlooks and capacities.	Increase variability by stressing individuality.
Stress cooperation so that individuals share in achieving a common goal.	Stress competition so that the able person excels as an individual.
Allow students to clarify their own positions on moral and controversial issues.	Instruct students in the values of moral and intellectual integrity rather than allowing students to engage in sophistry and personal indulgence.

employ. Some examples of conflicts in beliefs about learning are shown in Tables 4 and 5.

Criteria from Educational Technology

Recently, technologists studying instructional variables and procedures have gained great influence over the kinds of factors used in both judging and developing learning opportunities. Persons like Robert M. Gagné, Robert Glaser, and Benjamin Bloom have adapted constructs of programmed learning and behavioral and contiguity psychology to instructional development.[5] Hence psychological and technological criteria often overlap—practice and knowledge of

[5]Robert M. Gagné, *Essentials of Learning for Instruction* (Hinsdale, Ill.: The Dryden Press, 1974); Robert Glaser, *Adaptive Instruction* (Hinsdale, Ill.: The Dryden Press, 1974); Benjamin S. Bloom, "Learning for Mastery," *Evaluative Comment* 1, no. 2 (May 1968): 1–9.

TABLE 5

Closed View Learning Activities Should:	*Open View* Learning Activities Should:
Be under the direct influence of the teacher who demonstrates so that the learner will imitate and acquire.	Be removed from direct teacher influence, allowing self-actualization by finding meaning in a situation where the teacher is a resource person.
Be pleasant and comfortable for the student.	Allow for hardship and perplexity so that significant growth can take place.
Teach one thing at a time but teach it to mastery, simplifying the environment and giving enough instances to help the learner abstract desired generalizations.	Bring about several outcomes at once, helping students develop interests and attitudes as well as cognitive growth.
Allow the learner to acquire simple basic patterns before being exposed to higher orders of learning.	Allow the learner to grasp the meaning and organization of the whole before proceeding to study the parts.
Allow the learner to see and imitate the best models of talking, feeling, and acting.	Allow the learner to create and practice new and different ways of talking, feeling, and acting.
Feature repetitive practice on a skill not mastered. Don't let the learner practice error.	Feature novel and varied approaches to an unlearned skill. Recognize that learners can learn from error.

results can be both psychological and technological criteria. These persons accept the revolutionary idea that all students can master a learning task if the right means are found for helping the student. Chief among the means they turn to are careful analysis and sequencing of tasks so that prerequisites are provided. They make sure learners understand the task and the procedures they are to follow, and adapt instruction to the characteristics of individuals. One way to adapt to these characteristics is to give more examples, frequent testing with immediate knowledge of results, reteaching if necessary, alternative procedures, and variation in time allowed for learning.

The technologists' criteria are found increasingly in instruments for assessing instructional materials, as indicated in the following list of criteria selected from widely used instruments:[6]

1. The objectives for the activity or material are stated in behavioral terms including the type of behavior, conditions, and level of expected performance.
2. A task analysis—identification of components of a complex behavior—has been made and a relationship between the tasks and the final objectives has been specified.
3. Learning activities are directly related to the behavior and content of the specified objectives.
4. Evaluation procedures are comparable to these objectives:
    a. There is immediate feedback regarding the adequacy of the learner's responses.
    b. There are criterion-referenced tests that measure stated objectives.
    c. Attention is given to evaluating both process, by which the learner learns, and the product, or what the learner learns.
5. The product or activity has been carefully field-tested. A technical manual might cite sources of available evidence to document claims about effectiveness and efficiency, including reports of unintended outcomes.

Political Criteria

Some pressure groups have been very successful in promoting new criteria for guiding the adoption of instructional materials. Although many of these new criteria reflect the philosophical belief that every human being is important, legal and political actions were necessary before the portrayal of racial, ethnic, and cultural groups, the handicapped, and the sexes began to change nationally. Typical of criteria that reflect the political efforts of minorities are the following legal requirements:

1. Teaching materials must portray both men and women in their

[6]Louise L. Tyler, et al., *Evaluating and Choosing Curriculum and Instructional Materials* (Los Angeles, Calif.: Educational Resource Associates, Inc., 1976); Maurice J. Eash, "Developing an Instrument for Assessing Instruction Materials," *Curriculum Theory Network* (Toronto, Canada: Ontario Institute for Studies in Education, 1972), pp. 193–270.

full range of leadership, occupation, and domestic roles, without
demeaning, stereotyping, or patronizing references to either sex.
2. Material must portray, without significant omission, the historical
role of members of racial, ethnic, and cultural groups, including
their contributions and achievements in all areas of life.
3. Materials must portray members of cultural groups without
demeaning, stereotyping, or patronizing references concerning
their heritage, characteristics, or life style.

As a consequence of these standards, publishers and teachers are
counting pictures of boys and girls to be sure both sexes are depicted
in a range of roles, rather than traditional masculine and feminine
ones, and they are being careful not to attach a color to an animal
serving as the antagonist in a tale. They are also modifying the
language by making changes in affixes and other structures. They are
replacing the singular *he* with *they* and substituting *person* for *man*.

At macro levels, curriculum planners attempt to meet the political
criteria by designating new curriculum domains or areas such as
American Indian studies and Chicano studies. Curriculum planners
at a macro level also confront the special interests of conserva-
tionists, religious and veterans' organizations, auto-related industries, and other groups. Numerous admonitions to curriculum
developers are the direct result of such pressures. Curriculum
developers are told to present the responsibilities of individuals and
groups in preserving or creating a healthful environment, including
appropriate and scientifically valid solutions to environmental problems. They may be admonished to present the hazards of tobacco,
alcohol, narcotics, and drugs without glamorizing or encouraging
their use. Curriculum planners are all reminded that curriculum
should reflect and respect the religious diversity of people.

Practicality as a Criterion

At the macro level, practicality generally takes the form of
economy. Planners weigh the cost of providing a certain learning opportunity. In times of financial pinch, for instance, curriculum planners at macro levels might consider the cost of initiating an expensive
laboratory course prohibitive. Instead, they might suggest a science
course that features a less expensive instructional process such as a
lecture format. Curriculum programs can be expensive in many
ways. There are the outright costs of purchase of materials, the cost
of maintaining the materials, the costs of purchasing necessary sup-

plementary materials, and the costs of acquiring or training personnel.

It is important to weigh costs of purchase and installation against the expected level of goals or objectives to be achieved. If powerful forces outside the school are working against attainment of a goal, the purchase of new means for attaining that goal is impractical. In times of economic austerity, curriculum planners must also consider "diminishing returns" in learning opportunities. There is a level of educational attainment beneath which dollars invested show a return in student progress. Beyond that level, however, gain occurs only at rapidly increasing cost.

At both macro and micro levels, there are other practical concerns. Safety, durability, and adaptability of the activity must be considered. There also is the factor of *conditions of use*: Does it demand that a teacher interact with pupils or does it free the teacher from direct instruction? Is it appropriate for learners with given abilities and motivational levels?

Criticisms of Criteria for Selecting Learning Opportunities

Criticisms may be directed both at the criteria themselves and at their use. Simply having criteria does not take care of the problem of who will use them in making decisions; it may make a difference whether they are used by state curriculum committees, individual teachers, or boards of education. Further, little thought has been given to decision rules. Seldom are answers given to those questions: How many criteria must be satisfied before adoption? What should the planners do if two alternative opportunities meet the same number of criteria? Will the decision require agreement among raters?

It is often difficult to obtain agreement on the evidence that a particular criterion has been met. Criteria demanding few inferences, such as the specification that objectives be stated in behavioral terms, present little difficulty. Criteria requiring high levels of inference, however, such as the requirement that materials be appropriate for learners of given motivation level, allow for more subjective and varied judgments.

Many people also disagree on the relative merits of the respective criteria. Kenneth Komoski, president of the Educational Products Information Exchange Institute, would put primary emphasis on learner verification—data showing the learning effectiveness of the opportunities.[7] No clear basis exists for claiming the superiority of materials that have provisions for feedback, behavioral objectives, task analysis, or criterion-referenced tests; there is little conclusive evidence that these variables are directly related to attainment of particular goals and objectives.

One of the most useful analyses of the disagreement on criteria for determining "worthwhileness" of curriculum means and on their justification has been made by K.E. Robinson.[8] Robinson believes that the sources of disagreement may be found in the following five assumptions:

1. Worthwhile educational activities are conducive to but not necessarily the same as worthwhile activities in terms of the "good" life.
2. Worthwhile activities are not of universal value; their value is relevant to time, place, community, and individuals.
3. Activities deemed worthwhile in the past are not necessarily worthwhile today or in the future.
4. The justification of all activities said to be worthwhile will not necessarily spring from the same value premise, and the justification of some activities rests on more than one premise.
5. Trying to justify an activity on the grounds that it is instrumental to the pursuit of other ends leaves much to be resolved. The instrumental argument is of little consequence if the implied grounds for its ultimate justification cannot be sustained. By definition "ultimate" justification is not instrumental.

In his thoughtful essay, Robinson shows the strengths and weaknesses of different arguments for certain learning opportunities. He does, for instance, point out that a "transcendental" argument— justification for an activity on the grounds that it rises above mere partisan consideration—is valid but limited. This argument provides good grounds for justifying some activities some of the time for some people. When personal tastes and moral dispositions differ, however, Robinson would appeal to a *norm* and, when that does not suffice, he would appeal to expertise. There are people to whom we should listen because they have more experience and have reflected on it more than we outsiders have, he says. But ultimately, Robinson sees the decision as to whether the activity is worthwhile as our own. It

[7]Personal correspondence.

[8]K.E. Robinson, "Worthwhile Activities and the Curriculum," *British Journal of Educational Studies* 22, no. 1 (February 1974): 34–55.

will be tempered, of course, by considerations such as the range of our impulses that it satisfies, the degree to which it harmonizes the satisfaction of different impulses, and the extent to which it allows us to communicate with others, but it will still be our own decision.

DEVELOPING LEARNING OPPORTUNITIES

Selecting learning opportunities is not the same as developing them. Some people can apply criteria in deciding among various textbooks and other materials but are not able or willing to produce them. Similarly, the ability to implement opportunities in the interactive phase with learners calls for additional competencies. It is true that developers should keep in mind the criteria given for selection. Commercial developers do so because they want their products adopted. Development, however, is a creative art and allows for personal expression of the developer's values and style. As indicated in Part I of this book, techniques of development can be categorized by the four major curriculum orientations.

Social Reconstructionist Guidelines for Developing Learning Opportunities

The social reconstructionist wants the learners to use knowledge and intelligence to help improve the quality of public decision that determines the conditions under which they live. A particular model has been widely tried out and validated as useful for this purpose.[9] Teachers using this model stress ten considerations as they plan the opportunity.

1. *Select an idea for a learning opportunity.* The developer might reflect on a topic or problem such as public opinion, elections, media, or conservation, which makes sense to the students and is related to school and course goals. Issues and problems in the community are among the best sources of ideas for learning opportunities. Persistent struggles and value premises also suggest areas for learning. One might want to consider apathy toward general welfare or the importance of keeping informed on public issues and informing others.

[9]William S. Vincent, et al., *Citizenship Education Project: Building Better Programs in Citizenship* (New York: Teachers College, Columbia University, 1958).

2. *Explore the idea.* Here one must ask, "What can students do about the issue or problem besides studying about it?" A learning opportunity for the reconstructionist requires the students to take responsible action, whether working with community groups, informing people, or taking a stand on issues. Students may provide information to people about a public issue, try to influence people to a point of view, serve the community, or work with and as adult citizens.

3. *Plan for action.* Surveys, field trips, and interviews are not what the reconstructionist means by action. Although these activities may contribute to the action phase, they don't constitute *taking action* in a political sense. Since the essence of the civic act is carrying knowledge into action, a student activity that omits persuasion, decision making, and so forth, is not viewed as satisfactory. Planning means thinking of the action or project desired; for example, organizing a public forum and indicating how students will carry it out.

4. *Test the idea or project for realness.* Work in the community—helping to get out a vote, campaigning for a candidate, talking on issues—is real. Mock trials, mayor for a day, reading, and taking straw votes are not real to the reconstructionist; they are only role playing. To the reconstructionist, action must promise to contribute to the solution of the situation and be seen by students as important.

5. *Specify the instructional objectives that will also be served by the project.* The objectives might stress competencies such as persuasion, getting information, arriving at valid conclusions, predispositions toward recognition of others, acceptance of responsibility, or knowledge of function and structure in institutions.

6. *Limit the scope of the learning opportunity.* The project must be subject to reasonable limits of time and effort. Enough time must be allowed for students to complete the action phase. For most effective results, the project should be focused. One idea is to plan the project around the action of the city council on a particular issue rather than around some broad interest such as government. Include only those activities that are necessary to achieve the goals of the plan. Decide on the termination date at the outset and keep it in mind daily. The sixth consideration is met when teaching has limited student actions to a specific job, enumerated what students are to do, and reconciled the time needed for completing the project.

7. *Involve others in the project.* Get the school administrator and other persons in the community whose help is desirable.
8. *List the sources of firsthand information needed.* Consider interviews, polls, surveys, filming, and making visits.
9. *Select study materials.* Collect textbooks, pamphlets, films, and other materials on the subject matter of the project and pertinent to the instructional objectives.
10. *Plan for evaluation.* Select the evaluation devices that will be used to determine what gains and losses will have accrued as a result of the project.

Technological Guidelines for Developing Learning Opportunities

In Chapter 3, the technologists' product development procedures were delineated. The Northwest Regional Laboratory, for example, includes thirty-seven steps in its development process. A much more elegant set of guidelines for developing learning opportunities—more central to the problem and less compounded with matters such as strategies for effecting revisions—is found in the principles of programmed instruction. These principles illustrate the applicability of theory and experimental science of learning to practical problems of instruction. Basic documents regarding these principles are the works of Arthur A. Lumsdaine and Susan M. Markle.[10] These technologists identify four stages for developing learning activities:

1. *Specify terminal objectives.* The instructional objective must guide all development. This objective must be specific enough to remove ambiguity about what the learner will be expected to know and do in particular situations or classes of situations. A posttest or other procedure for indicating achievement of the desired terminal behavior is often produced in order to further explicate all dimensions of the learning task.
2. *Make a task analysis.* An effort is made to list all prerequisite skills and knowledge believed necessary before one can perform in accordance with the objective. After this list is prepared, the developer must indicate which of these prerequisites will be taught in the learning opportunity and which will be considered

[10]Arthur A. Lumsdaine, "Educational Technology: Programmed Instruction and Instructional Science," NSSE Yearbook, *Theories of Learning and Instruction* (Chicago: National Society for the Study of Education, 1964), pp. 371-401; Susan Meyer Markle, *Good Frames and Bad—A Grammar of Frame Writing* (New York: John Wiley and Sons, 1964).

"entry behaviors" (requirements that the learner is expected to demonstrate on entrance to the learning opportunity).

3. *Specify the intended population.* At this point, an idea of the anticipated learners can be gained. In addition to entry skills, characteristics such as cultural differences, learning styles, personality, interests, and the like are used to guide the developers.

4. *Formulate rules for development of the product.* These questions give direction to the developer and determine the characteristics of the product.

   a. *Concept presentation.* Will the concept be taught through examples leading to a generalization (inductive) or will a generalization be given followed by examples (deductive)?

   b. *Response mode.* Will the learner be actively involved by speaking, writing, touching? In addition to overt responding, are there anticipated covert responses? How often will learners be expected to respond overtly?

   c. *Elicitation of correct responses.* How will the learners be helped to make a correct response and learn? Will all answers be confirmed as right or wrong? Will they be confirmed with reiteration of the reasons for correctness? How? Will the learner be prompted to make the right answer by hints, as through visual cues, questions, metaphors, and other verbal means?

   d. *Learning sequences.* How will enroute objectives be ordered and reviewed? Will all learners be required to follow the same order? Will there be provision for "branching" (a point of choice at which students are sent to alternative material depending on their prior responses)?

Humanistic Guidelines for Developing Learning Opportunities

The humanistic curriculum has its roots in both the individual humanism of the Renaissance with its stress on personal culture, individual freedom, and development as the best way toward a full and rich life, and the naturalism of the eighteenth century which was a revolt against the cold, heartless aristocracy of intellect. The naturalists worshiped feelings and regarded education not as a preparation for life but as life itself. They believed that the activities which spring naturally from the interests of the pupils, from the needs of life, should make up the curriculum.

In contrast to other curriculum orientations, learning opportunities in the humanistic curriculum are not planned in the framework of a means-ends continuum. Indeed, many humanistic educators believe that only *after* an opportunity has been experienced can an objective be formed. How then does one create a more humanistic experience? The answers from the neo-humanists fall into three categories.

1. *Emphasize teaching procedures.* Instructional plans, textbooks, courses of study, and other artifacts designed to shape learners in specified ways are all seen as less important than the actual teaching. The teacher is seen as the primary learning opportunity; the interpersonal associations experienced with a teacher influence the pupils' growth. The humanists give more attention to method and the interactive phases of instruction than on advanced planning. Indeed, the planning of opportunities, activities, and experiences should be a cooperative process by students and teacher in which the pupil's own purposes are respected.

   This emphasis takes many directions. It may mean that the teacher will prepare by developing procedures of reflective teaching, group dynamics, and sensitivity training—methods that may be of value in releasing the creative capacity of learners. It may mean that teachers will anticipate what they will bring to students by "knowing" themselves. They will try to recognize their prejudices, biases, fears, loves, strengths, and other attributes that bear on the ability to care, feel, and relate to students.

2. *Create an environment that will not impede natural growth.* The most general guide to developing learning opportunities is focused on the conditions of learning. On the positive side, this includes attending to conditions such as: the characteristics, interests, and growth patterns of each child; a rich environment with many materials to manipulate; opportunities that stress wholeness, putting all our senses to work; human relations; opportunities to wonder and be puzzled; and opportunities for the learner to feel independent by facing problems alone.

   On the negative side, the admonishment implies that learners do not have to meet standards beyond their abilities, endure much tension, face destructive criticism, think in terms of previous solutions to problems, conform to meaningless tradition, regard achievement as the production of a similar rather than a unique product, nor be denied choices.

3. *Arrange situations in which learners determine what they will learn.* The teacher as arranger considers physical conditions including safe facilities as well as natural objects of beauty, and uses those from which the learner can benefit. The cultural environment, too, is a responsibility of the humanistic teacher. Cultural excellence in music, painting, and literature, and scientific equipment, musical instruments, and art supplies may constitute an invitation to learning. Arrangement of the social environment may also be planned. Association with others in a variety of shared enterprises may permit self-activated students to respond and, by their own urge toward self-realization, bring the learning process to fulfillment.

Academicians' Guidelines for Learning Opportunities

To the academician learning opportunities are chiefly textbooks, films, teachers' guides, as well as laboratory apparatus. The textbook is most important. Development of these tools is seen as an effort to convey the authenticity of content and method of given subject fields. Organizing centers, rather than instructional objectives, are central to academic developers. These centers are topics, questions, or problems that will guide the class activities. Until about the 1930s, for example, textbooks by scholars were descriptive and usually consisted of a mass of disconnected facts and primitive generalizations. Between the 1930s and the 1960s, textbooks were more often written by professional educators rather than by specialists in the disciplines. Their books were criticized as being too busy with many topics to treat any in depth. The student was given many conclusions but had little opportunity to understand how these findings were achieved and how they were interrelated. About 1960, distinguished scholars began to select and guide the development of textbooks as well as courses and materials. They used five steps.

1. *Choose organizing centers.* Organizing centers provide the story line that relates text, lab, films, and the context for study of a field over a year-long span. The following criteria should guide the selection of centers: Do they stress major achievements, that is, powerful ideas? Do they show ways in which the powerful ideas were conceived and sometimes improved on? Do they show how the ideas are interrelated?
2. *Lay out the ordering of the centers.* Usually this step rests on an assumed principle of dependency in which the basic concepts are

given so that the student can have the understanding necessary for further study. The presentation is through general concepts rather than specific definitions so that the students make some contact with the subject matter they will deal with later in greater depth.

3. *Develop suggested units of instruction.* Each unit deals with a particular topic and has its own purposes. Each unit also includes an outline of suggested information to be presented and a bibliography suggesting other sources of information.

4. *Recommend specific instructional content.* This content consists of a wealth of information for each unit. Some examples of recommendations are: ways to interpret data; suggested examples that will lead to important generalizations; background information that will encourage generalizations; opportunities for students to apply generalizations; suggested demonstrations that will show the limits of the generalizations; and listing of useful materials, such as maps, apparatus, and collections that might be used.

5. *Recommend teaching strategies.* Unlike the technologists, academicians do not specify in detail the methods teachers are to follow; their materials are not intended to be "teacher proof." Academicians do, however, prize the method of choice, learning how to inquire by doing it. Hence, they not only suggest different ways for students to discover important principles, they provide training materials, workshops, and films for use, aimed at helping the teacher move from didactic methods to those of discovery. Further, they preface with a variety of step-by-step solutions the experimental and theoretical problems presented to students. However, the communication of method has turned out to be one of the weakest aspects of the academic curriculum. Teachers who have never themselves developed skill in scientific reasoning and problem solving have difficulty in teaching methods of inquiry to others. Also, each teacher may have a favorite method, and will thus present different ideas and concepts than others will to students. The instructor interested in laboratory methods, for example, will emphasize this aspect. Teachers filter the materials through their own perceptions.

One can infer from the classic monograph on text material by Lee Cronbach that academicians and others don't know how to achieve a perfect learning opportunity in text materials. Cronbach thought, however, that creative developers might make real progress if they kept these questions in mind:

Does the text create readiness for the concepts and accomplishments to be taught in subsequent grades? Does the text assist the pupil to understand why certain responses are superior to others for given aims, rather than present them as prescriptions? Does the text make provisions for realistic experience, through narration, proposal of supplementary experiences, and laboratory prescriptions, so that students will be able to connect generalizations to reality? Does the text formulate explicit and transferable generalizations? Are the text explanations readable and comprehensible? Does the text provide for practice in application either by suggesting activities or by posing sensible problems in symbolic form? Do these problems call for the use of generalizations under realistic conditions and require the student to determine which principles to use as well as how to use them? Does the text provide an opportunity to use concepts from many fields of study in examining the same problems? Does the text help the learner recognize the intended outcomes from his work? Does it provide him with means of evaluating this progress along these lines?[11]

Does the classroom activity into which this text fits make it possible for the student to acquire emotional attitudes and skills of group membership? Does the text fit as closely as possible the readiness of the pupils for whom it is intended and does it develop readiness not now present?

Teacher Development of Learning Opportunities

In hundreds of ways, teachers modify curriculum for the needs of a given class—mimeographing materials, making arrangements for visiting speakers, creating learning games, designing learning packets, planning field trips, arranging original displays, suggesting individual studies, posing novel questions, and the like. Teachers recognize the inadequacies of available instructional materials in matching the requirements for each child. It is as if textbooks, curriculum guides, and other instructional material developed by those outside the particular classroom are highways, satisfactory for general planning, yet highways from which the teacher must at times turn off, taking a different route in order to provide something more appropriate for a learner or a group of learners. Usually the development and modification of curriculum by teachers is undertaken for the following reasons:

1. The particular learners require learning opportunities that are

[11]Lee J. Cronbach, *Text Materials in Modern Education* (Urbana, Ill.: University of Illinois Press, 1955), pp. 90–91.

closer to their present background and level of attainment. Pupils may need explanations drawn from familiar instances or more simple or more advanced tasks than have been provided. The development of a skill lesson in the language of a non-English-speaking child is a case in point.

2. The particular learners or their community have pressing questions or problems that require the experiences, facts, or the introduction of new activities and material.
3. Teachers desire to provide opportunities that are motivating. Hence, they create learning opportunities in accordance with motivational principles such as:

   choice—Learners choose from among activities. A range of opportunities is offered in order to accommodate to learners' style or mode of learning.

   utility—Opportunities encourage learners to use what is learned in satisfying unmet physical and psychological needs and to satisfy motives such as curiosity, exploration, and manipulation.

   link to other values—Opportunities place learners in contact with highly valued persons or activities.

   interests—Opportunities are related to special interests of learners at hand.

   models—Older peers, parents, and other significant persons are selected as exemplary models.

   success—Adaptations in conventional materials are made in order to ensure success, including prompting, flexible standards, and provision for learners to recognize their own success.
4. Teachers' interests, capabilities, and style make departures from standard materials desirable or necessary.

As an illustration of procedures used by teachers in developing learning opportunities, consider the development of a learning center (a learning center may consist of interesting activities that offer opportunity for children to practice and apply skills already acquired and to learn concept relationships). In general, the teacher begins with a view of learning from a child's perspective, including a predisposition or desire to be active, to manipulate—touch, grab, fondle—things, to socialize, to contemplate, to speculate, and to discover. Next, the teacher asks how concepts of math, art, science, and other subject fields can be presented so that they are consistent with children's predispositions. One answer might be to create a center that encourages manipulation in math, where a young child is asked to guess how many sets of four are in a plastic pill bottle containing twenty-four beads. The child can write down a guess, count the beads out into cups of an egg carton and check the answer against an answer card. After the beads are put back in the bottle, other written directions can ask the child to guess how many sets of three, eight, and six there will be. Or the task can be made harder by not disclosing how many beads are in the bottle.

Other answers might feature social interaction, making a product, speculating through "just suppose" activities, discovery through activities involving simple experiments, and knowledge of self through responsive activities whereby children indicate their feelings or reactions to stories, music, and the like, through their drawings as well as through oral and written comments.

In developing the learning center, the teacher answers such questions as:

1. What purpose will the center serve? What will children learn from it?
2. What subject area will be enhanced? What skills should be strengthened? Where is motivation the weakest? What attitudes are lacking? What concepts should be applied? What extra interests should be encouraged?
3. What kinds of tasks are appropriate—listening, recording, experimenting, writing, discussing, constructing, or what?
4. What materials are available?
5. To what extent should the activities of the center be designed so that children may proceed without the immediate presence of the teacher?
6. How long will each child or group have at the center? What will be the life span of the center?

As indicated previously, the teacher's curriculum orientation will reflect the planning procedures used. Those who begin with objectives follow a technological approach, those who commence with the quality of experiences use a humanistic procedure.

John A. Zahorik studied how teachers actually go about planning lessons and courses.[12] His findings indicated that teachers of adults were more likely to focus first on objectives or purposes than were other teachers. Secondary school teachers were more likely first to make decisions about materials or resources to be used, while elementary teachers first make decisions about pupils' readiness— ability and interest—for the particular lesson(s). Decisions about the

[12]John A. Zahorik, "Teachers Planning Models," *Educational Leadership* 33, no. 2 (November 1975): 134–39.

subject matter to be taught—fact, idea, content—are among the first decisions made by most teachers in their planning. The first and most frequently asked questions generally seems to be, "What are the ranges and particulars of the subject matter of the lessons that I must teach?"

Carol M. Jacko and Noreen M. Garmar say that teachers are instructional designers when they engage in such tasks as designing lessons for a particular grade or content area, writing a rationale for a specific instructional unit, or developing criteria for evaluating a commercial instructional program.[13]

Jean Helen Young cites recent studies indicating that teacher participation in curriculum decisions about goals and planning the scope and arrangement of a projected educational program for a school or district holds little or no attraction for classroom teachers.[14] According to Young, the major function of teachers is to implement district central office curriculum decisions in their particular classrooms and to select or create materials of instruction (means), rather than to participate in establishing district or schoolwide goals (ends). Only as teachers are relieved of full-time classroom responsibilities does their interest in curriculum decision making expand. The teachers' classroom orientation prevents the development of a long-range perspective and collegiativity that are essential to planning overall school or systemwide courses of study.

Young offers an alternative context for curriculum decision making that promises to enlarge teacher participation in curriculum making. Her proposal is to change the context for curriculum decision making from the school district to the individual school. Each individual school would have responsibility for development of the school's educational programs, money for development and implementation of the programs, and accountability for the results that follow. The proposal would require teachers to expand their role beyond their own classroom and to engage in curriculum making on an ongoing basis. All members of the staff would be expected to work toward common goals that they set with parents and others in the school community. There still would be such parameters as districtwide goals and required subjects in the curriculum of every school because the school district is responsible for the educational programs of the district. Teachers would, however, organize these

[13]Carol M. Jacko and Noreen M. Garmar, "A Search Through the Curriculum Maze," *NASSP Bulletin* 63, no. 425 (March 1979): 91–98.
[14]Jean Helen Young, "Teacher Participation in Curriculum Decision Making: An Organizational Dilemma," *Curriculum Inquiry* 9, no. 2 (Summer 1979): 113–27.

subjects, and possibly others, into a curriculum suitable for the particular community. The school staff would plan the ways in which it would achieve the common goals and how each subject would contribute to the total curriculum.

Unfinished Business: Relating Curriculum Plans to Teaching Models

The previous discussions should have illuminated the kinds of choices that can be made among the means available. What has not been made clear is that there should be some consistency between these different guides to instructional planning and both the curriculum domains and teaching modes to be employed. Just as failure to match a domain with the right learning opportunities makes an ineffective curriculum, so too does a mismatch between goals and teaching modes. Currently, for example, a teaching mode appropriate for teaching basic skills is being widely promoted as an exemplary teaching model. The inappropriateness of this mode for use with social reconstructionist, humanistic, and inquiry goals within an academic curriculum is not considered by the promoters. In evaluating this model, M. Frances Klein indicates the limited focus of a skills model for teaching and at the same time suggests that the use of activities representing a number of different curriculum orientations within a single classroom might be confusing to learners.[15]

A serious deficiency in curriculum planning is the gap between concepts for designing learning activities and concepts for guiding teacher preparation. Paradigms for teaching, such as those by technologists James Popham and Eva Baker,[16] humanists Maxine Greene and Arthur Combs,[17] and academicians Richard Suchman and Robert Karplus[18] are not often related to particular curriculum domains or to the wide range of criteria for selecting learning opportunities. Hence we see teacher training programs preparing teachers

[15]M. Frances Klein, "A Perspective in Curriculum and the Beginning Teacher Evaluation Study," *Newsletter 4 Beginning Teacher Evaluation Study* (Sacramento, Calif.: Commission for Teacher Preparation and Licensing, June 1979), pp. 1–7.

[16]W. James Popham and Eva L. Baker, *Planning an Instructional Sequence* (Englewood Cliffs, N.J.: Prentice-Hall, 1970).

[17]Maxine Greene, "Teaching the Question of Personal Reality," in *Staff Development: New Demands, New Realities, New Perspectives*, Ann Lieberman and Lynne Miller, eds. (New York: Teachers College, Columbia University, 1979), pp. 23–36.

[18]Donald C. Medeiros, et al., "Humanistic Teacher Education: Another View," *Educational Leadership* 36, no. 6 (March 1979): 434–38; and "Teacher Inquiry and Discovery," in *The Nature of Teaching*, Lois Nelson, ed. (Waltham, Mass.: Blaisdell Publishing Co., 1969), pp. 198–236.

in methodologies that do not correspond to the curriculum designs those teachers are likely to encounter or use in their particular school settings. Teachers are given methods for conducting inquiry lessons only to find themselves later responsible for designing and implementing didactic lessons or managing instructional systems.

One of the few persons to address this problem is Bruce R. Joyce.[19] Joyce has attempted to form engineering models by which specific teaching strategies, curriculum structures, and educational missions (ends) can be related. He would, for example, match the learning opportunity approach of Carl Rogers with the domain of personal development, the academic modes of Bruner with information processing and the goal of intellectual development. By clarifying alternative purposes and domains and by using the appropriate sets of criteria for developing the activities and instructional strategies, curriculum workers will be engineering a consistent curriculum. In the process, they will be encouraging broad conceptions of purposes and extending options in order to attain those purposes.

CONCLUDING COMMENTS

There were really two parts to this chapter. In one part we dealt with how best to select the learning activities by which the ends of educational programs can be attained. We also asked whether activities should be considered as means to ends or whether they should be judged as valuable or not in their own right. Differences were shown between the kinds of opportunities—categories or domains—commonly chosen at macro or societal and institutional levels and the kinds selected at micro or classroom levels. Several criteria for selecting learning activities were presented and there was an analysis of the strengths and weaknesses of different arguments used in justifying learning activities.

In the second part we focused on development of learning opportunities—products and materials. The ways in which social reconstructionists, technologists, humanists, academicians, and teachers develop learning opportunities were described, and attention was drawn to the special problems of relating curriculum plans to teaching modes.

Development of learning opportunities will continue at both

---

[19]Bruce R. Joyce, "The Curriculum Worker of the Future," NSSE Yearbook, *The Curriculum: Retrospect and Prospect* (Chicago: University of Chicago Press, 1971).

macro and micro levels. It is not known, however, which set of procedures will dominate. There is, for example, a question as to whether the technologists' more expensive procedures that have guided the developmental projects of regional laboratories will be adopted by publishers or whether less rigorous operational standards will prevail. We need to study what happens when different procedures are followed. Are different ends promoted by different approaches? Do some procedures pay off in demonstrably superior programs? What is the relative economic and procedural efficiency of the different approaches?

QUESTIONS

1. How do technologists, humanists, academicians, and social reconstructionists differ in their models for developing learning opportunities?
2. To what three criteria would you give greatest weight in selecting among textbooks?
3. How would you expect the issue of accountability to be treated by expressives and instrumentalists in their attitude toward learning opportunities? Accountability is defined here as the selection of goals and specific objectives, assessment of learner status with respect to these goals, efforts directed at improvement of weaknesses revealed in the assessment, and fixing of responsibility for results.
4. Contrast the nature of learning opportunities at macro levels of planning with that at micro levels.
5. Consider a learning opportunity that you might like to introduce as an innovation within a school system. What factors would you use in defending the proposed innovation? How would you justify the proposal, using costs as a criterion?
6. Consider a classroom objective that you think is important for a given learner. Describe a learning opportunity for this learner consistent with the objective, illustrating the following principles: (a) appropriate practice (opportunity to practice what is called for in the objective), (b) learning satisfaction (provision for the learner to find the opportunity rewarding), and (c) learner readiness (assurance that the learner has the necessary prerequisites for participating in the opportunity).

SELECTED REFERENCES

Briggs, Leslie J., ed. *Instructional Design: Principles and Application.* Englewood Cliffs, N.J.: Educational Technology Publications, 1977.
Dunfee, Maxine. *Eliminating Ethnic Bias in Instructional Materials.*

Washington, D.C.: Association for Supervision and Curriculum Development, 1974.

EPIC Report. *Improving the Selection and Use of Instructional Materials: A How-To Handbook*. New York: EPIC Institute, 1979.

Klein, M. Frances. *About Learning Materials*. Washington, D.C.: Association for Supervision and Curriculum Development, 1978.

Komoski, P. Kenneth. "The Realities of Choosing and Using Instructional Materials," *Educational Leadership* 36, no. 1 (October 1978): 46–51.

McNeil, John D. "The Design and Selection of Learning Activities," *Designing Curriculum: Self-Instructional Modules*. Boston: Little, Brown, 1976.

Read, Donald A. and Simon, Sidney, eds. *Humanistic Education Sourcebook*. Englewood Cliffs, N.J.: Prentice-Hall, 1975.

Schaffarzick, Jon and Hampson, David, eds. *Strategies for Curriculum Development*. Berkeley, Calif.: McCutchan, 1975.

Schultz, Richard E. "Learning About the Costs of Instruction and the Benefits of Research and Development in Education," *Educational Researcher* 8, no. 4 (April 1979).

Tyler, Louise. "Materials in Persons," *Theory Into Practice* 16, no. 4 (October 1977): 231–37.

Tyler, Louise, Klein, M. Frances, and associates. *Evaluating and Choosing Curriculum and Instructional Materials*. Los Angeles, Calif.: Educational Resource Associates, Inc., 1976.

7 / IMPLEMENTING CURRICULUM

The purpose of this chapter is to introduce the reader to several approaches for effecting curriculum change. Strengths and weaknesses of the approaches are presented. This chapter provides a perspective on serious issues such as whether curriculum change should start with a teacher, with an administrator, or with members of formal committees or professional reformers at local, state, and federal levels.

One might think that curriculum formulated by teachers for use in their own classrooms would be the easiest to implement. The teacher would clearly understand the objectives and have thought out the learning opportunities for attaining them. It is not that simple, however. Teachers may be reluctant to develop and execute curriculum for several reasons. They are constrained by time and load and they might perceive a climate of resistance to change from parents, peers, or a principal. Even if others are not actually opposed to teachers implementing a new curriculum, the anticipation of resistance may be enough to preclude innovation. Most curriculum innovations, further, do not affect a single classroom, but an entire school or school district. As was indicated in a previous chapter, teachers are more interested in planning for their own classroom rather than for the total school or district. Hence, it is difficult to effect a school system's curriculum revision through teacher initiation.

Administrators, on the other hand, often feel helpless in initiating a new curriculum, finding it difficult to persuade staff and others to respond enthusiastically and to carry out the proposed changes. It is not easy to control the classroom in specific ways when one is outside the classroom. Even when administrators have money to stimulate curriculum improvement, the results are frequently insignificant.

Those who develop curriculum at the state or national level also have problems. The first is how to get the curriculum adopted. There are difficulties in clearing the political hurdles of textbook committees, curriculum commissions, boards of education, and other groups so that the curriculum can be made available to teachers. An even bigger problem is how to get their products actually used as intended in the schools. A classroom study by Goodlad, Klein, and others concluded that practitioners did not have clearcut ideas of what was required to enact curriculum innovations of others. At best, the innovations are only partially implemented. The novel features often are blunted in the effort to twist the innovation into familiar ways of doing things.[1] Top-down planning generally fails because it does not generate the staff commitment necessary for project success and the planning does not take into account the special knowledge and suggestions of those who will be responsible for implementing the curriculum.

What is the answer to this state of affairs? What understanding and practical suggestions are available to help those who would implement curriculum changes? Theories of educational change, such as those by Robert Chin and Donald C. Ovich, give fresh interpretations of what is involved in getting change and suggest testable strategies.[2] Others, like David Shiman and Ann Lieberman, distrust solutions, models, and designs for change because they believe these strategies do not correspond with the reality of the school situations.[3] Rather than taking a single position on the argument over the need for conceptualizations of the change process or prescriptions for it, we will present both.

---

[1]John Goodlad, M.F. Klein, et al., *Looking Behind the Classroom Door*, rev. ed. (Worthington, Ohio: Charles A. Jones, 1974).

[2]Robert Chin, "Applied Behavioral Science and Innovation, Diffusion, and Adoption," *Viewpoints* 50, no. 3 (May 1974): 25–45; and Robert Chin and Donald C. Ovich, "Federal Educational Policy: The Paradox of Innovation and Centralization," *Educational Researcher* 8, no. 7 (August 1979): 4–10.

[3]David A. Shiman and Ann Lieberman, "A Non-Model for School Change," *The Educational Forum* 38, no. 4 (May 1974): 441–45.

CONCEPTUALIZATIONS OF THE CHANGE PROCESS

Kinds of Changes and Difficulties in Implementing Each

Behavioral scientists who interpret the change process have found it useful to look at five kinds of change.

1. *Substitution.* One element may be substituted for another already present. Substituting a new textbook for an old one is an example. This kind of change is readily made.

2. *Alteration.* Alteration occurs when a change is introduced into existing material in the hope that it will appear minor and thus be readily adopted. The curriculum person who modifies the activities accompanying a popular textbook in the interest of student initiative and independence as opposed to student dependency is engaging in alteration. Such changes are easily made but may lead to unanticipated consequences. For example, altered activities may be accepted but the initiative and independence may be counterproductive to other classroom objectives.

3. *Perturbations.* These changes are disruptive, but teachers can adjust to them within a fairly short time. Most teachers, for instance, can quite easily make allowances for a change in scheduling of classes and the length of time allowed for teaching.

4. *Restructuring changes.* These changes lead to modification of the system itself. Decentralization and new concepts of the teaching role are examples of restructuring. When students and parents begin to participate in selecting objectives and designing learning opportunities, there is a change in the system.

5. *Value orientation changes.* These are shifts in the fundamental value orientations of participants. When a school begins to be staffed with new teachers who value student personal growth or social reconstruction more than academic achievement, value orientations are changed.

Curriculum workers will find these conceptualizations useful in making decisions regarding the requirements for implementing particular innovations. Before introducing a change, they should classify it and recognize the probable difficulty and consequences. Such anticipation will facilitate planning of the resources necessary to effect the change. Indeed, in some cases, one will decide that the change should not be undertaken.

Sociological Findings About Change

Sociologists study stability and changes in organizations. They have found that both formal and informal channels of communication are features of curriculum change. They tell us that most curriculum innovations in a school are borrowed rather than invented. The borrowing may take the form of direct imitation or the importing of new personnel. The former is exemplified by those who visit another school or district to see an innovation, such as a new career guidance center, and subsequently start a similar one, perhaps avoiding many of the errors and costs associated with the initial development. Observation of results in classroom situations and the exchange of opinions with fellow teachers are also important in getting teachers to change, particularly when the validity of information is in doubt. Importing occurs when a group of persons from a subculture—for example, minority group members not previously represented—become members of the staff.

For teachers, there is little financial incentive for accepting an innovation. Indeed, punishment is often associated with such acceptance. The teacher might have to work longer hours in order to make the change and might attract criticism from those who are opposed to it. Hence, it is much more comfortable and a lot safer to be conventional most of the time. It is remarkable that many teachers are as open to innovation as they are, considering the basic reward system which discourages risk taking, experimentation, and responsiveness to some consumers.[4]

School administrators are viewed by sociologists as persons "in the middle," with little possibility of being primary advocates for major curriculum change. In the formal organization, school administrators must maintain equilibrium among different forces. They cannot alienate significant segments of the public and stay in business. Thus, institution of change cannot rest mainly with the administrator. To say that administrators may not be major advocates is not to say that they may not be key figures in innovation, however. On the contrary, when they are both aware of and sympathetic to a change, the innovation tends to prosper. When administrators are ignorant, apathetic, or hostile, an innovation tends to remain outside the

[4]William Lowe Boyd, "The Politics of Curriculum Change and Stability," *Educational Researcher* 8, no. 2 (February 1977): 12–18.

school. Implementation of new curriculum is directly related to immediate administrator support. Teachers alone cannot innovate and
implement. Department and grade level faculty, possibly under the
direction of a chairperson or team leader and operating with the
backing of the principal, often are influential.

One very real problem in effecting change is due to a paradoxical
situation involving mediation between the school organization and
its external environment. Often, for example, tension arises between
those who seek to maintain the values of the school staff and those
who would respond to the conflicting values of a changing
community.

A somewhat different paradox is due to conflicting pressures for
curriculum change on the part of those who want the curriculum to
be responsive to local concerns about relevancy to larger social
issues. At the same time that there is vigorous interest in local
autonomy over curriculum matters, wide sociocultural problems that
derive their significance from beyond the local area are evident.

Major curriculum decisions are being made at the national level
relating, for example, to career education, early childhood education, and multicultural programs. Few persons would deny that we
should be sensitive to national interests and to happenings in the
larger society. Professional reformers supported by federal and foundation funding have raised the consciousness of local communities
and influenced curriculum change in the interests of the non-English-
speaking, handicapped, sex discriminated, and other students. Yet
the concept of the school as a community operation is not dead.
Most of us sympathize with those who want to see local lay participation in curriculum planning. The school has been one of the few
institutions in which a scattered public could recognize itself and express its interests. Because citizens feel remote from much of civic,
national, and international affairs, it is desirable to preserve those
neighborly vehicles by which the individual can influence a crucial
public matter. Further, such participation makes possible the innovations and creations that are essential in implementing more general
plans. The task, therefore, is to find a way to interest the community
in curriculum change without jeopardizing the right of pupils to acquire the knowledge, skills, and attitudes necessary for participation
in a larger world.

Groups and individuals in the community can also aid in devising
supplementary learning situations. They can plan opportunities out
of school in which pupils can apply the intellectual skills being taught
and can attack those conditions shown to be detrimental to the instructional program. There is, however, a danger that in col-

laborating with the community, administrators will make incidental functions dominant and respond to pressures that attenuate the systematic organization of learning.

Six Aspects of Curriculum Change

Ronald Lippitt, a prominent social psychologist actively engaged in curriculum development, has found it helpful to identify six aspects of curriculum change. His model is more comprehensive than other models of change. Lippitt is one of the few to show the importance of involving pupils in the change and to specify the functions that lead to greater teacher acceptance and use of innovations. If the following guidelines for curriculum committees were followed, our schools would have many more effective curriculum materials.

Student Use of New Material. The decisions students make about their involvement with a new curriculum are the most crucial in the process of curriculum change. Such decisions are determined by *internal supports.* By way of illustration, students must perceive the learning opportunity as relevant to their world of meaning, value, interests, and curiosities. They must receive feedback from their responses. They must learn how to learn from the material and enjoy the fun that comes from active search and closure. Other determinants of student utilization are *external supports.* The innovator must take into account peer norms about such things as how active and how cooperative students should be in working with the teacher. To do this, curriculum workers may use models furnished by the older peer culture. Teachers also need to be aware of peer norms and to be willing to share leadership with peer leaders if pupils are to become involved. Also, the extent of collaboration of parents and other adults in the community will influence student involvement with the changed curriculum.

Teacher Use of New Material. In order to get teachers to use the new curriculum, it is recommended that the curriculum leader first involve the teacher in the review, evaluation, and exploration of the relevance of the new materials. This means asking teachers to apply criteria for evaluating learning opportunities and objectives. Second, the teacher should have freedom to explore the new skills needed for utilizing the curriculum material, to learn new concepts and new techniques, and to collaborate with colleagues in sharing practices and learning together. Third, the curriculum changes must equip teachers with the tools for diagnosing their own class responses and for involving the students in adapting the curriculum and inventing new procedures.

Adoption of New Material. A curriculum committee's adoption decision should include involvement of appropriate decision makers in a review of alternatives. There should be a review of the criteria to be used in making the decision and a plan to test alternatives, to judge feasibility, and to learn about the learners' responses to the material and method. Learners should be involved in evaluating the new materials. It is important that adoption committees analyze the needs for staff development that would follow if the materials were adopted.

The Search for Curriculum Innovations. In searching for new ideas, curriculum planners should start with the *home*, schools recognizing the creative curricula that are hidden with the local scene. Next, planners should consider *neighboring school systems*. They should break down the barriers that keep neighbors from sharing. Finally, curriculum workers should get information regarding promising innovations. Clearinghouse procedures for identifying creative innovations should be used in getting information. One should ask innovators questions about what they are doing and how, what they have discovered, how they have failed, what difficulties they have encountered, and what skills they have found necessary.

Distribution of New Curriculum. Diffusion of curriculum rests heavily on the staff development available for the teachers. Teachers must have the opportunity to achieve skills for using the new curriculum. They should also have the chance to get excited about and feel free to adapt the materials.

Development of New Materials. New material may be developed through the work of a team in a school system, the creative efforts of a single teacher, or the project staff of a research and development center. Curriculum development requires identifying priority objectives and core units of knowledge, and relating content to experience, interests, and competence of learners. Teachers should be helped to understand and use the resources skillfully and to evaluate the materials so that the curriculum may continue to improve.[5]

---

[5]Ronald Lippitt, "Processes of Curriculum Change," *Curriculum Change: Direction and Process* (Washington, D.C.: Association for Supervision and Curriculum Development, 1966), pp. 43-59.

DESCRIPTIVE STRATEGIES FOR CHANGE

The models that describe how curriculum change best occurs in school settings often conflict with one another. The Research and Development (R and D) model, for example, describes the change process as a top to bottom procedure, whereas the integrative development model starts with a teacher problem and moves out to an entire school system. There may be partial truth in all of the models, and we may gain from understanding each of them.

The Adoption Model or R and D Model

The R and D model has been popular among those concerned with implementing curriculum throughout the region or nation, because it describes processes for both development and diffusion. This model utilizes programs, research, and development projects from universities, regional laboratories, and other institutions to develop an innovative package of materials. Then the product is disseminated to a wide population. Effective diffusion requires that consumers be made aware of potential benefits and usefulness of the product and that influential persons in the schools be convinced that the innovation would strengthen the school. The model calls for a facilitator who performs first the role of "salesperson" and later a training role with school personnel so they can train others with the system, the "multiplier effect."[6] The innovator, together with school leaders, monitors and assists with problems that arise during initial installation.

Persuasive criticisms have been made of the R and D model.[7] It is not specific about the nature and function of the political factors that interfere with innovation. The model's developers seem to have assumed that good communications are enough. But one critic has shown, for example, that a teachers' union might oppose a given curriculum innovation because of increased paperwork and longer hours required of its members.[8] Further, the model is too vague and optimistic about the facilitators' roles.

[6] Ronald Hull, "A Research and Development Adoption Model," *Educational Administration Quarterly* 10, no. 3 (Autumn 1974): 33–45.

[7] Ernest R. House, *The Politics of Educational Innovation* (Berkeley, Calif.: McCutchan, 1974).

[8] Jack E. Thomas, "Why Revive the R and D Model of Innovation," *Educational Administrator's Quarterly* 11, no. 2 (Spring 1975): 104–08.

Mammoth federal experiments that suggest a curriculum design such as is provided for compensatory education, career education, or "Right to Read" often leave their advocates pensive. The instructional treatments within these curriculum innovations sometimes become distorted, lacking in standardization, and modified when used by teachers and pupils with different backgrounds. Between-school variation often wipes out any generalized effect of the innovation, making it difficult to say with certainty that the change is valuable.

Richard Schutz, however, is optimistic about the model as it is being revised to include attention to implementation—R D and I (I for implementation). Implementation requires attending to political, social, and economic considerations in addition to technical, scientific, and scholarly considerations. He sees a new era in which R and D will conduct participatory activity *with* the school community rather than *for* the school community.[9]

The Integrative Development Model

The strategy in the integrative development model is to deal with the immediate concerns of teachers and then move out of the classroom, perhaps even to reorganize the school system. An assumption underlying this approach is that a climate for eliminating clouded vision, fears, and threats must accompany change. The model calls for involvement by starting with the concerns teachers face. The first business in the strategy is to help teachers identify their problems. The problems selected, however, should be within the competence of the teacher. The second order of business is to study the cause of the difficulties. Using the analysis of the teachers' data, the curriculum leader introduces the teachers to new insights and abilities. The integration of theory with the analysis of problems stimulates bolder departures and the transition of general ideas into practice.

Difficulties with the approach include time and lack of expertise both to handle human relations procedures and to relate relevant theory to the problems selected. Changes in teacher attitudes and skills take time. The establishment of an experimental attitude is especially slow at first. Also, there are teachers who feel insecure about engaging in group problem solving. To lessen such problems, productive groups should be composed of persons with expertise in

[9]Richard E. Schutz, "Where We've Been, Where We Are, and Where We're Going in Educational R & D," *Educational Researcher* 8, no. 8 (September 1979): 6–24.

several areas: curriculum, principles of learning, the realities of the classroom, pertinent subject matter, inquiry skills, and the skills of human relations and group process.

The Change Agent Model

The absence of agents for promoting change has long been thought to be a factor in the slowness with which schools adopt innovation. Educational writers are fond of pointing to the agricultural extension agent's success in influencing farmers to modify their practices in accordance with scientifically derived information. The idea of creating a new professional role in education to do the same sort of things has often been proposed. After careful thought, however, it is noted that education, unlike agriculture, medicine, and certain governmental agencies, lacks (1) reliable knowledge, (2) a well-defined and respected communication channel for diffusing innovation effectively to the appropriate audiences, and (3) a definite authority to guide individual decision. Most important, educational practitioners are accustomed to adopting innovations without benefit of evidence of their effectiveness and without fully understanding how to implement curriculum innovation.

There is much disagreement as to who the change agent should be in curriculum implementation. Some people would have the building principal perform the role. Certainly at the building level, the principal can play the role of supporter of innovation. Yet it seems difficult for the principal to take on the additional roles of trainer and political advocate. Other people, like James K. Duncan, would have curriculum directors be responsible for generating the institutional response to widespread demand for change.[10] Duncan believes this should be so because the curriculum directors have authority. They have the legal right to make decisions that affect other people's behavior and the power to make those decisions, and they often have influence based on mutual trust. (Role responsibility, time and opportunity, and acknowledged expertise have also been suggested as the basis for a curriculum director's influence.)

The principal advantage of giving responsibility to curriculum directors is that they can influence all essential elements of the cur-

[10]James K. Duncan, "The Curriculum Director in Curriculum Change," *The Educational Forum* 38, no. 1 (November 1973): 51–77.

riculum event. These elements include artifacts (materials), actors (teachers, administrators, students, producers of materials), and operations (purposes, ends, intended outcomes). Curriculum directors relate these elements in the preinstructional phase, devoted to planning the curriculum, and the interactive phase, given to evaluating the consequences. Hence, attacking the problem of curriculum innovation means changing curriculum events either by changing the nature of the elements or by changing their relationships. Modifying artifacts, actors, and operations is a less dramatic way to change the curriculum than is creating entirely new events, but it may produce a more durable form of change.

The teacher as change agent is getting much attention of late. In Britain, much curriculum innovation has grown out of the imaginative work of classroom teachers. In the United States, however, curriculum innovation still tends to come from outside the classroom, through government and foundation-supported projects and commercial publishers.

Thelma Harms has proposed that the American teacher should have a role in curriculum innovation. She suggests that the teacher's role is to establish a *divergent curriculum*.[11] By this, she means a curriculum that reflects many different orientations. Harms wants the teacher to synthesize the many opposing learning strategies inherent in the different curriculum materials from outside the classroom. If separate materials feature open-ended democracy, guided discovery, self-corrective programmed materials, and imitation, for example, the teacher must see how many of these varying approaches to learning can be used in the classroom. In so doing, teachers "become their own consultants"; they look at themselves and at the learning environment they are creating. In short, innovations from outside are seen as setting the stage or challenging the teacher to study all strategies, take the best parts of them, and find the means to deal effectively with all areas of learning.

Impatient with the school's resistance to change, those outside the school have created new professional roles and involved sociologists as change agents working on both administrators and teachers. The sociologists have sought to direct communication from the very top levels of the system to the bottom with no intervening mediators. But

[11]Thelma Harms, "Change-Agents in Curriculum," *Young Children* 29, no. 5 (July 1974): 280–88.

this strategy has caused problems. As two sociologists who tried it said, "We went over [the supervisors'] heads on all of the major issues. We thus brought about their alienation from the program and criticism for whatever was done without their involvement."[12] However, their strategy is sometimes successful. One sociologist change agent asks teachers, "What materials would you like that you have never been able to get before?" Suggested materials are acquired for them with lightning speed. Principals are invited to "status meetings" with top officials and prominent community leaders. They thus have the feeling of being in the top circle of policymaking and, thereby, offer less resistance to the change proposals coming from the outside agent.

The Institute for the Development of Educational Activities (IDEA) of the Charles F. Kettering Foundation tried to introduce new professional roles into local school units. Among the new roles were those of director of research and development and director of demonstrations and disseminations. The director of research and development was to refine, evaluate, and further develop new practices within a league of innovative schools; the director of demonstrations and disseminations was to provide leadership in extending innovative practices to conventional schools and school systems. In general, the plan sputtered. As indicated by W.C. Wolf, Jr., competent, well-trained individuals could not be found to fill the new roles; in-service training opportunities offered by IDEA were inadequate; not all of the consortium schools offered innovative situations; IDEA did not provide the back up services needed by individuals in the new roles; the new roles were not clearly defined in terms of performance criteria; hence, they were subject to the whims of the individuals occupying them.[13]

The Nonmodel for Change

David Shiman and Ann Lieberman were participants in a five-year study of the process of change in eighteen schools. They sought to get the schools to look at their problems and to explore the question:

[12]Mario Fantini and Gerald Weinstein, "Strategies for Initiating Change in Large Bureaucratic School Systems." Paper presented to the Public Policy Institute, Teachers College, Columbia University, New York, April 1967.

[13]W.C. Wolf, Jr., "Change Agent Strategies in Perspective," in *Conceptual Base of Program I: Specialists in Continuing Education* (Northfield, Ill.: Cooperative Educational Research Laboratory, 1969).

"How does a school faculty attempt to cope with change?" Subsequently, these two researchers described the process of change as they thought it really occurs.

First, people talk about the possibility of bringing about some kind of change. Expectations rise and there is uneasiness when teachers feel pressure to do something. Second, some teachers begin to do something. They attempt to individualize their reading program. Third, justification for the teacher's new activity begins: "Why am I doing this?" "Is this better than what I did before?" Fourth, problems with the innovation arise. Individualization of the reading program makes it difficult to give the same spelling test to thirty-six children. Fifth, teachers now question the basic assumptions of the program. "What is the relevancy of the program for children?" "Is my teaching behavior consistent with the goal we're trying to accomplish?"

The researchers concluded that they had discovered something important, namely, that innovation should not start with goals, priorities, motivation, or evaluation, as suggested by most simplistic models. Instead, innovators should take each school where it is, and use its strengths in fostering disequilibrium, considering alternatives, raising philosophical questions, and helping in evaluation. Only by being sensitive to each school's particular situation can innovators effectively relate the intervention to the school's needs.[14]

W.C. Wolf, Jr., and John A. Fiorino also studied school persons who seemed interested and willing to make change. They found that changes were prompted by dissatisfaction with existing practices and a desire to expand present offerings. Those who were interested in change sought their alternatives from courses, professional meetings, articles, or salespeople from publishing house, not from the educators' own imagination. Initial interest in an innovation was maintained if it didn't cost too much and if it could be adopted without too much fuss. Most of the educators' energies were expended in behalf of innovations that were unlikely to alter markedly the status of conventional practice. The authors concluded that today's practitioner seems driven to change for the sake of change and that the changes made do not come through disciplined inquiry methods.[15]

[14]David A. Shiman and Ann Lieberman, "A Non-Model for School Change," *The Educational Forum* 38, no. 4 (May 1974): 441.

[15]W.C. Wolf, Jr., and John A. Fiorino, "Some Perspective of Educational Change," *The Educational Forum* 38, no. 1 (November 1973): 79-84.

PRESCRIPTIONS FOR IMPLEMENTING CURRICULUM CHANGE

Lessons from the Ford Foundation's Experience

Paul Nachtigal has reported on the Ford Foundation's Comprehensive School Improvement Plan, a $30 million project aimed at legitimizing the concept of innovation in schools and at testing various kinds of innovation.[16] The findings and conclusions of the Nachtigal report include some of the most valuable advice available for those who would effect curriculum change. Among the lessons drawn from the CSIP efforts are these:

1. Innovation takes hold best when the number of schools is limited and the objectives and techniques few and sharply defined. The most successful and permanent changes are started with a minimum of disruption within a single school or inside a few classrooms.
2. The size of the grant (money) has little to do with the ultimate success of the program. Large-scale change is more likely to occur when grantee and grantor agree on the purposes and nature of the project. Change needs commitment from parent districts as well as the foundation as an indicator of an intention that districts will stay with the program.
3. "Lighthouse" schools are not perceived by those in neighboring schools as innovative and exemplary. Districtwide influence is more likely when projects encourage innovation in schools throughout the district.
4. The directorship is the most crucial indicator. Projects that are most effective are those in which the director is present at planning and remains through implementation, evaluation, and adaptation.
5. The university as an institution is not a force for improvement. It is not seen as an instrument for reform. University faculty members who work with teachers function as part-timers—persons who cannot become involved in the nitty-gritty.
6. The less complex the school system's structure, the more easily innovations are introduced. Small schools change faster than large ones.

[16]Paul Nachtigal, *A Foundation Goes to School* (New York: Ford Foundation, 1972).

7. The most lasting innovations occur in middle-sized suburbs small enough to avoid divisive debate between powerful interest groups but large enough to require that the change be identified with more than individual or local concerns. Locally produced packaged curriculum and curriculum that requires a major change in faculty behavior are both usually discontinued.

8. Any significant process for curriculum improvement needs scholarly input to ensure intellectual rigor, expertise in learning to support methodologies, extensive testing evaluation and revision, programs for teacher training, and procedures for dissemination. In terms of both costs and student learning, the adoption of professionally developed curriculum produces far more change than in house curriculum development.

Suggestions for Successful Implementation

Newer views on staff development, along with modified organizational and role expectations, are among the answers to curriculum implementation. Curriculum innovations that rely heavily on technology tend to be short lived. Unlike business or industry, which seek to eliminate the need for human services, education is a labor intensive field that requires teachers more than machines. Hence, a key to educational change must include staff development.

Staff development is now at center stage in successful curriculum implementation. As a result of recent studies, staff development is taking the following directions. [17]

Intensive *staff development* as distinct from single one-day workshops is an important strategy. Staff development is seen as part of curriculum planning tied to a school site. The principal serves as the instructional leader in the context of strengthening the school curriculum by giving clear messages that teachers may take responsibility for their own professional growth. *Staff training* activities are skill specific, such as instruction in how to carry out a new reading program or how to introduce new mathematical material. This is in contrast to many old in-service programs where training activities were isolated from the teachers' day-to-day responsibilities, thus having

[17]Milbrey W. McLaughlin and David D. Marsh, "Staff Development and School Changes," in *Staff Development*, Ann Lieberman and Lynne Miller, eds. (New York: Teachers College, Columbia University, 1979), pp. 69–94; and Michael Fullan and Alan Pomfret, "Research on Curriculum and Instruction Implementation," *Review of Educational Research* 47, no. 2 (Winter 1977): 335–97.

little impact. There are *support activities*. In order that staff training result in more than transient effects, the contributions of staff training must be reinforced and extended through: (1) classroom assistance by resource personnel and outside consultants (provided these resource persons are perceived by teachers as being helpful), and (2) project meetings whereby teachers learn to adapt the new curriculum to the realities of the particular school and classroom. In addition to feedback between users and consultants, peer discussions seem to be vital for working through the problems of innovation. Teachers and administrators need one or more years to learn what innovation is needed and what the innovation should look like in the particular school. They need to learn what help is necessary and the skills to be acquired and applied. Significant curriculum changes usually require certain organizational changes, particularly in roles and role relationships of the staff and students. The redevelopment of roles is an example of a reconstructing change which is difficult to bring about. As a case in point, I recently visited a classroom where a teacher was trying to implement a curriculum that demanded much interaction among pupils. The furniture had been arranged to accommodate the small group work demanded by the new materials. The teacher, however, had not recognized the need for changing from a didactic role to a resource role. Consequently, the teacher was frustrated in her ability to control the attention of pupils working in groups with the new materials.

Curriculum innovation also may require a change in the principal's role. Teachers teach more of a new curriculum when the principal plays an active role in its implementation. New curriculum does not flourish when the principal remains in an office, verbalizes support, and lets the teachers struggle with the problems.

Active involvement of the teachers in the development process — in developing guides and materials — is more important in getting teachers to implement plans than participating on the curriculum committees that decide on the plans. The roles of students and parents as decision makers in relation to the degree of implementation have been largely unstudied.

James M. Mahan has written of his experiences in curriculum installation activity in more than sixty schools.[18] Among his generalizations for turning curriculum change into the reality of improved classroom instruction are these:

[18]James M. Mahan, "Frank Observations on Innovation in Elementary Schools," *Interchange* 3, nos. 2–3 (February 3, 1972): 144–60.

Monitor the curriculum in the classroom. Provide for prerequisite learning experiences. For example, grade K-1 materials may be introduced one year; other grade level materials in successive years. One should eliminate other curriculum in order to allow time for the new and try to follow the sequences when using hierarchically constructed programs. The teacher must be helped to learn how to transfer "inquiry" and "process" methods to the conventional curriculum. Teachers should also know at the start what types of evaluative data will be required.

Maintain the curriculum after it is no longer an innovation. A local plan for full continuing district support should be agreed upon at the beginning of the innovation. This plan might include a requirement that the district will hire only teachers who agree to teach the particular curriculum envisioned. It might also provide ways by which skilled teachers who have peer respect can assist other teachers.

Similar suggestions regarding the survival of new programs have been made more recently by others.[19]

Central policymakers should emphasize broad-based programs and provide support for local development of specific forms of implementation. Social experimentation should be encouraged during implementation to develop variants that are more appropriate in particular circumstances.

We should recognize that while professional reformers are rewarded for proposing controversial, innovative curriculum changes, school practitioners are usually rewarded for innovations that promote social stability. Therefore, professional reformers are likely to be frustrated in their efforts to sell the implementation of controversial curriculum.

In order to illuminate the problems that come with curriculum implementation, one need only reflect on these considerations: What is the desirable number of new curriculum installations for any one year? What should be the timing of installations and requisite experience of the staff? Must there be agreement on humanistic, technological, and subject matter orientations? What relations between administrators and teachers are necessary? In what way does a school district's history of innovation efforts influence the decision to innovate?

[19]Ronald S. Brand, ed., "Curriculum Implementation," *Theme Issue Educational Leadership* 37, no. 3 (December 1979): 204-65.

CONCLUDING COMMENTS

Reviewing the content of this chapter, a number of issues become clear. One issue arises in the approach to innovative curriculum: should it be from the user-teacher-student viewpoint, the developer's orientation toward the product, or consistent with the ideals of professional reformers? Recommendations that call for the involvement of students, parents, and community members in school curriculum development, staff problem-solving approaches, and the teacher as an agent of change favor one side of the issue. The manipulation of organization, social structure, specified competency-based approaches, and R and D adoption models favor the other side. Reformers and R and D developers want teachers to implement goal-focused curriculum in predetermined ways, although teachers may advise and indicate the factors that must be attended to in order to get fidelity to the given ideals and the specified plan or product. Those with a user perspective assume that users should at least codecide what innovations to implement and how to implement them.

A second issue relates to the values of theories in guiding the implementation process. Some people believe that practice is ahead of theory, and hence, is a more valuable guide to implementation. Opposing this notion are those who believe that theory is invaluable in directing the attention of practitioners to otherwise overlooked variables and to fresh conceptualizations of the change process.

Disenchantment with a single model probably rests on the fact that most settings for curriculum implementation are situation specific. In one case, the social environment or policy may be crucial to effecting the change. In another, group dynamics or individual personalities may be all-important. If this is so, then broadly conceived change models and histories of innovations should be in the curriculum specialist's repertoire.

Finally, the frequent triviality and faddishness of curriculum changes effected from both outside and inside the school would remind us of the continuous need to consider the value of proposed innovations. Decision makers should be sure about whether a proposed curriculum will best serve a specified target group of learners, or aid general education; contribute to interpretive or applied purposes; be relevant to the kind of world the students will live in when they finish school; and relate to the other domains of knowledge that are supposed to be provided by the school experience.

QUESTIONS

1. Preparing effective curriculum materials costs much money. Without broad dissemination, the impact of the materials is minimal. What are the implications of these facts for curriculum development?
2. Give examples for each of the following kinds of curriculum changes: *substitution, alteration, restructuring of the system, value orientation.*
3. Consider the relative strengths and weaknesses of the R and D adoption model and the integrative development model of curriculum change. Can you indicate how both models can be used together or when one or the other model might be more useful?
4. A curriculum change agent is sometimes defined as (a) one who holds a position of change agent, (b) one who is perceived by others as being a change agent, and (c) one who actually brings about change. Think of a situation familiar to you and identify those who meet the different definitions. How can they be found to be true for one individual?
5. John Goodlad believes that the school, with its principal, teachers, pupils, and parents, is the largest organic unit of and for educational change. On the other hand, Paul Nachtigal believes that although the most successful changes in teacher behavior start within a single school, the effect of such restricted and unrelated efforts is minimal. Who do you think is right and why?
6. What kinds of curriculum changes do you think can best occur at national, state, systemwide, school, and classroom levels?
7. Consider a curriculum program you might wish to initiate. Would you stack the deck so that only interested, dedicated, and creative participants were included in the initiation of the program or would you include an unselected group of participants so that the innovation has more credibility? Why?

SELECTED REFERENCES

Boyd, William Lowe. "The Politics of Curriculum Change," *Educational Researcher* 8, no. 2 (February 1979): 12–19.

Fullan, Michael and Pomfret, Alan. "Research in Curriculum and Instruction Implementation," *Review of Educational Research* 47, no. 1 (Winter 1977): 335–97.

Goodlad, John I. *The Dynamics of Educational Change: Toward Responsive Schools*. New York: McGraw-Hill, 1975.

Havelock, Ronald. *The Change Agent's Guide to Innovation in Education.* Englewood Cliffs, N.J.: Educational Technology Publications, 1973.

Lieberman, Ann and Miller, Lynne. *Staff Development: New Demands,*

New Realities, New Perspectives. New York: Teachers College, Columbia University, 1979.

Melton, Raymond G. "Change for the Practitioner," *Planning and Changing* 5, no. 4 (1975): 211–18.

Orlich, Donald C. "Federal Educational Policy: The Paradox of Innovation and Centralization," *Educational Researcher* 8, no. 7 (July / August 1979): 4–10.

"Realities of Curriculum Change," theme articles, *Educational Leadership* 36, no. 1 (October 1978): 27–70.

Sarason, Seymour. *The Culture of the School and the Problem of Change.* Boston: Allyn and Bacon, 1971.

Wise, Arthur E. "The Hyperrationalization of American Education," *Educational Leadership* 35, no. 5 (February 1970): 354–62.

8 / EVALUATING THE CURRICULUM

After studying this chapter, the reader should be able to match specific evaluation procedures with specific curriculum decisions, such as how to improve a course, how to decide which program should continue, and how to assess the long-term effects of the curriculum. A major issue raised is whether curriculum evaluation is best served by classical research models and experts in measurement or by adaptable procedures whereby students and teachers judge their own curriculum.

In addition to acquiring information about a number of evaluation techniques, the reader will learn about common errors that prejudice evaluative studies and make it difficult to judge the relative effects of different programs. It is hoped the reader will be able to take a personal stand regarding controversial technical issues on the role and form of objectives used in evaluation, the value of criterion-referenced and norm-referenced tests, and evaluation and invasion of privacy.

The word *evaluation* generates a host of responses. Fear of power and control is one. Local communities have been dismayed by those in government saying: Do your own thing, set your own goals; *but*, of course, your efforts must be evaluated by standardized tests in areas important to us. Another reaction is that of perceived reassurance. People often expect that evaluation will solve many pressing problems—the public who demand accountability, the decision maker who chooses curriculum alternatives, the developer who needs to know where and how to improve the curriculum product, and the teacher who is concerned about the effect of learning

151

opportunities on individual students all look to evaluation for their answers.

The field of evaluation is full of different views as to the purposes of evaluation and how it is to be carried out. Humanists, for example, argue that measurable outcomes form an insufficient basis for determining the quality of learning opportunities. They believe it naively simplistic to measure higher mental functioning, knowledge of self, and other life-long pursuits at the end of the school year. Curiously, however, they perceive no difficulty in evaluating the existential quality of life in the classroom. For them, the learning experience is itself "the event," not a rehearsal whose values will be known only on future performance. Technologists, on the other hand, perceive evaluation as a set of verified guidelines for practice. They believe that if curriculum workers use these procedures, essential decisions regarding what and how to teach will be more warranted.

David Hamilton has distilled the ideas and events in curriculum evaluation during the past 150 years, illuminating its relatively unchanging features.[1] According to him, curriculum evaluation falls within the sphere of practical morality. As such, it responds to both the ethical question, "What should we do?" and the empirical question, "What can we do?" He recognizes, too, that evaluation is heightened by social change and politics. Governments make evaluation compulsory, and curriculum evaluation can be seen as part of the struggle by different interest groups—educationalists, teachers, administrators, industrialists—to gain control over the forces that shape the practices of schooling. When more than one person is involved in the selection of criteria to be used in evaluating, agreement cannot be assumed.

At the present time, there are serious issues regarding the conduct of curriculum evaluation, or which particular evaluation model should be used. Technologists use *consensus* models and regard evaluation as a technical accomplishment—the demonstration of a connection between what is and what (all agree) ought to be. They require a consensus on the desired ends and on the rules of evidence. Given agreement on ends, the selection and evaluation of appropriate means are technical problems for them. In reality, technologists have been most active in determining achievement in basic skills and academic knowledge.

[1]David Hamilton, "Making Sense of Curriculum Evaluation: Continuities and Discontinuities in an Educational Idea," in *Review of Research in Education*, Lee S. Schulman, ed. (Itasca, Ill.: F.E. Peacock Publishers, 1979), pp. 318–49.

Social reconstructionists and humanists, however, have a *pluralistic* view of evaluation. This view holds that evaluators should be sensitive to the different values of program participants and should shift the locus of formal judgment from the evaluator to the participants. As evaluators, pluralists tend to base their evaluations more on program activity than on program intent and to accept anecdotal accounts and other naturalistic data rather than to rely on numerical data and experimental designs. For them, evaluation is an unfinished blueprint that can generate issues, not solutions. They are concerned about whether evaluation will be fair to all parties. They are more interested in the fairness of the curriculum than in its effectiveness as measured by, say, changes in test scores. Hence, those with a pluralistic bent advocate handing over control of an evaluation to those who have to live with the consequences and having it conducted *by* the participants rather than *for* the participants.

The paragraphs to follow contain an examination of the most promising roles of evaluation and illustrate where they are appropriate and inappropriate. Finally, several important technical issues in curriculum evaluation are treated. We will look at sampling, the value of behavioral objectives, standardized tests versus criterion-referenced tests, and the ethics of evaluation, including the measurement of affect.

CURRICULUM EVALUATIONS FROM A TECHNOLOGIST VIEW

In a general sense, curriculum evaluation to a technologist is an attempt to throw light on two questions: (1) Do planned learning opportunities, programs, courses, and activities as developed and organized actually produce desired results? and (2) How can the curriculum offerings best be improved? These general questions and the procedures for answering them translate a little differently at macro levels (for example, evaluating the citywide outcomes from several alternative reading programs) than at micro levels (evaluating the effect of a teacher's instructional plans for achieving course objectives). Classroom teachers often have an additional set of evaluation questions to guide them in making decisions about individuals:

1. *Placement.* At which level of learning opportunity should the learner be placed in order to challenge but not frustrate?

2. *Mastery.* Has the learner acquired enough competency to succeed in the next planned phase?
3. *Diagnosis.* What particular difficulty is this learner experiencing?

Decisions and Evaluative Techniques

If evaluation is to provide information useful to decision makers, evaluative models should be chosen in light of the kind of decisions to be made. In this connection, a useful distinction is made between formative and summative evaluation. Formative evaluation is undertaken to improve an existing program. Hence, the evaluation must provide frequent detailed and specific information to guide the program developers. Summative evaluation is done to assess the effect of a completed program. It provides information to use in deciding whether to continue, discontinue, or disseminate the program. Summative evaluation is frequently undertaken in order to decide which one of several competing programs or materials is best.

Guidelines for conducting formative evaluation have been given by Lee J. Cronbach in a classic article treating *course improvement* through evaluation. The following prescriptions are among the most important:

1. Seek data regarding changes produced in pupils by the course.
2. Look for multidimensional outcomes and map out the effects of the course along these dimensions separately.
3. Identify aspects of the course in which revisions are desirable.
4. Collect evidence midway in curriculum development, while the course is still fluid.
5. Try to find out how the course produces its effect and what parameters influence its effectiveness. You may find that the teacher's attitude toward the learning opportunity is more important than the opportunity itself.
6. During trial stages, use the teacher's informal reports of observed pupil behavior in aspects of the course.
7. Make more systematic observations only after the more obvious bugs in the early stages have been dealt with.
8. Make a process study of events taking place in the classroom and use proficiency and attitude measures to reveal changes in pupils.
9. Observe several outcomes ranging far beyond the content of the curriculum itself—attitudes, general understanding, aptitude for further learning, and so forth.[2]

[2]Lee J. Cronbach, "Course Improvement Through Evaluation," *Teachers College Record* 64 (May 1963): 672–83.

Formative evaluation does not require that all pupils answer the same questions. Rather, as many questions as possible should be given, each to a different sample of pupils. Follow-up studies to elicit opinions regarding the ultimate educational contributions of the course are of minor value in improving the course because they are too far removed in time.

Summative evaluation has several purposes. One purpose is to select from several competing curriculum programs or projects those which should continue and those which are ineffective. To this end, an experimental design is highly desirable. Donald Campbell and Julian Stanley have provided an excellent source for such designs.[3] Also, James Popham has illustrated ways of adapting these designs to meet various practical situations.[4]

There is, for example, the *pretest-posttest control group design*. As the design's name suggests, students are pretested on whatever dimensions are sought from the programs. Then, after receiving instruction, students in each of the competing programs are tested for their status on a common set of objectives. That is to say, effectiveness is noted for all objectives for which each program claims superiority. The posttest used must not be biased in favor of one program's objectives. Objectives important to others, but not those of the designers of a particular program, can also be assessed.

The students are assigned randomly. Each student has an equal chance to be assigned to any of the programs. Differences in the performance of students may be attributed to differences in the programs. However, evaluators may not always know whether the respective programs were carried out as planned. It is desirable to try each of the programs in many settings, since the experimental unit for analysis is likely to be schools or classrooms, not pupils. Only in within-classroom experiments, in which the pupils receive different programs, can the pupil be the unit of analysis.

Evaluators should not allow ideas about what must happen in a perfect evaluation to discourage them; they should remember that there have been no perfect evaluations. When faced with frustrations, like student absenteeism or the failure to give tests, they should remember that the curriculum evaluator is only responsible for providing the best information possible under existing circumstances.

One purpose of evaluation is to decide on the value of a curricular

[3]Donald T. Campbell and Julian C. Stanley, "Experimental and Quasi-Experimental Designs for Research on Teaching," in *Handbook of Research on Teaching*, N.L. Gage, ed. (Chicago: Rand McNally, 1963).
[4]W. James Popham, *Educational Evaluation* (Englewood Cliffs, N.J.: Prentice-Hall, 1975).

intervention within a course. An *interrupted time series design* is useful for this purpose. In this design, a series of measurements are taken both before and after the introduction of the intervention. Nonobtrusive records—absences, disciplinary referrals, requests for transfer—are frequently used with this design, although test scores and other data can also serve. A significant difference in pupil performance during and after the intervention may be taken as evidence that the intervention had a positive effect.

Another important purpose of evaluation is to decide on the long-term value of curriculum offerings. Longitudinal or followup studies are undertaken to indicate whether desired objectives are being realized and to reveal shortcomings. One of the better known longitudinal studies was conducted on a national level in Project Talent. This project was initiated in 1960 with the testing of 400,000 secondary school students. Such data as student interests, ability scores, and characteristics of a student's school, including courses offered, were collected. Fifteen years later, a representative sample of these persons were interviewed, and they reported on their satisfaction with their current status on different life activities. One overall generalization from the findings was that educational programs should be improved and modified to enable persons to achieve greater satisfaction in intellectual development and personal understanding.[5] Another example of the findings from Project Talent studies is that, whereas in 1960 47 percent of the graduating boys and 38 percent of the girls said their courses were not helpful in preparing them for occupations, eleven years later 46 percent of the men and 40 percent of the women still felt high school had been "at best" adequate.

National Assessment of Educational Progress is an assessment project designed to furnish information regarding the educational achievements of children, youth, and young adults, and to indicate both the progress we are making and the problems we face.[6] Unlike Project Talent, NAEP does not follow individual progress but does sample different age groups. The project includes plans for the assessment of each of ten study areas—reading, literature, music, social studies, science, writing, citizenship, mathematics, art, and career and occupational development—on four- or five-year cycles. Test

[5]John C. Flanagan, *Perspectives on Improving Education* (Los Alamitos, Calif.: Southwest Regional Laboratory for Educational Research and Development, 1979).

[6]National Assessment of Educational Progress, 1860 Lincoln Street, Denver, Colo. 80203.

results are reported by age group, sex, region, type of community, racial group, and level of parental education. An illustration of how the NAEP illuminates problems is the 1979 finding that many Americans are unable to use basic math to solve everyday consumer tasks ranging from balancing their checkbooks to deciding which size package is the cheapest. Too many students apparently fail to see the relationship between math courses in school and the use of math in everyday living. Even though 87 percent of the adults said they had managed to balance a checking account before, only 16 percent of those tested could solve a problem that included a subtraction error, a deposit error, service charges, and an outstanding check.

A Technological Evaluation Model

An example of a technological model for evaluation is the *CSE Model*, named for its origin at the UCLA Center for the Study of Evaluation. As described by Marvin Alkin and Carol Fitz-Gibbon, this model has five stages, each related to a particular kind of decision to be made.[7] The first stage is related to *problem selection*, in which the evaluator tries to find out the difference between what is and what is not desired in order to determine educational need and to identify educational goals. The procedures used in this stage are analogous to the curriculum needs assessment model for formulating outcomes. The second stage of the CSE model is related to the *selection of programs* that might be used to close identified gaps. This stage involves the appraisal of available instructional materials that might be used in a program for attaining goals and is analogous to the curriculum task of selecting learning opportunities. In this stage, the evaluator determines the likelihood of success with the different programs. The third stage is related to *modification of the program*. The evaluator provides information on the degree to which the program as carried out corresponds to the plan. Any departure must be duly noted. The fourth stage is also related to program modification. In this stage, however, the evaluator tries to find out the *relative success of the different parts* of the program as it is progressing. During stage 4, data collected according to the guidelines on page 154 help one overcome deficiencies. The final stage of the CSE model concerns *program certification* or *adoption*. In this stage information on the

[7]Marvin Alkin and Carol T. Fitz-Gibbon, "Methods and Theories of Evaluating Programs," *Journal of Research and Development in Education* 8, no. 3 (September 1975): 2–15.

achievement of goals from stage 1 helps the decision makers to determine whether the program should be modified, eliminated, retained, or disseminated more widely. Note that this model takes as its aim the improvement of rational decision making. The criteria used are in the interests of the total system rather than individual pupils or teachers.

PLURALISTIC MODELS OF EVALUATION

Evaluation models with the pluralistic concern of humanists and social reconstructionists have had as yet a relatively limited impact. Pluralistic procedures are less frequently used than research and technological procedures as applied by teachers in course improvement, by school managers in rational decision making, by government evaluators in auditing new social programs in the schools, and by statewide evaluators in monitoring the curriculum for accountability purposes.

Pluralistic evaluation models tend to be used only when research and technological models are less attractive for reasons of politics, costs, or practicality. These newer models are chiefly used with curriculum that is out of the mainstream—curriculum associated with aesthetic education, multicultural projects, and alternative schools. Pluralistic models are also increasing in supplementary experimental designs.

The Countenance Model. Robert E. Stake was one of the first evaluators to reflect the pluralist argument that the evaluator should make known the criteria or standards that are being employed and who holds them. His model differs from the older technological models by being more extensive in the types of data collected, more sensitive to the different values of program participants, and allowing more participation in the making of judgments. The countenance model calls for attention to three phases of an educational program: *antecedent, transaction,* and *outcome* phases. Antecedents are conditions existing prior to instruction that may relate to outcomes; transactions constitute the process of instruction; and outcomes are the effects of the program. Stake emphasizes two operations, descriptions and judgments. Descriptions are divided according to whether they refer to what was intended or what actually was observed. Judgments are separated according to whether they refer to standards used in arriving at the judgments or to the actual judgments. The model is depicted in Table 6.

As a pluralist, Stake believes that sensitivity to the perceived needs of those concerned with the evaluation is essential. Accordingly, he urges initial evaluations to discover what clients and participants actually want from the program evaluation. These concerns should be discovered prior to designing the evaluation project. Stake places less emphasis on precisely specified objectives than do technologists, for he wishes to describe all intentions, even those which are not explicated in terms of postinstructional learner behavior. The key em-

TABLE 6   Stake's Description of Data Needed for Educational Evaluation

	Descriptive Matrix		Judgment Matrix	
	Intents	*Observations*	*Standards*	*Judgments*
Antecedents (student and teacher characteristics, curriculum content, instructional materials, community context)				
Transactions (communication flow, time allocation, sequence of events, social climate)				
Outcomes (student achievement, attitudes, motor skills, effect on teachers and institution)				

Source: R.E. Stake, "The Countenance of Educational Evaluation," *Teachers College Record* 68 (1967). Reprinted by permission of Teachers College, Columbia University.

phasis in his model is on description and judgment. For him, an evaluator should report the ways different people see the curriculum. Hence the evaluator's principal activities include discovering what those concerned want to know, making observations, and gathering multiple judgments about the observed antecedents, transactions, and outcomes. A wide variety of persons—outside experts, journalists, psychologists—as well as teachers and students may participate in the conduct of the evaluation.

Educational Connoisseurship for Evaluating School Life

Elliot W. Eisner[8] has argued for an evaluation process that will capture a richer slice of educational life than do test scores. One of his procedures is educational criticism in which a critic asks such questions as: "What has happened during the school year in a given school? What were the key events? How did they come into being? How did students and teachers participate? What were the consequences? How could the events be strengthened? What do such events enable children to learn?"

Other vehicles for disclosing richness of programs, according to Eisner, are films, videotape, photography, and taped student and teacher interviews. These useful tools in portraying aspects of school life are, when supplemented by critical narrative, valuable channels for communication.

Connoisseurship is involved in noting what is and is not said, how something is said, tone, and other such factors that indicate meaning.

Another procedure recommended by Eisner is the analysis of work produced by children, including a critique to help evaluators understand what has been accomplished and to reveal some of the realities of classroom performance.

The fundamental thesis of the connoisseur approach is that the problem of communicating to some public—parent, board, state agencies—about what has happened in school—the good and the bad—can be usefully conceived as an artistic problem. It is the putting together of an expressive picture of educational practice and its consequences.

Connoisseurship and criticism—ways of seeing rather than ways of measuring—have been criticized as abstruse technology requiring

[8]Elliot W. Eisner, "On the Uses of Educational Connoisseurship and Educational Criticism for Evaluating Classroom Life," *Teachers College Record* 28, no. 3 (February 1977): 345-58.

special training in acquiring "interpretive maps" and ways to understand the meaning of what has been said. Judgments are established
externally by the nature of artistic virtues and tradition. This approach, though informative and highly adaptive to unique local conditions, is subjective and thus potentially controversial.

CONTROVERSIAL TECHNICAL ISSUES IN CURRICULUM EVALUATION

Measurement people, curriculum specialists,
teachers, and administrators often disagree regarding which techniques to use in evaluation. Many disputes about procedures occur
because the antagonists have different purposes and needs in mind.
They argue over the merits of procedures and instruments such as
formats for stating objectives, prespecifying goals, norm- and
criterion-referenced tests, sampling, and technical hazards. Their
controversies will not be resolved by taking an either-or attitude but
by showing the circumstances in which one approach is better than
another.

The Form of Objectives

During the last fifteen years, no issue in curriculum has received
more attention than the value of and proper manner for stating objectives. Part of the problem is philosophical. One extreme position is
that an objective must specify the exact overt behavior that a learner
is to display at the end of an instructional sequence. This overt
response is seen as important in itself. A more moderate behavioral
position is that the objective must specify behavior that will *indicate*
whether the objective has been attained. This position allows for
high-level covert responses on the part of the learner, but demands
that some overt behavior be specified to indicate whether the desired
(perhaps hidden) behavior has occurred. Another extreme position is
that there should be no stated objectives at all. It is said that objectives represent external goals and manipulation and that they in-
significantly indicate what a learner actually experiences from a
given situation.

Part of the problem is that the protagonists try to judge the form
and value of objectives without understanding their purposes. There
are many uses for objectives. They can communicate general direction at a policy level, provide a concrete guide for selecting and plan-

ning learning opportunities, and set the criteria for evaluating the learners' performance. To illustrate, there are at least four degrees of specificity for an objective. There are very general statements that are useful when trying to get a consensus on direction at a policy level. For this purpose, it is often sufficient to use *general goal statements*: "to learn to respect and get along with people by developing appreciation and respect for the worth of individuals"; "to respect and understand minority opinions"; "to accept majority decisions."

More specific objectives are useful when planning the learning opportunities for courses or when analyzing instructional materials. These objectives are called *educational objectives* and are illustrated in several taxonomies of educational objectives.[9] These taxonomies treat affective, cognitive, and psychomotor domains. The *Taxonomy of Educational Objectives: Handbook I*, for example, treats cognitive objectives and classifies them using six major categories and several subcategories. Categories range from simple recall of information to critical evaluative behaviors. One such category is *application*. Application is defined as using abstractions in particular and concrete situations. The abstractions may be general ideas, rules of procedures, or generalized methods. They may also be technical principles, ideas, and theories that must be remembered and applied. The taxonomy also gives sample objectives. The level of specificity of an educational objective can be seen in this example: "The ability to predict the probable effect of a change in a factor on a biological situation previously at equilibrium." The objective can be further amplified by an illustration of the kind of test or test item that would be appropriate.

The taxonomies have greatly influenced curriculum making. More attention is now given to affective, cognitive, and psychomotor domains. Also, curriculum workers are now more sensitive to the level of behavior expected from instruction. They are, for instance, more concerned now that objectives and test items treat higher cognitive processes like comprehension, application, and analysis rather than dealing only with recall of information.

There is an even more specific form for an objective; it is called an

[9]Benjamin S. Bloom, ed., *Taxonomy of Educational Objectives: Handbook I: Cognitive Domain* (New York: David McKay Company, 1956); David R. Krathwohl et al., *Taxonomy of Educational Objectives: Handbook II: Affective Domain* (New York: David McKay Company, 1956); Anita Harrow, *A Taxonomy of the Psychomotor Domain: A Guide for Developing Behavioral Objectives* (New York: David McKay Company, 1972).

instructional objective. This form is useful when teaching pupils a specific concept. It is often called a Mager-like instructional objective after the person who advocated its use.[10] These objectives specify the behavior to be exhibited by the student, a standard or criterion of acceptable performance, and the kind of situation in which the behavior is to be elicited. One instructional objective might be, "Given a linear algebraic equation with one unknown [the situation or condition], the learner must be able to solve the equation [behavior and criterion] without the aid of references, tables, or calculating devices [additional conditions]."

An additional degree of specificity can be found in the *amplified objective*, which is used when one desires to communicate to writers and consumers of criterion-referenced tests. Amplified objectives represent a set of rules to generate test items.[11] These rules describe (1) the stimuli or testing situations that can constitute or be used in constructing test items, including the potential content from which items can be generated and the directions to be given the learners; (2) the response options, including the nature of the distractors to appear in a multiple-choice test; and (3) the criteria of correctness (the bases for judging responses right or wrong).

Specific behavioral objectives seem valuable in providing guidance for evaluation of instructional materials and student performance. Other functions of behavioral objectives, however, such as giving direction in teaching and aiding learning, arouse much difference of opinion. It is charged that a teacher who uses specific objectives may not give enough attention to the immediate concerns of learners. The research on this issue, however, is inconclusive. Some studies on the effects of behavioral objectives on learning, for example, have shown facilitative effects, but an equal number have not shown any significant differences.[12] Objectives sometimes help and are almost never harmful. They seem to assist students in determining what is expected of them and in discriminating between relevant and irrelevant content. There remains, however, a question regarding the number of objectives provided the student. If the list of objectives is extensive and detailed, the student may be overwhelmed.

[10]Robert F. Mager, *Preparing Instructional Objectives* (Palo Alto, Calif.: Fearon Publishers, 1962).

[11]Popham, *Educational Evaluation*, p. 147.

[12]Philippe C. Duchastel and Paul F. Merrill, "The Effects of Behavioral Objectives on Learning: A Review of Empirical Studies," *Review of Educational Research* 43, no. 1 (Winter 1973): 53–69.

Measurement of Intended Outcomes
Versus Goal-free Evaluation

Years ago Ralph Tyler told evaluators that it was impossible to decide whether a particular test would be appropriate for appraising a certain program until the objectives of the program had been defined and until the kinds of situations that would give an opportunity for this behavior to be expressed were identified. Tyler recommended checking each proposed evaluation device against the objectives and constructing or devising methods for getting evidence about the student's attainment of these objectives.

More recently, Michael Scriven moved beyond Tyler's concern for data about intended outcomes to a concern for all relevant effects.[13] His approach is called *goal-free evaluation*. Such evaluation does not assess a situation only in terms of prespecified goal preferences. It is evaluation of *actual* effects against a profile of demonstrated needs. It is offered as a protection against the "tunnel vision" of those close to the program—against harmful side effects, missed new priorities, and overlooked achievement. To the extent that Scriven's approach is used, more evaluative measures will have to be employed. Selection of these measures will be difficult, for there are thousands of such devices. Practicality will probably dictate the use of measures that assess most intended outcomes and a limited number of possible side effects.

Norm-Referenced Tests and Criterion-Referenced Tests

Standardized achievement tests are norm-referenced. They are designed to compare the performances of individuals to the performance of a normative group. The purposes of these tests initially were to find the most able persons and to sort out those who would most likely succeed or fail some future learning situation. Only those test items which discriminate between the best and worst are kept. The assumption that everyone can learn equally well is rejected in norm-referenced testing. These tests, therefore, tend to correlate very highly with intelligence tests. In order to obtain items with high response variance, writers of norm-referenced tests are likely to exclude the items that measure well-taught concepts and skills of schooling.

[13]Michael Scriven, "Pros and Cons about Goal-free Evaluation," *Evaluation Comment* 3, no. 4 (December 1972): 1–4.

Although norm-referenced tests do identify persons of different ability, they are of questionable value in curriculum evaluation. They may not accurately measure what educational programs are designed to teach or reveal particular problems that are keeping pupils from achieving. Teachers can sometimes improve scores on such tests, but such improvement usually results from tricks like (1) telling children to respond to all items so that the possibility of getting more right answers is increased (a child needs to get only three to seven more items right to show one-year improvement on typical achievement tests); (2) testing at a different time of the year than previously to show apparent but not real gains; (3) capitalizing on regression effects that make the poorest scores look better on the second testing; and (4) teaching pupils how to respond to the items themselves and to the test format.

Criterion-referenced tests are meant to ascertain a learner's status with respect to a learning task, rather than to a norm. These tests tell what learners can and cannot do in specified situations. The tasks selected can be those which the curriculum emphasizes. The items used in the test match the set of learner behaviors called for in the objective and should not be eliminated, as in the norm-referenced tests, merely because most students answer them correctly. Hence, these tests can be sensitive measures of what has been taught.

Criterion-referenced tests are also useful in showing whether a student has mastered specific learnings. That is why they are popular in instructional settings using continuous progress plans or other individualized teaching approaches. The tests indicate what instructional treatments are needed by individual learners and also indicate when learners are ready to proceed to other tasks.

Criterion-referenced tests are sometimes faulted because they have been based on objectives that are too narrow. The multiplicity of tests necessary to accompany many objectives has been a management problem to teachers. Trends indicate that particular courses in the future will use perhaps eight to ten very important end-of-course objective-based tests of high transfer value rather than large numbers of objective-based tests as is now common. Tests that are curriculum embedded—that is, tests that have items dependent on particular materials or programs—will diminish. Other ways of improving these tests are to include a complete description of the set of learner behaviors that the test is to assess and to increase the number of items for each competency measured in order to have an acceptable standard of reliability.

Tests and Invasion of Privacy

The American Civil Liberties Union has taken up the cause of students who charge that tests are an invasion of privacy. Students have complained about the use of instruments, usually self-report devices, that probe their attitudes in such areas as self-esteem, interest in school, and human relations. Evaluators want such data in order to assess the effects of schooling. Protests against the use of tests to guide the learning process in academic areas are less frequent. ACLU lawyers argue that authorities have not made it clear that pupils may refuse to take tests that they believe to be invading their privacy. Pupils should also be told that the questions asked in a test might require self-incriminating responses.

This issue is related to a larger problem, that of the effect of tests on students. Do they affect motivation and self-esteem by producing anxiety and encouraging cheating? Do they create labels and determine adult social status? Marjorie C. Kirkland completed an extensive review of the research treating such questions. Her review throws light on test effects. She shows, for example, that how individuals think of themselves and what they believe about a test influences their test behavior. Other examples from Kirkland's review show that students' attitudes about tests in general are negative. The more interested persons are in their test results, the more they perceive positive consequences of tests. Systematic reporting of test results helps students to understand their interests, aptitudes, and achievements.[14] Anyone reading Kirkland's review will conclude that tests are powerful indeed and that their consequences are far-ranging.

TECHNIQUES FOR COLLECTING DATA

Newton S. Metfessel and William B. Michael have published a list of multiple criterion measures for evaluating school programs.[15] The list indicates the great range in ways of collecting evidence. One class of indicators of change in learners is associated with informal, teacher-made devices, incomplete sentence techniques, interviews, peer nominations, sociograms, questionnaires,

[14]Marjorie C. Kirkland, "The Effects of Tests on Students and School," *Review of Educational Research* 41, no. 4 (October 1971): 303–51.
[15]Newton S. Metfessel and William B. Michael, "A Paradigm Involving Multiple Criterion Measures for the Evaluation of the Effectiveness of School Programs," *Educational and Psychological Measurement* 27 (1967): 931–34.

self-evaluation measures, projective devices, and semantic differential scales. The authors also describe the many ways for assessing the effect of programs without influencing the outcomes. These noninfluencing ways are called *unobtrusive measures*; they include attending to absences, anecdotal records, appointments, assignments, stories written, awards, use of books, case histories, disciplinary actions, dropouts, and voluntary activities.

Creative indicators can be devised if persons will think beyond the use of formal tests. A useful scheme for generating indicators is to reflect on (1) learners' products—such as compositions, paintings, constructions; (2) learners' self-reports on preferences and interests; and (3) how learners solve problems, conduct discussions, and participate in physical games and dances. With these methods, the teacher or evaluator should use an accompanying checklist stipulating behavior to be exhibited by the pupil and the qualities to be found in the pupil's product.

Measuring Affect

Although it is a controversial activity, the assessment of affect is gaining interest. Special techniques are used for this task, because it is believed that individuals are more likely to "fake" their attitudinal responses. Hence, mild deception is often used so that learners will not know the purpose of the inquiry or that they are being observed. A student may be asked, for example, to respond to several hypothetical situations, only one of which is of interest to the examiner. The examiner may ask, "Where would you take a visitor friend from out of town—to the market, the movie, the school, the library, the bank?" If "school" is the answer, it is presumed that the respondent tends to value that institution. Another, less direct approach is to use high inference and theoretical instruments. The examiner might ask, "Would you play the part of a degenerate in a play?" or "Which of the following names (one of which is the respondent's own) do you like?" (The inference is that students with high self-concepts will play any role and will like their names.) Situations are sometimes contrived, and students' reactions are interpreted to indicate particular attitudes. Student accomplices may collect unobtrusive data and report their observations later, for example. Audio recordings are sometimes made of student small group discussions and analyzed later.

An illustration of a low inference self-report device follows. This device is an example of how affect can be assessed with criterion-referenced measures. Note how the objective stated in the general description is amplified by sections treating stimulus and response attributes.

Preferences in music[16]

General description

When given the names of a wide variety of types of music, students will select a response for each type that indicates whether they are familiar with it and, if so, the degree to which they like it.

Sample item

Directions: This is a survey of students' opinions about different kinds of music, such as bluegrass, gospel, and hard rock. If you are not familiar with a type of music, mark choice *a* on the answer sheet. For those types of music with which you have any familiarity, no matter how slight, select an answer from *b, c, d, e,* and *f* that states how much you like each one. Mark the letter of your choice on the answer sheet. In the item below if you have heard some *operetta* music and you *like* it, you would mark *e* on the answer sheet. Since this is an opinion poll, there are no right or wrong answers. Do not put your name on the answer sheet and do not worry if many of the types of music are not familiar to you.

  1. Operetta   *a.* unfamiliar
                                 b. strongly dislike
                                 c. dislike
                                 d. neutral
                                 e. like
                                 f. strongly like

Before answering any of the items below, please look over the names of all of the types of music.

Stimulus attributes

  1. Students will be given the names of categories or types of music.
  2. The types will be ones to which Americans are commonly exposed in the U.S. media or where they are living abroad. The categories will represent a wide range of music and will include those types that are currently popular with the student population.

[16]Drawn with permission from IOX *Illustrative Criterion-Referenced Test Specifications: Aesthetics K-12.* Los Angeles: Instructional Objectives Exchange, 1980.

The categories may have some overlap since borrowing among types is common and boundaries of types are not distinct.

3. At least 20 different categories of music will be included, of which at least 20 percent will be more formal types, such as classical and chamber. Test constructors will rely on their knowledge of local culture in generating types of music that are found in the home area. No more than 10 percent of the items will be specifically local ones. The following list may be useful in generating test items:

Big band (dance and swing)	Folk rock
Bluegrass	Gospel
Blues	Hymns
Cantata and oratorio	Indian (from India)
Caribbean (calypso, reggae)	Jazz
Chamber music	Latin American
Christmas music	Marches and military music
Classical: full orchestra	Musical show tunes
Concert band	Opera
Country and western	Operetta and light opera
Electronic	Pop (except rock)
Folk dances	Rhythm and blues
Folk songs: international	Rock
Folk songs: American	Soul

Response attributes

1. Students will respond by selecting one of six multiple-choice alternatives from the following set:
   a. unfamiliar
   b. strongly dislike
   c. dislike
   d. neutral
   e. like
   f. strongly like

2. Point values will be assigned to the response categories as follows: $a = 0$, $b = 1$, $c = 2$, $d = 3$, $e = 4$, $f = 5$, with informed dislike (choices b and c) scoring higher than complete unfamiliarity (choice a). Students may then be assigned three different scores on the survey, as follows:

   a. Average appreciation of familiar types of music: The average of all nonzero value (non-a) responses reveals the degree to which students like the categories of music that are familiar to them.
   b. Breadth of familiarity: The number of different types of music receiving responses other than a, divided by the total number of

types on the test, gives the proportion of types that the student is familiar with.

c. Average appreciation overall: The average rating for all categories, both familiar and unfamiliar, reflects in one score both the breadth and degree of students' likes.

Sometimes, too, individuals are offered ways to respond anonymously. It should be clear that in evaluating affective effects of curriculum, individuals need not be identified. One only has to know what effect the curriculum is having on students as a group. Further, the measures or scores obtained with most high inference instruments are not reliable enough for making predictions about individuals.

In an effort to improve the credibility of their findings, evaluators may use *triangulation* (the use of three different measures in concert). If a similar attitude is found by all three measures, they have more confidence in the findings. Locally developed instruments also are thought to be more valid when two or more persons score students' responses the same, and when several samples of student behavior are consistent.

Appraisals of Existing Instruments

There are several sources that both list and evaluate instruments. The Center for the Study of Evaluation, at UCLA, has four publications that describe and evaluate thousands of tests for elementary and secondary schools.[17] The Social Science Education Consortium has analyzed and catalogued 1,000 instruments for use in evaluating programs in the social studies.[18] Many measures of social and psychological attitudes are also described in a publication by John Robinson and Phillip Stover of the Survey Research Center Institute for Social Research at the University of Michigan. Data concerning criterion-referenced tests and instructional objectives can be obtained from the Instructional Objectives Exchange. *Tests in Print II*, by the late Oscar K. Buros, includes a bibliography of most known tests published for use with English-speaking persons, a classified index to the contents of mental measurement yearbooks, descriptions of the population for which each test is intended, and other features. Buros was also the editor of *The Eighth Mental Measurements Yearbook*.

---

[17]The Center for the Study of Evaluation, 405 Hilgard Avenue, Los Angeles, Calif. 90024.
[18]The Social Science Education Consortium, 855 Broadway, Boulder, Colo. 30302; Instructional Objectives Exchange, Box 24095, Los Angeles, Calif. 90024.

This yearbook includes, among other things, 798 reviews of 546 tests.[19] Future issues of *The Mental Measurement Yearbook* will be forthcoming from the University of Nebraska at Lincoln. Finally, the Educational Testing Service is a clearinghouse for tests, measures, and evaluation, offering information regarding a wide range of instruments.[20]

Sampling

Sampling is the practice of inferring an educational status on the basis of responses from representative persons or representative tasks. James Popham has said, "Sampling should make a Scotsman's values vibrate. It is *so* terribly thrifty."[21] It is controversial mainly because it is sometimes imposed in inappropriate situations. When students are to be graded on their relative attainment of common objectives, for example, it is not proper to assess only certain students nor is it valid to test some individuals on one set of objectives and other individuals on another set.

Administrators rightfully use sampling when they estimate the typical reactions of students from a few instances of their behavior. It is not necessary to collect all the compositions students have written in order to judge their writing ability. Samples will suffice—perhaps one at the beginning of the year and one at the end—to show change, if any, as a result of instruction. Similarly, to determine a student's knowledge in one subject, it is not necessary to ask the student to respond to all the items that are involved in this knowledge. A sample of what is involved is enough to draw an inference about the student's status. To find out whether the student can name all the letters of the alphabet, one can present only five letters at random from the alphabet and ask the student to name them. The responses will indicate ability to respond to the total population of letters. If all five are named correctly, there is a high probability that the child could name all of the letters. If the child cannot name one or more of the letters, obviously the objective has not been reached. Controversy arises over sampling because teachers have concerns that do not lend themselves to sampling. If sampling indicates that a child cannot name all of the letters of the alphabet, then the teacher wants to

[19]Oscar K. Buros, ed., *Tests in Print II* and *The Eighth Mental Measurements Yearbook* (Highland Park, N.J.: Gryphon Press, 1978).
[20]ERIC Clearing House, *Tests, Measures, and Evaluation* (Princeton, N.J.: Educational Testing Service, 1980).
[21]Popham, *Educational Evaluation*, p. 218.

know specifically which ones must be taught. Sampling is unlikely to reveal this information.

Controversy may also arise between legislators and others who want achievement records of individuals and evaluators who prefer to use a technique like *matrix sampling* to determine the effects of a program. In this sampling technique randomly selected students respond to randomly selected test items measuring different objectives. Thus, different students take different tests. The advantages of the technique are many: reduced testing time required of the student, attainment of information concerning learners' knowledge with respect to many objectives, reduced threat to students since examinees are not compared. The disadvantage is that sampling does not tell us the status of an individual on all the objectives. But again, this is not necessary to get an indication of abilities within groups of students.

Technical Hazards

Donald Horst and colleagues of the RMC Research Corporation have identified twelve hazards in conducting evaluations. Each hazard makes it difficult to know whether or not students do better in a particular program than they would have done without it.

1. *The use of grade-equivalent scores.* One should not use grade-equivalent scores in evaluating programs. The concept is misleading; a grade-equivalent score of 7 by fifth-graders on a math test does not mean that they know sixth- and seventh-grade math. Such scores do not comprise an equal interval scale and, therefore, "average" scores are not interpretable. Procedures for generating these scores make them too low in the fall and too high in the spring.

2. *The use of gain scores.* Gain scores have been used to adjust for differences found in the pretest scores of treatment and comparison groups. Using them in this way is a mistake, because raw gain scores (posttest scores minus pretest scores) excessively inflate the posttest performance measure of an initially inferior group. Students who initially have the lowest scores will have the greatest opportunity to show gain.

3. *The use of norm-group comparisons with inappropriate test dates.* A distorted picture of a program's effect occurs when pupils in the new program are not tested within a few weeks of the norm group's tests. Standardized test developers might collect performance scores in May for the purpose of norming the

test. If the school's staff, however, administers the test during a different month, the discrepancy might be due to the date of testing rather than to the program.

4. *The use of inappropriate test levels.* Standardized norm-referenced tests are divided into levels that cover different grades. The test level may be too easy or too difficult, and thereby fail to provide a valid measure of achievement. Ceiling and floor effects may also occur with the use of criterion-referenced tests. Hence, one should choose tests on the basis of the pupils' achievement level, not their grade in school.

5. *The lack of pre- and posttest scores for each treatment participant.* The group of students ultimately posttested is not usually composed of exactly the same students as the pretest group. Eliminating the scores of dropouts from the posttest may raise the posttest scores considerably. Conclusion of a program's report should be based on the performance of students who have both pre- and posttest scores. The reason for dropping out should also be reported.

6. *The use of noncomparable treatment and comparison groups.* Students should be randomly assigned to groups. If they are not, students in a special program may do better or worse than those in other programs, because they were different to start with.

7. *Using pretest scores to select program participants.* Groups with low pretest scores appear to learn more from a special program than they actually do because of a phenomenon called *regression toward the mean.* Gains of high-scoring students may be obscured.

8. *Assembling a mismatched comparison group.* The correct procedure for matching groups is to match pairs of pupils and then randomly assign one member of each pair to a treatment or comparison group. If, for example, one wants to control for age, one should choose pairs of pupils of the same age. Each member of the pair must have an equal opportunity to be assigned to a given treatment. Do not consciously try to place one member in a certain group.

9. *Careless administration of tests.* Pupils from both treatment and comparison groups should complete pre- and posttests together. Problems arise when there is inconsistent administration of tests to the two groups. If, for example, there is a disorderly situation in one setting and a different teacher present, the results may differ.

10. *The assumption that an achievement gain is due to the treatment*

alone. The Hawthorne effects—unrecognized "treatments," such as novelty—may be responsible for gain. Plausible rival hypotheses should be examined as a likely explanation.

11. *The use of noncomparable pretests and posttests.* Although conversion tables allow one to correct scores on one test to their equivalent on other tests, it is best to use the same level of the same test for both pre- and posttesting. Often it is possible to use the identical test as both pre- and posttest. Obviously, this will not suffice if teachers teach to the test and if there are practice effects from taking the test.

12. *The use of inappropriate formulas to estimate posttest scores.* Formulas that calculate "expected" posttest scores from IQ or an average of grade-equivalent scores are inaccurate. The actual posttest scores of treatment and comparison groups provide a better basis for evaluating treatment effects.[22]

CONCLUDING COMMENTS

Measurement is a waste if appropriations of the data are not drawn and acted on in modifying the curriculum. Looking at test scores and filing them away mocks the evaluative process, although admittedly, there are latent functions for evaluation. Results are sometimes used to gain support of parents and others. Evaluation may be undertaken because it is a necessary basis for requesting federal monies. The principal purpose for using the data, however, should be improvement of the curriculum. Hence, some schools now have curriculum groups that study the findings and then make plans both for the whole school and for individual teachers.

Scores or descriptive terms that summarize learner performance give study groups the opportunity to see the strengths and weaknesses of their programs. Analyses of different populations of pupils are done, and teachers attempt to find out from the data what needs individual students have. Diagnosing needs becomes a basis for giving personal help. Study groups also discuss the reasons for a curriculum's strengths and weaknesses. Members try to explain results in terms of particular learning opportunities, time spent on an objective, the ordering of activities and topics, the kinds and frequency of

---

[22]Donald P. Horst et al., *A Practical Guide to Measuring Project Impact on Student Achievement,* Monograph Series on Education, no. 1 (Washington, D.C.: U.S. Office of Education, 1975).

responses from learners, the grouping patterns, and the use of space and interactions with adults. Explanations are verified by seeing whether all the data lead to the same conclusion. Plans are made to modify the curriculum in light of deficiencies noted and the cause of the deficiencies.

The results from evaluation should be used in at least two ways. First, they can be used to strengthen ends. Results can be the basis for inferring new instructional objectives aimed at meeting revealed needs. If evaluation of a program or particular learning opportunities results in the selection of more important objectives than were originally held, the experiences were valuable. Dewey put it well: "There is no such thing as a final set of objectives, even for the time being or temporarily. Each day of teaching ought to enable a teacher to revise and better in some respect the objectives arrived at in a previous work."[23]

Results can also be used to revise means. They can serve as a guide to the need for new learning opportunities and arrangements that might close gaps. That is, evaluation pinpoints needs and guides one in the selection of new material, procedures, and organizational patterns. These innovations in turn must be tried out and their results appraised. In short, evaluation is only a link in a continuing cycle.

QUESTIONS

1. How would you respond if faced with the choice of getting important data about the learner through deception or getting less important data in a straightforward manner?
2. What kinds of student progress are best revealed by (a) products of learners, (b) self-reports, and (c) observations of pupil behavior?
3. The National Assessment of Educational Progress is a federal project that administers tests called objective-reference exercises to small groups of representative pupils and young adults (a sample) across the country. Many persons, however, do not consider the assessment information helpful, saying they can cite no program changes based on assessment reports. Further, the assessment data do not tell whether the results are good or bad, nor do they pinpoint the reasons for the percentage scores. What kind of information should national assessment provide if it is to affect the decision-making process?
4. Compare the purposes and manner of construction of norm-referenced and criterion-referenced tests.

[23]John Dewey, *The Sources of a Science of Education* (New York: Horace Liveright, 1929).

5. Think of a learning opportunity that you might select for learners (for example, a particular educational game, lesson, field trip, experiment, textbook article, or story selection). Then indicate what you would do in order to find out whether or not this opportunity produced both intended outcomes and unanticipated consequences.
6. How might a teacher or principal gain information regarding the end-of-year progress of students with respect to a large number of objectives without subjecting students to a great deal of testing?
7. What are the major advantages and disadvantages of objectives from the point of view of *curriculum* (the designation of worthwhile ends), *instruction* (the designing of instructional sequences), and *evaluation* (the determination of accomplishment and judgment of the program's worth)?
8. Whose criteria should operate in an evaluation situation known to you—experts, participants, those affected by its consequences?

SELECTED REFERENCES

Apple, Michael W. et al. *Educational Evaluation.* Berkeley, Calif.: McCutchan, 1974.

Bellack, Arno and Kliebard, Herbert. *Curriculum and Evaluation.* Berkeley, Calif.: McCutchan, 1977.

Eisner, Elliot W. "The Forms and Functions of Evaluation," in *The Educational Imagination.* New York: Macmillan, 1979, pp. 168–89.

"Evaluating Educational and Social Action Programs," *Journal of Research and Development in Education* 8, no. 3 (Spring 1975): 20–25.

Hamilton, David. "Making Sense of Curriculum Evaluation," in *Review of Research in Education* 5, Lee S. Schulman, ed. Itasca, Ill.: F.E. Peacock Publishers, 1979, pp. 318–49.

Popham, W. James. *Educational Evaluation.* Englewood Cliffs, N.J.: Prentice-Hall, 1975.

McNeil, John D. *Designing Curriculum*, Module 4. Boston: Little, Brown, 1976.

Willis, George. "Studied Naivete: A Review of Handbook of Curriculum Evaluation," *Curriculum Inquiry* 1, no. 9 (1979): 27–36.

III / ORGANIZING THE CURRICULUM FOR EFFECTIVE LEARNING

Organization in curriculum refers to the sequencing ordering, and integrating of learning opportunities so that intended outcomes are achieved or learners otherwise profit from the opportunities presented. Persons attend to organization because they believe that the relating of learning opportunities to one another makes a difference in both what is learned and how easily it is learned. Organization may make a difference in the way students view their studies, their attitudes toward learning, their ability to learn on their own after leaving school, and on other important consequences. To some persons a curriculum consists of ordered experiences that would not occur by chance; instead, the experiences are extended in systematic fashion. The school is a place where students pursue a restricted number of studies without the distraction of too many competing demands.

Curriculum organization must make possible the illumination of essential but nonobvious attributes, generalizations, and the like. Events should be carefully ordered so that patterns rather than individual entities are seen. Organization must also contribute to learning by providing sufficient opportunities for practice and enlargement of significant concepts and skills. In a sense, the organized curriculum is like a time-motion camera in which events that take months, years, or centuries in nature are arranged so that the learner can grasp their significance and pattern within a brief period of time. In another sense, it is like a giant chessboard in which the pieces take on meaning because of their relations to one another and to a larger design.

The two chapters to follow present first, what theory we have regarding curriculum organization and second, concrete exemplars and prescriptions for organizing curriculum both for the total school and within the individual classroom.

9 / PRINCIPLES OF CURRICULUM ORGANIZATION

The idea that curriculum purposes, activities, and structure should be related leads to what is often called a curriculum design. A number of concepts have been evolved to effect these relationships. There is, for example, the notion of an *organizing element* or thread by which learning activities are selected and ordered to extend in breadth and depth important qualities that the learner should acquire from the program. This chapter deals mainly with concepts and principles that have been used in organizing the curriculum. The reader is asked to look at organization as a problem in curriculum and to ask how the different schemes proposed might influence the efficiency of instruction.

There is no fully adequate theory of curriculum organization, but there are several important concepts and principles necessary for both theory and practice. It is assumed that curriculum workers who adhere to these principles of organization will develop programs that are more comprehensive, consistent, and effective. If nothing else, the interpretations, descriptions, and issues of what is involved in curriculum organization will help us to understand and judge the alternative patterns and details of organizations.

RELATING LEARNING ACTIVITIES

Two Dimensions of Curriculum Organization

Ralph Tyler has written much about the "vertical" and "horizontal" relations of learning opportunities.[1] When we consider the relationship between opportunities in one week's work and those in a second week's work, we are considering *vertical* organiza-

[1] Ralph W. Tyler, "The Organization of Learning Experiences," *Toward Improved Curriculum Theory* (Chicago: University of Chicago Press, 1950).

tion. When we consider the relationship among opportunities in concurrent classes, in subject matters, and in situations both within and out of school, we are considering the *horizontal* organization of learning opportunities. These two dimensions guide us in producing a curriculum that has a cumulative effect. When there is vertical and horizontal continuity, learning opportunities reinforce each other so that the learner acquires both deeper and broader understanding of important elements.

Organizing Elements

In order for opportunities to be related, whether vertically or horizontally, there must be some common element between them. Elements are the threads, the warp and woof of the fabric of curriculum organization. They need to be woven together, or organized. If they are not, we will have this situation, described by Edna St. Vincent Millay:

> Upon this gifted age, in its dark hour,
> Rains from the sky a meteoric shower
> Of facts . . . they lie unquestioned, uncombined.
> Wisdom enough to leech us of our ill
> Is daily spun; but there exists no loom
> To weave it into fabric. . . .[2]

Let us look at some of the more common elements used as the basis for organization.

Concepts. Many curriculum plans are built around such key concepts as culture, growth, number, space, entropy, and evolution.

Generalizations. Generalizations are conclusions drawn from careful observations by scientists. Two generalizations are: "In stable societies all educative influences operate consistently upon the individual; in heterogeneous societies, there are inconsistencies and contradictions." "A person is both participant (subjective) and observer (objective) in all human behavior."

Skills. Skills are generally regarded as proficiency plans for curriculum organization. They are commonly used as the basis for building continuity in programs. Elementary schools, for ex-

---

[2]From *Collected Poems*, Harper and Row. Copyright, 1939, 1967, by Edna St. Vincent Millay and Norma Millay Ellis. Reprinted by permission.

ample, sometimes organize learning experiences around word recognition or comprehension skills, fundamental skills of operations in mathematics, and the skills for interpreting data.
Values. Philosophical values are cherished beliefs that are not to be questioned but taken as absolutes for the governance of behavior. Examples are: "respect for the dignity and worth of every human being regardless of race, nationality, occupation, income, or class" and "respect for self." When organizing a curriculum plan around values, most of the activities must be designed so that they reinforce the particular value selected.

The understanding of organizing elements is a distinguishing attribute of curriculum expertise. A child may be immediately aware of learning activities only in their concrete form, but the insightful teacher or curriculum writer is always conscious of their deeper significance. When one asks children what they are learning, they are likely to respond, "We're learning about the Indians" or "We're learning to speak a foreign language." The curriculum person however, sees, in addition to such direct learnings, the key abstractions to which the present activity points. The activity dealing with Indians may be pointing toward a generalization about basic needs that all people have always had. Learning to speak a foreign language may be most important for what it illuminates about one's own language, language in general, learning to learn any language, or some element even more fundamental, such as communication among people.

Organizing elements are, of course, selected in light of the goals, objectives, and intended outcomes for the curriculum. When the curriculum goals are technical and vocational, skills are an appropriate element to use. When the curriculum goals emphasize moral and ethical domains as the integrative function, values are the preferred element for organization.

Table 7 gives an example of the use of organizing elements in relating an objective vertically to experiences or opportunities.

Objective: Given new situations from everyday life, the learner can indicate the likely effect of technology on these situations. Characteristics, limitations, and capabilities of modern technology will be used by the learner in determining the effect.

Within the first center or unit of instruction—defining technology—students are introduced to systems approaches for reducing complex problems. One definition of technology is acquired. In the next unit, students get glimpses of the ways technology helps people,

TABLE 7

Organizing Centers or Units of Instruction

Organizing elements	Defining technology	People	Jobs	Society	Environment	Quality of life
Technology (concept)	X	X	X	X	X	X
Value of persons (value)		X	X	X	X	X
Relation of natural resources to quality of life (generalization)			X	X	X	X

of the limits to its use, and of its side effects. The concept of technology is further extended and the student begins to judge how technology decreases or enhances the value of people. Subsequent units involve students in problems about applying technology to human uses and jobs to be accomplished, to societal needs, to nature and manmade environments. Prior elements are extended and a new element—the relation of resources to the quality of life—is introduced. Opportunity for students to assess the future effect and value to persons is given in all subsequent units. The quality of life unit allows for an unusually large number of activities related both to individuals and to societal values. As indicated in the matrix, no provision is made for treating value in the first unit; and the relation of natural resources to quality of life is not dealt with until the third unit.

To illustrate the horizontal dimension of organization—sometimes called *correlation*, *integration*, or *concurrency*—consider how learners taking a course in technology might be helped if their other courses were integrated with the course in technology. In their math course, they could acquire other basic concepts for understanding technology and systems, such as algorithms, probability, and binary systems. In their English course, they might be able to examine the interaction between technology and society in the mass media. They could appraise American societal values as reflected in newspapers, advertisements, and modern fiction. They could be helped to see how language is related to thought in both persons and machines.

PRINCIPLES OF VERTICAL ORGANIZATION

Traditional Principles of Sequence

Principles for sequencing learning opportunities go back hundreds of years. Comenius in 1636, for example, admonished teachers to order activities from the simple to the complex. The principle *simple to complex* means introducing learning activities involving a few factors before activities involving many factors. It also means going from a part to a whole or from general to more detail. There are other traditional principles of sequence. Generally, it is best to go from *familiar to unfamiliar*. Activities that involve what the learners know should precede completely novel activities. Children should study their neighborhood before learning about their state and nation, and about foreign lands, for example. One should also progress from *concrete to abstract*, by presenting opportunities for children to see, touch, taste, hear, or smell instances of a phenomenon before asking them to verbalize and categorize. It is also best to teach *dependent factors* first. Addition and subtraction, for example, should precede multiplication. There are also several ways of sequencing a series of facts or subjects. Ordering by *chronology* means presenting events as they occurred in time. Ordering by *usefulness* means teaching particular school subjects at the time they are needed in everyday life.

In Chapter 14, there is a discussion of the *theory of culture epochs*, which was used as the basis for sequencing studies at the turn of the century. This theory states that the learning processes of children follow the same pattern as the learning process of the human race. The notion is still very much alive. Some modern curriculum writers in the field of music are interested in the ideas of Carl Orff, a German composer who developed new plans and materials for teaching music to children based on the cultural epoch hypothesis. Orff reasoned that primitive people used free bodily movement in dance and also simple rhythmic drum patterns, so children should begin with drums suited to their size and skill. Bodily movements should be combined with the beat of the drum and rhythmic chants should synchronize the spoken rhythm with other movements.

Since primitive peoples first employ only one or two pitches before finally progressing to the use of the five-tone scale, the musical experiences planned for children should include songs with only two or three notes and, at most, five notes from the pentatonic scale. Melodic vocabulary includes other steps only after many opportunities with the simple melodies.[3]

Newer Principles of Sequence

Some recent principles for sequencing learning come from psychological models like those of Robert Gagné,[4] and from developmental schemes like those by Robert Havighurst, Jean Piaget, Erik Erikson, and Lawrence Kohlberg.

Gagné's View: Knowledge as a Hierarchy of Ideas. Gagné is concerned with ordering activities according to types of learning. He believes that children learn an additive series of capabilities; that is, the simpler, more specific capability must come before the more complex and general one. Gagné would order learning activities in this fashion:

1. *Multiple discrimination.* The student learns to make different responses to stimuli that are similar in appearance. Children in kindergarten, for example, learn to tell the difference between the letters *d* and *b*.
2. *Concept learning.* The student makes a common response to a class of stimuli. A student may learn, for example, to classify or identify different types of literature or to recognize consonant–vowel–consonant spelling patterns.
3. *Principle learning.* The student acquires a principle, rule, or chain of concepts. The student learns, for example, to predict what word will follow in a given sentence structure according to rules for sequencing English.
4. *Problem solving.* The student learns to combine two or more principles to produce a solution and in the process acquires the capability to deal with future similar problems with greater facility.

---

[3]Carl Orff and Gunhill Keetman, *Orff-Schulwerk: Musik für Kinder*, 5 vols. (New York: Associated Music Publishers, 1950–53).

[4]Robert Gagné, *The Conditions of Learning*, 2nd ed. (New York: Holt, Rinehart and Winston, 1971).

Gagné believes the child comes to school with many capabilities for making multiple discriminations and building further concepts and higher order capabilities. He also realizes that the order of attaining complex behavior is not universal, that it is possible to subordinate capabilities.

Curriculum ordered in accordance with Gagné's theory, like AAAS *Science—a Process Approach,* a number of commercial programs using a cumulative approach to the teaching of reading and mathematics, and mastery learning strategies, sequence learning opportunities according to assumed hierarchies. Children at different levels of a hierarchy are given opportunities to learn prerequisite subordinate and superordinate capabilities as appropriate.

Robbie Case believes that Gagné's model is deficient in one respect. It does not take into account the unique ways children look at a task.[5] Children differ from adults not only in the form of previously learned subskills, but in the number of subskills they are capable of coordinating at one time and in their ability to avoid applying incorrect subskills or concepts. In making a task analysis or hierarchy, Case would analyze the structure of the task *from the learner's point of view.* When such an analysis shows a mismatch between the capacities of the learner and the demands of the task, the sequence should be redesigned either to reduce the hierarchy span or to provide more opportunities to discriminate among concepts that are confusing children.

The Developmentalists' View: Orderly and Sequential Growth. Developmental tasks form an important basis for sequencing curriculum events. Robert J. Havighurst created the concept of a developmental task from (1) the idea that the maturation of the biological organism sets the conditions for learning social tasks, (2) the fact that social and cultural patterns demand that certain things be learned at a given time, and (3) the fact that there is often a sequential pattern of preferences and dislikes dictated by the individual personality. He defined a developmental task as "a task which arises at or about a certain period in the life of an individual, successful achievement of which leads to his happiness and to success with later

[5]Robbie Case, "Gearing the Demands of Instruction to the Developmental Capacities of the Learner," *Review of Educational Research* 45, no. 1 (Winter 1975): 58–89.

tasks, while failure leads to unhappiness in the individual, disapproval by society, and difficulty with later tasks."[6]

Hence, the activities selected for the late childhood curriculum might be those which help one form friendships with peers, learn rules and abstractions for fairness, identify with peers of same sex, and accept a changing body. Developmental tasks of the adolescent might be forming new relations with age mates of both sexes, gaining emotional independence from parents and other adults, selecting an occupation, and preparing for marriage.

In a simple way most schemes outlining developmental stages and tasks support the commonsense notion that health, safety, and physical survival must be attended to first; then can come opportunities that will enable learners to gain the capacity for economic self-maintenance in maturity, which, in turn, is likely to bring the ability to maximize cultural values like morality, prestige, wealth, and self-realization.

Erik Erikson has been credited with originating the idea of charting both the desires of the learners and the demands placed on them by cultural expectations.[7] Erikson's chart of life cycle states, from infancy through senescence, has been proposed as a way to organize the curriculum. Children would be given opportunities to deal with the emotional issues that are salient at particular stages of the life cycle. Children in the latency period (about 8 to 12 years), for example, whose central growth crisis is "mastery versus defeat," would be given opportunities to use newly acquired skills in logical thought to interpret a long-standing conflict with one of their parents.[8] Erikson has defined crucial tasks for each of the major seven life states. The ordering of learning activities addressed to these crises might better serve the needs of learners.

Lawrence Kohlberg, too, has created a developmental scheme for ordering learning opportunities in the area of moral judgment. According to him, learning opportunities must take into account both the learner's existing stage of development and a next higher stage.[9]

[6]Robert Havighurst, *Developmental Tasks and Education*, 3rd ed. (New York: McKay, 1973).

[7]Erik H. Erikson, "Growth and Crises of the Healthy Personality," in *Personality in Nature, Society, and Culture*, C. Kluckholn et al., eds., rev. ed. (New York: Knopf, 1955).

[8]Richard Jones, *Fantasy and Feeling in Education* (New York: New York University, 1968).

[9]Lawrence Kohlberg and Phillip Whitten, "Understanding the Hidden Curriculum," *Learning* 1, no. 2 (December 1972): 10–14.

Kohlberg believes that changes in moral thinking progress step by step through six stages and three levels.

Preconventional Level

Stage 1. Goodness or badness is determined by whether or not one will be punished for an act (punishment and obedience orientation).

Stage 2. Right action is that which satisfies one's needs (instrumental relativist orientation).

Conventional Level

Stage 3. Good behavior is that which pleases others and is approved by them ("good boy–nice girl" orientation).

Stage 4. Right behavior consists of doing what family, group, and nation expect ("law and order" orientation).

Postconventional Level

Stage 5. Right action means obeying legal standards agreed on by the whole society and, in areas where there is no agreement, following personal values and opinion. Right action also includes taking action to change the law (social contract, legalistic orientation).

Stage 6. Right action is exercising one's conscience in accordance with universal principles of justice and rights (universal ethical principle orientation).

Developmentalists have the central idea that development—physical, social, intellectual, and emotional—is fairly orderly and internally regulated. This idea has generally had a salutary effect on curriculum. It has kept before us the fact that some things can be more easily learned after minimum levels of maturity. It may be dangerous, however, to give too much credence to the view that capacities are genetically predetermined and unfold automatically. By manipulating environmental factors, we may alter the concept of readiness—the assumption that there is an optimal age for every kind of learning.

The idea of a developmental sequence sometimes leads to a self-selection practice in curriculum organization, whereby children's interests are taken as an adequate index of their developmental needs. Consequently, learning opportunities are planned in accordance with these interests. However, such interests may reflect an inadequate curriculum or a lack of desirable prior experiences more than maturational deficiencies. The tyranny of fixed age level norms can both lower our sense of what is possible under different learning conditions and keep us from remembering large individual variations.

Jean Piaget's ideas on the stages of mental growth are probably the best known among developmentalists. He has postulated the following stages: a *sensory motor stage* (birth to about 2 years), in which the child begins to "symbolize and to represent things by words or gestures"; *representational stages* (approximately 2 to 4 years), in which the child learns to represent objects by symbolic means and (4 to 7 years) in which the child begins the initial stage of logical thought and can group objects into classes by noting similarities and differences; a *concrete operations stage* (approximately 7 to 11 years), in which the child learns to solve physical problems by anticipating consequences concretely; and a *formal operations stage* (usually 10 to 15 years), in which the youngster learns to use hypothetical reasoning and to perform controlled experimentation.[10]

One implication of Piaget's stage theory of mental development is that learning opportunities should match or nearly match the child's thought structure. This means analyzing each opportunity in terms of the level of reasoning required and then testing to see whether the intended learner has this level of ability. It is often assumed that learning can be induced when the learning activity requires reasoning that is slightly above the predominant level at which the child is operating. However, about the only way one could develop a curriculum that would allow for matching (in most classrooms, children will be at different operational levels) is to provide opportunities that have solutions at each level and let each child choose the level at which he or she will experience the activity.

Developmental schemes for sequencing learning opportunities are subject to two criticisms. First, there is a question about the validity of the principle underlying the scheme. Not everyone believes that Piaget has established valid stages of growth. Contrary to Piaget, there is evidence that young children can think reflectively, recognize fallacies in logic, and make and apply generalizations.[11] Second, there is difficulty in relating developmental sequences to the sequences of learning opportunities. The variation in individual needs,

[10]Jean Piaget, *The Psychology of Intelligence* (New York: Harcourt Brace Jovanovich, 1950).

[11]Robert H. Ennis, "Children's Ability to Handle Piaget's Propositional Logic: A Conceptual Critique," *Review of Educational Research* 45, no. 1 (Winter 1975): 1–43.

interests, and levels of thinking makes it necessary to test all intended learners across a wide range of interests and concepts to assess individual developmental profiles.

In her review of experimental curriculum derived from Piaget's developmental stage sequences and other developmentally based programs, Deanna Kuhn illuminates ambiguities in developmental theory and difficulties in trying to apply it.[12] Her analysis shows the problem of selecting principles that are both effective in the teaching of particular subject matter and important in promoting cognitive development. Definitions of cognitive competencies are not precise enough for constructing curriculum, and we lack knowledge of measuring strategies that characterize a given developmental stage across a range of subject matter.

Categorizing Sequencing Principles

George Posner and Kenneth Strike have derived a scheme for showing how different principles of sequence relate to views of knowledge, views of learning, and views of how content is to be used.[13] By way of example, the category for *relating content to phenomena*—people, events, things—includes:

Space. Principles of closest to farthest, bottom to top, east to west (for example, used in relating such diverse content as parts of a plant, geography, and positions on a football team).

Time. Principles of cause and effect, chronological—early to most recent events (for example, used in relating content of history).

Physical attributes. Principles of softness to hardness, smaller to larger, order of size, greatest to least brightness, less to more complex structure (for example, used in teaching the properties of things in the natural world; science).

The category of sequence principles useful in the *teaching of concepts* includes:

Class relations. Principles that call for teaching about a general class before teaching about its members (for example, teach about mammals before teaching about specific animals in that group).

[12]Deanna Kuhn, "The Application of Piaget's Theory of Cognitive Development to Education," *Harvard Educational Review* 49, no. 3 (August 1979): 340–60.

[13]George J. Posner and Kenneth A. Strike, "A Categorization Scheme for Principles of Sequencing Content," *Review of Educational Research* 46, no. 4 (Fall 1976): 665–90.

Sophistication. Principles by which the less abstract matter is presented first (for example, real numbers before imaginary numbers) and basic ideas before refinements (for example, Newton's laws before Einstein's refinement of these laws).

Logical prerequisites. The principle that ordering of concepts depends on the relations among concepts rather than the relations among their referents (for example, teach the concept of set before the concept of number).

The category of *inquiry-related* sequences includes principles for sequencing learning activities for generating, discovering, or verifying knowledge:

Logic of inquiry. Principles of sequencing based on induction (instances before generalizations) and principles based on deduction (hypotheses before evidence is collected).

Empirics. Principles calling for a general survey of an area before consideration of special problems.

Learning-related content sequences are similar to those mentioned previously as coming from the works of psychologists like Gagné, Piaget, and Erikson. Learning sequences stress ordering of experiences according to familiarity (most familiar to most remote), difficulty (less difficult before more difficult), interest (most interesting first), development (according to developmental stages), and internalization (opportunity to recognize certain features in others before recognizing it in themselves).

The category of *utilization-related* sequence principles includes:

Procedure. Principle of sequencing steps in the order in which they will be used when carrying out a procedure (for example, teach golf grip before teaching address of the ball).

Frequency. Principle of basing sequence on predictions of likely future encounters (for example, teach the use of chi square and correlation coefficients before factor analysis; teach a television repairer how to change a tube before teaching how to change a resistor).

You will note how the above categorization system corresponds to different conceptions of the curriculum. Those with an academic conception use the categories of sequence for (1) relating content to phenomenon, (2) development of concepts, and (3) generating and discovering knowledge. Those with a technologist orientation select sequencing principles from the category of learning-related sequences, such as those of Gagné or Bloom, and from the category of utilization, when their interest is in developing curriculum for vocational training. Humanists tend to draw their sequencing principles from the developmental category, such as the sequences for moral development, values acquisition, and stages of growth. Some humanists are trying to apply John Dewey's principles for sequencing of curriculum content by attending to the individual learner's prior experiences—the cumulative result of the learner's using knowledge gained from one experience to understand more fully the meaning of the next experience.[14] Although social reconstructionists might find the sequencing principle of internalization useful, they give less attention to sequence than to integration of the curriculum. One principle of sequencing sometimes used by reconstructionists, however, is the *principle of graduated responsibility* in ordering learning opportunities for children. This principle is illustrated as follows: observe→ play act→perform useful service→work as equal partners with adults→carry responsibility for a project on a limited budget of power→exercise full adult responsibility.

PRINCIPLES OF HORIZONTAL ORGANIZATION

Integration

Curriculum integration is a response to the desire to make curriculum socially relevant and personally meaningful. The criterion of integration is valued by those who see society as justification for the organization of knowledge. Proponents of curriculum integration argue that if knowledge is to be important and relevant to students growing up in present-day society, there must be a departure from traditional forms and organization. Exploration of topics of crucial social and personal concern, such as relations between the sexes, life in cities, war, and the like, requires introducing content and organizational patterns not found in conventional subject areas. An interdisciplinary approach is required.

Integration of subject matter becomes controversial because it usually means giving up fixed subject matter boundaries and conventional content, emphasizing breadth rather than depth and showing

[14]Chiarelott Leigh et al., "Basic Principles for Designing Experience Based Curriculum," paper presented at annual meeting of American Education Research Association (AERA), San Francisco, Calif., April 1979.

✱ horizontal

more concern for application of knowledge than for the form of knowledge.

There are several schemes for effecting curriculum integration. In some schemes, academic content is fixed and in others the individual student has much freedom of choice. The teacher is a generalist in some schemes; in others each teacher contributes as a specialist while team teaching. There are also integrated schemes within a discipline, such as integrated science, as opposed to schemes whereby all kinds of subjects—science, art, technology, and so forth—are combined.

Integration is a logical problem when we allow a rigid view of knowledge to dominate curriculum planning. As indicated in Chapter 4, there are those with a narrow academic conception of curriculum who view knowledge as fixed and "not there" to be created. Such persons will oppose curriculum reorganization along integrated lines for epistemological reasons. On the other hand, social reconstructionists and humanists who view knowledge as tentative and "person made" favor integration as a way to ensure that knowledge and curriculum fit changing social and human needs.

We have fewer principles for integrating activities than for sequencing them. Horizontally, the curriculum must be organized in order to relate subjects with one another, to relate curriculum with out-of-school experiences, and to relate curriculum with personal needs and interests. Horizontal relationships call for applying organizational elements to an ever widening variety of situations.

Organizing principles commonly in use call for increasing breadth of application and range of activities, and for putting parts into larger and larger wholes. Sometimes the learner's problems and interests serve as the framework or organizing centers within which knowledge from many fields can be brought together. Similarly, opportunities to attack social problems and to conduct projects call for integrating concepts and methods from different fields of knowledge. This content is then featured, not as a system of ideas or concepts, but as ideas that have relevance to a practical problem. *The Chicken Book*, a popular nonfiction book, is an excellent example of how an organizing center, the chicken, can be used to bring together a wonderful compendium of history, literature, science, medicine, religion, technology, economics, fact, and lore.[15] Indeed, one of its authors teaches an in-depth course on the fluctuating fortunes of the

[15]Page Smith and Charles Daniel, *The Chicken Book* (Boston: Little, Brown, 1975).

fowl dedicated to the idea that that which is divided may once more be made whole.

The use of such elements as "great ideas," "broad concepts," and methods of inquiry may effectively interrelate courses and out-of-school experiences. Organizing centers and elements are not principles, however. Many principles for integration are more like administrative and organizational guides for facilitating integration, such as:

Concentration. Students are not expected to take more than four courses at any one time so that they may gain the depth of preparation necessary for seeing the ramifications of each subject on the whole curriculum.

Correlation. Subjects keep their separate identities, but the concepts of one subject are related to the concepts of another (for example, concepts from history and literature are taught at the same time to reinforce each other).

Integration of a tool subject. Skills learned in one subject are used as tools in another field (for example, math concepts are used in social science).

Fields of study. Fields or areas of study differ from forms of knowledge and disciplines in that they do not have a distinctive rational structure of knowledge (for example, the fields of geography and health draw on mathematics, the physical sciences, and the human sciences).

Comprehensive problem solving. Problems such as those of energy and conservation are predicted which require the drawing together of skills and knowledge from such forms of knowledge as science, mathematics, and philosophy in optimizing solutions.

ORGANIZING STRUCTURES

Organizing structure is the way the time spent in the school is divided to provide a series of periods for activities. The kinds of curriculum structures used depend on (1) the level (institutional or classroom) at which the curriculum making is to occur; (2) the conception of curriculum (academic, social reconstruction, and so forth); and (3) the curriculum domains or functions (self-awareness, specialization, exploration, general education). At a broader level, structure consists of *specific subjects*, like biology,

English, or reading, or *broad fields*, like social studies, language arts, or mathematics. The structure may also be a *core curriculum* that draws content from a range of content to general problems and unifying themes. Structure, too, may be a *free form* in which there is a potpourri of offerings to reflect changing tastes. At an intermediate level, there are structures that feature discrete courses (such as modern dance), as well as courses that are part of a complete program (first-year science, second-year science, and third-year science). Common organizing structures at the classroom level are the lesson, the topic, the project, the module, the minicourse, the unit, the learning center, and the learning packet.

Organizational Designs

An organizational design is a statement of the relationships among purposes (functions, domains, goals, or objectives); organizing structures (subjects, courses, topics, and so forth); organizing elements (skills, values, concepts, and so forth); specific learning opportunities or activities; and the principles to be followed in order that learning

FIGURE 1

Outline of a Curriculum Design

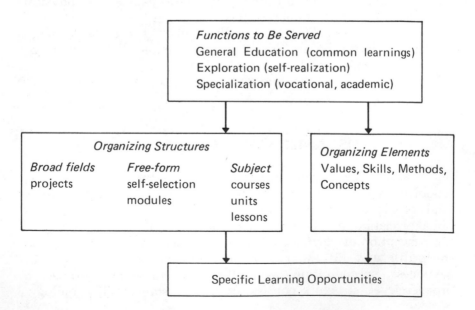

opportunities have a cumulative effect (simple to complex, and so forth). Such a design is shown in Figure 1. The school using such a design indicates that it has a wide range of purposes, domains, and objectives. Hence, there is also a range of organizing structures. The design includes broad fields to serve the function of general education, undifferentiated or open structures that relate to the self-realization domain, and subjects or disciplines to serve the specialization function.

The organizing elements that are derived from purposes indicate the kinds of learning opportunities that must be provided within each organizing structure. The design does not indicate the principle by which the opportunities are to be ordered.

Organizing Centers

Particular topics, problems, questions, themes, projects, and the like serve as organizing centers within each structure. The structure itself influences the choice of center. That is, a subject structure usually is centered on some concept or topic of importance to an academic discipline or trade; a broad field structure within a social reconstructionist orientation typically uses a social problem as an organizing center; a free-form structure with a humanistic orientation will likely feature centers derived from the personal needs and interests of the particular learners. Further, just as the specific learning opportunities are linked to one another by organizing elements, organizing centers are sequenced to produce a cumulative effect. Centers may be ordered to advance both the level of content and the level of mental operations. Detailed examples of curriculum organizational designs for major curriculum orientations were given in the chapters of Part I.

One organizational problem that has not received sufficient attention is how to relate whole curriculum domains to one another. Back in 1962, the National Education Association arranged for a disciplines seminar at which many scholars met to study the effective use of the discipline. The recommendation from this seminar called for reconciling the demands of the discipline with the demands of the learners and society:

> One part, to be called the *nuclear* curriculum, would contain materials from the disciplines, selected to fulfill those objectives of education which are determined primarily by the needs of the developing child and the aims imposed by our culture and society. . . .

The second or *cortical* component of the curriculum would be chosen by contrary and complementary principles. It would consist of materials chosen specifically because they are representative of the major disciplines.[16]

The scholars did not give the details by which these two components would reinforce each other, and practitioners never brought the two together. Programs in the specialization domain are separate from those in general education, and organizing structures and elements by which the two could be mutually supporting did not evolve. The idea, however, is a sound one. One step that should be taken in order to make it a reality is the preparation of new integrative textbooks as opposed to textbooks that reinforce only the subject matter divisions. A second step would involve teacher preparation and the development of team approaches by which teachers would learn how to reinforce curriculum elements in cortical and nuclear components.

ISSUES IN CURRICULUM ORGANIZATION

Curriculum organization is in trouble because the fields of knowledge have not been organized in a way that makes them useful in daily life. Also, those in different disciplines express their findings in different terms so that the consumer does not know how to relate the findings. Curriculum efforts to integrate concepts from various disciplines have not been very successful.

Practical problems of curriculum integration center on (1) teachers' loss of identity and security as isolated teachers of English, science, history, or other subject fields; (2) the need for flexible scheduling during the school day along with freedom for student choice of work and movement within the school building and community; (3) the need for material resources that go beyond the normal stock of books and equipment found in separate subject matter departments; (4) the difficulty of acquiring the teaching roles—skills and attitudes required by curriculum; and (5) meeting the objections that an integrated curriculum will not prepare students for external examinations based on separate subject matter.

[16]National Education Association, *The Scholars Look at the Schools* (Washington, D.C.: NEA, 1962).

Curriculum integration is now an overriding concern. The curriculum reform movement of the 1960s extended the scope of content to include new areas of knowledge, but neglected to evolve unifying purposes. Pluralistic and humanistic interests of the 1970s extended even further the range of electives and the scope of content. As a result, today there is curriculum fragmentation. We are in a wave of curriculum organizational reform which developed as a response to the criticisms of fragmentation and irrelevance. Some idea of the difficulty involved in responding to this situation and to the lack of shared skills and values is seen in Peter B. Dow's report of efforts to build an integrated curriculum.[17] Dow and his colleagues in the Education Development Center in Newton, Massachusetts, tried to organize learning opportunities around interests that appear to be important to the prospective students—child-rearing practices, love and affection, expressions of fear and anger, parent-offspring conflict. Using these interests, the staff sought content from different disciplines (biology, anthropology, psychology, sociology, linguistics) that would help students to meet these interests and at the same time gain an understanding of their own uniqueness, of their kinship with others of the culture, and of the characteristics that unite the human race as a whole.

The curriculum developers found that no academic discipline was adequate to cope with the questions they wanted to raise. They also found that academics from different fields use different words to discuss similar phenomena and that these words are invested with different meanings. A biologist speaks of "bonding" when examining relationships between male and female or between parent and offspring; a psychologist may use words like "love" and "attachment" to describe the same relationships. A third problem was that the disciplines not only represented separate languages and tools of analysis, but also drew from bodies of data that did not overlap. A final and deeper problem was the difficulty of trying to combine different points of view regarding human nature. There is, for example, much conflict over whether cultural evolution proceeds independently of biological factors or whether biological forces determine the direction of evolution.

Several solutions have been proposed to the curriculum problem that life is not encompassed by a single discipline. Philosophers of science have argued that integration can be achieved by using con-

[17]Peter B. Dow, "Science, Schooling, and Society: The Search for an Integrated Curriculum," *EDC News* 5 (Winter 1975): 1–3.

cepts of knowledge about knowledge. One can draw from disciplines the content that represents the field as a whole. The curriculum person can select ideas and instances that exemplify the method of inquiry in these disciplines and offer instruction in *synoptics*—the integrative fields, like history, religion, and philosophy. These disciplines have as their function the making of coherent wholes.

A second proposal is to live with the fact that the scholars in any one discipline are incapable of resolving any complex human problem. In other words, students should try to examine personal and social problems from multiple perspectives, realizing that no one of these views is entirely satisfactory. Perhaps the conclusion students reach after attending to the different perspectives will be more valuable than any one discipline's answer to real-world problems.

A third proposed solution is to forget about curriculum organization as a way to effect meaning for students. Even when there is a careful attempt to simplify and relate content so that students can follow it, the organization will fit any one student imperfectly. Students individualize their experiences anyway. This position puts the burden on the learners to make sense out of learning opportunities in any order. More positively stated, it challenges individuals to pose their own questions, seek their own answers, make their own synthesis, and find satisfaction in so doing. How else will learners begin to organize their own experiences?

Curriculum organization has been accused of preventing learners from comprehending content in any other order and from learning content that is incompatible with adaptive teaching. Underlying most organizational issues, however, are disputes about purpose. Curriculum workers who favor specialization orientation value organization as it relates to sequencing for depth, but they are not impressed by integrative or breadth arrangements. Those who seek integrated approaches, usually humanists and social reconstructionists, distrust prearranged sequences within a single field.

This chapter would be incomplete without presenting a final, very different point of view about the problems of integration. An English educator, Frank Musgrove, has written about the political danger of unified and integrated curricula and their corresponding organizational structures. He sees the integration of separate subjects and the destruction of subject departments in schools as a shift of power from the staff in separate fields to the administrator who directs the new master plan. Further, Musgrove does not agree with social analysts who see homogenization as the dominant trend of our times. He believes instead that postindustrial societies are more segmented, differentiated, and diversified. Hence, for schools, Musgrove prefers fluid, flexible, improvisational styles of organization with power on the periphery. He wants a curriculum to have many subjects and specialists coming together to decide on common objectives.[18]

CONCLUDING COMMENTS

Several technical terms and principles were defined and illustrated in this chapter, such as organizing elements, organizing centers, principles of sequence, and principles for curriculum integration. Alternative organizing structures for institutional and classroom levels were presented.

Emphasis was given to the concept of a curriculum design as a plan indicating the relationships among purposes, organizing structures, organizing elements, specific learning activities, and the principles to be followed in order that learning activities have a cumulative effect.

It was discovered that curriculum organization is not fixed. Controversies over the merits of different organizational schemes were examined and practical problems encountered in trying to act on organizational principles were related.

QUESTIONS

1. Think of a familiar learning task such as tying shoes, operating an automobile, playing a game, composing a musical or literary piece. Into what a priori units would you divide the task you have in mind? In what order would you teach these steps? What principle of sequence determines your ordering?
2. State an organizing element—a concept, value, or skill—that you would like to build on throughout a number of activities in a course or program of interest to you.
3. Curriculum constructed in accordance with hierarchical theories (that is, curriculum where there is an attempt to specify prerequisites and to place them in a simple-to-complex order) is sometimes criticized for being boring and ineffective. Critics charge that there are too many unnecessary steps for some learners and that many learners who successfully complete the enroute steps fail at transfer tasks at the end of the programs. What is your response to this criticism?

[18]Frank Musgrove, "Power and the Integrative Curriculum," *Journal of Curriculum Studies* 5, no. 1 (May 1973): 3–12.

4. What consequences (good or bad) would be likely from a curriculum in which learning opportunities are ordered on the assumption that there is an optimal age for acquiring particular capacities?
5. Arno Bellack once suggested a program that would include basic instruction in the humanities, natural sciences, and social sciences together with a coordinating seminar in which students dealt with problems "in the round" and in which a special effort is made to show the relationships between the systematized fields of study as materials from these fields are brought to bear on a topic. What are the likely advantages and disadvantages of Bellack's suggestion? What conditions would have to exist in order for the proposed plan to work?
6. Assume that you are a member of a planning committee charged with a new curriculum organization for a school. You have been asked whether or not the new organization plan should attempt to provide for integration of subject matter and, if so, how it can best be achieved. What is your reply?

SELECTED REFERENCES

Barrow, Robin. "Integration," in *Common Sense and the Curriculum.* Hamden, Conn.: Linnet Books, 1976, pp. 27–32.

Fiasca, Michael, ed. "In Search of Unity," special issue, *School Science and Mathematics* 75, no. 659 (January 1975).

Gibbons, J.A. "Curriculum Integration," *Curriculum Inquiry* 9, no. 4 (Winter 1979): 321–37.

Kelly, A.V. "Curriculum Integration," in *The Curriculum: Theory and Practice.* New York: Harper and Row, 1977, pp. 79–101.

National Society for the Study of Education. *The Integration of Educational Experiences.* Chicago: University of Chicago Press, 1958.

Posner, George J. "Extensiveness of Curriculum Structure: A Conceptual Scheme," *Review of Educational Research* 44, no. 4 (1974): 401–07.

Posner, George J. and Strike, Kenneth A. "A Categorization Scheme for Principles of Sequencing Content," *Review of Educational Research* 46, no. 4 (Fall 1976): 665–90.

10 / CURRICULUM ORGANIZATION IN PRACTICE

Curriculum organization as conceived by administrators is the first subject discussed in this chapter. Contrasts in school organization during the 1960s and 1970s and the present are described and evaluated. There is, for example, a description of the radical free school movement's influence on the formal public school and the contrasting organizational demands brought by those in the accountability movement and those who favor options in school programs. There is also a critical treatment of the organizational changes proposed by various national commissions concerned with school reform. A second subject is the classroom teacher's view of organization. In discussing this view, we present illustrations of the many organizing structures used by teachers, and look at the controversial organizational ideas associated with open education and the back-to-basics movement.

It is hoped that the reader will both gain knowledge about the many organizational options represented in present practice and relate particular patterns of organization to curriculum purposes.

ADMINISTRATIVE APPROACHES TO ORGANIZING THE CURRICULUM

The chief items manipulated by administrators in organizing the curriculum are the grouping of students, the teacher's role, schedules of instruction, time arrangements, and the ordering of instructional modes. Changing views regarding the needs and functions of schooling require that each of these factors be altered frequently. This requirement can be illustrated by looking at organization during the 1960s, 1970s, and the present.

Traditional Administrative Arrangement

A typical small high school in the early 1960s was divided into three or four nine-month grade levels. Each level offered semester or year-long courses. Each course met five days a week for forty-five minutes, and each student took five or six courses in a number of subjects or departments, usually math, social studies, English, physical education, foreign language, science, homemaking, or fine, industrial, or commercial arts. All students were expected to take some required courses, like tenth-grade English, world history, and physical education.

However, different sections of the required academic courses were established. Hence, students of lower and higher academic, social, and economic background were separated by being assigned to different sections of the required courses where the content and method differed considerably; this was called *tracking*. Tracking also occurred when students were counseled into either a vocational or college preparatory program. Further separations of students occurred when they elected a "major," a subject area in which one completed continuing work of three- or four-year duration.

There were opportunities within the typical school of the early 1960s for students to explore their interests in electives and through student activities. Often there were courses within departments, which were designed to introduce students to a certain dimension of a field (for example, drama or ceramics in the arts). Student activities—clubs, sports, games, hobbies—were usually considered extracurricular. They seldom carried credit and usually took place before or after school. Some of these activities, however, such as student council or the Annual staff, had curriculum status.

Organization Innovations During the 1960s and 1970s

Several different scheduling and staffing approaches were advocated by the Ford Foundation and by persons like J. Lloyd Trump.[1] Let us examine the most important of these changes.

[1] J. Lloyd Trump and Delmas F. Miller, *Secondary School Curriculum Improvement* (Boston: Allyn and Bacon, 1968, revised edition, 1973); J. Lloyd Trump, *A School for Everyone* (Reston, Va.: National Association of Secondary School Principals, 1977).

Grouping. Instead of grouping thirty-five students with one teacher on the basis of ability or achievement, one can use different sized groupings for three different purposes. There is *independent study,* allowing for an individual activity or, on occasion, for two or more pupils to work together. It may take the form of remedial or advanced work in the library, at resource centers, in conference areas, and in outside work experiences or study projects. There is *large-group instruction* by which presentations are arranged that are motivational (stimulating), informational (giving information not available elsewhere), and directional (clarifying assignments). Large-group instruction is often followed by independent study and small discussion groups. The size of the class does not matter and is often 100 or more. There is *small-group discussion* in which students deal with issues and learn how to apply the knowledge gained in large groups and from independent study. Twelve to fifteen student members usually constitute a small group. Membership, however, may change weekly, monthly, or at other intervals depending on the nature of their study. The groups are supervised by a teacher, although students may assume leadership. Such groups usually meet once a week for about forty minutes.

Scheduling. It is possible for some classes to have more time than others or to meet less often, but for longer periods of time, on certain days. Consider the *modular concept* of flexible scheduling, in which there is a fifteen-, twenty-, or thirty-minute time module adopted within a twelve-, sixteen-, or twenty-four period day. Various subjects are scheduled for a different number of modules. Schedules can be rotated by days and periods, and students can take more than six subjects by scheduling subjects to meet fewer than four times a week. True flexible scheduling depends on a nongraded sequence of content and large blocks of time for independent study. Sachem High School, for example, introduced ten-week minicourses and scheduled them in the middle of the day. These courses were regarded as extensions of the main curriculum stream and as exploratory areas. Students could choose from among courses in genetics, sports in literature, local political issues, vocabulary building, preparation for college examinations, home maintenance, and others. In addition, courses were offered during one period a day for a full year or in a double period block for half a year. Half-year courses were joined and taught in tandem blocks during the year as well as in their conventional time segment. Hence, students had more opportunity to alter their schedules to meet career needs. Further, the summer school program was broadened to continue the school year, allowing for a modified trimester system plan. A broadening of course offerings was also made possible by offering independent study via an educational contract system. The system allowed a teacher and student or group of students to set an objective in agreed-on areas. The plan, in turn, was approved by the department chairman and principal. Both vocationally oriented and college-bound students could move at a pace other than that of the conventional program. Self-scheduling allowed parents and students to assume more responsibility and allowed departments to make their courses more appealing. Indeed, seventy-five new courses were introduced during a two-year period.[2]

Team Teaching. Team teaching occurs when, for example, six teachers accept responsibility for 180 students for a two-hour block of time each day. This allows the staff to assume different roles, such as planning, lecturing, leading discussion, and counseling. A given teacher in a team may be involved with a large class, with a seminar-sized group of fifteen, or with pupils engaged in individual study. Teaching teams determine in advance what pupils they need to teach, in what size groups, for what lengths of time, and with what materials. Team leaders provide information for preparation of a master schedule for student guidance. Often, in a daily twenty-minute period, pupils determine their own daily program from the choices available on the master schedule.

One brand of interdisciplinary teaming is found in some middle schools where there are four-person teams composed of one specialist from among the areas of language arts, math, social science, art, or science. Each specialist serves as the resource person for an area, doing much of the planning and teaching of that subject. Each teacher on the team, however, teaches all four of the academic subjects. The advantage of this arrangement is that correlation of subject matter areas is easier and teachers are better able to attend to individual students.

Team teaching is not supposed to be a labor-saving device, like cooperative or rotating turn teaching. It is intended to bring about clear joint acceptance of objectives and better conditions for achieving them. Teams of teachers and groups of students can be together, for example, for approximately three hours each day in what is called a *fluid* block. Two of the hours are devoted to interdisciplinary ac-

²Richard A. Berger et al., "A Redesign Experience for Sachem High School," *The Clearing House* 49, no. 2 (October 1975): 84–87.

tivities, and the additional hour is given to one or more open labs in a variety of subcourse content. With twelve teachers operating across three teams for at least two of the three different hours, as many as twenty-four different minicourses can be offered during a nine-week period. Students from each of the three fluid blocks are able to schedule the minicourse of their choice. The fluid block team also schedules large-group, small-group, and individual student activities, always having a free-floating option for student placement in the open labs, which operate concurrently on an individual instructional format. The balance of the school day is given to elective courses such as physics and typing, or to a vocational block in any of a number of different areas (see Table 8).

Each student is assigned to a specific team or faculty member for the entire day, hence meeting accountability concerns. The organization of the team, advisement, and individualized labs offer several ways to meet student needs.

Supplementary Personnel. Pupil tutors, adult volunteers, and inexpensive paraprofessionals allow teachers to serve more pupils effectively and efficiently. Cross-age tutoring, whereby older students tutor younger ones to the benefit of both, has become very popular

TABLE 8 A Team Teaching Outline

	Fluid Block	Individualized Labs
Hour 1	Fluid block: 100–120	Music
2	students in course	Math
3	(minicourses or	Driver Ed.
	planning)	Art
		Drama
		Typing
		etc.
4	Elective	
5	Elective	or three-hour
6	Elective	vocational block

Source: Gerald C. Ubben, "A Fluid Block Schedule," *National Association of Secondary School Principals Bulletin* 60, no. 397 (February 1976): 104–12. Reprinted by permission of the National Association of Secondary School Principals.

across the country. Indeed, no other innovation has been so consistently perceived as successful. Ideally, tutoring is a regular class assignment rather than a voluntary activity. Instructional modules are selected that will induce academic growth of the tutor as well as tutees. Ninth-graders, for example, may teach fractions to fourth-graders if the "sending" ninth-grade teacher believes the tutors need to learn and practice fractions and the "receiving" fourth-grade teacher would like his or her students to learn fractions.

Scheduling of one-to-one tutoring can occur when two classes get together regularly on two or three occasions per week. A room set up with pairs of desks (carrels) is most desirable, but regular classrooms, cafeterias, or libraries will suffice. The sending teacher prepares the tutors in special training sessions. In these sessions, tutors learn exactly what they are to teach. They may also role-play their methods and prepare materials such as flash cards and tests for their tutees.

The tutoring sessions themselves should be supervised by the teachers concerned. Tutors should be free to ask for assistance, and the teacher can check that the work is being taught correctly.

Nongrading. Nongrading occurs when content and experience are offered on the basis of learner interest and ability and are not restricted to a given grade level. The lack of grade levels permits students to progress at different rates and lets them take advanced or additional courses. A student may wish to take correspondence courses, for example, or participate in advanced placement programs, taking college level courses for credit while in the secondary school. Also, instead of offering world history, United States history, and problems of democracy to tenth-, eleventh-, and twelfth-graders respectively, schools may offer one of these courses each year to all students.

Facilities. Building, grounds, supplies, and equipment should follow from both the educational objectives and the means by which teachers and pupils achieve these objectives. Facilities for independent study means pupils must have a place to work and a place to use the special materials of the subject matter they are learning. There may be a need for places in which to view films, read, practice music, and work with metals and clay.

Classroom walls should not define the limits of the learning environment. Facilities should encourage communication, and there should be variations in lighting—less in small group discussion space than in independent study rooms. The budget for supplies and equipment should be increased as the cost of school building increases. Unlike industry, which wisely puts only 25 percent of total capital outlay into structure, schools have put 75 percent of capital outlay into the building shell and only 25 percent into instructional tools. Although modernization procedures are less costly than building new structures, the politics of education usually means that school persons are vulnerable to the pressures of real estate and building contractors for expensive sites and buildings that are not necessary.

The Middle School. A major institutional change with implications for curriculum organization is found in the rise of the American middle school. This type of school has grown from a smattering of schools in the 1950s to more than 5,000 in 1979. This school is characterized by service to the eleven- to fourteen-year-old age group. Typically, such schools are child centered rather than subject centered. The schools usually offer the design components of a subschool within a larger middle school and an interdisciplinary teaching team. The team operates as a small four- or five-teacher school. The same group of students in the subschool may stay together for a period of three or four years. Another team of teachers offers a related unified arts program to students from all subschools. The unified arts program gives all students experiences in such subjects as art, shop, homemaking, music, physical education, as well as focusing on career opportunities. Exploratory experiences on a nongraded basis are also provided to enrich and supplement the identified needs of the students.

Alternative Free and Specialized Schools. Modular scheduling, team teaching, flexible group instruction, and the like did not prove to be ideal solutions or lead to more effective implementation of curriculum. Some call these innovations "superficial tinkering" and are demanding much more basic reform.

Active groups began to take daring steps toward the reorganization of schooling in the late 1960s. Convinced that public schools were instruments of racist and oppressive society, some community activists opened storefront schools that emphasized both basic skills and black culture. They also tried to enlist school dropouts from the street and prepare them for college. These "freedom schools" were financially supported by foundations and dedicated individuals. A free school movement developed with the opening of these schools.

Radical leaders opened small schools, often characterized by a close, nonauthoritarian teacher-pupil relationship and a "do your own thing" concept for learning, and in which content focused on the ills of the capitalistic society.

By 1971, there were over 200 free schools, but with the quietude of the early 1970s and the loss of available monies during economic slumps, the free school movement lost much of its steam. It had its influence, however, on public education. John Bremer, for instance, the first director of the Parkway Program in the Philadelphia schools, borrowed free school ideas to create a "school without walls" in which effective use was made of community resources. Many of those who started the alternative schools within the public school system were not sure whether they should try to remake the educational system alone or the entire society. Although alternative schools had no uniform philosophies, they continued to increase in number. In 1977, the National Education Association reported 10,000 alternative schools in 5,000 districts across the country.

It is impossible to generalize accurately about alternative schools. By definition, each one is different. Much of the movement is directed toward making schools effective for students who have been school dropouts. Some alternative programs are organized to allow the kinds of options that permit students to work in a congenial atmosphere consistent with their own work style. Most people in alternative schools today are not working as social revolutionists but as humanists who want pupils to have a choice, not only in what is to be studied, but in styles of learning.

Alternative schools have made us conscious of whether or not we should allow students to select freely a formal or an informal school; a structured or an individualized curriculum; a demanding or an encouraging environment. An alternative school—whether a separate institution or a unit within a comprehensive school—is an organizational answer to the old problem of trying to fit the curriculum into the enormous range of talents and traits students bring to school and the diverse expectations they and their parents have for schooling.

Today's alternative school movement has broadened the definition of an elective from a choice of a subject to a choice in ways of working. Generally, people in the movement recognize the need for structure, sequence, and discipline but assert that, for many students, a choice of the degree of structure in a learner's school life is as crucial as a choice between studying Spanish or stenography.

In some of the alternative schools, students seldom enter a classroom. They pursue their individual interests outside. They may study the stars at an observatory, work with computers at a local firm, learn to make bread at the corner bakery, and discuss medicine with a physician—all for academic credit. The Parkway Program in Philadelphia, for example, allows students to travel daily from place to place in the city, learning from a variety of paid and unpaid teachers. Robert Wegmann tells of interviewing a Parkway student who was taking physics at Temple University, Elementary Functions and World Cultures from the Parkway staff, Contemporary American Literature and French II from students at the University of Pennsylvania, Museum Methods from the Park Service staff, and Understanding the Stock Market from a broker.

Recently the term *options* has been introduced. This term refers to the way in which choices are made. In an options system, the choice of school curriculum—methods, activities, or environment—is left to individual students and their families. Instead of a single alternative to an existing program, there are many options. In Minneapolis, for instance, students may attend the school selected by themselves and their parents. In most large cities, there are "magnet" schools which are consistent with the concept of options. These schools offer an especially strong curriculum in some areas, such as science, individually guided instruction, or business education, as a way to further court-ordered integration by attracting students from different ethnic and socioeconomic populations.

Unlike the early 1960s, today there is an incredible variety of new public schools that are available to students, parents, and teachers on the basis of voluntary choice. There are schools that emphasize different instructional approaches (open schools, Montessori schools, continuous progress schools, behavior modification schools, and the like); schools that feature distinctive curriculum (centers for world studies, environmental study centers, career learning centers); schools that offer unique resources (vocational training centers, health profession schools, maritime schools); and schools that focus on special students (maternity schools, bilingual schools, schools for the gifted and the dropouts). Yet, throughout the country, high schools are putting more emphasis on basic skills, career planning, and personal relations. Concerns are expressed that optional and elective courses may have gone too far. A return to some degree of homogeneity and uniformity is a trend. Alternative classes are being established, however, for students who fail competency exams in reading, math, and writing.

DIRECTIONS IN ORGANIZING
THE SECONDARY SCHOOL

Two directions of organizational reform have emerged out of the ferment over social policy dilemmas and the innovations both from those who would make the school more humane and from those who would make it more productive. Various commissions and study groups bent on studying secondary schools in order to restore them to full strength and vitality agree on two directions.

First, reduce barriers between adolescents and opportunities in the community. Work or volunteer experience outside the school building is seen as desirable in increasing students' independence and helping them to encounter a broader range of people and experiences. Students' time should, however, be well planned, and off-campus programs should be organized to allow for reflection. The study groups also realized that tracking can occur outside as well as inside the school. A combination of action and reflection is believed necessary in order for adolescents to mature in an integrative manner.

Second, create smaller schools or subschools characterized by more specialized courses of study. Students who are unlikely to get training beyond high school should leave school with enough skill to procure a job. Rather than each offering training in fifteen or twenty skills, different schools might each offer three or five trades in depth. To facilitate such specialization, the school,. satellite, or cluster within schools should be smaller, with each unit focusing on fewer but more specific areas and skills. Basic academic subjects would still be offered in all schools, but students would select a magnet school on the basis of the training it offers.

Teachers within smaller schools, with some of their students on alternating work and study programs outside the school, would have more time to spend with fewer students. They also would perform more varied roles, like that of advisor, work supervisor, and model. The reports from the various commissions and panels trying to reform secondary education emphasize options in high school organization and the need for instruction in informal settings. These reports are not truly plans for curriculum development because they fail to attend to the questions of what should be taught and how. If we return to our metaphor of curriculum as a game, as found in chapter 5, we might say that the authors of these reports fail to pick up all the curriculum pieces. Like so many administrators and policymakers, they make the mistake of assuming that if the structure and organization are changed, or if the setting and scene of schooling are moved, then appropriate and effective education will result. This is not so. The learning of the various settings must be coordinated with that of the school, and one should not assume that all work settings are appropriate for learning. The task of improving learning of students in terms of specifics has yet to be done. Unfinished, too, is the development of a conceptual framework for guiding the creation of learning activities and the training and deployment of personnel.

Concurrent with the movement toward alternatives or options in the secondary school is the accountability movement. Whereas the former implies different goals, the accountability movement demands minimum competencies (presumably the same competencies) for all students. Accountability demands arise for a number of reasons: concern that students are graduating without the skills necessary for survival in our society, fear that encouragement of pluralistic values instead of a stress on common values will result in a divisive society, and efforts by professional reformers at federal and state levels to control the curriculum at the institutional and classroom level. These two conflicting movements require different organizational plans— one, a fixed structure toward narrowly focused ends; the other, open structure toward a wide variety of ends. The orchestrating of these conflicting requirements is an uncompleted task.

DIRECTIONS IN ORGANIZING THE ELEMENTARY SCHOOL

Three terms are associated with organizational reform within the elementary school: open education, individualized instruction, and back-to-the-basics.

Open Education

Open education rests on the belief that children learn best when they are placed in a stimulating environment and allowed to choose activities for exploring and developing. Children are treated with much respect, and efforts are made to have the school a place in which children live as happy human beings while preparing for the future. Children are free to move and interact with others as they play and carry out purposeful activities. An abundance of materials is accessible for children's manipulation and use, but not for waste.

Open education is based on many of the organizational principles of the activity curriculum of the 1930s,[3] although many mistakenly believe that such practices arose only with Jean Piaget's development theories or Lady Plowden's account of the British primary schools. Among these principles is the importance of play, both as a normal behavior of children and as a valuable area of human activity. Children should have an environment that stimulates them to ask questions, explore, and observe. The importance of construction should be stressed, and children should make things from paper, rope, seeds, wood, metal, and other materials. Many activities should be brought together by a center of interest. Children's interests should be classified in order to reduce their activities to manageable terms.

Management is a central organization problem in the open curriculum. There are few concrete strategies for sustaining the involvement of many children in activities. When several children are engaged in separate open-ended tasks, it is difficult for a teacher to help them all extract important learnings from these activities. The problem of making an interesting and motivating activity educative has not been fully resolved. One type of answer is found in *Olson's Toy*. David Olson has reported on the development of a nonverbal toy that teaches preschoolers to conceptualize diagonality and other spatial models in order to construct them, but at the same time makes no demands on the teacher.[4] Devices of this kind may be helpful in open classrooms, leaving the teachers free to address the demands of management. Children must feel that the teacher is in charge but, at the same time, that information has been arranged to reach them without the teacher's intervention. Children must know that they can check their own and others' work in an independent manner and can consult the teacher when there are problems they cannot meet by themselves.

There are other souces of answers to the problem of management. The California Elementary School Improvement Program features one adult for every ten children, with aides, volunteers, and parents

---

[3]B. Othanel Smith et al., "The Activity Curriculum: Problems, Practices, and Criticisms," *Fundamentals of Curriculum Development* (Yonkers, N.Y.: World Book Company, 1957), pp. 292–310.

[4]David K. Olson, *Cognitive Development: The Child's Acquisition of Diagonality* (New York: Academic Press, 1970), chapter 9.

assuming teacher roles. Cross-age tutoring, described on page 205, is a successful way to attend to individual needs and interests. Intraclass procedures are also helpful. Such procedures include the *integrated day*, during which pupils select their learning tasks without set time periods for the different areas of instruction; *family groupings*, which bring together in a single class pupils of different ages; and *friendship and interest groups*, whereby "learning bays" or "stations" are equipped for study of different topics and volunteer adults guide the activity.

Individualized Instruction

Individualized instruction is a method used to serve the interests of those with different curriculum orientations. Whether you want to stress academic mastery, tool skills, personal development, mastery learning, or social development, you can find some kind of organizational plan that can be labeled "individualized." However, these plans differ significantly.

Technologists and other people who stress mastery of particular skills and concepts utilize a programmed instruction approach to individualization, in which students proceed individually through sequences of learning units assigned according to results of pretests; the activity, program, or lesson, and a posttest are all related. Mastery is the criterion for advancing to each succeeding unit. The chief organizational features of the technological approach apply to intraclass arrangements within a heterogeneous grade level or several grade levels. Whole class and subgroup teaching are largely replaced by tutorial or self-instructional lessons within such areas as reading, math, science, and language arts. Temporary pupil clustering occurs when teachers identify pupils who have a common deficiency and then group them to receive instruction in the required learning task.

Technological approaches individualize chiefly by varying the *pace* (for example, the number of frames to be completed in a given period of time); the number of *examples and amount of practice* required (those who can acquire the skill or concept with a "lean" program need not complete supplementary exercises or attend to additional explanation); or the *tasks required*. Pupils need to take programs only when a pretest indicates that the objective is not already within the learner's repertoire.

Organizational variations in the technological approach often are found in plans where specific objectives and matching criterion-referenced tests are used to define *what* is to be learned and a wide range of materials from many sources are brought together to serve as the *means* for achieving the objectives. The placing of particular collections of material in a central location by objective tends to break down the self-contained classroom. Instead, children come to a learning center that focuses on a given skill they need, regardless of their age or grade level.

Humanists view individualization as self-seeking. Their approach is to advance self-determination through individualized plans in which pupils choose tasks and make decisions about how and when to perform them. Such features are seldom found in programs with carefully structured sequences. Humanists believe that personal and social objectives are best met in individualized programs that involve pupil participation in projects of their own choosing.

Contracts in which teacher and student agree on objectives also occur in individualized instruction. Students may determine the resources from which they will learn and select the group techniques necessary for sharing what they have learned from others. Future direction in individualized instruction probably lies in matching learning style with learning activities. Little has been done in this respect. Rita and Kenneth Dunn have drawn attention to the possibility of matching by noting such factors as: the time of day when a pupil is most alert; whether a pupil works best in quiet or with music; whether one learns more effectively in leisure or under pressure; and whether the pupil has a need for reward or incentives.[5]

Competency-based Programs

The pendulum swing that is pushing an accountability orientation in the direction of minimum standards that students must meet to graduate from high school is affecting the organization at the elementary school level. Competency-based programs are found increasingly in elementary schools. Children are given tests to assess whether they have acquired the skills thought necessary for achievement at a particular grade level, and, in some cases, minimum standards are set as a requirement to be met in order to move from grade to grade.

On the positive side, the results of competency exams may serve to identify instructional deficiencies and to initiate effective remedial instruction. On the negative side, competency exams may encourage too much emphasis on the teaching of isolated skills—more cur-

[5]Rita Dunn and Kenneth Dunn, "Learning Styles—Practical Applications of the Research," *PAR Phi Delta Kappan Newsletter* 1, no. 3 (March 1979): 2–3.

riculum fragmentation—and the false expectation that all children should acquire the skills at the same time. If the test results become the principal basis for deciding whether to retain or promote a child, they may have harmful social and instructional effects for that child.

Competency-based curriculum is adding to what is already, in many schools, a confused organization picture. In a recent study, for example, Gail McCutcheon found disjointed, unharmonious programs, lacking a coordinated design.[6] She attributed the incoherence to piecemeal decisions made in response to the demands of many diverse groups—the legislature concerned about competence, minority groups advocating multicultural education, federal programs aimed at mainstreaming, and the mismatch between textbooks adopted and the philosophical orientation of the school. In one school, for instance, the mathematics program offers metrics through conversion, while the science program stresses metrics through inversion. In another school, an experiential science program that requires extended time for the conduct of experiments cannot be implemented as intended due to schoolwide scheduling of twenty-five minutes a day for science. The twenty-five minutes a day regulation was adopted to allot more time to reading and math in hopes of raising low achievement scores.

ORGANIZATIONAL PLANS AND THE CLASSROOM TEACHER

The organizational plan adopted by the school will influence the patterns teachers adopt in working with pupils. Nominally, a school that features flexible scheduling, team teaching, and open and nongraded organizational patterns offers teachers more options in choosing and scheduling and in grouping of pupils. It is easier, for example, to arrange swimming lessons, neighborhood projects, intercultural exchanges, and other activities associated with a broadened curriculum when the school organization provides for sharing community recreational and cultural facilities. Adventure areas within the school are more likely when the school's plan encourages indoor-outdoor work areas such as garden plots, animal pens, weather stations, and bird feeders. Yet the curriculum the child will experience depends on the attitudes of teachers regarding

[6]Gail McCutcheon, "The Curriculum: Patchwork or Crazy Quilt?" *Educational Leadership* 36, no. 2 (November 1978): 114–16.

children and instruction. The organization and curriculum structure within classrooms reflect teachers' educational predispositions.

Open and Individualized Classrooms

Time, space, materials, and human resources are ordered by aides, teachers, and parents in open classrooms. Informal materials are created, such as laminated learning task cards, and reading or math games. Instructors plan the integrative experiences that will allow learners both to bring together the skills learned in isolation and to advance social goals. There is likely to be candle making and pottery, volley ball, folk dancing, and singing.

A good example of how a teacher in a school can provide a very individualized and personalized program in an open environment has been reported by Alan Wheeler who described the Beavers Lane School:

> The curriculum is divided into three major areas: language, numbers, and drama. Each teacher is responsible for her particular area, but has the opportunity to explore as many areas as possible. The thrust of most activities is to interest children in such a way as will involve them in their own learning.
>
> As one observes and works in the school, he senses a tremendous enthusiasm on the part of both teacher and pupils as they work together in small groups or as a total group, depending on the activity or activities . . . .

The Integrated Day—A Number Class

> In the number class three children were measuring flour, water, and orange juice in order to make cookies. After measuring the ingredients, they became involved with additional number activities by cutting out squares for each member of the class. After these three children finished their project, other children became involved with the same procedure.
>
> At the same time, another child was coloring numbers, another was counting, two other children were painting and finishing their projects, four children were individually taking a number count regarding the upcoming football match between Chelsea and Liverpool, four other children were working with counters with the teachers. There was an abundance of activity, interest, and sustained effort on the part of each of the 31 children in the classroom. Those children who were not involved were questioned by the teacher as to their activity or lack of it. The room was alive with number concepts and activities, but also there was ample evidence of language and creative activities pres-

ent, such as science interest centers, art projects, writing, and verbalization. Other activities which the author encountered included:

Measuring each other to find the tallest, and the shortest, boy or girl
Measuring hand spans—number of hand spans—needed to fill the inside of a truck
Motor skill development
Questions on who wants to be a nurse, a hairdresser, a fireman, or a policeman
Art
Drawing pictures of their concept of football players on the field
The flower shop—using tissue to make flowers, and selling them, which entails using money
Using the water table to measure water—how many cups in a gallon jug, etc.

A visual diagram shows what this author perceived to be a usual day in a number class.

Flow of Activities in a Number Class

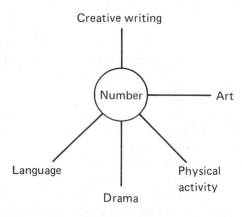

The same type of diagram could be drawn for language and/or drama. A typical day at Beavers Lane Infant School is arranged according to a schedule which allows each child intensive involvement with all three areas—language, number, and drama. At the same time the schedule allows each teacher the opportunity to explore any other area that she and the pupils decide upon.

9:00–10:30   language
number
drama

10:30–11:00	free play
11:00–12:00	language number (change) drama
12:00– 1:30	lunch
1:30– 2:35	number (change)
2:35– 3:15	play and activity

Structured Openness

The use of the integrated approach, coupled with vertical grouping (that method of organization in which individuals of different ages are placed together in the same class), ensures heterogeneity and expands opportunities for freedom of choice, flexibility, facilitation of PIES (Physical, Intellectual, Emotional, and Social) development, and individualization of instruction. Furthermore, progressiveness and personalization of learning experiences are enhanced through this type of school organization. The integrated day approach, or unstructured day, can be achieved only by having a highly organized classroom which, in turn, relies on a highly structured environment.[7]

Another organizational plan for classroom individualizing is the arrangement of the day's activities into laboratory, individual, large- and small-group settings. Thus a pupil's daily plan in an area of reading might include several of the following:

Individual listening station. There is a work station, for example, where a child might hear taped instruction regarding a reading skill, where a child might learn to listen for details in learning to read, or hear literary selections.

Activity center. There may be a diorama where a group of children learn to find common attributes—what things go together—a skill related to reading comprehension.

Directed lesson. For example, a teacher may present a lesson treating "signal" words indicating cause and effect.

Individual work. The child may use independent self-instructional booklets or learning packets that offer practice in selected reading skills such as finding main ideas in paragraphs.

Library center. This center offers free choice to the learner and gives opportunity to practice reading skills.

[7]From Alan H. Wheeler, "Structuring for Open Education," *Educational Leadership* 31, no. 3 (December 1973): 251–53. Reprinted by permission of the Association for Supervision and Curriculum Development and Alan H. Wheeler. Copyright © 1973 by the Association for Supervision and Curriculum Development. All rights reserved.

Tutor session. This can be an opportunity for the child to receive a sequenced lesson in reading from a cross-age tutor. The lesson usually takes less than twenty minutes.

The newer organizational plans described above markedly change the teacher's role. Instead of devoting so much time to the planning of teacher-directed lessons, the teacher designs activities, such as learning centers, by which pupils learn without the direct presence of the teacher. There is a diminishing of the didactic teaching role and an increased emphasis on the role of curriculum development. Further, the teacher must become a manager of other instructors, such as aides, parent volunteers, and tutors. This manager role requires supervision as well as curriculum development and team planning skills. It is true, too, that the modern teacher is expected to do more diagnosing of the learner's need for specific skills and matching of this need to given instructional treatments.

Controversy About the Open Classroom

Like other organizational plans, open classrooms depend on the attitudes of the teachers, parents, and pupils involved. The quality of the classroom environment is particularly dependent on the attitudes held by teachers. The open classroom teacher should be more person-centered than content-centered. The structure is related to the curriculum conception that the process of learning may be more important than the acquisition of particular knowledge and skills. Hence, the teacher's task is viewed as setting up opportunities for learning in and out of the classroom where the teacher can watch children and see what they respond to. The questions generated by children in these opportunities become the basis for the curriculum. Correct answers are not valued as highly as good questions.

Children are allowed to pursue their interests without feeling that they are wasting time. The hope is that they will find the excitement of learning more from self-initiated activity than from the teacher's direction. This is not to say that the teacher should not make suggestions and establish requirements to help students become self-directed.

Conventional organization with more uniformity and greater control is easier for most teachers to manage. Not all children welcome opportunity to explore a variety of materials, to make choices, and to pose their own problems. Although an open classroom gives the children more freedom, it also gives them more responsibilities.

Sometimes open education attracts teachers who are unwilling to exercise their intellectual authority. Children respond with anger when they sense a teacher's lack of leadership as insecurity, forcing the teacher to assume a detested authoritarian role. Also, as noted before, an open classroom requires a structured or planned environment. There must be opportunities for children to learn.

Parents and the community also often expect to see each child under the teacher's control at all times. For these and other reasons, only a few of America's classrooms are open, although there is a growing interest in open structure in all parts of the country.

Conventional Self-Contained Classrooms

Organization within classrooms staffed by one teacher and thirty or more pupils may reflect any number of curriculum orientations—technological, humanistic, academic, social reconstructionist. Many teachers believe that all the talk about cross-age tutoring, learning centers, and other devices is just reinventing the pedagogical wheel. They have always used such devices in individualizing their classrooms. Further, some teachers within self-contained classroom organizations do not fit the stereotype of one who lectures, dominates all activities, and prescribes curriculum with the same assignments for all. Indeed, many teachers have always practiced flexible grouping by interests, friendships, and needs. They have long created supplementary activities appropriate for individual learners in a given community and have put children in touch with resource persons who possess a variety of competencies and outlooks.

ORGANIZATIONAL STRUCTURES
OF SHORT TIME DURATION

Most teachers have relied on curriculum guides, courses of study, and textbooks in different fields to provide scope and sequence to the curriculum as well as to suggest learning opportunities. Few teachers have the time or ability to select organizing elements that relate to long-range goals and to sequence interest centers and activities spanning several years of instruction. Nearly all teachers do, however, organize their lessons, learning centers, and other classroom structures within a restricted time frame.

The following paragraphs offer a description of currently popular structures prepared by teachers. It is suggested that teachers give more attention to designing these structures in accordance with particular curriculum orientations and with a regard to the principles of continuity and integration.

Learning Centers

Learning centers are a popular structure for classroom instruction. They are incorporated into classroom settings as alternative approaches to teacher-directed lessons. Their major principle is to allow a teacher to provide a pupil with a self-directed learning experience that furnishes the child with immediate feedback. Moreover, they can reinforce a previously acquired skill or concept, stimulate children to explore other subjects, and disclose information on the workings of a process, while providing activities that are interesting and challenging.

The learning center is most effective when used by one student or a small group of students. Behavior standards for the center should be set at the beginning of the school year, either formally or informally. Use of the center by one student should not ordinarily be for more than forty-five minutes. A good instructor gears the length of time at the center to the attention span of the students. A constant rotation of activities and skills helps the child maintain interest. A teacher must take into account the students' interests, what the students talk about most outside of the classroom, and the subjects that seem to turn students off. Students who enjoy reading the "funnies" would probably enjoy a learning center that allows them to create and produce their own comic strips. They should be encouraged to produce stories for others to read and enjoy, since creative writing is an important part of any language arts program. A science center could be established in which the reproductive cycle of the human body is discussed and explained. Whatever centers are developed, they must be relevant to the pupil's everyday classroom needs and to the teacher's philosophy.

Because the learning center is a pupil-directed experience, it should be independent of any type of assistance from the teacher while it is being used. Materials and equipment for the learning center should be tried beforehand in order to perceive any possible difficulties. The centers should be designed and located in an area of the classroom that will not cause disturbance to other learners. If possible, learners should be allowed to help in the actual physical construction of the center. Allowing the pupils to be so involved gives them a chance to develop their own needs and interests. The standard paper and pencil routine is not necessary for the learning center experience. Instead, every available resource, such as filmstrips, records, and puzzles, might be considered in order to help stimulate interest. An evaluation system should be built into the entire program so that students can continually check their progress. Confirmation of correct responses may be given through cassette players, answer sheets, or other devices.

Learning centers have many possible variations and often serve more than one function at a time. A center can cause children to interact socially, while also teaching them a basic skill or concept. Some centers (such as a science center) that are designed to help children make discoveries combine manipulative devices to help promote this discovery. Others are designed to change the negative attitude many children have about previously acquired subjects.

A learning center is not a substitute for a teacher; it is an instrument that allows children to have a self-directed learning experience and gives a teacher more independence in the mode of instruction. It is a step away from mass education and a step toward personalization of instruction, which is so needed today.

The Lesson Plan

The lesson plan is one of the most important tools of the educational trade. Teachers of all ages and experience devise plans. Just as ground plans are necessary for construction work and maps are necessary for planning a trip, lesson plans are a must for any instructional endeavor.

Lesson plans are strategies for teachers. They may be written formally or informally according to the teacher's need. Teachers differ with respect to their need for frameworks with which to help them anticipate the exigencies of their lessons. A lesson plan should not inhibit teaching to the point where an instructor becomes totally dependent on it during the lesson. Some teachers prefer to make complete lesson plans, which include most of the questions they expect to ask during the lesson as well as providing for anticipated problems. Others make outlines of the steps or agenda to be followed in a lesson. Whatever lesson plan is used, teachers should be able to incorporate it in their teaching with ease.

Those with a technological or academic orientation prepare their plans in the following manner. The first step is to state and describe clearly the purpose and objectives of the instruction. The objectives must ensure continuity for the total instructional unit. Next, the procedures for carrying out the lesson must be listed. (What will the teacher and learners have to do in order to complete the lesson?) Creative strategies and activities for stimulating the learners should be well thought out. The selected procedures need to match the instructional objectives of the lesson and should include substantial appropriate practice. The procedures must also be feasible for use within the desired time limit of the lesson. Variation of the activities is important, and alternative methods must be provided in case an activity should fail to produce the desired results.

Objectives of a lesson should be specific and should relate to the broader objectives and goals of the educational unit. Many teachers, in trying to put together lesson plans, fail by trying to accomplish too many objectives within a given lesson time or by producing objectives that are not mutually associated. In addition, some lesson plans teach toward the same objective day after day without any variation of planned activities. The lesson plan provides the instructor with an organized method for obtaining desired results. A typical lesson plan from the technologist orientation follows.

A Sample Lesson Plan from
A Technologist Perspective

Teacher's Purpose

To teach the children the principle of light rays. That is, to help children understand the manner in which light rays bend. They should know that light rays traveling in a low density medium (air) will *converge* when they strike a denser medium (glass) whose surface is shaped one way and will *diverge* when striking a differently shaped surface. They also should know that a reverse pattern occurs as light rays go from the denser glass to the less dense air.

Instructional Objective

Given a diagram containing parallel light rays, air, and convex and concave lenses, the student will indicate whether the light rays will converge or diverge by circling the correct term. (*The objective is not vague.*)
Example: "If you think the light rays will converge, put a circle around the word *converge*. If you think the light rays will diverge, put a circle around *diverge*."

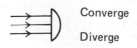
Converge

Diverge

Teaching Procedure

1. Stress the general notion that the path of light rays depends on two factors, curvature of the lens and change in density of the material it goes through. (*The teacher does not help students perceive a purpose to the learning task, which might be a weakness in the plan*).
2. Be sure pupils understand the meanings of "converge" and "diverge." *Con* means with, or together, as in convene (bring together), concur (in agreement), or converge (come together). *Di* means separate, as in divorce (separate or break up) or diverge (spread apart). (*There is attention to prerequisite tasks*).
3. Draw pictures of simple lenses, showing how a lens makes light rays converge.

a.   b.

4. Draw pictures of convex and concave lenses. Then ask students what happens to the light rays as they go from air to glass. (*There is appropriate practice. The teacher should give feedback to responses*).
5. Ask students what will happen to the light rays as they go from glass to air.
6. Ask students to draw a lens that would make the rays converge when entering the lens and diverge when leaving the lens.

Evaluation Procedure

Administer this test:
"For each diagram, decide if the light rays will converge or diverge. Put a circle around the word that is the answer." (*The evaluation samples what the objective calls for.*)

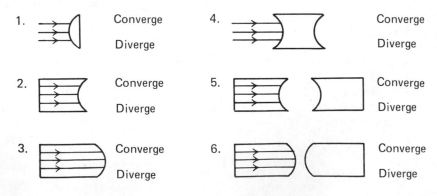

1.   Converge   4.   Converge
                     Diverge   Diverge

2.   Converge   5.   Converge
                     Diverge   Diverge

3.   Converge   6.   Converge
                     Diverge   Diverge

Teachers with a humanistic orientation are less likely to value the goal-focused lesson plan as an organizational structure. They think it may cramp creativity, and they prefer to do their planning with respect to the selection of a learning opportunity that is likely to give rise to many qualitative responses, not stimuli to elicit prespecified objectives. Teachers with a social reconstructionist orientation prefer that daily plans be cooperatively developed in relation to the project and purposes to which students and others have previously committed themselves. In short, the demands of the task set the daily procedure.

Educational Games

Students prefer games to other classroom activities. This finding holds true for students from elementary school through high school.[8] Games can often detour the boring repetition of drill learning. Rheta De Vries and Constance Kamii have shown, too, that in group games the child accepts an external system and regulates his or her behavior to it and then coordinates his or her own logic with that of others. The first response is part of the child's moral development; the second is a dimension of intellectual development.[9] Games can provide fun and excitement in the classroom situation as well as emphasize the concepts of "team work," "fair play," and "cooperation." Probably the most apparent factor of games is motivational. It is not often that you have to push a child into playing a game.

In simulation games the rules help students model a real-world process. We usually think of simulation in connection with flight simulators and other apparatus for training pilots and human engineers. In the classroom simulation consists of learning opportunities that allow students to carry out roles called for by political, economic, and social situations. In simulations, players learn their roles as the game progresses through following the rules and the changing aspects of the situation. *Democracy*, for example, is a game in which participants assume the roles of legislators who are trying to get reelected. Log-rolling, lobbying, the balancing of conflicting interests, and other political realities are faced by the players.[10]

[8]James Coleman, Keith Edwards, Gail Fennessey, Steven Kidder, and Samuel Livingston, "The Hopkins Games Program: Conclusions from Seven Years of Research," *Educational Researcher* 2, no. 8 (August 1973): 6.

[9]Rheta DeVries and Constance Kamii, *Why Group Games? A Piagetian Perspective* (Urbana, Ill.: Publications Office, ERIC, University of Illinois, 1975).

[10]James S. Coleman, *Democracy* (New York: Western Publishing Company, 1974).

Postgame discussion is considered as valuable as the simulation itself. The economical and motivational aspects of simulation games are clear. There are also disadvantages. Simulation requires much preparation. The teacher must be familiar with the details of simulation and anticipate what is likely to arise as it is carried out. It is not always easy to relate what is being learned to the other purposes and content in the curriculum. Occasionally, too, it has been wondered whether or not simulative games might give students distorted views of reality and influence them to see life as a game.

Teachers must take time to discuss the purpose of the game with the students. Students should be taught to take responsibility for the game. Directions on how to use it as well as the maintenance involved should be announced. A good idea is for the teacher to play a sample game with some of the students.

Occasionally, winning becomes too easy for some of the students. In that case, the teacher may ask the children to form partnerships for playing the game, or they may group the faster students together to play more advanced games. In the same vein, some students will always seem to be losers. Then, the teacher might decide to add a game that relies heavily on the elements of chance, thereby giving all learners an opportunity to succeed.

Elementary teachers often make their own games, many of which rest heavily on questions and answers. The following is an illustration of such a game.

What Do You Know?

Pupils move their game piece along a path by answering questions and rolling a die. The game can be applied to any subject area and age group. Three or more can play. Equipment consists of a game board, one die, some markers, question cards, chance cards, and an answer sheet. The question cards consist of thirty or more numbered questions. Chance cards are of the same size and number, and they are drawn when a player lands on a chance space on the game board. Examples of chance cards are: "You are cooperative—go ahead two spaces" or "You forgot something—go back one space." The game board should provide for twenty-four spaces from start to finish with several chance spaces.

The answer sheet is kept by a neutral player who affirms the correctness of the answers. The numbers on this sheet correspond to the respective question cards.

Rules. The first player takes the top card and tries to answer the question. If correct, he or she rolls the die and moves his or her piece the indicated number of spaces. Other players can challenge an answer. If it is a correct challenge, and the challenger can supply a better answer, he or she gets an extra turn. If it is an incorrect challenge, the challenger misses his or her turn. The play moves clockwise, and the player getting to "finish" wins.

Questionable Organizational Practices at the Classroom Level

There are two questionable classroom practices associated with organization. One of these is to rely on a continuum of instructional objectives within separate subject matters as the organizational plan. Although the sequence of skills and activities as given, say, in a textbook series for kindergarten through eighth grade has merit and a continuum of skills in reading or math may help a teacher provide for continuity in a child's learning, such plans have weaknesses. They are based primarily on principles for vertical organization. Thus the curriculum is characterized by (1) separate subject matter divisions, (2) a closed and narrow skill focus of objectives, and (3) a lack in opportunity to apply the skills in the child's daily living. Some hierarchies of skills lack validity—the enroute objectives are not essential prerequisites for the skills to which they point. Further, they tend to keep teachers and pupils from generating their own purposes, sequences, and applications.

A second questionable practice is that of offering one activity—learning center, game, and the like—after another without noting the consequences and without planning for the next steps in light of the observed consequences. In a way, some classrooms seem to be programmed like television, with a number of stimulating events, but not organized so as to enhance analytical or cumulative effects.

CONCLUDING COMMENTS

This chapter shows clearly that organization in the secondary school is very different from that in the elementary school. The difference may reflect the secondary school's academic elitist tradition and the elementary school's origin in a popular desire for education. Organizational change at the secondary school level has been chiefly concerned with administrative structures characterized as attempts to make different subject matters more accessible to students. Flexible scheduling and the introduction of modules and minicourses are cases in point. Most of these changes can be implemented within the traditional school framework. Expansion of opportunity has also come through independent study (in which students contract with faculty to carry out special interests), the waiving of prerequisites for course enrollment, work experiences within cooperative programs with community employers, optional courses that will satisfy a subject matter requirement imposed by the state legislature, correspondence courses, advanced placement, and short interim course sessions in which students can engage in remedial study, career internships, guidance sessions, and the like.

Nevertheless, the high school remains subject-oriented and departmentalized. Organization is based around the four traditional areas of the language arts, social studies, mathematics, and science. The traditional unit of accrediting high school work, the Carnegie unit, which demands 120 hours of classroom work per unit of credit, continues to influence the scheduling patterns of courses. The greatest organizational change has been in the addition of electives and vocational education. The subject-centered structure precludes broad efforts toward interdisciplinary programs, student participation in curriculum planning, extensive independent study, and community service projects. Well-publicized accounts of computer scheduling and student self-scheduling do not reflect what happens in the majority of schools. The often criticized use of minicourses occurs in only 12 percent of the high schools. Most schools have remedial labs, over half have media production labs, and nearly half use occupational training centers. Eighty percent of secondary schools report an increased emphasis on teaching basics during the years 1970 through 1978.[11]

A great deal of attention is given to the need for reforming the secondary school. Nine major commissions, committees, councils, panels, task forces, and agencies have been involved in studying the conditions of the American public high school.[12] Their reports have pointed to the desirability of restructuring secondary schooling so that it will accommodate young people who are able to begin the transition to adulthood. There are calls to put the high school in touch with the community and with the many institutions that can

---

[11]*Education USA* 20, no. 5 (August 1978).

[12]Examples of reports emanating from national commissions are: B. Frank Brown, *The Reform of Secondary Education: A Report to the Public and the Profession*. Kettering Commission Report. The National Commission on the Reform of Secondary Education. (New York: McGraw-Hill, 1973); John H. Martin, *Report of the National Panel on High School and Adolescent Education*. National Panel on High Schools and Adolescent Education. (Washington, D.C.: U.S. Office of Education, 1974); *This We Believe*. NASSP Report. The Task Force on Secondary School in a Changing Society. The National Association of Secondary School Principals. (Reston, Va., 1975); Maurice Gibbons, *The New Secondary Education*. Phi Delta Kappa Task Force Report. (Bloomington, Ind.: Phi Delta Kappa, 1976).

contribute to the education of the young. We do not yet know how this concern for reform will be implemented in the secondary schools. The idea that young people should be involved in work experiences, in community affairs, and in tutoring of younger children seems to have merit. On the other hand, the public at large does not yet share the need for reform as stated in the various committee reports. The 1979 Gallup poll of the public's attitudes toward the schools shows that a sizable percentage of respondents want more emphasis on the basics—the 3 Rs—and higher standards. Thus the unfinished task of organizing the secondary school curriculum will probably involve balancing demands for a core curriculum of common knowledge, a continuous progress arrangement for achieving literary skills, and a variable curriculum component that will help all students excel in unique directions.

New patterns of organization are found in the elementary schools. There is much more team teaching, individualized instruction, and nongrading. The latter is implemented by offering multilevel instruction within a heterogeneous classroom, assigning children to instruction according to performance levels, and by regrouping children from time to time in order that they may work at different levels under different teachers. Learning centers, self-instructional materials, cross-age tutoring, and learning games are now commonly found in classrooms. There are also more frequent uses of volunteers—parents, senior citizens, and college students. Most of these innovations have been wed to conventional goals of reading, writing, and computing.

Organization for open education in the elementary school has been less well received. This person-centered approach does not rest on predetermined objectives but on the child's active involvement in answering questions of personal importance. The learners are free to gather information in whatever sequence is most meaningful to them. Open education rests on the assumption that children are intelligent enough to create their own way of understanding a particular subject. The teacher studies the way the children solve problems by themselves and provides materials to assist as necessary. Although only a few classrooms are truly open in America today, such aspects of open education as pupil movement, interaction, opportunity for creative expression, and manipulation of materials have been widely borrowed. Many curriculum organizers are at a loss in dealing with open education, because it seems to negate their established concepts of curriculum development such as scope, sequence, continuity, articulation, priorities, and preconceived purposes.

Open education need not be antagonistic to such principles. On the contrary, by getting the full meaning of each present experience, the learner is better prepared for that which will follow. Finding activities that will appeal to children is only the first step. These activities should stimulate new ways of observing and judging, thereby effecting continuity and articulation of facts and ideas. It is not enough that activities be "interesting," they must be linked cumulatively to each other. As John Dewey said, "The central problem of an education based upon experience is to select the kind of present experiences that live fruitfully and creatively in subsequent experiences.[13]

QUESTIONS

1. Curricula organized in accordance with "open" structure are not more likely to produce cognitive gains than traditionally organized curricula. What do you think best explains this finding? Is it that the individual teacher's attitude is more important than the curriculum or is it that tests used to measure cognitive gain do not reflect the progress that has been made? Is it possible that a program based upon the individual's own needs and interests cannot be measured by a test of common skills? Can it be that open structure is designed more to affect the attitude of the child rather than his or her cognition?
2. Indicate which of the organizational forms is both economical and effective for given purposes.

	Purposes		
Organizational forms	*Acquisition of unusual information*	*Production of a creative product*	*Active commitment to a group or cause*
Independent study			
Group discussion and decision			
Lecture			
Tutoring or private conference			

[13]John Dewey, *Experience and Education* (New York: Macmillan, 1939), p. 17.

3. Indicate which organizational approach is most appropriate for the
   listed purposes.

	Approach			
Purposes	Broad fields	Mini- course	Structured course	Affective curriculum
Continuity in a subject field				
Study of a specific problem or discrete skill				
Study issues that require extended time and draw from many disciplines				
Personal learning focusing on feelings				

4. How might a school known to you implement the recommendation that
   barriers between adolescents and community opportunities be reduced?
5. Indicate how you might schedule typical activities in either a self-
   contained or individualized classroom.

SELECTED REFERENCES

Barr, Robert D. and Bennett, Christine I., ed. "Secondary Education: A
Time of Crisis and Creativity," *Viewpoints in Teaching and Learning* 55,
no. 2 (Spring 1979).

Dunne, Faith, Rogers, Elliott, and Block, Andrew. "Beyond the Cities:
Expanding the Sense of Option Among Rural Adolescents," *Curriculum
Inquiry* 10, no. 1 (Spring 1980): 3–28.

Glatthorn, Alan A. *Alternatives in Education: Schools and Programs*. New
York: Dodd, Mead, 1975.

Lounsberry, John H. and Vars, Gordon E. *A Curriculum for the Middle
School Years*. New York: Harper and Row, 1978.

Mitchell, Douglas E. and Spady, William G. "Organizational Contexts for
Implementing Outcome Based Education," *Educational Researcher* 7,
no. 7 (August 1978): 9–17.

Newton, Robert R. "Models of Schooling and Theories of Discipline," *The
High School Journal* 63, no. 5 (February 1980): 183–91.

Rogers, Vincent R. and Church, Bud, eds. *Open Education: Critiques and
Assessment*. Washington, D.C.: ASCD, 1975.

"The Patchwork Curriculum," theme issue. *Educational Leadership* 36,
no. 2 (November 1978).

IV / ISSUES
AND TRENDS

   In the next three chapters we will examine curriculum in a wider context. Chapter 11 deals with some of the most pressing issues confronting those who would develop programs for American schools. Multicultural education, moral education, the hidden curriculum, and mainstreaming are among the issues that have implications for the conduct of the curriculum enterprise. Chapter 12 describes changes in conceptions of the academic subject matters. In most ways these conceptions articulate the culture of the moment. They also stand as early-warning devices, signaling developments that have not been generally recognized. Chapter 13 treats the policy-making complex in curriculum making. Curriculum policy refers to guides to action, including requirements about what and how to teach. This chapter tells how curriculum policy is made and explains the potential sources of conflict among policymakers.

 A study of the politics of curriculum making may help the reader become more concerned about the decision-making processes that go on at different levels. The reader should begin to ask, Who are the interest groups making curriculum decisions? What are the consequences of political solutions to curriculum questions?

11 / CURRENT ISSUES DEMANDING CURRICULUM RESPONSES

Five crucial curriculum issues—the hidden curriculum, moral education, cultural pluralism, mainstreaming, and career education —are examined in this chapter. These issues are crucial because their resolution will move the curriculum in very different ways. Here, we will give no definite set of solutions to the issues. Instead, we offer a range of views with respect to each, so that the readers will discover for themselves the grounds for choosing one position rather than another. The purpose is not to argue for one favored view but to consider all the factors that apply. A sixth issue, the international studies, is less crucial, but it is of interest to people in many countries and suggests how international cooperation can contribute to the solution of curriculum problems.

Although each issue is important in its own right, you may regard those discussed here as a sample from a large population of issues demanding curriculum responses. We recommend, therefore, that you use the descriptions of these issues as opportunities to apply the curriculum orientations you have acquired thus far. In this way you will not only be thinking about the particular issues, but also developing your ability to deal with these and any other issues from the point of view of a curriculum specialist. You may wish to examine the issues from the perspective of different curriculum conceptions or note how traditional curriculum questions are being answered by the proponents involved, for example. Using your knowledge of curriculum conceptions, you might try to analyze critically the matter of the hidden curriculum from the perspective of a social reconstructionist or criticize different views of moral education from the humanistic perspective. You may wish to treat the issue of cultural pluralism by comparing the likely responses of those with academic, technological, and social reconstructionist conceptions. If you choose to use traditional questions as a procedure for examining the issues, you might ask: "Does mainstreaming advance the ideal of a common curriculum for all? How is the subject matter of moral education related to method? Are principles of sequence applicable in the hidden curriculum?"

THE HIDDEN CURRICULUM

The term *hidden curriculum* indicates that some intentional outcomes from schooling are not formally recognized; these are unofficial instructional influences, which may either support or weaken the attainment of manifest goals. (Some curriculum specialists consider unintentional, frequently counterpositive outcomes as pects of hidden curriculum). The hidden curriculum gives rise to several important questions. Does it educate or miseducate? Whose interests are best served by it? Should curriculum workers control the hidden curriculum so that it is either harmless or a tool to further formally stated ends? Should we leave it unstudied, hidden, a natural and consummatory aspect of school experience? First, however, we should understand what is meant by the hidden curriculum. There are several definitions.

Sociological Views of the Hidden Curriculum: Informal and Nonintentional Learning Within the School

Sociologists are interested in social structures and systems. They study positions, roles, and the interactional patterns among different people. They study the uses of power and authority, and the norms and sanctions that guide behavior. Sociologists are also interested in goals and processes. They think of the schools as having functions, such as the socialization of children and preparing the young for adulthood. They distinguish between *manifest* and *latent* functions; the latter serve ends not publicly recognized or approved.

C. Wayne Gordon was one of the first to reveal the nature of an informal school system that affected what was learned—a system with a hidden curriculum. In *The Social System of the High School* Gordon advanced the idea that the individual behavior of high school students is related to their status and their roles in the school.[1] Fur-

---

[1]C. Wayne Gordon, *The Social System of the High School* (Glencoe, Ill.: The Free Press, 1957).

ther, he understood that the informal system is a subsystem within the community and the still larger complex of American society. He found that the students were involved in three "subsystems": (1) the formal scheme, curriculum, textbooks, classrooms; (2) a semiformal set of clubs and activities; and (3) the informal half-world of unrecognized cliques, factions, and other groups. He found that such unrecognized groups controlled much of adolescent behavior both in school achievement and in social conduct such as dating. There was, in fact, a network of personal and social relations. Status in this adolescent system ranged from the "big wheel" at the top to the "isolate" at the bottom. It was a powerful system, which presented a constant source of conflict to the teachers. Teachers sometimes indicated the conflict by such comments as, "Jones and his gang terrify me."

Gordon believes that teachers must recognize the expectations set by the informal system, which determines the prestige of the students, and integrate them with the formal system and its demands that students learn specific kinds of subject matter. However, any teacher's ability to adapt to this conflict is determined in part by the extent to which the principal will support the formal expectations of the system. The principal must back up the teacher when there are disturbances or disorders, for example. Also, in order to deal with the hidden curriculum of the informal system, teachers must have insight into the informal system. They should be able to identify the roles operating in informal groups (boss, brain, clown), the motivations of different cliques, and the individuals within these cliques. Armed with this knowledge, the teacher can make different responses in relation to that system. The teacher may decide, for example, to advance goals that are not part of the formal system by showing more interest in students whose value orientations are not those of the formal system. Or the teacher can consciously decide to maintain objective or "fair" relations with all students and thereby run the risk of having conflicts with potent informal student groups. The teacher may also decide to diffuse affective and other rewards selectively.

There are new trends in adolescent society today. Whereas the earlier social structure was an elaborate status system built around school-based activities, the new youth society is organized around off-campus activities and is strongly influenced by popular figures in music, art, and television. Today's youth are more concerned with self-identity than with status and conformity. Unlike former youths, they are now more likely to break with established values and beliefs, and not merely to rebel against authority. These characteristics have the following implications for curriculum: (1) Students would be unlikely to respond favorably to prescribed topics and methods that feature competitive achievement and dependence on teacher authority. Hence, cooperative methods and self-selection would be in order. (2) The values being promoted by popular figures must be examined through the curriculum. (3) More attention must be given to ways in which to evolve a value system and to judge the relative strengths of systems.

If the context of adolescent society is a most important source in determining what is to be taught as well as how it is to be taught, then a major curriculum task is to analyze the context of adolescent society in order to develop programs. This does not mean that the curriculum must reinforce what is present in the adolescent society. It may mean an attempt to weaken the power of that society. In any event, curriculum planners must keep closely in touch with out-of-school experiences of students in order to focus on the ethical situations students are facing and to offer content that will be of value to them.

Robert Dreeben, too, has written about the social setting of the school, indicating that there is more to school than experiences derived from formal structural arrangements.[2] He believes that the school has produced different outcomes than expected because of the strategies learners discover in dealing with the school's regime. Different atmospheres may produce cheats, conformists, rebels, and recluses. Pupils derive their principles of conduct from their experiences in responding to school tasks. The principles acquired vary with the particular setting. Hence, a school staff should concern itself with socialization and other effects that follow from particular elements of their hidden curriculum. The staff should ask, "What kind of character is being produced by our practices of grading, grouping, eligibility, promotion, detention, and the like?"

The Sociology of Knowledge

A quite different sociological view of the hidden curriculum comes from those who study the sociology of knowledge. By sociology of knowledge, we refer to the notion that the school is not an open

[2]Robert Dreeben, "Schooling and Authority: Comments on the Unstudied Curriculum," in *The Unstudied Curriculum*, Norman Overly, ed. (Washington, D.C.: ASCD,1970).

marketplace for ideas but that particular kinds of knowledge are selected and incorporated into the curriculum.

M. F. D. Young in England and Michael Apple in the United States are prominent for their contention that specific social groups are unduly generating and distributing particular content and that this content affects the thinking and feelings of students in support of existing social institutions. Accordingly, curriculum materials bear ideological messages to which most of us are unconscious. Jean Anyon, for example, examined the knowledge in history textbooks and inferred that after reading these books students would be lead to believe that governmental reform and labor-management cooperation are successful methods of social recourse, whereas confrontation and strikes are failures; that the poor are responsible for their own poverty, and poverty is a consequence of the failure of individuals rather than of the failure of society to distribute economic resources universally; that there is no working class in the United States—workers are middle class. The author argues that just as the school curriculum has hitherto supported patterns of power and domination, so can it be used to foster autonomy and social change.[3]

The sociology of knowledge extends our definitions of the hidden curriculum by the assumption that there are hidden messages in curriculum materials—messages that influence by showing the world as certain social groups want the world to be seen by students.

Other Views of the Hidden Curriculum

Lawrence Kohlberg has proposed that the hidden curriculum can be a vehicle for moral growth.[4] He would have teachers and administrators get beyond the ideas that respect for law and order constitute moral character and that the ultimate end of moral education is loyalty to the school. Kohlberg would use the hidden curriculum to reflect an atmosphere of justice, giving all a chance to share in planning and executing activities, and in gaining the rewards of what they have accomplished as part of fair play. Benson Snyder, a psychiatrist, reinforces the importance of attending to the hidden curriculum but does not prescribe what the teacher should do. He has said that he knows of no school that is without a hidden curriculum that affects students and faculty. He believes that this curriculum, more

[3]Jean Anyon, "Ideology and United States History Textbooks," *Harvard Educational Review* 49, no. 3 (August 1979): 361–86.

[4]Lawrence Kohlberg, "The Moral Atmosphere of the School," in *The Unstudied Curriculum*, Norman Overly, ed. (Washington, D.C.: ASCD, 1970).

than the formal curriculum, determines to a significant degree all participants' sense of worth and self-esteem.[5]

The hidden curriculum has been found to be one of the determining factors in integration. Robert Wolf and Rita Simon, for example, completed a sociometric study showing how seven years of busing affected friendship groups.[6] Their findings suggest that both white and black children want to feel a part of the mainstream and that they will select friends on that basis. The greatest number of cross-racial friendships occurred when black and white children were bused in from the same neighborhood. The data from the Wolf and Simon study also suggest that more than busing or placing children in the same institution is necessary to achieve integration. Busing children into a "good" school, one noted for its responsiveness to the needs of individual children, produced few reciprocal friendships. White children did not tend to select black children as their friends, despite the fact that blacks often chose them. Integration requires attending to the hidden curriculum by manipulating both formal and informal systems through conscious and well-intentioned nurturance of pupil interactions. The staff must create specific programs and strategies for interactions across race, not leaving friendships, communications, and cultural understanding to chance. There are practical suggestions on how to help children make friends. One effective way to encourage cross-racial choices, for example, is to provide situations in which children can discover similarities of interests and attitudes or work together for a common good.

There is one final and quite different view of the hidden curriculum. Many school offerings have latent functions that serve special interest groups outside the school more than they serve the pupils themselves. Some courses, for example, may have the hidden or unrecognized purpose of creating student demand for commercial products. It is likely that driver training programs, which use late model cars, increase learners' desire to purchase cars, especially cars of a recent vintage. Indeed, Frederick McGuire and R. C. Kersh found that driver education courses in high schools do not lead to the prevention of accidents.[7] They concluded that the interests of automobile-related industries were being served. Similarly, many high school home economics courses may be kept well equipped with

[5]Benson Snyder, *The Hidden Curriculum* (New York: Alfred A. Knopf, 1970).
[6]Robert L. Wolf and Rita J. Simon, "Does Busing Improve the Racial Interactions of Children?" *Educational Researcher* 4, no. 1 (January 1975): 5–11.
[7]Frederick McGuire and R.C. Kersh, *An Experimental Evaluation of Driver Education* (Berkeley, Calif.: University of California Press, 1970).

the latest appliances in order that young persons will expect to purchase such items when establishing their own homes.

Suggestions for making the hidden curriculum more consistent with the ideals of the formal curriculum have been proposed by Henry Giroux. He recommends such actions as doing away with those properties of the hidden curriculum that are associated with alienation—rigid time schedules, tracking, control through tests, fragmentation in content, and competitions.[8]

MORAL EDUCATION

Moral concern is in the present American atmosphere. The American people are raising questions about what is right or wrong and what values should guide them to right actions. Conflicts of conscience are found in such issues as sex, race, drugs, politics, and death. People are becoming increasingly aware that without a moral base, no governmental, technological, or material approach to these issues will suffice. Hence, curriculum developers, too, are animated by an undercurrent of moral concern. The question, however, of how best to take advantage of this creative moment is not a simple one. A number of possible outlooks can be used to guide our conceptions of a moral curriculum.

Philip Phenix has pinpointed the basic question in moral education as one about the values, standards, or norms that are to be used and the sources and justification for these norms.[9] He sees four orientations that one can take: the nihilistic, autonomic, heteronomic, and telenomic positions.

The nihilistic position is a denial that there are any standards of right or wrong, of better or worse. Nihilists hold that all human endeavor appears meaningless and without purpose. This position is contrary to the notion of education as a purposeful activity and to its improvement.

The autonomic position is the view that there are norms or values and that their source of justification is the person who makes them. It is the individual who invests existence with meaning. The holder of this view believes that values are manmade and that all standards are relative to the persons and societies that make them. This position's

[8]Henry A. Giroux, "Developing Educational Programs: Overcoming the Hidden Curriculum," *The Clearing House* 52, no. 4 (December 1978): 148–52.

[9]Philip H. Phenix, "The Moral Imperative in Contemporary American Education," *Perspectives on Education* 11, no. 2 (Winter 1969): 6–14.

implications for curriculum are many. Inasmuch as human beings make their own values, their schools should *not* teach people how they *ought* to behave. All one can teach is how a particular person or group has decided to behave. Students then learn to display skill in adjusting to the varieties of values present so as to maintain a somewhat congruent social scheme. As Phenix says, "It is not a question of learning what is right or wrong, but what is socially expedient." This position transfers value issues to the political area without reference to moral ends. It is not a question of what is good or right but of who has the power to prevail. Also, it causes the curriculum to be judged in terms of its effectiveness in promoting autonomous interests and demands.

The heteronomic position asserts that there are known standards and values that can be taught and that provide clear norms of judgment for human conduct. People do not make values, they discover them. These moral laws are sometimes seen as originating with the divine. Sometimes they are regarded as rationally and intuitively deduced demands apprehended by moral sensibility. Curriculum persons who hold the heteronomic position urge the adoption of strong programs of a religious or ethical nature in order to restore lost values to the young. They also have a pedagogical commitment to transmit established standards of belief and conduct.

Phenix himself believes that each of the above positions fails to provide a basis for moral education; each is wanting. The nihilistic position cuts the nerve of moral inquiry and negates moral conscience. The autonomic position substitutes political strategy for morality and allows no objective basis for judging the worth of human creations. The heteronomic position is characterized by ethnocentrism and is untenable in light of the staggering multiplicity of norms by which people have lived.

Phenix's answer is a fourth position—the *telenomic*. This is a theory that morality is grounded on a comprehensive purpose or "telos" that is objective and normative, but that forever transcends concrete institutional embodiment or ideology. It rests on the belief that persons should engage in a progressive discovery of what they ought to do—a dedication to an objective order of values in the domain of human choices. The moral enterprise is seen as a venture of faith, but not in the sense of a blind adherence to a set of precepts that cannot be rationally justified. People preserve what is right through the imperfect institutions of society. They know, however, that these institutions will be subject to criticism and held up to an ideal order that can never be attained. A curriculum in accordance with the telenomic outlook would foster dialogue to make moral inquiry a life-long practice. One would want to do right, not merely be satisfied in getting one's own way. One would also see that what is right is a complicated matter, that personal judgments are made on the basis of one's own experience, and that these judgments are extremely partial and unreliable. Hence, a person needs to associate with others who can correct his or her misunderstandings and bring other perspectives to bear. The learner, too, would perceive that every value determination is subject to further scrutiny and revision in light of new understandings.

In the domain of moral education, the schools should develop skills in moral deliberation through focus on personal and social problems, bringing to bear relevant perspectives from a variety of specialized dimensions. Sex education, for example, would be considered with the knowledge of biologists, physicians (conception, abortion, pathologies), psychologists (affects, motivation, sublimation), social scientists (family, patterns of sexual behavior in diverse cultures), humanists (literary meaning of sex, historical perspectives), and philosophers and theologians (creation, nature, and destiny of the person, meaning of human relatedness, sanctity of the person, significance of loyalty). In the end, individuals would respond in conscience to the persuasion of the right that commends itself to them. What matters from an educational standpoint is that the decision emerges from a well-informed mind, not from haphazard impulses and accident of personal history.

Much of the current writing regarding moral education in schools features the work of two men, Lawrence Kohlberg and Sidney Simon, who are having an effect on practice. Their approaches, however, are not as comprehensive as Phenix's, which deals with all dimensions of moral behavior, not just the intellectual. As indicated in Chapter 6, Kohlberg has attempted to define stages of moral development ranging from the learner's response to cultural values of good and bad to the making of decisions on the basis of universal principles of justice.[10] He regards his stages as stages of moral reasoning. Thus, his assessment of the learner's status is made by analyzing the learner responses to hypothetical problems or moral dilemmas. Kohlberg admits that one can reason in terms of principles and yet not live up to these principles. He defends his work by claiming that the narrow focus on moral judgment is the most important factor in

[10]Lawrence Kohlberg, *Hypothetical Dilemmas for Use in the Classroom* (Cambridge, Mass.: Moral Education Research Foundation, Harvard University, 1978).

moral behavior. Other factors, which admittedly bear upon moral behavior, are not distinctively moral because there can be no moral behavior without informed mature moral judgment.

Kohlberg is now moving away from attempts to verify his stages and is beginning to tell us how to stimulate moral development. He would, for instance, expose the learner to the next higher stage of moral reasoning, present contradictions to the child's current moral structure, and allow for dialogue in which conflicting moral views are compared in an open manner. Further, he is now engaged in a four-year curriculum in English and social studies centering on moral discussions, on role taking and communication, and on relating the government, laws, and justice of the school to those of the American society and other world societies.[11]

The chief criticism of Kohlberg's view of moral education is that he has omitted important dimensions of moral education. He does not allow for utilitarian ideas of morality in which principles of justice can be problematic. He does not give enough emphasis to the need for conventional morality among all citizens in order for our society to function. He fails to appreciate that moral rules often have to be learned in the face of counter-inclinations. He has not attended to the affective dimensions of morality such as guilt, remorse, and concern for others, and he offers no suggestions for developing other factors, such as will, which are necessary in moral conduct.[12]

Louis Raths and Sidney Simon have another approach to moral education called *value clarification*. In value clarification the teachers elicit the child's own opinion about issues in which values conflict, rather than imposing their own opinions.[13] Value clarificationists see the exploration of personal preferences as helping people: (1) be more purposeful because they must rank their priorities; (2) be more productive because they analyze where their activities are taking them; (3) be more critical because they learn to see through other people's foolishness; and (4) have better relations with others. The approach is limited, however; it does not go much beyond helping one become more aware of one's own values. Value clarification assumes there is no single correct answer. Learners discuss moral dilemmas to reveal different values. One criticism of value clarifica-

---

[11]David Purpel and Kevin Ryan, eds., *Moral Education . . . It Comes with the Territory* (Berkeley, Calif.: McCutchan, 1976).

[12]Richard S. Peters, "A Reply to Kohlberg," *Phi Delta Kappan* 56, no. 10 (June 1975): 678.

[13]Louis E. Raths, Merrill Harmin, and Sidney B. Simon, *Values and Teaching*, 2nd ed. (Columbus, Ohio: Merrill, 1978).

tion centers on its reliance on peer pressure, the bias of many of the questions used in the process, a premature demand for public affirmation and action, and its moral relativism. Surely, morality is more than a matter of undebatable personal feelings.

Both Kohlbergians and value clarificationists are beginning to respond to their critics and now admit that there is moral content to their programs. Value clarificationists, for example, say they value rationality, creativity, justice, freedom, equality, and self-esteem.

Andrew Oldenquist, however, has raised more serious criticism of both approaches to moral education.[14] Neither approach has been able to show that the values and morality they wish to teach are rationally justifiable. The value clarificationists do not believe in rational justification and Kohlberg does not show teachers how actually to do moral reasoning. Oldenquist says that both the value clarification and cognitive development point of view lead to indoctrination, not moral neutrality. They indoctrinate by pretending to be neutral in moral discussions while subtly inculcating their own values and moral outlook without reasons or argument. Oldenquist wants students to acquire a morality composed of (1) personal virtues such as courage, temperance, and a willingness to work for what one wants but lacks, and (2) moral attitudes such as honesty and the abandonment of violence and theft that a safe and satisfying society requires. His justification for these moral qualities is straightforward and in order to accomplish these moral goals, he looks to teachers who are themselves morally earnest, self-confident about moral education, and capable of engaging in moral reasoning.

In short, although there is much agreement that programs of moral education would strengthen the curriculum, there is great division as to what such a program should be. People disagree on the relationship between a moral judgment and actual conduct. Some people are not satisfied with having pupils learn only to recognize the right thing to do; they want pupils to do the right thing. A number of different expectations can be held for a curriculum in moral education. Curriculum makers must decide whether they want learners to act for a reason, to respect other people's interests, to be logically consistent, to identify their own and others' feelings, or to act in accordance with the laws. In developing moral curriculum, it is a good rule, however, to stress the principle of respecting persons and considering the harm or benefit that the adoption of particular moral rules might have.

[14]Andrew Oldenquist, "Moral Education Without Moral Education," *Harvard Educational Review* 49, no. 2 (May 1979): 240–47.

CULTURAL PLURALISM
AND THE CURRICULUM

Boards of education historically have resisted a differentiated curriculum for Italians, blacks, Chicanos, and other ethnic, racial, and religious groups. Indications of a reversal in the "melting pot" concept appeared in the early 1970s. At this time, ethnic minority studies appeared in many schools. These were usually studies established in response to black, Mexican-American, Puerto Rican, or Oriental demands for content sensitive to their cultural experiences. American history was updated and interpreted from different points of view, which revealed the mistreatment of minority groups by the dominant white culture, the contributions of the minority groups and their leaders, and the social problems they face. These studies were offered as supplementary units, and as enrichment within existing courses such as literature or history.

Such ethnic studies soon lost their popularity for various reasons: rivalry among minority group members regarding what the content should be, fear that the studies were increasing the minorities' isolation, and the failure of our institutions to recognize the studies as intellectually viable. Eventually, efforts were made to refocus the studies. The refocusing led to new content treating intricate cultural patterns of different minority groups and the factors that account for their cultural distinctiveness with the idea of helping students learn how and why minorities think, behave, and perceive as they do. Curricula included plans to teach the black, Mexican-American, or Oriental student reading, social studies, math, and other subjects in terms of each child's own cultural perspective. Also, multicultural studies were seen as valuable for all students. Acquisition of different perspectives on personal and social problems were thought to be helpful in understanding the conflicts in values that paralyze our nation. It was recommended, too, that students become aware of the many ways in which all human groups are alike, both biologically and culturally.

By 1974, cultural pluralism embraced many aims. Among them were mutual appreciation and understanding of various cultures in the society; cooperation of the diverse groups in the society's institutions; coexistence of different life styles, language, religious beliefs, and family structures; and autonomy for each subcultural group to work out its own social future without interfering with the rights of other groups.[15] Bilingual education in which students learn to speak, read, and write in both their native language and a second language also gained in popularity. Not all schools moved in these directions, however. Indeed, individual schools could be placed at different points along a separatism–cultural pluralism continuum. James Deslonde at Stanford University identified six stages by which schools could be characterized.[16]

1. *Separatism.* Schools voluntarily separate along ethnic racial lines. The staff emphasizes academic preparation, cultural identity, ethnic studies, studies of inequality, and a matching of the programs to the community's cultural style.
2. *Segregation* Schools involuntarily separate students. School leaders tend to deny the problems of diversity and try to maintain a status quo. Persons in these schools devote attention to operational concerns, giving more attention to bus schedules and pupil placement than to modifications in the curriculum. Teachers may receive cultural sensitivity training.
3. *Desegregation.* Schools physically rearrange children and try to fit the child to the school environment. Some children are bused. In early stages of desegregation, much energy is spent on processes and little on the curriculum. Usually, when rearranging children, districts find that just putting children side by side does not do the job. There may be preliminary ethnic study activities.
4. *Post-desegregation.* Schools have new goals programs, such as social studies, that include content aimed at the prevailing minority group. Teachers acquire new skills. The Third World child takes part in either skill development programs or cultural awareness sessions. There is emphasis on diagnosing academic weaknesses.
5. *Integration.* Achievement problems of Third World children are attacked in the following ways: more appropriate evaluation techniques, in-service training of teachers, low-level community involvement, and alternative classroom organizational patterns. Curriculum content is revised to include ethnic studies, cultural

[15]Robert J. Havighurst, "The American Indian: From Assimilation to Cultural Pluralism," *Educational Leadership* 31, no. 7 (April 1974): 585–89.
[16]James Deslonde, "Distinctive Features of a Minority-Oriented Needs Assessment," address at Conference on Administrative Strategies for Pluralistic Education sponsored by Far West Laboratory for Educational Research and Development, Phoenix, Arizona, April 17, 1975.

infusion, nontraditional content, affective concerns, and different kinds of teaching strategies.

6. *Cultural pluralism.* Schools have new instructional goals, including the acquisition of cooperative skills and social analysis techniques. There is less concern about achievement. Cultural differences are emphasized. Students conduct inquiry into human development. They ask, "What makes us ethnically unique?" There is heavy focus on values and how they are formed. The traditional role of teachers is changed. There is much community and parent involvement. Dysfunctional structural impediments to learning are removed. There are new organizational patterns to meet cultural and ethnic differences of children.

By studying the continuum, the curriculum person can see where a given school lies and where it must move if the multicultural ideal is to be fulfilled. In treating the issue of cultural pluralism as applied to curriculum, it is well to think of alternatives. We can have some common ends and common means. Interpersonal skills and cross-group friendships are common ends. Activities for achieving these ends require the same experiences or learning opportunities for all. We can consider having common ends and different means. Students of all races, for example, should feel positive about the school, but the means for attaining this goal may differ. In order to reduce alienation and anxiety about the school, attention must be given to ethnic perceptions of what is taking place. A staff might want to modify traditional competitive ways of working to allow for newer cooperative patterns more consistent with minority expectations. It might also want to introduce new activities that are more rewarding to minority students to give them a better chance of reaching the common goal.

We can propose the controversial idea of having both different ends and different means. Ethnic groups that consider it desirable that children discipline their own expressions in the presence of an elder might request the school to treat their children accordingly. Teachers might use culture-matching strategies such as the use of nonverbal acceptance. They might consider, for example, a greater use of touch with the Mexican-American child.

We can avoid trying to apply generalizations about ethnic and cultural groups and let each learner freely choose the ends and means he or she wants. In order to do this, we must recognize the danger of stereotyping individuals on the basis of group membership. We will need a range of goals, and procedures for achieving them. We will need to ask how best to introduce or generate the options so that the learner can best make a considered rather than a random choice.

The current overriding cultural pluralistic issue centers on bilingual education. Advocates of bilingual education claim that it (1) reduces academic retardation by allowing non-English-speaking students to learn in their native languages immediately; (2) reinforces the relationship of the school and the home; (3) offers the minority student an atmosphere conducive to the development of personal identification, self-worth, and achievement; and (4) preserves and enriches the cultural and human resources of a people. Those who oppose bilingual education fear that encouraging the use of languages other than English and foreign cultural values will be divisive to American society, furthering political divison along ethnic lines and hindering the assimilation of minority students into the mainstream of American life.

A much discussed question is whether bilingual programs should regard the use of another language as *transitional*—a temporary means of instruction until the child acquires enough English to profit from instruction in English—or whether the bilingual program should be *maintained*, extending the child's language development in the native language and the child's acquisition of the culture associated with it.

The matter of whether bilingual/bicultural education programs should be only for non-English-speaking students or those with limited English is also pressing. Some advocate that the monolingual English-speaking student should be included in such programs. Indeed, the Commission on Multicultural Education of the Association for Supervision and Curriculum Development (ASCD) has stated:

> Implementation of multicultural education is vital at this point in our history. All our aspirations toward improvement of education for *all* children are tied to the success of multicultural education. Multicultural education is a tool for elimination of diverse forms of discrimination in regard to race, class, age, physical size, and handicaps.[17]

Briefly, minority group pressure for equity in education has been greatly accelerated by federal legislation for bilingual and ethnic studies. There are a variety of extant curriculum approaches to multicultural education—special programs for culturally different

---

[17]Carl A. Grant, ed., *Multicultural Education: Commitment, Issues, and Applications* (Washington, D.C.: ASCD, 1977), p. 4.

students, programs where all students learn about cultural differences, programs that try to preserve and extend cultural pluralism
into American society, and programs that try to produce learners
who can operate successfully in two different cultures.

MAINSTREAMING

Mainstreaming is another kind of integration: it is the
inclusion of handicapped children in the mainstream of child care
and education. Mainstreaming is partly a response to legislative and
judicial decisions, but many people believe that it can benefit both
the handicapped and the so-called normal. There are, however,
ethical and practical issues related to successful mixing.

In practical terms, mainstreaming means that many mildly handicapped children are integrated into regular classes on a part- or full-
time basis. Each handicapped child is provided with an Individualized Education Program (IEP) consisting of (1) a description of the
child's present level of functioning, (2) short- and long-term educational goals, (3) specific services to be provided, (4) starting time and
expected duration of services, and (5) evaluation criteria to be used in
determining whether objectives are being achieved. IEPs offer flexibility in programming. Children may remain in a regular program
for those subjects in which they have strength, while at the same time
receiving remedial assistance in a special setting. Parents, teachers, a
learning specialist, and, if appropriate, the child together prepare the
IEP.

Arguments for Mainstreaming

Equal opportunity for all is the overriding premise that courts use
in ruling that physical and mentally different children have the right
to share with others in education. Instead of being confined to special
education classes and specialized institutions such as schools for the
deaf, handicapped children can now be placed with normal children
so that they can learn to make inevitable adjustments to the larger
world, to play and work with all manner of people, and to gain self-
confidence. Some think it is good, too, for the intellectually dull to
learn about the weaknesses of the gifted and for the gifted to learn the
humanity of the dull.

Mainstreaming is seen as a way to meet the special needs of the
handicapped child within the integrated classroom. Some educators,

too, see the placement of those with obvious special needs in conventional classrooms as a device to draw teacher attention to everyone's individual differences. They view mainstreaming as an innovation with the potential for changing the system to better serve all children. It is also assumed that the general conditions for optimizing physical, emotional, and intellectual growth are pretty much the same for everyone.

Problems in Mainstreaming

Thus far, the benefits promoted by the early mainstreaming movement have not been shown.[18] Discussion of the problem focuses on the fact that both the term *mainstreaming* and the term *least restricted environment*, which was actually used in legislation effecting national policy on the education of all handicapped children (Public Law 94-142), do not provide specific enough mandates to provide a single course of action. The problem of implementing a least restrictive environment, or alternative environments, centers on the distinction between a model of instruction versus a mode of instruction. The former implies a method for delivering services; while the latter implies the method, techniques, tactics, and strategies used to effect change in the learner's behavior. Current models of the least restrictive environment serve more to identify administrative arrangements than to specify appropriate modes of instruction.

The majority of mainstreaming programs use a variation of (1) the learning disability group model (student receives additional assistance in the regular classroom); (2) a combination class model (student is placed in a regular small-group classroom where special materials are available); (3) a resource room model (student leaves the regular classroom for special instruction for certain periods of the day); and (4) a partial integration model (student spends part of the day in both regular and special classrooms).

Implementing the principle of placing handicapped individuals in the least restricted setting required and appropriate for the individual's needs is difficult because (1) there is little likelihood of creating least restrictive environments a priori without reference to the particular individual to be served, and (2) there is little agreement on the part of educators, parents, and children regarding what constitutes an acceptable standard for success in least restrictive settings.

Most opposition to mainstreaming centers on teacher concerns and

[18]Ted L. Miller and Marvey N. Switzky, "PL 94-142 and the Least Restrictive Alternative," *Journal of Education* 161, no. 3 (Summer 1979): 60–80.

the lack of a sufficient service-delivery model. Not all teachers are willing to mainstream handicapped children. The opposition of many of these teachers can be overcome by informing them about the limitations and assets of these children. Teachers need to be acquainted with the background of the specific disabilities involved and helped to see the strengths and weaknesses the child has as an individual. Teachers must be equipped to deal with such problems as caring for the handicapped without shortchanging others. They need to learn how to provide for safety and arrange learning situations so that all children have frequent opportunities to succeed. Most of all, they need help in establishing an accepting attitude among all of the children. There are, however, some teachers who should not receive handicapped children. These are teachers whose reactions make it difficult for the so-called normal children to be natural, understanding, and accepting.

The lack of a suitable service-delivery model could be remedied by better communication between teachers and special educators, who might assist in classrooms. Special educators could inform teachers of assistance available from outside agencies such as the United Palsy Association and local therapists. A good service-delivery model might provide for itinerant teachers who could help the regular teacher acquire needed skills. The model should offer administrative options in terms of resource rooms and other partial day plans. The teachers should have opportunities to learn about placement and reintegration procedures, and they should have the help that parents can give regarding how best to work with their own children.

Mainstreaming and the Curriculum

Frank Hewett at UCLA is an educator in special education who has spoken of the curriculum implications of intergrating the mildly retarded child into regular classrooms. Hewett believes that we must broaden our conception of curriculum. Instead of emphasizing the skills of reading, writing, and arithmetic, he says, we should aim for such important and generalizable skills as learner participation—overt responding and attending. Other goals of importance to Hewett are persistency and the ordering of tasks; the learner should show improvement in finishing something and arranging parts into wholes. Priority should be given to teaching retarded children how to make independent decisions. They should acquire social competencies, learning, for example, when and when not to make certain kinds of comments to others (how to keep from putting one's foot in one's mouth). In short, Hewett's curriculum would upset many current and probably overdrawn notions about what are fixed characteristics of the retarded (that they are rigid, iterative, insensitive, and dependent). Instead, a new curriculum would aim at showing the strengths of the handicapped and the peaks and valleys that all of us have.

The attainment of these new goals would occur as the classroom is orchestrated by the teacher. The classroom would offer multisensory stimulation and movement, which are powerful reinforcers for the child's active participation. There would be order centers, in which puzzles, pegboards, matching tasks, and other activities would help pupils acquire basic concepts. Orchestration would incorporate academic lessons into social studies projects and crafts activities. It would include schemes for forming friendship groups and situations in which retarded children can observe peers who are socialization models. Too often, we let the handicapped see only what they should not do.

Mainstreaming is a social experiment. The philosophical commitment is ahead of research and practice. In order to understand better the potential of all our learners we will need both fresh conceptions of what to teach and the creative orchestration of learning environments.

CAREER EDUCATION

Spokespersons for career education have defined it differently. Some emphasize the opportunities it gives the learner to experience work directly in formal and informal situations. Others define it as a plan by which individuals can be oriented to the world of work and become more productively involved in the work force. Still others regard career education as a total effort of school and community to help all persons become familiar with the values of a work-oriented society. According to this perspective, career education is an attempt to move beyond the aim of producing uncritical workers for a labor market. It is helping expanding minds to dissociate work from economic exploitation and material acquisition and to regard careers as viable sources of human dignity and freedom.

However, several characteristics seem essential to career education. It should be provided to all students and involve all educators. Further, it is a system that should make available a life-long continuum of educational opportunities.

Some proponents of career education have as a goal that every student, particularly at the high school level, should leave school with a salable skill (yet, predicting the salability of vocational skills is less than 50 percent accurate). Still others see career education as a guidance-oriented approach that aims at helping individuals make decisions about careers and how to achieve them. Accordingly, it involves participation of "academic" and "vocational" educators, home, business, industry, labor, and personnel agencies in programs ranging from kindergarten through the university. Others, such as James O'Toole, argue that schools are failing to prepare youth for workaday life, and that this failure occurs, not in vocational skills, but in the prime educational functions of teaching young people to read, write, and behave ethically.[19]

Career education has received strong support. Vocational educators, secondary school principals, members of chambers of commerce, directors of educational testing services, and leaders in the Department of Health, Education, and Welfare have promoted its ideals. These supporters have cited several benefits that will come from its use. They say that it will improve motivation of students and improve learning. Students will see that English, reading, writing, and math are not busy work or abstract intellectual exercises but have direct usefulness. It will give success to those individuals who now fail when judged exclusively on their academic abilities. It will help individuals find careers that are more likely to be satisfying and rewarding. It will break down the walls between academic and vocational education. It will make better use of the community's educational resources. School and community facilities will be open for longer periods of time and for more days per year. Capital expenditures may be reduced or offset. And lastly, the supporters of career education say, the involvement of the total community in the education process may restore public confidence in schooling.

Opposition to career education is found among some education professors and members of such groups as the Council for Basic Education, labor organizations, women's organizations, and spokespersons for minorities who see the concept as a weapon of oppression. The opposition argues that career education's focus on occupational preparation for all is antiintellectual and will result in a watering down of academic excellence. They also accuse it of being antihumanistic and subverting the development of the individual to the

---

[19]James O'Toole, "Education is Education, and Work is Work," *Teachers College Record* 81, no. 1 (Fall 1979): 5–21.

mechanistic aims of business and industry. As two educators observe: "The heart of the career education movement is an ideological commitment to a corporate social order."[20] Minorities fear that career education is likely to channel people into narrow occupational tracks, thus continuing to deny certain racial groups and women full access to all career fields. And, the opponents say, career education is going to be costly and take away resources from other more valuable programs.

Many states and local communities are clearly serious about creating a total integration of occupational and academic programs featuring the characteristics of career education. Federal, state, and local funds are being allotted to career education. New partnerships between education and industry are being formed. Among those states leading the career education movement are New Jersey, Arizona, Oregon, Maryland, Ohio, North Carolina, Wisconsin, Texas, Washington, Michigan, California, and Louisiana. Career-oriented materials are being produced; school laws are being rewritten to allow young people to engage in work experiences as part of their educational program; and interdisciplinary teams of teachers are being trained to relate their content areas to a broad spectrum of career clusters. Thus far, however, the ideals of career education have not been fully implemented in a single system.

Several states have programs at all grade levels. In elementary schools, it is common to combine technical activities with the usual elementary subjects. Classrooms feature learning center modules, some of which include hand tools and portable power tools. Students work with a variety of materials in "learning episodes" that range from writing poems for silkscreen reproduction to exploring electricity. In keeping with the idea that career education must be liberating, elementary teachers are asked to invent ways of teaching that reflect the value of human development over technological skill and subject matter expertise. A teacher may capitalize, for example, on the tentative career choices of pupils, using the motivation inherent in their choices to encourage exploration.

The following are illustrations of the concepts taught in the elementary classroom:

People have many kinds of careers.
Every occupation contributes to society.
Every person can have a meaningful career.

---

[20]Robert J. Nash and Russell M. Agne, "Career Education: Earning a Living or Living a Life," *Phi Delta Kappan* 54, no. 6 (February 1973): 373–78.

Careers require different knowledge, abilities, and attitudes.

Individuals develop their own ways of working, such as a preference for working alone or in the company of others, and some careers suit these preferences better than others.

These concepts are advanced through such activities as having children collect hats that are worn in certain occupations from parents and friends. The hats are placed in a large box. Children draw them out one at a time and tell where they have seen someone wearing the hat, what the person did, and how this work contributed to life in the community. Children might be asked to demonstrate or act out the occupations associated with the respective hats and the occupational requirements and rewards of the worker.

At the middle or junior high level, students usually explore occupations in different cluster areas by going on field trips, talking to resource persons, and working in the shop. Occupational work adjustment programs for fourteen- to sixteen-year-old students who are likely to drop out of school are also undertaken in order to prove to such students that they are worth something and to encourage them to stay in school. Career education is often seen as a way of meeting the individual needs and interests of the middle and junior high student. Hence, the curriculum provides experiences that enable students consciously to elicit information about themselves in relation to the broadest possible range of career-oriented activities.

Often, students first explore broad occupational groups such as service, business, outdoors, technology. Next, they explore occupational "families" within groups; and last, they get acquainted with clusters or single occupations within a "family." The following objectives for career education are commonly used at the junior high level:

1. Knowledge of characteristics and requirements of different courses and occupations. The student should know the relationship between the school curriculum and occupational "families," for example, and be able to identify some jobs that might become obsolete and to tell why.
2. Knowledge of the relationship between personal characteristics and occupational requirements.
3. Ability to communicate, use numbers, interact with other people, and use other skills related to a field of interest.
4. Possession of positive attitude toward work.

It is recommended that exploration activities be fused into school subjects through resource units so as to facilitate both career development and subject matter objectives. Most existing courses would be greatly strengthened by relating subject matter to application in work through such activities as projects, interviews, visitations, and simulated and direct work experiences.

Senior high schools feature "quick shot" vocational minicourses for seniors, community learning programs in which students earn academic credits in field experiences within the community, and skill centers for training in various occupations. The practice of establishing vocational schools for secondary and postsecondary school students continues, although it is at odds with the career education goal of blending the academic and vocational offerings.

The goals of career education are modified gradually from seventh grade to tenth grade in the direction of specificity. These goals call for graduates from formal schooling to have knowledge of the value of work, a personal set of work values, one or more clusters of occupations in which to build a career, a salable skill, and knowledge of where additional training and experience can be acquired in the pursuit of desired careers.

In a high school course students might study newspapers to help them in setting career education goals. One activity might be to study two editions of forty or so daily newspapers from various parts of the country, using the same two dates for all papers. Students compare the information in the various newspapers, noting aspects of the locales that might influence career choices (for example, cost of living, quality of life, employment opportunities). This activity affords a chance to discuss subtle aspects of life style, such as the effect of climate, and to apply most school subjects. One would use math for comparing wages and costs of living, science for studying efforts to control pollution and weather, social science for investigating social attitudes, and language arts for comparing writing styles.

The issue of career education allows us to clarify our values of work. We can view work as necessary but unpleasant. Educating persons toward this view would most likely develop a cleavage between their expectations of life and their behavior, making it difficult for personality to achieve integrity. Such a negative outlook may result from the failure to match the work required with the interests and abilities of the individual person. In contrast, we can affirm that work is a satisfying opportunity for personal fulfillment—a privilege. Persons can be educated to view work as an attractive and enjoyable pursuit. This affirmation assumes that work contributes to a person's sense of the meaning of life. A sense of meaninglessness arises from the failure to connect what one does with what one thinks is important.

Critics of career education are afraid that prevailing social powers are not dedicated to the optimum fulfillment of the individual person and that work will be demanded that is destructive of fundamental human characteristics. Work is humanizing or dehumanizing depending on whether workers use tools or are themselves merely a tool. The attitude toward career education seems to be "it depends." If career education will focus on ways to change careers so that they improve people's lives, it will hasten progress. Students might be helped to select careers on the basis of whether the work promises human enhancement rather than power, profit, and prestige. If work emphasizes only the values of the corporate state—the skills and attitudes of production, competition, and conformity—it will not be liberating.

INTERNATIONAL STUDIES

International studies have raised curriculum issues about whether the school can be effective in some areas—such as science—but not in others. Educators have become disturbed by findings from the studies suggesting that many prized notions, such as size of class, teacher characteristics, and instructional methods, are not correlated with achievement. The methodology used in the studies has become an issue in itself.

Since 1959, the International Association for the Evaluation of Education has been engaged in survey research describing what children know in different countries of the world. The association's aim is to explain the factors that account for cross-national differences and to predict the consequences of certain arrangements. The Six Subject Survey, for example, completed in 1973, covered practically all of the principal academic subjects in the secondary curriculum, except for classical languages, in some twenty countries. Three aspects of the studies are of particular interest: the results, the generalizations that have implications for curriculum, and the complexities of the problems in cross-cultural measurement.

Comparative achievement in the academic subjects has been reported in several volumes of International Studies reports.[21] One

[21]L.C. Comber and J.P. Keeves, *Science Education in Nineteen Countries: An Empirical Study, International Studies in Evaluation I* (Stockholm: Almqvist and Wiksell, 1973); A.C. Purves, *Literature Education in Ten Countries: An Empirical Study, International Studies in Evaluation II* (Stockholm: Almqvist and Wiksell, 1973); J.B. Carroll, *French as a Foreign Language in Seven Countries* (Stockholm: Almqvist and Wiksell, 1974); E.G. Lewis, *English as a Foreign Language in Ten Countries* (Stockholm: Almqvist and Wiksell, 1974); R.F. Farnen et al., *Civic Education in Ten Countries* (Stockholm: Almqvist and Wiksell, 1974).

fact shown is the gap in achievement between children in the wealthy developed nations and children in the poor developing countries. In economically advanced countries, the tests of fourteen-year-olds showed Japan, Hungary, and Australia first, second, and third, respectively, in science; the United States ranked fifth. On reading comprehension, New Zealand and Italy were first and second, with the United States, Finland, French Belgium, and Scotland tied for third. Reading scores in three developing nations—Chile, India, and Iran—are so low in comparison that fourteen-year-old students seem almost illiterate. The tests show that the performance of more able students is not adversely affected when more students are retained in the upper grades. Growth in achievement from ages ten to fourteen and fourteen to eighteen appears to be primarily due to maturation.

Among the most important generalizations from the findings are these:

1. Home background is the best predictor of achievement.
2. Science learning seems more school-based than other subjects, and achievement in this field is associated with the amount of time the learner gives to studying it.
3. Students' preferences for literature are related to culture and to the teacher's preferences.
4. The ability to read plays a central role in determining achievement in the subject matter fields.
5. Most school variables, such as organization, size of class, teacher characteristics, and methods of instruction, do not correlate with achievement.
6. Although many educators profess high-level objectives in classrooms throughout the world, they actually emphasize specific information to be remembered (low-level cognitive processes).
7. In spite of differences in curriculum, the top 5 percent of students in all countries are roughly comparable in achievement.

The implications from the findings are controversial. Also, many of the abundant data require further analysis. It is clear that increased learner time in instruction is likely to increase achievement, but we do not know what is the most economical way to increase time. The use of mass media for instruction, the development of new curriculum materials, changes in preservice and in-service education of teachers, each has yet to be evaluated. Further, the first-mentioned finding, regarding the power of the home curriculum, brings new challenges. It means we must find out how school and home should relate to each other in order to serve the best interests of child and society. It might mean that curriculum persons must assume responsibility for programs directed toward parents of young children whose verbal ability is not being developed in the home.

With respect to methodology, the Six Subject Survey has been criticized for finding out only what *is* taught rather than what *ought* to be taught. The investigations have been faulted for relying on standardized tests and for not attending to noncognitive behaviors such as self-concepts, tolerance for other people, and aesthetic abilities. Evidence suggests that the tests emphasized reading ability, Western concepts, and familiarity with a given test format. Shortcomings of the IEA Surveys are well described by Torsten Husén.[22] One great value of this pioneer work is in its strategies for getting people across cultures to cooperate on persistent educational problems. Cross-cultural studies allow us to make wider generalizations and give us a better picture of schooling in the real world than do other studies. The decade-long research effort sponsored by IEA has resulted in nine official volumes so far and the research and reanalysis of data continues.

We can expect more research on how to develop instruments for measuring outcomes in non-Western societies and developing countries. Constance McCullough, for example, wants future studies to place special attention on such factors as inclusion of reading passages and test items from more languages. She would like to see more culturally representative tests (so that all respondents have an equal degree of cultural unfamiliarity) and more care in the choice of translators.[23]

A second international study[24] will be conducted in the Northern Hemisphere in 1980-1981 and in the Southern Hemisphere in 1981-1982. This planned study will go beyond the information provided by questionnaires and examinations. A component of this study is curriculum analysis, which will provide a context for interpreting the data obtained from questionnaires and tests. A second component is emphasis on what teachers do in the classrooms and associated pupil outputs.

Curriculum analysis in the second international study of mathema-

---

[22]Torsten Husén, "An International Research Venture in Retrospect," *Comparative Education Review* 23, no. 2 (October 1979): 370–85.

[23]Constance M. McCullough et al., "Discussion Review of Reading Comprehension Education in Fifteen Countries," *American Education Research Journal* 11, no. 4 (Fall 1974): 409–14.

[24]Kenneth J. Travers, "The Second International Mathematics Study: Purposes and Design," *Journal of Curriculum Studies* 11, no. 3 (July-September 1979): 203–10.

tics will attempt to show the end results (both in terms of objectives and content of the curriculum and student cognitive and affective outcomes) of countries importing curriculum versus countries devising their own syllabi, courses of studies, and textbooks. Each country will be asked about the status of the curriculum and for assessment of how it came to be.

Other questions that the international study may answer are: How successful have been curriculum efforts in preparing students for postsecondary study? What changes have taken place in organization and philosophies of schooling? What shifts have occurred in proportions of students enrolling in preuniversity math courses? What changes have occurred with respect to student aptitude and achievement as compared with fifteen years ago? What is the relation between student attitudes and the use of instructional strategies?

In some countries, the influence of some mathematicians may be great—textbooks may focus on math as a self-contained body of knowledge with little application in the "real world." Other countries may promote a study of math which emerges out of the learner's experience. Should such differences in curriculum approaches be found, then the approaches can be related to outcomes such as interest, attitude, understanding, and problem-solving capabilities.

There is some doubt as to whether large-scale curriculum studies such as those represented by the early IEA studies will occur again. Funding is problematical and increased methodological sophistication might convince researchers to avoid projects on the scale of this classical study. Instead we may see more international studies such as those by M. Frances Klein, which focus on more limited aspects of education.[25] In her study of curriculum making in eighteen selected countries, Mrs. Klein, in collaboration with John Goodlad, surveyed respondents in curriculum centers—agencies under ministries of education or institutes of education—regarding their responsibilities for curriculum making and the levels at which curriculum decisions are made. Among the findings from this study are the following.

The processes used in curriculum development are a one-way street from the ministry, university, and center down to the local school, teacher, and finally to the student. Schools, teachers, and students appear to be more passive recipients than active agents in the processes of curriculum development. The national governments seem to be the greatest single source of curriculum influence. A recur-

[25]M. Frances Klein in collaboration with John Goodlad, *A Study of Curriculum Making in Eighteen Selected Countries* (Los Angeles: IDEA Research Division, September 1978).

ring theme in the data was the need for professional personnel with preparation in curriculum development and research.

CONCLUDING COMMENTS

The hidden curriculum points up both the opportunity to strengthen the formal curriculum with desirable aspects of youth culture and our need for attending to miseducative experiences that are fostered in our schools. The moral curriculum raises age-old curriculum questions: What is the meaning of morality? Should morality be taught? Can it be taught? Cultural pluralism is important because it fits in with a growing interest in the rights of children, and because it gives us a chance to redefine the purpose of schools. The issue of career education forces us to make a choice: we can see all education as vocational—helping persons become more truly human—or we can see it as serving the needs of the corporate state.

The international studies were meant to resolve controversy by answering questions such as: Does a nation hinder the achievement of the gifted by encouraging the education of the nongifted? The answer was that retention of large numbers of students did not adversely affect the gifted.

Most of these issues are instances of two fundamental concerns. Dedicated persons have sensed that aspects of the curriculum are not consistent with the premise that every human being is important regardless of racial, national, social, economic, or mental status. Exploitation of learners by the hidden curriculum, the denial of minority values in the curriculum, and the failure to stimulate the retarded are cases in point. Also, more persons today are aware that the opportunity for wide participation in the cultural resources of the society is a fundamental right. Hence, career education, mainstreaming, and multicultural education are offered as ways for identifying new resources and encouraging more people to appreciate them.

QUESTIONS

1. Describe aspects of a hidden curriculum in a school familiar to you. How should the staff respond to this situation?
2 . Tell what sources of values, norms, or standards you think should be used in planning a moral curriculum.

3. What are the likely consequences of using each of the following approaches to moral education:
   a. Cognitive. Students are stimulated to operate at higher levels of moral reasoning.
   b. Commitment. Personal and social action projects help students *do* something in relation to their values.
   c. Inculcation. Students observe good models and are reinforced for certain desirable social human behavior.
   d. Clarification. Through such exercises as thinking about things in their lives they would like to celebrate, students are led to define their values.
4. Which of the following purposes for undertaking international surveys of achievement seem most likely to be attained?
   a. To describe the salient factors that account for national differences.
   b. To determine the factors that are associated with achievement in all lands as a guide to practice.
   c. To compare curriculum endeavors within and among a number of countries.
5. Using James Deslonde's six stages of cultural pluralism (page 247), locate the stage that represents a school familiar to you.
6. State two working hypotheses, one describing situations in which mainstreaming will be successful and the other describing situations in which it will fail.
7. Identify one or more common elements among these issues: the hidden curriculum, moral education, career education, cultural pluralism, and mainstreaming.
8. Should programs of career education encourage students to enter the corporate (industrial-technological) growth sector or careers that respond to personal and social problems? Give reasons for your answer.

SELECTED REFERENCES

The Hidden Curriculum

Apple, M.W. "Power and School Knowledge," *The Review of Education* 3 (1977).

Bidwell, Charles E. "The Social Psychology of Teaching," in *Second Handbook of Research on Teaching*, Robert M.W. Travers, ed. Chicago: Rand McNally, 1973.

Gordon, C. Wayne. *The Social System of the High School*. Glencoe, Ill.: The Free Press, 1957.

Jackson, Phillip B. *Life in the Classroom*. New York: Holt, Rinehart and Winston, 1968.

Overly, Norman V., ed. *The Unstudied Curriculum: Its Impact on Children*. Washington, D.C.: ASCD, 1970.

Taxel, Joel. "Justice and Cultural Conflict: Racism, Sexism, and Instructional Materials," *Interchange* 9, no. 1 (1978–1979): 56–84.

Vallance, Elizabeth. "Hiding the Hidden Curriculum," in *Curriculum and Evaluation*, Arno Bellack and Herbert Kliebard, eds. Berkeley, Calif.: McCutchan, 1977, pp. 590–607.

Young, M.F.D., ed. *Knowledge and Control: New Directions for the Sociology of Education*. London: Collier MacMillan, 1971.

Moral Education

Beck, Clive. *Moral Education in the Schools: Some Practical Suggestions*. Toronto, Canada: Ontario Institute for Studies in Education, 1971.

Chazan, Barry I. and Soltis, Jonas F., eds. *Moral Education*. New York: Teachers College Press, 1973.

Cohen, Adir. "The Question of Values and Value Education in the Philosophy of Martin Buber," *Teachers College Record* 80, no. 4 (May 1979): 743–70.

Hall, Robert and Davis, John. *Moral Education in Theory and Practice*. Buffalo, N.Y.: Prometheus, 1975.

Mosher, Ralph, ed. *Moral Education*. New York: Praeger, 1980.

Phenix, Philip. *Education and the Common Good: A Moral Philosophy of the Curriculum*. New York: Harper and Row, 1961.

Purpel, David and Ryan, Kevin. *Moral Education . . . It Comes with the Territory*. Berkeley, Calif.: McCutchan, 1976.

Raths, Louis E., Harmin, Merrill, and Simon, Sidney B., *Values and Teaching*, 2nd ed. Columbus, Ohio: Merrill, 1978.

International Studies

Andreas, Kazamias, ed. "What Do Children Know," special issue. *Comparative Education Review* 18, no. 2 (June 1974).

Bloom, Benjamin S. "Implication of the IEA Studies for Curriculum and Instruction," *School Review* 82, no. 3 (May 1974): 413–37.

Inkeles, Alex. "The International Evaluation of Educational Achievement," in *Proceedings of the National Academy of Education* 4 (1978): 139–200.

International Association for the Evaluation of Educational Achievement (IEA). *International Studies in Evaluation*, 9 vols. New York: Wiley (Halstead Press), 1976.

Platt, William. "Policy Making and International Studies in Educational Evaluation," *Phi Delta Kappan* 55, no. 7 (March 1974): 451–56.

"On the International Education Achievement (IEA) Studies: A Symposium," *Comparative Education Review* 23, no. 3 (October 1979).

Walker, David A. *The IEA Six Subject Survey: An Empirical Study in Twenty-one Countries*. New York: Wiley (Halstead Press), 1973–1976.

Cultural Pluralism

Cultural Issues in Education—A Book of Readings. National Multilingual-

Multicultural Materials Development Center. Pomona, Calif.: California State Polytechnic University, 1978.

Dawson, Martha E. "From Compensatory to Multicultural Education: The Challenge of Designing Multicultural Educational Programs," *Journal of Research and Development in Education* 11, no. 1 (1977): 84–100.

Epps, Edgar G., ed. *Cultural Pluralism*. Chicago, Ill.: National Society for the Study of Education, 1974.

Hornby, Peter A., ed. *Bilingualism: Psychological, Social and Educational Implications*. New York: Academic Press, 1977.

Valadez, Concepcion M. "Bilingual Education: An Overview of an American Experiment in Progress," in *Basic Skills and Urban Schools*. St. Louis, Mo.: CEMEL, August 1979.

Valverde, Leonard A., ed. *Bilingual Education for Latinos*. Washington, D.C.: ASCD, 1978.

Wynn, Cordell, ed. "Multicultural Education," *Journal of Research and Development in Education* 11, no. 1 (Fall 1977).

Mainstreaming

Ashcroft, S.C., ed. "Special Education," *Theory Into Practice* 14, no. 2 (April 1975).

Gickling, Edward E. and Theobald, John T. "Mainstreaming: Affect or Effect?" *The Journal of Special Education* 9, no. 3 (Fall 1975): 317–28.

Hendrickson, Barbara. "Teachers Make Mainstreaming Work," *Learning* 7, no. 2 (October 1978): 104–20. (A special issue about mainstreaming.)

Career Education

Heyneman, Stephen P. "The Career Education Debate: Where the Differences Lie," *Teachers College Record* 80, no. 4 (May 1979): 659–88.

Preli, Barbara S. *Career Education Teaching/Learning Process*. Washington, D.C.: U.S. Government Printing Office, 1978.

Peterson, James A. and Park, Dick. "Values in Career Education: Some Pitfalls," *Phi Delta Kappan* 56, no. 9 (May 1975): 621–24.

Rossi, Robert J. "Career Education," *Teachers College Record* 80, no. 4 (May 1979): 629–58.

Thompson, Albert S. "Career Education—What It Involves," *Teachers College Record* 80, no. 4 (May 1979): 689–94.

12 / DIRECTIONS
IN THE SUBJECT FIELDS

The material in this chapter is arranged chronologically, although more in the sense of trends than as a detailed recital of events. The chapter is intended to reveal what various subject fields were like in the past, describe the directions they are now taking, and indicate the forces that will shape them in the future.

There are two approaches to keeping abreast of innovations in the subject fields. One of these has already been outlined in chapter 4, in which common trends were interpreted with respect to purpose, content, method, organization, and evaluation in the academic curriculum orientation. A second approach is to analyze recent developments in curriculum offerings associated with specific school subjects as revealed by lay and professional journals, yearbooks of national scholarly organizations, textbooks, and curriculum materials in the subject fields. The results of such an analysis are reported in this chapter.

A startling conclusion is drawn from this analysis. Despite recent political and legal actions intended to assure equal educational opportunities, it is clear that in each subject field, the able and talented students are given one curriculum and those students who are judged less able are given a very different one. When tracking occurs through a differentiated curriculum, there is no school integration in practice, although school desegregation may be the social policy. This differentiated curriculum tracks some children into programs leading only to low-status jobs and restricted opportunities for advanced education. This is not to say that all students must have the same curriculum in order to ensure equality of opportunity. It is possible, for example, to have science programs that differ in their approach with regard to the degree of abstraction or concreteness; yet both can be effective in helping pupils acquire useful knowledge and outlooks from science. Both approaches, however, must be shown to lead to outcomes that are equal in educational value.

The discerning reader will note how swings in emphasis within the subject fields reflect a difference of opinion about the nature of knowledge—whether it is viewed as something to be raided as a tool for resolving social problems or as a series of disciplines to be acquired for developing the intellect. Further, one will note how the conflicts in curriculum orientation preclude universal trends.

MATHEMATICS

Before the 1950s, schools commonly taught mathematics around one central theme; student mastery of basic computational skills. This practical yet simplistic approach to math instruction was unable to accommodate the nation's increasing need for theoretical mathematicians and scientists. By the early 1960s, a new trend in math instruction had emerged—student acquisition of mathematics as a discipline. Two influences helped set this trend in motion.

The first influence reflected the above-mentioned need for competent and creative scientists. The other influence on math curriculum was the belief that everyone could profit by acquiring knowledge of mathematics as a discipline. Briefly stated, the belief was that subject matter fields should introduce students to the general concepts, principles, and laws that members of a discipline use in problem solving.

The new math consisted of the fundamental assumptions and conceptual theories on which every scientific enterprise is based. Unfortunately, it was deprecated for being abstract, just as the old math was criticized for being boring. For the average student, sophisticated conceptual theories had little practical relevancy. Instruction in topics such as set theory and use of bases other than the generally used base 10 replaced practice in the basic skills needed for everyday problem solving. Developers of the new math paid too little attention to the practical uses of mathematics in the student's present and future life. Hence, many specialists in mathematics argued that the school should stress a knowledge of mathematics as an end in itself, as a satisfying intellectual task. On the other hand, in order for knowledge to be meaningful, it must be applied. As Stanley Bezuszka suggests, the main question facing mathematics teachers is whether they "can share the conviction that math is useful both in the intellectual order and for the necessities of a technological era and still avoid

a meaningless idealism on the one hand and an all-pervading voca-
tionalism on the other."[1]

Both modern and traditional math are found in today's secondary
schools. The move toward traditional mathematics results from the
emphasis on basics such as computational skills, while the move
toward modern math results from a concern about understandings
for high ability students. A survey of the status of mathematics in today's secondary schools indicates that traditional math courses —
courses that feature drill and practice, computation, and memorization — are taken by slower and non-college bound students, not by
students who tend to major in math.[2] The latter still take modern
mathematics, algebra, geometry, and optional fourth year courses
which place strong emphasis on structure, learning by discovery, definitions, properties, sets, rigor, proofs, statistics, calculus, trigono-
metry, and other abstract concepts.

In order to facilitate the application of knowledge, three new directions have been suggested for future math trends. The first is integration of math with other subject matter. Opponents of the new math
from its inception have proposed that math be studied not as a
separate theoretical discipline, but rather as an integrated part of
liberal education. Integration of subject matter facilitates the application of math skills to a variety of situations. The importance of math
skills in all subjects from homemaking to physics should be stressed.

Increased use of educational technology is a second means by
which math can be made more relevant. The United States Office of
Education has funded a $4 million program to develop a television
math series designed to show how mathematics may be applied to all
occupations and problem-solving situations. The series would supplement the teacher, who would continue with regular computational skills. Plans call for the series to be staged in a local drugstore,
with characters using basic math skills to solve problems relating to
measurement, quantity, estimation, and so forth. Technology in the
larger sense is also having an effect on the mathematics curriculum.
A hand-held calculator era is here. Young children will be expected to
understand negative numbers and exponents. The use of calculators
in all classes will require emphasis on the language of calculators — on
decimals, fractions, and algebraic symbols. The availability of
calculators will allow expansion of the traditional program to include

[1]Stanley Bezuszka, "Math Rx," *Learning* 3, no. 7 (March 1975): 27–35.
[2]J. Phillip Bennett, "Modern Mathematics: Perceptions of Secondary
Mathematics Department Chairpersons," *School Science and Mathematics* LXXVIII,
no. 8 (December 1978): 691–96.

numbers of greater magnitude. Teachers will be able to spend more time on concrete representations of concepts since they can check instantly for student understanding. Patterns can be more easily detected.

Surveys among parents and teachers regarding attitudes toward calculator usage in schools indicate negative feelings about the use of calculators in grades three to eight, but positive feeling about their use in grades nine to twelve.[3] Parents believe that teachers should require students to be competent in both calculator and pencil-and-paper solutions—that calculators be used to aid mathematical understanding but not to eliminate computational skills.

Community participation in curriculum planning and implementation is a third way being taken to increase the relevancy of math instruction. Use of parents as tutors, teacher aides, and resource persons not only helps to reduce per-pupil cost, but also provides a balance between classroom and community perspectives. Visiting lecturers and opportunities for work experience can narrow the gap between classroom theory and practical application. Bridges between the school and family will be built as parents share the responsibility for helping young people relate to life.

Concerns about curriculum content and about ways to develop ideas appropriate to the child's level persist. In their attempts to attain goals in computation, some people ignore concepts and processes for developing proficiency, defining the curriculum as a series of isolated skills to be taught by drill. Also, the role of application and problem solving is far from clear. Incidentalists argue that systematic instruction in abstractions should be replaced with general problem-solving experiences from the real world. Others advocate experiences in mathematical areas that closely resemble the physical world, such as measurement and geometry.

The immediate solution for these issues and concerns seems to be in the direction of a balanced curriculum. Content will be broadened beyond the teaching of whole number ideas in the primary grades. Ideas of symmetry and congruence will be explored. Shapes will be discussed and classified, and measurement and graphing will be popular. Metrics, of course, will be necessary. Informal experiences with important mathematical ideas may contribute to greater success in future learning and to application in daily life. A balanced point of view also implies the use of different instructional procedures. No

[3]Bernard R. Yvon and Davis A. Downing, "Attitudes Toward Calculator Usage in Schools," *School Science and Mathematics* LXXVIII, no 3 (June 1978): 410–16.

single mathematics program will fit all children. Briefly, the balanced curriculum means overcoming an undue focus on skills, mathematical content, or application. Instead, teachers who follow the policies of the National Council of Teachers of Mathematics stress the interdependence of these three elements. There must be techniques designed to help learners focus on specific elements and techniques in which less guidance is given. A variety of thinking strategies or ways to solve problems should be encouraged. Children should be given opportunities to relate events to mathematical models by estimating, applying estimating abilities in other situations, developing criteria for comparing lengths, noting the regularities of the coordinate system in the real world, and modifying or imposing order on a real situation and then summarizing in mathematical form.

SCIENCE

All branches of the scientific enterprise depend on the principles and laws of mathematics as a foundation for both theory and methodology. Because of this dependency, curriculum trends in the sciences often parallel those applied to mathematics. Science subject matter in the early 1960s was shaped by the same forces that influenced mathematics, namely, the discipline proposal and the push for specialization. These forces particularly affected the sciences because it was felt that advancements in a technological society required the training of highly skilled scientists and technicians.

Science subject matter at this time was conceptually and theoretically sophisticated. Students were introduced to the principles, of science by the discovery process of simple experimentation. This instructional approach replaced the more traditional process of memorizing theorems and laws. It was hoped that this approach would endow students with the inquiry mode of thought used by specialists in the scientific disciplines. Science projects in the early 1960s were heavily funded and resulted in a number of new programs. Children were encouraged to participate in scientific research on a very theoretical level. Science fairs enabled more advanced students to gain recognition as practicing members of the science discipline.

During the late 1960s, the discipline approach to science instruction was criticized for dwelling too long on theory and ignoring the need for practical application. Science in schools had been too specialized to be successfully applied to anything other than scientific research. For students uninterested in pursuing science as a career, the new subject matter had little practical relevancy. The average student could not identify the role of science in the common affairs and problems of people. Also, Americans were becoming increasingly concerned about societal implications of the scientific enterprise. Prior demands for research relating to space exploration and national defense had blinded scientists to the very real problems of air pollution, overpopulation, and depletion of natural resources. Scientists had neglected to study the relationship of research to the total person in the total universe. As a result of this neglect, a new trend to humanize the sciences emerged in the 1970s.

The trend to humanize curriculum led to a multidisciplinary approach to instruction. This approach applied basic laws of science to a variety of problem situations in subjects other than science. Science teachers sometimes worked in teams with teachers from other disciplines and helped students relate principles of science to current social, political, and economic problems. Students majoring in social science frequently studied the relationship of scientific discoveries to industrial and technological revolutions. The role of the scientific enterprise in international policymaking was sometimes studied in political science courses.

By the late 1970s, science's heyday in the schools was past. A 1979 National Science Foundation study reported that 90 percent of teachers have now returned to the traditional textbook approach.[4] Enrollment in high school science courses has been steadily decreasing. More than half of high school students today take no science at all after the tenth grade. High school programs are replete with courses such as earth science, ecology, marine biology, and anthropology, not chemistry, physics, and biology. Only 4 percent of classes in elementary school science are taught in special science rooms and more than a third of the instruction is done with no special science equipment. At all levels, lecturing and reading from a single textbook is the dominant method of teaching. The use of laboratory instruction, an important part of inquiry-based curriculum, is disappearing.[5]

Pupils are given the idea that science is a set of conclusions rather than a method of inquiring about the world. In large cities, much of

---

[4]Edward B. Fiske, "Science's Heyday in the Schools Is Past," *The New York Times*, section 12 (April 22, 1979): 1, 14.

[5]"Inquiry-Based Science Studies Are Giving Way to Rote Learning, NRC Says," *Phi Delta Kappan* 61, no. 3 (1979): 225.

the responsibility for scientific literacy is being taken over by science museums. The Lawrence Hall of Science, University of California, Berkeley, has opened its facilities to the public to provide a close look at and firsthand experiences with science activities, for example.

Considering the curriculum of the 1980s, science will likely only become important when the public recognizes the need for understanding the methods, content, and limitations of modern science — when the idea that science is basic is accepted. A scenario for the future science curriculum features a multidisciplinary approach involving inquiry and outreach to the community.

The multidisciplinary approach serves two purposes. First, it brings new depth to all disciplines. Second, it reminds us of science's relation to the political, economic, and social affairs of humankind. A major goal of science teachers in the 1980s will be to provide students with the basic problem-solving skills they will need to cope with an often dehumanizing technological society. One effort in this direction is the Inquiry Training Project of Port Colborne, Ontario, Canada. The aim of this project is to improve the ability to solve problems that a person might encounter in the course of everyday life now and in the future. To this end, instead of teaching students a single direct path between questions and answers, teachers in the inquiry project teach students to deal with questions that give rise to a number of plausible alternatives whose desirability must be thought out and ranked. The program attempts to teach children to analyze cause and effect relationships, a technique that has been profitable in the sciences. With respect to method, children are given simple scientific equipment and materials from the world around them and are encouraged to experiment. A typical activity is the raising of green plants under different conditions and observing and recording the results. Another favorite practice involves fermentation. In this project, pupils are given yeast, sugar, tubing, and a few other materials. They are asked to keep track of how the rate of fermentation is affected by changes in the amount of water used and the temperature, in order to learn about control of variables and effects of such controls. Ecological projects are also popular in science courses. As they progress, children using the discovery method are exposed to the basic concepts of many sciences, from botany and biology to physics, chemistry, and astronomy.

Questions about the effectiveness of the inquiry method have been raised in light of test scores showing a decline in science knowledge. Defenders of the inquiry method say that the tests used do not measure the ability to perform experiments that the new courses emphasize. There is, however, no serious backlash against the new courses using the discovery approach, and the broad recommendation is toward more inquiry in the science class. Two obstacles are economic and instrumental (teacher deficiency) considerations. Initial investment in equipment for courses emphasizing experimentation can run as high as $500 per classroom. Teachers must know enough about the principles and teaching materials involved to have confidence. One of the biggest problems in teaching science in the early grades is the teacher's insecurity with the subject matter.

Secondary schools are likely to continue to offer a few science courses of high quality for the most talented students. These courses will probably be organized around the traditional topics of biology, chemistry, and physics. Such programs are now designed for a minority of students. Indeed, data from the National Longitudinal Study of the High School Class of 1972 show that entry into prestigious fields of biological science, business, engineering, physical sciences, and math can be predicted by the science and mathematics courses taken in high school.[6]

There are several recommendations for improving the traditional courses. It is suggested that new materials be developed for use by the 70 percent of students now being inadequately served. These materials would deal with new areas of modern science. They also would contain less of the encyclopedic content and details that have little bearing on students' present problems of living. Instructional activities would be tied to the ongoing scientific enterprises in the community. Science would be treated less as an end in itself than as a field that is related to other aspects of life. There would be more emphasis on the power, responsibilities, and limitations of science.

The idea of having the local community serve as a learning laboratory is another recommendation. Education Development Center in Newton, Massachusetts, for example, is already developing science projects related to issues with social implications. In one such project, The Family and Community Health Through Care Giving, students have health care giving experiences in schools, families, and agencies in the community. Units treat such topics as adolescent pregnancy, drinking, stress, environmental and consumer health. Such projects combine ideas and skills from the natural sciences, humanities, and social sciences.

[6]Samuel S. Peng and Jay Jaffe, "Women Who Enter Male-Dominated Fields of Study in Higher Education," *American Educational Research Journal* 16, no. 3 (Summer 1979): 285–94.

PHYSICAL AND HEALTH EDUCATION

In the early 1960s, President John Kennedy proposed that a national standard of physical fitness be established. Shortly thereafter, most elementary and secondary students were required to participate in annual assessments of physical fitness. This period also saw the flourishing of international sports events. Participation of highly trained foreign athletes in these events aroused American interest in the development of physical education programs.

Unfortunately, physical competition as part of the 1960s sports ethic produced disappointment and humiliation for many children. Being good was often not good enough; excellence was the goal. Physical education offerings were limited to traditional team sports, and often aggression and competitiveness were the prerequisites of sportsmanship.

Throughout the 1960s, physical education offerings gradually expanded. Communities requested that more emphasis be placed on life-long sports. As a result, courses in scuba diving, bike riding, and golf were added to the curriculum. The direction was not away from strenuous exercise, but simply away from the harshness of competition. Competition as an American virtue was slowly being replaced by individualism.[7] Physical education has now established a new flexibility in course offerings. Less rigid sex roles are also opening new opportunities for girls. Students, for the first time, may choose from a variety of programs best suited to their interests.

The role of physical education in the classroom has become a controversial issue nationwide in the face of budgetary cutbacks and the demand for renewed emphasis on basic educational forms. A 1979 New York State Education Department study, for example, found that most kindergarten through sixth-grade schools offered physical education only two days a week.

The American Alliance for Health, Physical Education and Recreation (a 50,000-member professional organization) has suggested five guidelines for future physical education programs:

1. Break down current mass education techniques.
2. Increase flexibility of offerings and teaching methods.
3. View sports as more than athletic competition.

[7]Stuart Miller, "Is Your School a Training Ground for Gladiators?" *Learning* 3, no. 3 (May–June 1975): 57–64.

4. Increase coeducational classes, sailing, camp counselor training, self-defense.
5. Promote physical activities that support the desire to maintain physical fitness throughout life.

The association recommends that teaching methods emphasize activities that can serve as vehicles for education of the whole person. Activities should be designed to introduce students to the subtle and often overlooked potentials of the human body. Here are some suggested activities:

> *Movement education.* The objective is to develop an understanding of creative and expressive movement. Five-year-olds can be asked to proceed down a marked line in any fashion they desire. Some balance carefully, some run, some crawl, but all experience their own style.
> *Centering oneself.* Here the student develops a state of alert calm by becoming aware of physical energy in and outside of the body.
> *Structural patterning.* Students become aware of variations in the way people move.
> *Relaxation techniques.* By means of rhythmic breathing, the student learns how to gain control over habitual tensions.

Illustrative of newer curriculum in health is the Health Activities Project (HAP) developed by the Lawrence Hall of Science, University of California, Berkeley. This program offers an activity-centered health curriculum for pupils in grades five through eight. The goal of the project is to create a positive attitude toward health by giving pupils a sense of control over their own bodies and by imparting understanding about the body's potential for improvement. HAP activities, organized into modules treating such topics as fitness, interaction, growth, decision making, and skin, supplement existing programs in health, physical education, and science.

ENGLISH

English as a school subject is relatively young, hardly over 100 years old. In 1865, there was a variety of studies of English—rhetoric, oratory, spelling, literary history, and reading. In the following decades, these traditional offerings were united under the teaching of a single subject—English—with literature, language, and composition forming the major components.

Early in the twentieth century, there were efforts to emancipate the teaching of English in the high schools from the college program. These efforts took the form of rejecting a traditional body of literature as the sole purveyer of culture, giving up an analytic approach to literary studies in favor of studying "types" of literature. In the early 1920s, there was a functional emphasis on English; committees attempted to identify the skills learned in English classes that were most useful to people in a range of social positions. An experience curriculum in English was introduced. It featured an abandonment of formal grammar in favor of functional instruction through activities in creative expression, speaking, and writing.

The 1940s saw teachers of English trying to adapt their content to adolescent needs, the problems of family life, international relations, and other aspects of daily living. English became guidance. In the late 1950s, there was an academic resurgence, with attacks on English as "life adjustment." English as a discipline in the high schools followed the model of academic work in the college. There was a stress on intensive reading, the Great Books, and literary rather than personal pursuits. Language, literature, and composition remained the tripod of English. Teachers were expected to teach pupils how to give close analytic attention to what was read, asking questions about form, rhetoric, and meaning. Literary values once again prevailed over other considerations.

The middle 1960s saw the beginning of a counter movement with concern about making the English curriculum more relevant and meaningful to the disadvantaged. The emphasis again shifted to contemporary writing, including selections by black authors. In literature, there was a move away from the traditional historical and biographical approach that had been preoccupied with the social context, and toward topical units in the junior high school and thematic units in the senior high school. A theme like justice as treated by poets, playwrights, and novelists over the years often served as the basis for deeper study by the student. Reading literature was considered more important than reading what was said about it.

English teachers and curriculum workers still wonder whether courses should feature great works of literature or emphasize contemporary problems and modern psychological interpretations. The popular response is to try to have both traditional and contemporary. One chooses important themes dealing with the human condition, such as guilt, and then selects material from traditional and modern American and British literature, folklore, and mythology that helps illuminate the theme. A danger in this approach is that it may induce a premature sophistication with respect to literary works. No single course can cover all centuries. Selectivity should govern both the scope and the details selected.

A conference on the teaching of English at Dartmouth College in 1966 brought American specialists in English in contact with British influences. The British offered the Americans a model for English that focused on the personal and linguistic growth of the child. Hence, many teachers of English began to copy the British practice of offering improvised drama, imaginative writing, personal response to literature, and informal classroom discussion. Like the Britishers, they gave less attention to textual analysis, to the study of genres, to literary periods, and to chronology. Parallel with the reemphasis of English as a humanistic subject came technological influences. Behavioral objectives in English aroused much controversy. The skills thought necessary for speaking, listening, reading, and writing could be specified and taught. How these skills could be related to the "higher" goals of expression or response to literature is unfinished business.

There are mounting concerns about the new English as graduating students find that they are not equipped with the basic reading and writing skills needed for employment. College entrance exam scores continue to decline, and many freshmen are required to take a basic grammar course before enrolling in college English. The failure of the new English to provide working skills has resulted in a back-to-basics movement. This return to the teaching of fundamental skills has gained support among students, teachers, parents, and administrators. Some minority members are also supporting the back-to-basics movement. Courses for studying the contributions of minority groups to literature engendered racial pride but often did not prepare minority students for the demands of a society in which standard English is the criterion for social advancement.

The back-to-basics movement in English is seen in a demand for more history of classical literature, more traditional grammar, and a greater emphasis on formal rather than personal writing. There is a return to the workbook and hard cover anthology.[8] Elective programs are being dismantled (they are accused of fragmenting and diminishing the goals of an integrated approach to English); the new

<hr/>

[8]Marilyn Sobelman and Martha Bell, "Curriculum Concerns for the E J Reader," *The English Journal* 68, no. 6 (September 1979): 89–93.

linguistics is gone; "personal growth" and "creativity" are disparaged. Opponents of this movement urge English teachers not to succumb to pressures that would have them teach trivia because trivia can be easily measured, but to teach that reading and writing will help students find personal meaning in life. Modernists also urge including a critical study of the media, particularly television, because the media are so closely related to our quality of life.[9]

As a compromise, The Center for Urban Education, in Amherst, Massachusetts, suggests that basic English skills be taught in conjunction with general literature themes that affect all humanity. The great theme approach focuses attention on the most profound and humane questions of all time, for example, people's response to nature, the nature of beauty, the relationship between fate and free will. Those who teach isolated skills often neglect to show how these skills relate to current social realities. Those supporting the back-to-basics movement will have to consider how skills may be applied in situations relevant to the students' lives. The acquisition of basic skills alone does not ensure communication of ideas. Communication of ideas requires both skill and interest. Indeed, some specialists in English believe that when subject matter is relevant to student interest, motivation to acquire skills is high. The late Professor Mina Shaughnessy of the City University of New York, for example, believed that even if one is motivated to write and is equipped with the skills needed to write, there is still "no way of learning how to write unless you write."[10] She required students to write no less than 1,000 words a week. Writing activities included a journal, essays on topics of interest, timed class writings, and term papers. To keep up with the paperwork, Dr. Shaughnessy suggested the use of peer group teaching. Students could exchange essays and help each other to recognize areas of weakness. There is a strong belief on the part of many language arts instructors that the focus in the teaching of writing should be on designing experiences that systematically develop the students' abilities, including their sense of audience and purpose. It has been shown, for example, that even young children can be taught to formulate their writing intentions—to amuse, to inform, to praise someone or something—and to differentiate their writing according to genres such as narrative, dialogue, exposition,

[9]Vernon H. Smith, "Beyond Flax and Skinner: A Personal Perspective on Teaching English 1954–Present," *The English Journal* 68, no. 4 (April 1979): 79–85.
[10]Lee Dembart, "Capitalizing on Poor Writing," *The New York Times*, section 12 (May 4, 1975).

and voice—to tune their language to suit different audiences.[11] Attaining knowledge of stylistic conventions—paragraphing, punctuation, and so forth—leads to writing in order to affect the reader. Once students start writing for others, they read their own writing, thereby improving it.

Recently there has also been a shift from "relevant" literature. There is a rising tide of criticism and displeasure about the reading material taught in schools. Book banning has risen remarkably in America during the last five years. It remains to be seen whether there will be a focus on improving taste at the expense of fostering response. Inasmuch as the teaching of literature is a political act, goals for this curriculum are likely to reflect one's prior assumptions about the nature and purpose of education.

In brief, current trends in the teaching of English reflect three conflicting conceptions. Teachers who value an academic orientation base their instruction on what scholars are doing in the field. Those who think of education as personal growth attend to a pedagogy associated with oral expression, projects, popular media, contemporary literature, and social commentary. Those who think of English as a set of mechanical skills in language use are focusing directly on reading, spelling, and writing.

THE TEACHING OF READING

The curriculum for the teaching of reading in America from 1600 to the present has reflected different goals. The initial goal was religious. Children were expected to learn to read the word of God directly. With the forming of a new nation, reading was taught to help build national strength and unity—to instill patriotism. The teaching of reading as a means for obtaining information was the primary goal during the period from 1840 to 1890. This emphasis on enlightenment was an extension of nationalism—from patriotic sentiment to the ideal of an intelligent citizenry. To awaken a perennial interest in literary material was the overriding goal in the late 1890s and until about 1918. Thereafter, utility rather than aesthetics had priority. Reading selections were oriented more to the events of daily living than to literary appreciation.

Currently, there are two emphases in the teaching of reading. One

[11]Carl Bereiter, "Development in Writing," in *Cognitive Processes in Writing*, Lee W. Gregg and Erwin R. Steinberg, eds. (Hillsdale, N.J.: Erlbaum, 1979).

of these focuses on the development of intellectual skills for word recognition and reading comprehension. These skills are taught without considering the purpose for which they will ultimately be used. The other emphasis focuses on the specific kinds of situations in which the student is to apply reading skills—reading want ads, Yellow Pages, job applications, and newspapers. The latter emphasis reflects a concern for those who are functionally illiterate—who lack the reading competencies necessary to function successfully in contemporary society. Accordingly, there is increasing interest in the teaching of reading at the middle and senior high school levels.

Trends in the teaching of reading during the past decade followed those in the other language arts. Instruction in reading was influenced by scholarship, technology, and humanistic concerns. The influence of scholars in linguistics, for example, can be noted in more natural language in preprimers, controlled spelling patterns rather than a controlled vocabulary in texts designed for teaching word recognition skills, the use of language patterns to signal the meaning of what is written (for example, word order patterns), and greater acceptance of the learner's own articulation and substitution of words. On the other hand, the influence of the technologists is seen in today's instructional materials which feature task analyses, specific objectives with matching criterion-referenced tests, relevant practice, provision for feedback to the learner, and mastery of prerequisite tasks before proceeding.

Readiness to read is now conceived of as mastery of prerequisite skills rather than an assumed maturational level. Based on a diagnosis of the learner's skills, a reading program is prescribed which presumably meets the child's individual reading needs. Basal readers are now supplemented by a variety of self-paced reading materials, which enable students to advance along a continuum of competencies at their own rates. Greater emphasis is given to decoding skills, the relating of letters with sounds. Basal readers now feature phonic patterns to illustrate the sound and spelling regularities of English rather than emphasizing "sight words" and the irregular features of the language. More varied sentence structures are employed in beginning reading materials and some teachers use a language experience approach whereby children learn to read by reading what they themselves have spoken.

Future directions in the teaching of reading will respond to the following agenda of interest to researchers and policymakers:

1. Misuse of instruction based on hierarchical models. This reflects a

concern that unfavorable consequences may arise from over-reliance on diagnostic-prescriptive approaches that rest on hierarchies that are not fully validated.

2. Relation of instructional tasks to developmentally determined abilities and cultural differences of children.
3. Ways to increase comprehension in reading. There will be greater study, for example, of the effect of child-to-child tutoring on learning both to understand and use what is read.
4. Ways to match reading materials to the cognitive development of adolescents and adults.
5. Specific training in the skills required for reading job-related materials such as schematics.
6. More formal instruction in reading in the high school.

HISTORY AND SOCIAL STUDIES

History

The "new" history of the 1960s, both in subject matter and methodology, evolved from the same forces that had affected other subject matter fields, that is, the discipline proposal and the push toward specialization. The subject matter of history was chosen in order to provide students with a conceptual foundation on which specialization could be based. Emphasis was placed on historians' methods of research, analysis, and interpretation. Students were no longer required to memorize sheer facts or chronology, but rather to express an understanding for general sociological theories. This conceptual approach encouraged students to doubt and openly criticize textbook interpretations of history. Students drew their own conclusions and often found previous perspectives biased and unreliable.

Campus demonstrations in the late 1960s reflected a general lack of confidence in politicians and governmental agencies. Students had been taught to examine, analyze, and interpret, and they freely applied these skills to national policymaking. The Vietnam War was history in the making, and students were determined to make known their interpretations of the facts.

Public concern about campus protests resulted in a demand that history be taught in a manner that would make it applicable to constructive resolution of community problems. To accommodate this demand, curriculum specialists suggested integrating the study of history with studies in other subjects. Emphasis is now being placed on providing a basic understanding for historical influences on community life. Suggested learning activities include studying the influence of science and technology on historical periods; identifying the relationship between historical movements and developments in the arts; and investigating the effects of business and industry on local history.

A current appraisal of elementary and secondary history textbooks is negative.[12] They lack realism; although they show the present as a "tangle of problems," paradoxically, they are sanguine about the future. Economic history is conspicuously absent; an analysis of ideological conflict is missing from discussions of American wars; and they lack continuity. "Politics is one theory to them, economics another, culture a third. . . . There is no link between the end of Reconstruction in the South and the Civil Rights movement of the sixties. . . . History is just one damn thing after another. It is, in fact, not history at all."[13] Frances Fitzgerald attributes the lack of interest in academic competence in history to the societal demand that the curriculum promote good social behavior and learning for strictly practical purposes.

The 1970s demonstrated America's dependence on international economy and policymaking. Interdependence among nations for natural resources, economic stability, and environmental control is sure to increase in the 1980s. History courses need to emphasize the importance of economic, social, and political awareness in shaping the history of the future as well as understanding historical periods of the past.

There is another way in which the history curriculum is likely to change in the years ahead. Persons such as Martin Sleeper are arguing that curriculum design in the field of history must be based on cognitive-developmental theory rather than concentrating solely on the predefined meaning of history as a field (the logic of the scholar) or focusing only on the concerns of the students and how history can help them.[14] Sleeper would have the meaning and function of history change as children interact with each stage of their development. Young children consider history to be a collection of stories and unrelated events. As they grow older, they define history in concrete terms and think it to be objective. As adolescents, they understand interpretations and hypotheses in history. Although for the young

---

[12]Frances Fitzgerald, "Prizewinning Author Changes History Textbooks' Present Distorted Picture," *ASCD News Exchange* 21, no. 4 (Summer 1979): 1, 7.

[13]Ibid., p. 7.

[14]Martin E. Sleeper, "A Developmental Framework for History Education in Adolescence," *School Review* 84, no. 1 (November 1975): 91–107.

child history had to happen as recorded, the adolescent can imagine alternatives and contemplate different outcomes. The future purpose of history in the school may be to encourage developmental transitions, helping adolescents to meet their need for identity, to recognize both a sense of continuity with their own lives and an assurance of significance within their community. An adolescent trying to be less egocentric and learning to relate to others might use history to reveal the basis for the cultural differences of others, for example.

Social Studies

Social studies is a covering term for several subject matters including history and the social sciences. Originally, the purpose of the social studies curriculum was the "creation of rich and many-sided personalities, equipped with practical knowledge and inspired by ideals so that they can make their way and fulfill their mission in a changing society which is part of a world complex."[15] Today, there is disenchantment with the stated purpose. It is too vague, and there is doubt that those in the social sciences are able to furnish knowledge with which to resolve complex social issues like racial strife, war, and economic depressions. Indeed, Robert Nisbet, professor in humaties at Columbia University, believes that social scientists have inflated hopes and made promises beyond the means of their knowledge and capacities.[16]

In the 1950s, the curriculum of the social studies was varied. The authors of some programs aimed at social literacy. They wanted learners to understand social change as responses to the problems and needs of human beings throughout the world. Others said their mission was to help learners develop socially desirable behavior, to demonstrate social processes, or to promote understanding and skill in dealing with social problems. A common curriculum premise of that time was that the social studies program should combine both content and process. Students should have the opportunity to make decisions regarding personal and social problems using the generalizations from the social sciences.

In the 1960s, more than forty major social studies curriculum projects were financed by the federal government, foundations, and institutions of higher learning. Authors of these projects all emphasized an academic structure but did not share a common view as to what

[15]Charles Beard, *The Nature of the Social Sciences* (New York: Charles Scribner's Sons, 1938), p. 179.
[16]Robert Nisbet, "Knowledge Dethroned," *The New York Times Magazine* (September 28, 1975), pp. 34–60.

the structure was. They tended to define structure loosely as generalizations, concepts, or modes of inquiry. There was little agreement on which concepts or ways of working in the social sciences are most fruitful and representative of structure. Like most other curriculum programs of the 1960s, social studies projects stressed inductive teaching. Students were expected to find generalizations from data. Typical goals for the social studies during this period were to interpret problems of world citizenship using concepts from the behavioral sciences; to interpret social behavior using concepts from anthropology; to analyze problems of social change using concepts from a variety of "disciplines"; to analyze public controversies using the method of discussion and argument; and to recognize objective evidence using concepts from philosophy, psychology, law, and other social sciences.

Today, the social studies curriculum is in disarray. On the one hand, there are those who advocate drawing substantially from a wide range of social science disciplines in developing new social studies programs. On the other hand, others recommend studying non-Western societies and organizing curriculum content around the study of world cultures and international affairs.

The social studies curriculum in school is still more social studies than social science, with history, government, and geography the dominant subjects. In the elementary schools, the social studies receive little attention, serving primarily as another opportunity to teach reading and writing skills. Citing a National Science Foundation study of the social studies curriculum, Gerald Ponder gives this picture: at all levels the social studies curriculum is a textbook curriculum; the textbook is used to organize courses and students encounter the content of the text.[17] Few teachers have ever heard of approaches oriented toward the social sciences, and fewer still use them. Despite repeated cues for greater relevance, content relevance is not dominant. The back-to-basics movement has weakened efforts to promote inquiry and problem analysis. There is little agreement among teachers, advocates, or analysts within the field as to what ends the social studies should serve or the most appropriate subject matter to teach.

Problems concerning the social studies curriculum of the future center on the following observations. Rational discourse, critical inquiry, opportunity to exercise the skill of autonomous judgment, and other featured values in social studies programs seem to be no

17Gerald Ponder, "The Status of Social Studies," *Educational Leadership* 36 (April 1979): 515–18.

guarantee of behavioral change or even increased happiness of the individual or society. Inasmuch as human beings act irrationally with impulse, emotion, pride, and passion, we should not expect social studies programs that feature only facts and interpretations to contribute much to making students more reasonable about human and social behavior. Consequently, there will be a movement in the direction of the affective realm. Values and attitudes will become more important, and efforts will be made to involve students in ecological and political matters of personal interest. There will be a return to the project method, stressing ways to participate in acts of citizenship and to improve and perfect our governmental system. (This emphasis is also necessary in order to overcome students' loss of confidence in the American political system.)

The need to construct a more livable world will force those in the social studies to focus on social problems rather than on transmitting knowledge. These kinds of problems require that the student draw the best current thinking from both the natural and social sciences. Hence, we will see attempts at an integrative curriculum. The task will be difficult. Teachers, for example, are not always comfortable with the inquiry methods and concepts of a single social science. Now they will be asked to gain competency in several disciplines. Also, we know that scholars in a single social science have difficulty in agreeing on the objectives and content for course materials. Greater difficulty will be experienced in getting agreement from scholars in different fields about what should be taught.

Pressures will continue to make the social studies curriculum respond to the needs of special groups. Law interests will demand school courses on law; business interests will influence legislators to mandate instruction in the free enterprise system; Jewish groups will seek legislation to make mandatory detailed study of the Nazi holocaust. It looks as if the social studies curriculum across the land will be a hodgepodge of programs.

FOREIGN LANGUAGE

Six years before Sputnik, the Modern Language Association of America expressed the conviction that we were not teaching enough people foreign languages. National concern for the advancement of scientific and technological research in the late fifties accentuated the need for international exchange of knowledge. Hence, study of one or two foreign languages became a requirement of most secondary schools and universities. Indeed, over 8,000 elementary schools began to offer instruction in foreign languages.

An instructional method sometimes called the American method or the audiolingual approach for teaching foreign languages became popular at this time. This method was derived from the science of structural or descriptive linguistics that had proved useful in courses offered to the military during World War II. The basic principle of the method is that language must be learned as a system of communication by sound from mouth to ear. Student and teacher who used this method spoke the foreign language; they did not only talk about it. The first 300 to 400 hours of language learning were devoted to acquiring a skill rather than a body of facts. During this initial period, students began to comprehend the spoken word and to speak after listening; reading and writing were not emphasized. Students then practiced actively and aloud until they gained some control over the language patterns. The opportunity for such practice was generally provided by language laboratories in which the students heard recordings of a native speaker and tried to model their speech after the speaker's.

Interest in foreign languages began to decline in the mid-1960s as the national concern for space exploration subsided, and with it the push for communication with foreign scientists. Studies in language were criticized for being too specialized to be applicable. Foreign language requirements were eliminated in many colleges and secondary schools. There was a decline of nearly 10 percent in college enrollments in foreign language classes between 1965 and 1975. Parents do not pressure school authorities to have languages taught.

The American Council on the Teaching of Foreign Language reported that in 1974, of the 13.6 million students in public high schools, only 3.1 million were studying a modern foreign language and fewer than 175,000 were taking Latin. In 1976, a presidential commission reported that only 4 percent of pupils graduating from high school had studied a foreign language for as long as two years. One-fifth of United States public high schools offer no courses in foreign language at all. Among those that do, Spanish, French, and German are the favorites, in that order.

A national sampling by the University of Michigan found that more than 52 percent of Americans questioned would like to study a foreign language in the future, but nearly 49 percent opposed making it a requirement in high schools.

The foreign language disciplines are now being faced with budget cuts, as they are placed lower on the scale of school priorities. To counteract this pressure, advocates of foreign language are attempting to humanize their discipline in hopes of regaining student interest. Language departments are expanding their course offerings in order to meet the needs and interests of students. In discussing ways to do this, teachers typically suggest integration of language study with other subject matter areas, early introduction of language arts, and student participation in curriculum development. Subject matter integration is accomplished by introducing students to the contributions of language to all subject areas. English classes study the contribution of foreign languages to the development of American English, music classes study lyrics of foreign folk songs, and art classes share their work with those in foreign countries.

Bilingual-bicultural programs are currently increasing, and the early introduction of foreign languages has gained general support from everyone concerned with the development of language skills. Young children between the ages of four and ten have been found to be very successful in learning foreign languages. Children are usually flexible, uninhibited, and eager to explore different languages. Early introduction of languages also enhances cultural awareness among children. Languages may be used to explore the everyday experiences in different cultures (cooking styles and names of foods, folk songs, games played in foreign countries). Among the innovations suggested for stimulating language learning are bilingual nursery schools, home visits by bilingual teachers, play tutoring of younger children by trained school-age peers, and mobile classrooms to teach foreign languages.

Students are now being encouraged to participate in the planning of new language courses. The trend emerged from the need to make the language arts relevant to the needs of students. In addition, it is now realized that optimum learning takes place when the learner is meaningfully involved in determining what is to be learned or how it is to be learned, or both.

Language subject matter for the 1980s probably will include emphasis on basic speaking skills as well as those needed for reading and writing. Study activities will be designed to ensure relevancy and applicability. Speaking skills will be related to foreign cultural topics ranging from dating customs to urban problems. Use of current periodicals will also enhance relevancy of reading skills.

Resource persons can bring life to the languages. Non-English-speaking persons in the community may be invited to participate in classroom learning activities. Community businesses that employ bilingual persons may be encouraged to offer internship experiences.

Field trips and opportunities for travel can be used to introduce students to language in action, making language studies alive, vital, and relevant.

THE ARTS

The broad direction of curriculum revision needed in the arts was set in 1958. At that time, the American Council of Learned Societies' panel on curriculum made two recommendations. First, that the basic approach be creative, allowing the student in studios and workshops to be personally involved. Second, that historical matter be incorporated to develop the student's sense of heritage in the arts. Instead of survey courses, an attempt should be made to involve the student in the study of art as it represents various epochs and cultures and as it might affect his or her own creativity. Critical judgment is to be developed by practice, seeing good examples, reading, and hearing about original works.[18]

Subsequently, some educators based their curriculum on aesthetic theory; others, mindful of learning theory's emphasis on conceptual structure, turned their efforts toward defining the structure of art in terms of concepts. The pronouncement that any subject could be effectively taught to any child at any stage of development had eventually influenced curriculum developments in art as it had in other subjects.

Art curriculum of the mid-1960s was designed to provide students with an appreciation for the basic aesthetic themes expressed in all art forms. Subject matter covered basic concepts such as rhythm, movement, harmony, and texture. These concepts were to be experienced through listening (music appreciation), performing (acting, playing traditional instruments), and composing (emphasizing classical techniques). The main weakness of this instructional approach was that it served the needs of only a small portion of the student population. Subject matter was too specialized for the average student's basic artistic needs. The narrow range of course offerings could not encompass growing interest in art forms of ethnic minorities, use of a wide variety of musical instruments, art forms of different countries, and use of new art media.

To help show the usefulness of art, curriculum specialists are sug-

[18]American Council of Learned Societies, "Secondary School Curriculum Problems," *Newsletter 9*, no. 9 (1959).

gesting integration of subject matter fields. If integration is accomplished, music instruction may include an examination of
cultural and historical influences on music. Development of lyrics
may be studied in English courses. The Columbus, Ohio, public
schools are known for their integration of the arts with other areas of
the curriculum. Music in many of the schools, for example, is used in
the teaching of poetry (rhythm), history (songs of people in history),
math (patterns and frequencies), and science (the physics of sound).
Students studying future utopias might examine the authenticity of
the proposed systems in science classes. Later, they could write a play
in conjunction with a creative writing course. Finally, their play
could be produced in drama class.

Instruction in the arts should be related to real-life experiences.
Students will have increased interest and will be able to see how the
arts can become an intrinsic part of life. Resident artists can help
students plan a career in the arts. In 1969, a $100,000 national en-
dowment was endorsed by the United States Office of Education for
placement of six visual artists in secondary schools during the school
year 1969–1970. Now similar programs extend to all states. Local artists are participating in school art curriculum programs. Poets, musi-
cians, sculptors, actors, craftspersons, designers, environmental
planners, and filmmakers are a sample of the artists bringing the outside world to the classroom.

Use of peer group and cross-age teaching is also gaining support as
a possible trend for the 1980s. Dr. Robert Pace, chairman of the
piano department at Columbia University's Teachers College, has
developed a system for music training which maximizes peer
teaching. Groups of eight to ten students of varying ages learn the
techniques of music by participating in sight-reading games, ear-
training musical drills, and exercises in musical improvisation. The
program is cost effective, and children enjoy sharing their musical
development with peers.

New methods are being developed for the teaching of music based
on the interests and capacities of the average child. There are schools,
for example, that offer programs, commencing in kindergarten,
based on children's natural affinity for jazz. Other schools teach rock
music and electronic music. Guitars have become major teaching
tools. An art curriculum specialist faces only one fear for art in the
1980s: "Will art, music, dance, and drama be regarded as frills by an
increasingly cost-conscious public?"

The back-to-basics movement is a threat to courses in arts
although the Council for Basic Education thinks art is among the

basics. There are disagreements over the reasons for art in the curriculum—for self-expression, appreciation, a future career? Or for artistic intellectual content, historical importance, or a role in culture? In an essay that is highly critical of the vague, lofty, and unexamined list of aims for teaching art, Jacques Barzun says we do not have to have eighteen reasons to justify it in the schools. One way in enough: "Art is an important part of our culture. It corresponds to a deep instinct in man; hence it is enjoyable. We therefore teach its rudiments."[19]

Harry S. Broudy, on the other hand, believes that the schools should cultivate the aesthetic mode of experience, not because it is a delight, but because it is necessary for the development of the intellect. He argues for teaching how to be sensitive to the appearance of things, how the expressive properties of color, sound, texture, and movement are organized into aesthetic objects, and how to perceive and construct images that portray intimations of reality in forms of feeling.[20]

CONCLUDING COMMENTS

Most subjects are influenced by the same social, economic, political, and technological forces. Hence, it is no great surprise to see most of them moving in the same direction. All fields are attempting to individualize instruction. Sometimes the learner is offered choices among topics and learning activities. Sometimes individualizaton means allowing each pupil to proceed at his or her own pace, with self-instructional materials aimed at teaching a skill that the pupil needs. At other times, individualization means giving attention to the learner's characteristics as a basis for deciding what and how to teach.

One problem that has become more serious is that of curriculum organization. Offering learners choices of new studies and new approaches leads to competition with older studies and may give rise to charges of frivolousness, triviality, and lack of coherence. Curriculum makers in all fields are trying to relate subject matter to the developmental stages of different learners and to the human conditions. This effort is putting curriculum makers ahead of academic

[19]Jacques Barzun, "Art and Educational Inflation," *The Education Digest* XLV (September 1979): 12–16.

[20]Harry S. Broudy, "Arts Education: Necessary or Just Nice?" *Phi Delta Kappan* 60, no. 5 (January 1979): 347–50.

specialists in the reconceptualizing and integration of subject matter. Curriculum makers and academic specialists in every field are divided on the issue of whether traditional cultural experiences or a body of content should be transmitted or whether more concern should be given to the dynamic needs of learners. Curriculum planners find it difficult to agree on priorities among such goals as the development of reason, guidance, and adjustment, and the acquisition of the structure of the disciplines. Many are preoccupied with the knowledge required for teaching newer conceptions of school fields. Thus both major research and training for the teaching of school subjects are moving to the classroom.

There is a growing interest in mission-oriented teacher centers for staff development. Teachers in these centers select a specific goal for their own development (for example, the implementation of a specific curriculum). The center then acquires the materials and arranges for the training needed to implement and adapt the curriculum to local conditions.

Four forces seem certain to shape the teaching of subject fields in the future. One force is the growing insight into the developmental crises of learners and the need for applying subject matter to these crises. A second force is the knowledge that is expected to come from current studies of the relationship between the attainment of specific objectives and the achievement of long-term competencies and attitudes of learners. If the present practice of teaching to specific objectives does not result in the attainment of desired qualities of mind and character, many current programs will be rejected. The third and fourth forces are presently at cross purposes. There are social pressures to have the subject fields exercise a progressive influence by challenging and redefining conventional beliefs. Other social forces, however, expect the curriculum to serve the need for continuity and stability in a society fraught with moral dilemmas, shifting perspectives, and conflicting views. The latter view is expressed in the back-to-basics movement.

The back-to-basics and accountability movement means a shift from the curriculum theory that emphasized the structure of the disciplines toward a sociological theory that places more importance on socially useful skills. A return to the basics also means a movement away from the psychological or needs-of-the-child theory, as associated with some alternative schools and open classrooms, and toward more traditional programs aimed at quiet, order, control, and the preparation of students to take their place in the world of work. Most proponents of the movement want more emphasis on the common skills and abilities used in everyday reading, writing, and arithmetic.

Whatever changes are made in response to the proponents of the back-to-basics movement will probably fail to satisfy. The profound social changes in the structure of the family, community, and the world have made it impossible for children to experience what many adults want them to experience.

It is clear that the conservative movements in education—minimum competency testing, an emphasis on the acquisition of textbook information, the practice of teaching isolated skills of reading, writing, and arithmetic—together with attempts to make subject matter relevant to current social problems are resulting in one kind of curriculum; while college and university requirements, together with academically oriented teachers, are influencing a second trend aimed at intellectual development. The first curriculum is given to the majority of students, including minorities, slow learners, and the unmotivated. The second curriculum—which stresses understanding of a discipline and approximates the procedures and content of the field itself—is given to those perceived as able for and committed to advanced study and leadership. Offering differentiated programs to those from different socioeconomic backgrounds has not resulted in equal educational opportunities.

QUESTIONS

1. Sometimes trends are regarded as bandwagons—efforts to influence a desired future; at other times they are viewed as red flags—warnings of something that should be stopped. Identify some trends that you feel are bandwagons and some that you see as red flags.
2. Try your hand at anticipating a likely future trend in a subject field by (a) identifying or analyzing a political, economic, or other social factor that has the potential for shaping curriculum and (b) indicating how this force might affect the curriculum in this field.
3. Although much has been made of the common trends among the subject fields, they differ somewhat in the directions they are taking. For example, English is taking a somewhat different direction than the sciences. What are some of the differences? How do you account for their departures?
4. Select the curriculum trend of most interest to you and then try to stipulate some of the implications of this trend. Consider, for example, some of the consequences of this trend for the community, other social agencies, business and economic interests, and the school's bureaucratic structure.

5. Subject matter was probably never really viewed as an end in itself. The learning of particular subject matter has usually been justified as useful for some social purposes. What social purposes or interests were the disciplined approaches meant to serve? What purposes and interests are being attended to in the current curriculum of the subject fields?

SELECTED REFERENCES

Applebee, Arthur N. *Tradition and Reform in the Teaching of English: A History*. Urbana, Ill.: National Council of Teachers of English, 1974.

Boykin, Wilfred E. "The Next 10 Years' Trends for Mathematics Education," *NASSP Bulletin* 62, no. 422 (December 1978): 101–10.

Fiasca, Michael, ed. "In Search of Unity," special issue, *School Science and Mathematics* 75, no. 659 (January 1975).

Gibney, Thomas and Karns, Edward. "Mathematics Education—1955–1975: A Summary of the Findings," *Educational Leadership* 36, no. 5 (February 1979): 356–61.

Judy, Stephen N., ed. "English Since Sputnik," *The English Journal* 68, no. 6 (September 1979): 7–95.

Judy, Stephen N. and England, David A., eds. "An Historical Primer on the Teaching of English," *The English Journal* 68, no. 4 (April 1979): 6–85.

Kaufman, Irving et al., eds. "Curriculum in Art," special issues, *Curriculum Theory Network* 4, issues 2, 3 (1974).

Kiernan, Owen B., ed. *Where Will the Schools Be?* Reston, Va.: National Association of Secondary School Principals, 1974.

Mirsky, Jerome G. "Goals Clarification: Curriculum, Teaching, Evaluation," The 1975 Northeast Conference, *The Modern Language Journal* 59, nos. 5–6 (1975): 275–79.

Purves, Alan C. "Trends and Counter Trends in the Teaching of English," *NASSP Bulletin* 63, no. 427 (May 1979): 87–93.

Sabar, Naama. "Science, Curriculum and Society Trends in Science Curriculum," *Science Education* 63, no. 2 (April 1979): 257–69.

Sidwell, Robert. *Building Instructional Programs in Music Education*. Englewood Cliffs, N.J.: Prentice-Hall, 1973.

Stake, Robert E. and Easley, Jack A. *Case Studies in Science Education*. Washington, D.C.: U.S. Government Printing Office, 1978.

13 / THE POLITICS OF CURRICULUM MAKING

When members of the National Institute of Education quizzed officials from more than sixty education and citizen groups, they found the officials are more worried about who makes the decisions on school curriculum than about what is being taught. Although NIE's respondents unanimously agreed that it is better to leave the ultimate decisions on curriculum to the local arena, opinions differed sharply about who is making curriculum decisions, federal and state roles in curriculum development, and how curriculum materials get into the schools. This chapter is addressed to such questions. The reader will learn about the influence of textbook publishers, testing organizations, and other special groups. The roles of teachers, students, board members, principals, and superintendents are also included in this analysis of curriculum policymaking. The discerning reader will recognize an underlying struggle between complex political and professional reform apparatus at the national level and "loosely coupled" educational systems at other levels aimed at preserving local values and interests.

The Politics of Curriculum Decision Making

Curriculum decision making is political. Pressure groups of all kinds are proposing competing values concerning what to teach. A state board must decide, for example, whether to give in to efforts to have the biblical version of human origin—the creation theory—become part of the content in the school or to follow the pressure of those who want only the Darwinian evolutionary theory to be taught. Members of state and local public agencies legally responsible for these decisions regularly are accepting and rejecting different values in some way. They may bargain and permit new values to enter as modifications in the program on a piecemeal basis. They may give lip service to the new values, indicating their importance in general terms but not providing concrete ways for fulfillment. They may reject a proposed curriculum because it does not meet their view of a school's functions. The decision to accept or reject a proposal often depends on the decision maker's own view as to whether the school should emphasize individual growth and enrichment, transmission of subject matter, or preparation for life in the community. Curriculum policy is not always rational or based on research. Decisions, that is to say, are not often based on careful analysis of content in the discipline and of societal needs, or on studies of the learning process and concerns of learners.

Some idea of the complexity of curriculum policymaking can be gained from this paragraph by Kirst and Walker:

> A mapping of the leverage points for curriculum policy making in local schools would be exceedingly complex. It would involve three levels of government, and numerous private organization foundations, accrediting associations, national testing agencies, textbook-software companies, and interest groups (such as the NAACP or the John Birch Society). Moreover, there would be a configuration of leverage points within a particular local school system including teachers, department heads, the assistant superintendent for instruction, the superintendent, and the school board. Cutting across all levels of government would be the pervasive influence of various celebrities, commentators, interest groups, and the journalists who use the mass media to disseminate their views on curriculum. It would be very useful if we were able to quantify the amount of influence of each of these groups of individuals and show input-output interactions for just one school system. Unfortunately, this is considerably beyond the state of the art.[1]

DECISION MAKING ABOUT
WHAT WILL BE TAUGHT

There are several definitions of curriculum that would alter most analysis of curriculum making. To say, for example, that the curriculum is what the learner actually experiences from schools—the outlooks, predispositions, skills, and attitudes—im-

[1]Michael W. Kirst and Decker F. Walker, "An Analysis of Curriculum Policy Making," *Review of Educational Research* 41, no. 5 (1971): 488. Copyright 1971, American Educational Research Association, Washington, D.C. Reprinted by permission.

plies that the learner personally has a major role in determining the curriculum. Individual learners can decide to some extent at least what they will learn. To say that curriculum encompasses everything that influences learning in the schools increases the range of curriculum makers by including peers, custodians, visitors, and cafeteria workers. Further, the definition means that anyone whose actions affect the school experience—either fortuitously or by plan—is engaging in curriculum making.

For this analysis, we will treat curriculum decisions as conscious policy choices that affect what is learned. These decisions pertain to the nature of programs, preinstructional plans, materials, or activities that delineate organized educational programs of the school or classroom. They are made with the intent of controlling purposes, subject matter, method, and order of instruction. Curriculum policymaking is indeed anticipatory. However, plans and materials are not always used as intended. And learner differences make it difficult to ensure that all will derive the same meaning from a common experience or opportunity.

Not all who make curriculum do so in the same way. A school superintendent who persuades his or her board to install a program of career education is influencing the curriculum. Testing agencies that determine what will be called for on standardized tests, thereby guiding the instructional program, are also making curriculum decisions. When deciding to substitute value clarification activities for those involving ecological studies, the teacher is engaging in curriculum policymaking, because each of these learning opportunities probably will lead to different outcomes. The authoritative decision to advance one outcome over another is policymaking.

CONCEPTS FOR INTERPRETING THE PROCESS OF POLITICAL DECISION MAKING

Certain ideas and issues provide a framework for understanding the politics of curriculum decision making. Some of these come from studies by sociologists, and some from insightful educators observing how curriculum decisions are being made.

The Professionalization of Reform

Daniel P. Moynihan is credited with the idea of "the professionalization of reform"—the notion that efforts to change the

American social system (including schools) have in recent years been undertaken by persons whose profession is to do just that.[2] National curriculum reform has been spearheaded by persons like Jerrold Zacharias, Mario Fantini, and B. Frank Brown. Professional reformers tend to measure their success by the number of changes they get started.

Examples of professional reformers in action are found in: (1) J. Hottois and N.A. Milner's study citing evidence that the initiative for introducing sex education came from educators, although the educators themselves claimed that sex education was added in response to public demands for it;[3] (2) D. Nelkin's complaint that, in connection with the nationwide introduction of the curriculum Man: A Course of Study, "an elite corps of unrelated professional academics and their government friends run things in the school;"[4] (3) Norman Drachler's account of how a United States commissioner of education established the Right to Read Program with overtones of a political manifesto, including demands for accountability, minority teachers, cultural pluralism in the curriculum, bilingual education, vouchers, and competency-based teacher certification;[5] and (4) description of the Reverend Jesse Jackson's Push for Excellence Program with funding from such sources as the Ford Foundation and the federal government.[6] Unlike other professional reformers, Jackson does not call for radical curriculum reform but instead emphasizes the changing of students' attitudes and performance.

In his analysis of professional reformers, William Boyd sees them as a controversial new force in educational policymaking. He describes them as pursuing their visions of equal opportunity and a more just society convinced of their expertise and its prerogatives, armed with "solutions looking for problems," assisted by an educational research establishment with its built-in incentive to discover failure, which justifies even more research, supplied by federal and foundation funding, and stimulated by the civil rights discovery of new classes of disadvantaged students and forms of discrimination,

[2]Daniel Moynihan, *Maximum Feasible Misunderstanding* (New York: The Free Press, 1969).

[3]J. Hottois and N.A. Milner, *The Sex Education Controversy* (Lexington, Mass.: Heath, 1975).

[4]D. Nelkin, "The Science-Textbook Controversies," *Scientific American* 234, no. 4 (April 1976): 36.

[5]Norman Drachler, "Education and Politics in Large Cities, 1950–70," in *The Politics of Education, NSSE Yearbook 1977* (Chicago: University of Chicago Press, 1977), pp. 188–219.

[6]Barbara Sizemore, "Push Politics and the Education of America's Youth," *Phi Delta Kappan* 60, no. 1 (1979): 364–70.

such as the non-English-speaking, handicapped, and victims of sex discrimination.[7]

Forces for Stability

In contrast to professional reformers, many communities, school boards, school administrators, and teachers are more interested in maintaining social values of the current curriculum and the structure of the schools. To them, implementation of the curriculum changes proposed by professional reformers is seen as too costly in terms of coordination, unpredictability, conflict, and the like. It may be that the power of the forces for stability is now undergoing erosion, yet Lawrence Iannaccone and Peter Cistone testified in 1974 to the strengths of a constraining policy in innovation by saying, "Two decades of effort in the area of race, equality, and curricular revision with more federal input than impact speak loudly enough for those who will listen. Schools today are more like the schools of twenty years ago than they are like anything else."[8]

Constraints on policy for curriculum innovation occur through *non-decision making, conflict avoidance*, the *threat of controversy*, and *loose coupling*. Non-decision making refers to the ability of powerful interests to control the decision-making agenda, preventing the discussion of "undesirable issues." Wilson Riles, the California State Superintendent of Public Instruction, along with leaders from the California educational establishment tried, for example, to avoid public exposure of a campaign to place a school voucher initiative on the 1980 ballot. A low profile strategy was laid out at a meeting of educational groups where they also agreed to step up propaganda efforts to improve the public image of public education. Riles turned down numerous invitations to debate the voucher question, saying, "If we were to get into a knock-down drag out fight, it would get attention. If they [voucher advocates] are going to get publicity, they are going to have to do it on their own."[9] Non-decision making is a formidable barrier to change by keeping potential issues from being discussed or recognized.

[7]William L. Boyd, "The Politics of Curriculum Change and Stability," *Educational Researcher* 8, no. 2 (February 1979): 15.

[8]Lawrence Iannaccone and Peter J. Cistone, *The Politics of Education* (Eugene, Oregon: ERIC Clearing House on Educational Management, University of Oregon, 1974), p. 64.

[9]Quote taken from *Los Angeles Times*, October 15, 1979, p. 1, in an article written by Jack McCurdy, "Subdued Drive On To Stop School Voucher Initiative."

Conflict avoidance refers to educators' unwillingness to introduce curriculum changes that conflict with community values and are, therefore, likely to arouse controversy and opposition. William Boyd found that the degree of latitude for local educators in effecting curriculum change depends on the community.[10] In general, rural school districts and those in the "sun belt" of the United States are more restrictive about the content of courses such as social studies, literature, and biology. Methods of teaching reading or mathematics are sometimes a matter of public controversy, especially in conservative communities.

The *politics of controversy* is a technique used by those with a minority viewpoint to control the majority. Using a squeaking wheel tactic, those opposed to a curriculum innovation create a controversy in the hope that school authorities will back off from it. Textbook publishers, for example, are known to be sensitive about introducing into their materials content that is likely to be controversial. Thus the threat of controversy results in nonpublication and weak pablum in the curriculum.

Loose coupling is recognition that the goals set by reformers—the ideal curriculum—may not be faithfully followed by local school boards—the formal curriculum—and certainly are not likely to be attained by the procedures of teachers in the classroom—the perceived and operational curriculum. Awareness of loose coupling, or the inability of policymakers to implement their curriculum plans and to effect their desired outcomes, has resulted in what Arthur Wise calls "hyper-rationalization."[11] Since teachers have failed to attain the goals, they must be made accountable for the goals. Classroom methods and procedures for treating handicapped and bilingual children, for example, are now specified in detail by federal and state agencies and by the courts. Compliance is sought through program evaluation, site visits, reviews of classroom records, and learner verification—pupils both displaying desired competencies and reporting to authorities about teachers' practices. Policymakers in federal or state governments now mandate measurable goals (narrow, selective, and minimal) and demand frequent testing of pupil achievement with respect to these goals. Additional control over the curriculum occurs through special staff development of experienced teachers and competency-based education for novices—both types

[10]Boyd, "The Politics of Curriculum Change," p. 15.
[11]Arthur E. Wise, "The Hyper-rationalization of American Education," *Educational Leadership* 35, no. 5 (February 1978): 354–62.

of training programs consistent with the curriculum goals of the centralized planners.

PARTICIPANTS IN DETERMINING CURRICULUM POLICY

Teachers

At the classroom or instructional level, most teachers have the opportunity to define instructional objectives within an overall framework that indicates what is to be taught. Often they can also design and order learning activities to achieve these ends. They make important curriculum decisions when they decide to group activities around particular organizing centers such as problems, a project, an area of inquiry, subject topics, and units. However, a teacher's freedom in curriculum development varies. Many years ago, Virgil Herrick proposed three different degrees of teacher responsibility for making curriculum decisions.

His ideas can be seen in Table 9, adapted from 'The Concept of Curricular Design."[12] In Table 9, Degree I gives the teacher least responsibility and the children none. The teacher is concerned about the interests, questions, and problems of children only incidentally as they can be brought into the discussion of the textbook material.

At Degree III, the teacher is still relying on an outside source (for example, a subject matter expert), to determine the concepts to be taught. On the other hand, a teacher at this level is engrossed in such questions as: What questions do these children have that can be used in developing the concept? What learning activities, materials, and processes can be used in dealing with the concept?

A particular teacher's degree of responsibility depends on the teacher's competency, willingness to accept responsibility, and the teaching role encouraged by the leadership in the school. Educators usually stress the role of teachers in curriculum making. Teachers are admonished in the professional literature to bring the school into closer relations with home and neighborhood, to set objectives that will have significance in the child's own life, to base objectives for each learner on his or her powers and needs. Frequently, however, there are restraining forces on the teacher. Some teachers may be reluctant to innovate a curriculum change because they are ap-

[12]Virgil E. Herrick, "The Concept of Curricular Design," in *Toward Improved Curriculum Theory* (Chicago: University of Chicago Press, 1950), pp. 37–50.

TABLE 9   Degrees of Teacher Responsibility in Making Curriculum Decisions

Areas of Decision	Degree I	Degree II	Degree III
Concepts to be taught	Text or workbook	Text and course of study	Subject specialist
Experience, facts, activities, materials	Text, workbook, and teacher	Text, teacher, groups of pupils	Teacher, pupils, community
Timing and schedules	Text, workbook, teacher, and school program	Teacher and school program	Teacher, pupils, school program
Evaluation	Text, workbook, teacher, school evaluation program	Teacher, concepts to be learned, evaluation program	Teachers, pupils, school evaluation
Continuities and next steps	Text, workbook, and activities of school program	Text, courses of study, teacher	Teacher, pupils

prehensive of resistance from students, colleagues, parents, and administrators.

In earlier periods, teachers were more involved in courses of study preparation. Teacher participation in curriculum revision was not new even in 1922. Gary Peltier, for example, tells about a program of curriculum construction at that time using teacher participation. The account brings forth most of the arguments in favor of teacher participation in curriculum decision making. As a result of this participation, teachers became better informed about the aims of education and better able to interpret programs for the people, and they accepted suggestions for new methods more readily. Their courses of study then reflected newer views of subject matter, social needs, and attention to the learner.[13]

A radical proposal for curriculum decision making was made by Hilda Taba in 1962. She called for a deliberate inversion of the com-

[13]Gary L. Peltier, "Teacher Participation in Curriculum Revision: An Historical Case Study," *History of Education Quarterly* 7, no. 2 (Summer 1967): 1209–15.

mon procedure. Instead of starting with a general design in which curriculum began at the societal level and rippled down through institutions to the classroom, Taba proposed that curriculum making start at the teaching level with the planning of specific units of instruction. The results of experimenting with these units then would provide a basis for a general design to be created later. Taba's strategy was calculated to infuse theory into the operation of the practitioner from the outset.[14] As indicated in Chapter 8, Jean H. Young has a similar notion. However, school or districtwide coordination of curriculum by teachers is unlikely because of their focused interest in unique classrooms.

Teachers are likely to influence curriculum policy in the larger political arena through their unions. Teacher organizations are beginning to look at curriculum issues. Accountability procedures, differentiated staffing, voucher plans, and other innovations affecting teachers force them to take positions on what shall be taught. Until recently, however, demands from such organizations focused primarily on staff benefits such as pay, class size, or extra assignments. But today, there is an expectation that teachers will use this organized power in the interests of curriculum. Ronald Corwin, for instance, questioned secondary school teachers in the Midwest and found that they wanted to exercise authority over such matters as textbook selection. They wanted to establish minimum knowledge that students enrolled in particular courses should derive from the courses and to determine what concepts and values were to be taught in a particular course. Teachers also wanted the authority to name the appropriate method for teaching the course.[15]

A national survey found that 45 percent of teachers had no direct involvement in selecting textbooks for use in their classrooms.[16]

Teachers are beginning to influence other curriculum decisions through collective bargaining. The bargaining away of innovative programs in preference for smaller classes and guaranteed jobs for experienced teachers is a case in point. Van Geel, for instance, raises the issue of whether boards of education should be in the position of having to pay an economic price to a private group (the teachers'

[14]Hilda Taba, *Curriculum Development: Theory and Practice* (New York: Harcourt Brace and World, 1962), p. 529.

[15]Ronald Corwin, "The New Teaching Profession," *NSSE Yearbook 1974, Teacher Education*, Part II (Chicago: University of Chicago Press, 1975), pp. 230–64.

[16]P. Kenneth Komoski, "The Realities of Choosing and Using Instructional Materials," *Educational Leadership* 36, no. 1 (October 1978): 48.

unions) in order to keep control of what they were established to do.[17] Indeed, collective bargaining has raised the issue of whether public interests in curriculum—the interests of students, parents, and others—might be trampled on if disproportionate powers are given at the bargaining table to board and teacher groups.[18]

Teachers' organizations also have much influence at the state and federal levels. Teacher political action committees are active in nearly all states raising funds for politicians friendly to teachers' causes. Teacher center legislation, for example, which states that teacher centers must come under the operation of a policy board whose members are represented by a majority of practicing elementary and secondary teachers, was lobbied for and supported by the teachers unions.[19]

Principals

Despite the formal job description as curriculum leader, the principal tends to be little more than a middleman between the central office, parents, and the staff in implementing curriculum. Principals are burdened with such a multitude of managerial activities that it is extremely difficult for them to devote the time and effort required for innovation on a substantial scale. Principals can be actively engaged in curriculum making only in schools where their planning responsibilities can be carried out without heavy operating responsibilities.

The role of the principal in curriculum making is not settled. Some people think that the principal should initiate curriculum change. Others believe that principals can be more effective and influential by implementing curriculum decisions already made. One would expect principals working in centralized school systems, as opposed to those in decentralized systems, to be more likely to accept the latter role. To date, however, this has not been shown. Although the principal now has the power to make some decisions that were formerly made at the central office, accountability is still directed upward, not toward the community. Decentralization has probably made some principals more responsible to their communities and more attentive

[17]T. Van Geel, *Authority to Control the School Program* (Lexington, Mass.: Heath, 1976), pp. 178–79.

[18]Douglas E. Mitchell, "The Impact of Collective Bargaining on Public and Client Interests in Education," *Teachers College Record* 80, no. 4 (May 1979): 695–717.

[19]S.J. Yarker and G. Yarker, "And So We Asked Ourselves About Teacher Centers," *Theory Into Practice* 37, no. 3 (1978): 248–57.

to systematized goals and to ways of tailoring local school objectives to meet these goals. Esra Staples, for instance, has found that, under decentralization, the principal's influence has been the greatest in selecting materials, altering programs in content areas, and in determining the school goals.[20]

Mainly, curriculum development has not improved in decentralized school systems because teachers and principals lack the technical skills for curriculum making and refinement of their roles. Decision making has been placed at the local level with very little guidance for the principal. Meanwhile, we continue to hear the platitude that the "greatest amount of power to change and improve the curriculum lies in the hands of local administrators." Older studies in support of this belief are found in the work of Henry Brickell and of Paul Mort and F.G. Cornell, who reported that administrators were the vital force in the initiation of change and that neutrality on the part of principals prevented changes.[21] The reason for this conflicting assessment of the principal is that the older studies were referring to the legal authority of the principalship as a power in effecting change. The newer view attends to the principals' lack of expertise, which impedes their ability to make wise decisions about curriculum. Also, as curriculum has become increasingly legalized because of the growing body of legislation, regulation, and judicial doctrine, the principals have had their authority to initiate curriculum diminished.

Superintendents

The superintendent influences curriculum policy by responding to matters before the board of education, initiating programs for the inservice education of teachers, making district personnel aware of changes occurring in other schools, and moderating outside demands for change. The superintendent must take the curriculum demands from state and federal governments and make them acceptable to the local population. Existing studies of the superintendent are quite old. The data we have, however, indicate that school board members tend to feel that superintendents are rather poor in curriculum planning. Superintendents also rate themselves weakest in curriculum

[20]Esra I. Staples, *Impact of Decentralization on Curriculum: Selected Viewpoints* (Washington, D.C.: ASCD, 1975).

[21]Henry Brickell, *Organizing New York for Education Change* (Albany, N.Y.: State Department of Education, 1961); Paul Mort and F.G. Cornell, *American Schools in Transition* (New York: Teachers College, Columbia University, 1941).

and instruction, as opposed to performance in finance or plant management.[22] Nevertheless, the superintendent is the key figure in curriculum innovation and educational decision making.[23] In large cities, assistant superintendents for curriculum and instruction attempt to influence the curriculum through their work with committees of teachers and their preparation of guidelines, bulletins, staff development sessions, and the like.

The superintendent, like the principal, is losing control over the curriculum to the centralizing forces of state and federal legislators and to the courts. On the basis of his review of research over the past two decades, on the other hand, William Boyd concluded that one of the most effective means for local control of the curriculum occurred by communities having superintendents whose values were consonant with those predominant in the district.[24] Superintendents were fired when they strayed from community values. Recent developments in taking control out of the hands of local superintendents, however, may be eroding the last power of local control.

Students

Students seldom have formal influence over what they learn. There are, of course, schools in which provisions are made for some genuine self-government by students. Student officers can be elected and appointed to policy boards. They may even approve faculty appointments and determine course offerings and academic requirements. The extent of control given students is usually a function of maturity they have attained and the nature of the particular community. Student policymaking is generally derived rather than absolute, a privilege granted by higher powers and subject to revocation by them. Often student government is an administrator's or teacher's means of securing student cooperation.

Informally, however, students have much influence over what is taught. Often they can "vote with their feet" by refusing to enroll in courses that feature the curriculum of academic specialists. The

[22]Neal Gross, *Who Runs Our Schools?* (New York: John Wiley and Sons, 1958), p. 195.

[23]Gordon M. MacKenzie, Harmon Zeigler, et al., "Communication and Decision-Making in American Public Education," in *The Politics of Education,* Jay Scribner, ed., *NSSE Yearbook 1977* (Chicago: University of Chicago Press, 1977).

[24]William L. Boyd, "The Changing Politics of Curriculum Policy Making for American Schools," *Review of Educational Research* 48, no. 4 (Fall 1978): 622.

failure of students to respond to the Physical Science Study Committee's "Physics" was an argument for curriculum change. Alternative schools and underground newspapers are other instances of student power. The late 1960s saw both college and high school students dissenting against their role as a captive audience and asking for both a social curriculum that would confront the facts of war, racism, power structures, and a personal curriculum to help them answer the question, Who am I?

Local School Board

Political analysis shows local boards of education playing a diminishing role in actual decision making.[25] Members of these boards often rubber stamp the professionals' recommendations. Board members usually lack the technical competencies they need to decide on specific curriculum programs. Hence, they vote on intuition or the advice of others. Also, growing state and federal pressure has weakened local jurisdiction, and in large districts at least, the less specific policies are not carried out according to the board's mandates. Usually the smaller the community, the more likely the public is to believe that school board members are primarily concerned with the welfare of children. Residents of large urban centers tend to see board members as individuals seeking prestige and power.

Lee K. Davies has described how the actions of legislators, judges, and lay groups are draining control from local school boards.[26] She documents the courts as the major players in the current struggle for control. Special interest groups prefer to go to court if board policies are not to their satisfaction rather than to discuss board policy at public meetings of the board. Similarly, legislatures are viewed as a court of last resort for the citizen who is in opposition to the local board. The instances of Massachusetts legislation effected by parents in Boston seeking redress for local policy on assignment of pupils to special classes and of Florida legislation in opposition to Orange County's policy regarding sex education are cases in point.

Briefly, it appears that federal, state, and local professionals are determining the curriculum and the board is serving as an advisory or sounding board. The realities of implementing federal directives

[25]David K. Wiles and Houston Conley, "School Boards: Their Policy-Making Relevance," *Teachers College Record* 75, no. 3 (February 1974): 309–18.
[26]Lee K. Davies, "The School Board's Struggle to Survive," *Educational Leadership* 34, no. 2 (November 1976): 95–99.

and court orders tend to make board members more dependent on experts, especially those with legal expertise.

Local Communities

The role of the local lay community in formulating curriculum is minimal. The public knows little about course content and is not involved with general curriculum issues. Vandalism, drugs, and discipline tend to be seen as problems, not as curriculum issues. Until very recently, local communities left curriculum planning to professionals. Only occasionally did the public get involved in curriculum. These occasions are viewed as episodic issues which emerge under special conditions and shortly subside. Thus it is not textbooks that cause concern, but a particular textbook under a special set of circumstances.

Community participation in local curriculum making was thought to increase because of the establishment of such innovations as local school advisory bodies charged with representing community needs and interests and local school site management. To date, however, study of such councils has shown that most participation has come from parents of successful learners and that not much has been improved by virtue of the school councils. This may have been due to school boards' lack of specificity in stating what they mean by "participation" or to the reluctance of educators to share in decision making.

Jon Schaffarzick found that citizen participation in curriculum policymaking tends to be minimal, perfunctory, and reactive.[27] Citizen participation is usually superficial. Citizens take part very early when general goals are being established or very late when most of the preparation for change has been completed. Citizens can, however, be influential when they become activated. When there are significant conflicts between citizens and school board, lay groups usually win. Most active parent groups represent special interests in the curriculum, working for such programs as those in behalf of the handicapped or those that will strengthen the fields of athletics, art, and music. Together with the professional educator associated with those particular programs, they engage in campaigns to protect and enhance their programmatic interests.

[27]Jon Schaffarzick, "Teacher and Lay Participation in Local Curriculum Change Considerations." Paper presented at the American Educational Research Association Annual Meeting. San Francisco, Calif., 1976.

Most citizen groups active in school affairs are not parents, however, but members of noneducational organizations, such as business people's associations and property owners' groups. They are more interested in school policies bearing on taxes and prestige of the school as a factor in property values than in decisions about course content.

Regional and State Agencies

States exercise leverage on the curriculum in many ways. State legislatures frequently prescribe what shall be taught. Driver training and courses on the dangers of alcohol and narcotics are commonly mandated. Insurance, oil, and automobile interests, too, have made their influence felt in such matters as strong driver education legislation. Professional organizations, like those of vocational, special, and physical educators, and home economics teachers, use their state-affiliated chapters to maintain their interests by influencing state requirements. Representatives of these special interest groups long ago cemented linkages within state departments of education.

The most noteworthy evidence of state control of curriculum is seen in the national minimum competency movement which has influenced most states. This movement is concerned with assessing the basic academic skills of students at the high school and grammar school levels, and, ultimately, with establishing competency standards which all students must meet. By 1980, most states had either adopted legislation with respect to testing such skills or had enacted regulations through their state boards of education. The remaining states, whether through legislative or state board activity, are contemplating some form of action with respect to minimum competency testing.

The roles of state departments of education and state boards of education vary. In New England, the local schools have had much freedom from state control, whereas in most southern states, textbooks and courses of instruction are mandated by the state. The manner of control has also differed. Some states, like New York, have long exercised control through required tests and examinations. Others, like Texas and California, exercise their leverage through state adoption of textbooks and instructional systems. In Texas, for example, the state commissioner nominates the members of the State Textbook Committee and the State Board of Education has final authority in the selection of texts. State education department personnel specify the criteria for selecting the books, including the topics to be covered. Books that have been selected are distributed to schools at state expense. Districts that want to use other texts must do so with their own local money.

In 1974, California adopted, for the first time, a multiple list of textbooks in a field instead of a single or very limited list. Further, the criteria used in California reflected new influences on the curriculum, such as women's rights and ethnic or racial groups. Evaluators were mainly concerned with the structure of the materials, and with portrayal of race and minority relationships. These concerns, in turn, had an effect on the publishing houses, many of which modified their material.[28]

Six years later in California an attempt to return to a very limited list of textbooks was under way. State Senator Rodda, who represents state employees working in the state textbook printing house, is seeking to restrict the number of approved textboks to those printed by the state. He has encountered little opposition from other legislators because he chairs the powerful finance committee. Thus we can see how it is possible for political pork barrel interests to dominate curriculum decisions.

Some states use accreditation procedures to maintain a particular curriculum. Accreditation may be done by the state department itself, by an association of professional educators (such as the National Association of School Principals), or by a private regional accrediting organization (such as the North Central Association). Usually these agencies require site visits and evidence of a school's adherence to each of their detailed standards. One of their standards might read, "English courses are organized by themes or experiences with a minimum of emphasis on type or chronology." A standard for social studies might read, "Social studies offerings assist pupils in understanding ideologies that differ from democracy."

Testing Agencies

Testing agencies have helped make a "national" curriculum. Standardized tests for college admission have pretty well defined what students going to college must know in the way of understanding and reasoning. Further, national standardized reading and math tests given in the elementary schools determine much of the specific content of the curriculum. The Educational Testing Service, with an an-

---

[28]Barbara Crane, "The California 'Effect' on Textbook Adoption," *Educational Leadership* 32, no. 4 (January 1975): 283–85.

nual budget of $52 million, dominates the testing industry and administers a broad range of vocational and college placement tests. Its Scholastic Aptitude Test is considered the most important test the company has. About 1½ million students take the test each year. The test publishers say they try to "hold a middle ground"; they try not to freeze the secondary school curriculum and not to adopt innovations too quickly. Their practice of involving professionals from secondary schools and colleges in the preparation and review of the tests is intended to keep the achievement tests abreast of important trends.

Textbooks and Other Curriculum Materials

Most teaching in our schools is from textbooks or other curriculum material, such as guides, workbooks, and laboratory apparatus. Decker Walker and Jon Schaffarzick have found that student achievement—what students acquire from instruction—mirrors to a substantial extent the content in the textbook: "Students are more likely to learn what they have been taught than something else."[29] Once an item of content has been included in a text as important for children to use, Walker and Schaffarzick say,

> the multiple resources of the curriculum in use—and the variety of active student learning processes combine to produce a level of achievement that is usually greater than any additional increment that might be produced by any further refinement of the curriculum or any improvement in teaching style or method or medium of instruction or organizational change in the school or classroom.[30]

Often the textbook publisher is only a disseminator, and the actual product is developed by professionals in regional laboratories, universities, and nonprofit organizations paid by agencies of the federal government, private foundations, and professional and scientific associations. At other times, the publisher contracts directly with teachers to develop the company's products. Reference has already been made to the pressure on publishers from state curriculum commissions and groups demanding certain emphasis on content. Publishers also use their sales organizations for information and guidance in the revision and production of texts. "Strangely enough this network of salespeople is the only reasonably depend-

. [29]Decker Walker and Jon Schaffarzick, "Comparing Curriculum," *Review of Educational Research* 44, no. 1 (1974): 97.
   [30]Ibid., p. 101.

able comprehensive mechanism for compiling the preferences and prejudices of schools on curriculum matters."[31]

The Federal Government

The federal government has become a very powerful influence on the kinds of materials used in schools. Mainly through the National Science Foundation (NSF) and the United States Office of Education (USOE), it has dwarfed all previous curriculum development efforts by states, local systems, and private enterprise. Federally supported regional laboratories, academic scholars, and nonprofit organizations have produced curriculum materials that have been used in most of our schools. Generally, this material has modified the content of existing subject matter—math, science, English, reading—rather than introduced new disciplines into the school. Also, by specifying the use of standardized tests for evaluating the projects they finance, federal agencies have fostered national objectives.

Initially the government seemed to be interested in increasing the number of curriculum options available to schools. Later, however, there were deliberate efforts to ensure that schools used the new curriculum through evaluation requirements and special monies given to disseminate materials developed with federal funds. The government became more interested in producing change than in merely making change possible.

The partnership between government and certain subject matter specialists has had effects on the curriculum, some of them dire. Jerome Bruner and Jerrold Zacharias are two professional reformers who have been sponsored by National Science Foundation funds. Zacharias gave much of the impetus to the so-called curriculum reform movement of the 1960s, in which subject specialists took it on themselves to define the structure of subject matter worth teaching to pupils. He argued then that a discipline-based curriculum was necessary because "our real problem as a nation was creeping anti-intellectualism from which came many of our educational deficiencies."[32] Dissatisfaction with the scholars' curriculum came under attack for reasons ranging from economics to ideology. Evaluation in terms of pupil achievement failed to demonstrate its worth. Test scores declined considerably as did student interest in further study of the subjects taught. Zacharias, the physicist who was partly

---

[31]Kirst and Walker, "An Analysis of Curriculum Policy Making," p. 497.
[32]J. Koerner, *Who Controls American Education?* (Boston: Beacon Press, 1968), p. 62.

responsible for the academic emphasis, reversed his judgment and admitted that the impact of the new math, for example, was "on the whole negative." Along with other critics, he said that the proponents of the reform curriculum were too concerned with pure subject matter and paid too little attention to the practical uses of mathematics in the children's present and future lives. Subsequently, Zacharias conceived a new project and received $4 million from the USOE to develop a television series, which stressed the power of math as a tool to cope with such common tasks as baking a cake, leaving a tip, and estimating the amount of paint needed to paint a room.

In 1977 the National Institute of Education (NIE) shifted its budget from curriculum development to support for basic and applied research and efforts to stimulate and coordinate the research and development (R and D) work of other educational agencies. This change in federal reform strategy occurred because of the high costs of curriculum development as carried out by regional laboratories and other R and D agencies, and because of public concern over the nature and effects of federal support for curriculum development. Jon Schaffarzick and Gary Sykes have discussed this shift in government priorities.[33] They recall the issues of federally backed revision efforts—the argument that federal involvement in curriculum contributed to nationalization of the curriculum versus the argument that such efforts increased the alternatives from which to choose.

The 1977 NIE policy established equalization of educational opportunity for minorities, women, the non-English-speaking, the poor, and the geographically isolated as the focus for federal curriculum development (instructional improvement) efforts. NIE recognizes that there is little consensus about the proper role of government in curriculum development, particularly in the areas where values are so prominent—social studies, moral education, and sex education. There is much fear among the educational community that federal sponsorship of development, demonstration, dissemination, and teacher training activities is an illegitimate attempt to influence state and local control over the school curriculum.

Foundations

The foundations are a major source of funds and influence on the curriculum. The Ford, Rockefeller, Carnegie, and Kettering founda-

[33]Jon Schaffarzick and Gary Sykes, "A Changing NIE: New Leadership, A New Climate," *Educational Leadership* 35, no. 5 (February 1978): 367–72.

tions have been very active in curriculum development. Some indication of the direction and effect of their influence is found in *A Foundation Goes to School*.[34] This report tells of deliberate efforts to change the habits of school systems and to modify the curriculum, both by putting into practice the curriculum reform movement of Zacharias and Bruner and by underwriting the production of locally made materials. The foundations' effort was only partially successful, mostly in suburban school districts. The effort to package curriculum seemed to bog down because teachers wanted to create their own materials under the rationale of local uniqueness. Yet, in many instances, overproduction of inadequate curriculum units at the local level occurred because of failure to estimate the difficulties of curriculum construction.

In terms of both cost and learning, the adoption of professionally developed curricula produced far more substantive change than in-house curriculum development. Without systematic teacher preparation, the use of new curricula tended to be superficial, sporadic, and ephemeral. The most lasting application seemed to occur in middle-sized suburbs, which were small enough to avoid the divisive debate between powerful interest groups but large enough to require that innovative movements be identified with more than individual or simple localized concerns.

Pressure Groups

Kirst and Walker have differentiated between two separate policymaking processes: normal policymaking and crisis policymaking. Groups such as the John Birch Society, Chamber of Commerce, National Association of Manufacturers, and AFL-CIO are regarded as relatively weak in normal policymaking but very powerful in crisis policymaking.[35]

Sputnik, drug abuse, war, depression, violence, energy, and natural disaster are examples of the everlasting crises which draw the response of different groups. Then there are organizations like the Council for Basic Education, which lobbies consistently for the teaching of fundamental, intellectual subjects. Also, there are causes that invite the combined pressures of many different groups. Virtually every organization working for the advancement of Afro-Americans, whether militant, moderate, or in between, has de-

---

[34]Ford Foundation, *A Foundation Goes to School* (New York: Ford Foundation, 1972).
[35]Kirst and Walker, "An Analysis of Curriculum Policy Making," p. 498.

manded a more adequate treatment of blacks in books and courses dealing with the history of the United States.

CONCLUDING COMMENTS

Many groups and individuals are interested in having a say about what should be taught. No single source believes that it has enough influence or power. Each tends to feel that another element is in charge. In reality, it is a standoff. The curriculum decision of a board of education, a federal agency, a state department of education, or a legislature can be changed in spirit and in fact by principals and teachers. Although students are often thought to be without much power in deciding what will be taught in schools, they have a great deal to say about what is learned.

The political linkage of special interest groups within professional education to those in government is not too different from the more exposed business-government ties. Most curriculum decisions, however, reflect conflicts among persons and groups. Like most political solutions, the curriculum comes about by compromise, bargaining, and other forms of accommodation. It is clear that the making of curriculum policy does not follow a tidy rational procedure resting on the evidence from research. It is also clear that general ignorance of the curriculum experience of learners will match the expectations of policies made outside the classroom.

QUESTIONS

1. Do you opt for the possibility of a "moral, principled, legal" model of curriculum making, in which curriculum decisions are made by authorities on the basis of logic and with the guidance of experts? Or do you prefer a model that is highly political and that seeks no more than an imperfect justice because there is no other kind?
2. Should professional curriculum workers, supervisors, teachers, and principals exert more influence in the control of curriculum? Why? Why not? Consider in your answer such matters as whether educators have the unity as well as the necessary intellectual and moral authority.
3. What evidence can you supply that the discretionary power of local boards of education is being whittled away?
4. The efforts of singleminded groups and individuals operating at local, state, and national levels have been able to gain support for special interests such as retarded children and health and consumer education. What has been the effect of these efforts on the total curriculum plan?

5. Some people feel threatened by our present national efforts to influence the curriculum; others see federal influence as desirable. What evidence do you have that one or more of the following consequences are associated with federal actions?
   a. Stifling inventiveness.
   b. Increasing range of local options.
   c. Stimulating local effort.
   d. Denying local needs and interests.
6. What new political alliances do you envision in state efforts to shape curriculum policy through competency-based examinations? Who is formulating the skills to be measured and who is setting the standards that determine passing?
7. What forces appear to have the greatest effect on what is taught in a situation familiar to you?

SELECTED REFERENCES

Boyd, William Lowe. "The Changing Politics of Curriculum Policy Making for American Schools," *Review of Educational Research* 48, no. 4 (Fall 1978): 577–629.

———"The Politics of Curriculum Change and Stability," *Educational Researcher* 8, no. 1 (1979): 12–19.

Dias, P.V. and Hauf, T. "Politics—Education," *Comparative Education Review*, special edition 19, no. 1 (February 1975).

Kirst, M.W. and Walker, D.F. "An Analysis of Curriculum Policy-Making," *Review of Educational Research* 41, no. 5 (December 1971): 479-511.

Koerner, J. *Who Controls American Education?* Boston: Beacon Press, 1968.

"Politics and Education," theme issue. *Educational Leadership* 34, no. 2 (November 1976): 87–132.

Scribner, Jay. *The Politics of Education*, Part II, NSSE Yearbook. Chicago: University of Chicago Press, 1977.

"State, Federal Role in Curriculum Development," theme issue. *Educational Leadership* 35, no. 5 (February 1978): 339-74.

V / RESEARCH THEORY AND CURRICULUM

A popular publication a few years ago carried the title *The Curriculum—Retrospect and Prospect*. The title would be a good one to apply to this part. The emergence of curriculum as a professional study is treated in a historical chapter. The views of a number of influential curriculum theorists and developers are examined to cast light on the nature of curriculum and the central concerns of curriculum specialists. A second chapter is devoted to appraising curriculum as a field of inquiry today, giving attention to future directions. The work of curriculum scholars is described, making it possible to see successes, gaps, and trends in curriculum research and development. The reader will find specific suggestions by which research in curriculum can be most fruitfully pursued.

14 / A HISTORICAL PERSPECTIVE OF CURRICULUM MAKING

The curriculum field's past can give some shape and meaning to the confusing number of activities that go on under the rubric *curriculum*. By looking at the efforts of a particular group of educators identified as curriculum specialists, one can find central questions that characterize the field. Historical consideration of curriculum thought and practice may also help us to be more reflective in greeting new curriculum proposals. We will see that many of these proposals are not "new" at all in a fundamental sense. Armed with a historical perspective, we will be better able to judge the consequences of curriculum ideologies. Another value of looking at our inherited ways of resolving curriculum problems is that we may be more critical of the old as well as the new.

HISTORY AND CURRENT CURRICULUM PROBLEMS

There are at least two reasons for attending to the history of curriculum thought and practice. First, a review of the past can help us identify problems with which dedicated persons have struggled and are struggling.

Admittedly, we will still have to decide whether these problems are unsolvable, and therefore should be abandoned as unfruitful areas of inquiry, or whether their very persistence makes them worthy of our attention. Consider the issue of curriculum correlation. Correlation is the relating of ideas from different subject matters; for example, mathematics may be taught as a tool in science. As early as 1895, the issue of correlation was central. Some viewed correlation with suspicion and as a threat to the inviolability of the basic divisions of subject matter. Others saw it as an answer to the problem of an overcrowded program of studies and of value in helping the child's untrained mind relate an enormous number of topics.

Today, the issue of correlation is still important. The recent popularity of competency-based curriculum, whereby pupils focus on a hierarchy of skills within a single subject rather than attend to relating skills from different subjects, is anticorrelational. Also, the use of curriculum materials prepared by academic specialists—anthropologists, physicists, historians—tends to make the school's program of studies fragmental and piecemeal. Now, as in 1895, some people ask not so much whether there should be correlation of subject matter but how. Should we group subjects around pupils and problems, using the facts from one discipline to illuminate another? Should be put within a comprehensive course the important generalizations from many fields?

A second reason for studying the history of curriculum thought and practice is that we can get a clearer understanding of the processes of curriculum making by examining the work of prominent exponents in the field. By examining what curriculum meant to those who developed the field during this century, we can see more clearly what "curriculum" means. Few issues are more important to today's theorists than the formulation of an adequate concept of curriculum. Theorists believe that its clarification may contribute to improvement of curriculum and that it will increase our understanding of curriculum phenomena. Some concepts of curriculum are:

1. A set of guidelines for developing products, books, and materials by which learning will occur.
2. A program of activities. A listing of course offerings, units, topics, content.
3. All learning guided by the school.
4. The process by which one decides what to teach.
5. The study of the processes used in curriculum making.
6. What learners actually learn at school.
7. What one plans for learners to learn.

In 1890, there was no extensive professional preparation for curriculum making, and there were no curriculum experts in the United States. Yet less than fifty years later, curriculum was a recognized field of specialization. One way to illustrate this development and at the same time illuminate the nature of the specialization is to look at the work of the individuals who have been most associated with curriculum making. The persons chosen for review span a period from 1890 until the present, and represent a much larger group of equally important specialists. One basis for selecting them is that they studied the theory of curriculum and engaged in making curriculum.

HERBARTISM AND THE McMURRYS

Charles A. McMurry (1857–1929) and his brother, Frank W. McMurry (1862–1936), taught for several years in elementary schools before going abroad to study at the University of Jena in Germany, which was a mecca for educators in the late 1890s. There they became profoundly influenced by the pedagogical theory of Johann Herbart whose *Outlines of Educational Doctrine* was the basis for many of the ideas and practices at Jena.[1]

Essentially, Herbartism was a rationalized set of philosophical and psychological ideas applied to instructional method. It rested on the assumption that only large, connected units of subject matter are able to arouse and keep alive the child's deep interest. Hence, it stressed "the doctrine of concentration," which occurs when the mind is wholly immersed in one interest to the exclusion of everything else. This doctrine was supplemented with "the doctrine of correlation," which makes one subject the focus of attention but sees to it that this subject receives support from related subjects.

Specifically, Herbartians recognized five steps as essential in the procedure of instruction:

1. *Preparation.* To revive in consciousness the related ideas from past experience that will arouse interest in the new material and prepare the pupil for its rapid understanding.
2. *Presentation.* To present the new material in concrete form, unless there is already ample sensory experience, and to relate it to the students' past experiences, such as reading, conversing, experimenting, lecturing, and so forth.
3. *Association.* To analyze and to compare the new and the old, thus evolving a new idea.
4. *Generalization.* To form general rules, laws, or principles from

[1]Johann F. Herbart, *Outlines of Educational Doctrine*, Alex F. Lange, translator (New York: Macmillan, 1904).

the analyzed experience, developing general concepts as well as sensations and perceptions.

5. _Application_ To put the generalized idea to work in other situations, sometimes to test it, sometimes to use it as a practical tool.

Herbart's followers believed that moral action was the highest educational goal and that education should prepare one for life in an idealized culture. Further, they believed that some subjects, such as history and literature, were superior for the development of moral ideas. They thought that if learners were guided by correct ideas and motivated by good interests, they would be prepared to discharge life's duties properly. Among the interests or motives to be advanced were sympathetic interest (a kindly disposition toward people), social interest (participation in public affairs), and religious interest (contemplation of human destiny).

The McMurrys recognized in Herbartian pedagogy a systematic method of selecting, arranging, and organizing the curriculum, something that had been missing in American schooling. On their return from Germany, they joined with others to apply the Herbartian methods and ideals in American schools. During his career, Charles McMurry wrote thirty books and prepared a course of study for the eight elementary grades describing how to select and arrange ideas for instruction. Principally, he addressed himself to teachers. His own teaching in the schools of Illinois and at George Peabody College for Teachers centered on the making of lesson plans according to the Herbartian five formal steps. He also concerned himself with the special instructional methods required for the teaching of specific subject fields.

Frank McMurry taught and wrote at Teachers College, Columbia University. His students were chiefly teachers who would train and supervise other teachers. His course in general methods reflected the Herbartian concern about the ends of education, the means for their attainment, the relative worth of studies, and the doctrines of correlation and interest. Both brothers participated in national organizations devoted to the study and improvement of school programs. The effect of their efforts was great. Charles's course of study provided an overall framework for teachers, giving details for conducting lessons, the types of studies, and the special methods thought best for organizing the content in each subject. Their influence on lesson planning was especially noteworthy. In the period between 1900 and 1910, "every good teacher was supposed to have a lesson plan for each class period, and the five formal steps were much in evidence."[2] Even today military instructors are expected to design their lessons according to the formal steps outlined by the McMurrys. Analysis of the McMurrys' work shows the questions and answers which define the nature of curriculum thought in this early period.

What Is the Aim of Education? The McMurrys broadened Herbartian concerns for the moral development of the child to include the desire to lead children into the ways of good citizenship and into a wise physical, social, and moral adjustment to the world.

What Subject Matter Has the Greatest Pedagogical Value? Initially, the McMurrys regarded literature as most useful in bringing the aesthetic and the intellectual into helpful association; they saw geography as the most universal, concrete correlating study. When the development of good character was the primary aim, they saw literature and history as the most important subjects. Later, the McMurrys differentiated between subjects that primarily helped the learner to express thought and those which primarily helped the learner receive or furnish thought. They noted that about one-half of schoolwork (that is, beginning reading, writing, spelling, grammar, music, numbers, modeling, drawing, and painting), depends on the other half for its motive and force. In their latter years, the McMurrys came to see that new subjects would claim favor. These new studies were nature study, science, industrial arts, health, agriculture, civics, and modern languages. Indeed, the introduction of new branches of knowledge and activity was seen by them as one of the greatest achievements of the age.

How Is Subject Matter Related to Instructional Method? The McMurrys believed there were formal elements of method and concepts for each subject, whether it be geology, arithmetic, or literature. They insisted that the child learn to think with these elements just as the specialists did in these fields and that the learner develop a consciousness of the right method of thinking in each subject. They saw that teachers at that time were not equipped with the fundamental concepts of each subject and, therefore, found it difficult to order instruction to clarify concepts in the respective fields.

[2]William H. Kilpatrick, "Dewey's Influence on Education," in *The Philosophy of John Dewey*, Paul A. Schilpp, ed. (Evanston, Ill.: Northwestern University, 1939), p. 465.

They were disturbed when curriculum workers ignored the fact that subject matter makes particular demands on the organization of the curriculum.

What Is the Best Sequence of Studies? The McMurrys thought that suitable subject matter varies according to age and stage of development. Initially, they believed in the *theory of the culture epochs*. This theory holds that the child passes through the same general stages of development through which the race or culture has passed. Hence, what interested humanity at a certain historical stage would appeal most to a child at the corresponding stage of development. It was thought, for example, that teachers should present the stories of Ulysses to younger children. *The Odyssey* was seen as a means by which the heroic impulses of childhood could be related to an ideal person who achieved what the child would like to achieve. This work was deemed of pedagogical value, because it portrayed the primitive human struggle and at the same time revealed a higher plane of reason. Similarly, *Robinson Crusoe* was viewed as a good source for showing humankind's struggle with nature and at the same time helping the learner see that myths were attempts to interpret nature. Myths, legends, and heroic tales were followed by biography and formal history.

By 1923, Charles McMurry, at least, saw the culture epoch idea as vague in its implications and admitted he knew of no sound basis for the placement of studies. For him, any particular scheme for placement of subject matter had come to be no better than the broad plan for organization that was in back of it. The importance of organizing studies in relation to the child's mode of thought was seen as the more pressing problem.

How Can the Curriculum Best Be Organized? Faced with new school studies and activities, the imposition of scholarly works on children, and the isolation of each study, Charles McMurry gave highest priority to organization of the curriculum. His first answer was to organize the school studies on a life basis. Knowledge from different subject fields was coordinated into a single project or unit of study. Pupils were to become absorbed in pragmatic life problems or centers of interest. There was, for instance, applied science, like "the problem of securing a pure milk supply"; there were geographic projects like "the Salt River Irrigation project in Arizona"; and there were historic projects like "Hamilton's project for funding the national debt." Most of these projects drew on history, geography, science, mathematics, and language. Also, each project or series of projects was to reveal the scope and meaning of a larger idea, which "like a view from the mountain top, at one glance brings into simple perspective and arrangement a whole vast grouping of minor facts."[3] The idea of evolution, for example, derived from a series of animal studies, becomes a principle of interpretation for use in other studies of animals and plants. A well-devised continuity of thoughts was kept steadily developing from grade to grade. The growth of institutions in history, for example, was one element chosen to effect continuity over the span of several years of study.

Charles McMurry saw that the central problem of curriculum was to select the right centers of organization. These centers were to be consolidation points where older forms of knowledge and new studies could be combined. The relation of centers of organization to the aim of education was most important. Further, he was concerned about who would develop the big topics or themes or organize them into effective instructional plans and materials. It seemed that experienced teachers were too absorbed with their teaching duties; scholarly specialists were too involved in the academic instruction of university students; and the pedagogical specialists were identified as members of an educational cult dealing solely in generalities and verbal distinctions.

THE INSTRUMENTAL VIEW OF KNOWLEDGE: JOHN DEWEY (1859-1952)

In his own laboratory school at the University of Chicago, John Dewey introduced manual training, shopwork, sewing, and cooking on the ground that the traditional curriculum no longer met the needs of the new society created by the forces of industrialism. He wanted the school to take on the character of an embryonic community life, active with occupations that reflect the life of the larger society.

Younger children in the school played at occupations with some degree of realism, simplifying but not distorting adult roles. Older children followed the Herbartian idea of recapitulating primitive life, but in a childhood social setting as they reconstructed the social life of other times and places. These children were expected to relate their

[3]Charles A. McMurry, *How To Organize the Curriculum* (New York: Macmillan, 1923), p. 76.

own activities to the consequences of those activities. Primitive human life was supposed to reveal to the child the social effects of introducing tools into a culture. Still older children reflected on the meaning of social forces and processes found in occupations. They were to sense questions, doubts, and problems and to study how to resolve them.

Dewey used his experiences in the laboratory school in formulating philosophical views that were different than those of the Herbartians. He insisted that the Herbartian interpretations of morality were too narrow and too formal. He protested the teaching of particular virtues without regard for the motives of children. Instead, he proposed that moral motives would come when children learned to observe and note means-ends relations in social situations. It was not enough for the teacher to be the model of moral behavior for the children to emulate. Children should be asked to judge and respond morally to their present situations, which are real to them. Indeed, Dewey wanted life in the school to offer opportunities for children to act morally and to learn how to judge their own behavior in terms of the social ideals of cooperation, participation, and positive service. Thus, Dewey challenged the view that morality was an individual matter between oneself and God.

Dewey attacked the view that one's social duty should be done within a traditional framework of values, proposing instead that the method of social intelligence be a critical and creative force. The method of social intelligence involves deciding what is right and best through experimental procedures and the judgment of participants. It requires recognition of varying points of view and accommodations of one's own perspective. Whereas the Herbartians relied on ideas as the basic guide to conduct and conceived of knowledge as something to be acquired, Dewey thought more in terms of the child's discovery and evaluation of knowledge than of mere acquisition. He recommended that the learner become the link between knowledge and conduct. His was a relative view of knowledge, not a fixed one. In contrast to the Herbartians' assumption that there was a body of known knowledge, which was indispensable and which could be made interesting to pupils, Dewey argued that subject matter was interesting only when it served the purposes of the learners. Hence, he emphasized learners' participation in formulating the purposes involved in what was to be studied.

By setting purposes, Dewey meant, however, not only expressing desires but studying means by which those desires can best be realized. Desire was not the end, but only the occasion for the formulation of a plan and method of activity. Thus, Dewey would not have the curriculum start with facts and truth that are outside the range of experience of those taught. Rather, he would start with materials for learning that are consistent with the experience learners already have and then introduce new objects and events that would stimulate new ways to observe and to judge. Subject matter was not to be selected on the basis of what adults thought would be useful for the learner at some future time. Instead the present experience of the learners was to become the primary focus. The achievements of the past (organized knowledge) were to serve as a resource for helping learners both to understand their present condition and to deal with present problems.

In short, Dewey did not believe that the curriculum end should merely be the acquisition of subject matter. Instead he believed in a new curriculum end, namely, that organized subject matter become a tool for learners to use in understanding and intelligently ordering their experiences. He generated many of the fundamental questions that guide our inquiries today. What is the best way to relate the natural view of the child and the scientific view of those with specialized knowledge? How can knowledge become a method for enriching social life? How can we help learners act morally rather than merely have ideas about morality? How can the curriculum best bring order, power, initiative, and intelligence into the child' experience? How can the teacher be helped to follow the individual internal authority of truth about a learner's growth when curriculum decisions are made by external authority above the teacher?

SCIENTIFIC CURRICULUM MAKING: FRANKLIN BOBBITT (1876–1956) AND WARRETT W. CHARTERS (1875–1952)

Scientific curriculum making is the attempt to use empirical methods in deciding *what* to teach. The history of the scientific movement in curriculum making shows very well that curriculum cannot be separated from the general history of American education nor divorced from the broader stream of cultural and intellectual history. Both Franklin Bobbitt and Warrett Charters were greatly influenced by these developments in their lifetimes.

Industrialism. Large numbers of persons began engaging in manufacturing instead of agriculture, and changes were wrought by a technological revolution, including a concern for efficiency and economy. For the first time, there was a societal interest in the systematic study of jobs, practices, and working conditions as related to objectives. There was also a concern about how to set standards for both products and processes.

Changing concepts of school. From an institution with fixed subject matter and concerned primarily with improving intellectual ability by disciplining the mind, the school was increasingly conceived as an agency with no less a goal than satisfying individual and social needs.

Scientific methods and techniques. The nineteenth century was characterized by great developments in the pure sciences such as biology, physics, and chemistry and in the application of science to agriculture, manufacture, and almost every other phase of practical life. Yet it wasn't until early in the twentieth century that the spirit of scientific experimentation began to push its way into the thinking of educators. Bobbitt and Charters brought a scientific way of thinking into the emerging field of curriculum making.

Much of what was called scientific at the time is now labeled scientism, mere technology, or nose counting. Modern critics like to say pejoratively that educational scientists of those days equated efficiency with science. It is true that these early educational scientists were attempting to solve educational problems by means of experimental and statistical techniques. They particularly emphasized the measurement of ability and achievement with their development of intelligence and achievement tests. The zeal for measurement brought forth an abundance of facts about school buildings, school finance, pupil achievement and pupil traits, and learners' physical, emotional, intellectual, and social growth. The field of curriculum also caught this zeal for measurement. Data were collected about the content of textbooks, courses of study, school subjects, and appraisal of results. Studies were undertaken to find out how pupils learn and to design new methods for overcoming pupil difficulties.

Two ideals were frequently associated with the scientific movement in education. One was the idea of an open attitude, the expectation that the school staff would be willing to consider new proposals and be alert to new methods and devices. Teachers, for example, were expected to join their pupils in asking questions. Second, there was an assumption that natural laws govern not only things and their forces, but also humans and their ways. Hence, it was the duty of education to shape the will into a desire to move in harmony with these laws. Science was seen as a guarantor of social progress.

Franklin Bobbitt's Contribution

Franklin Bobbitt articulated for the first time the importance of studying the processes for making a curriculum. He realized that it was not enough to develop new curricula; there was also a need to learn more about how new curricula can best be developed. This insight came through long experience in curriculum matters.

In his book, *The Curriculum*,[4] Bobbitt tells of a personal experience that caused him to look at curriculum from the point of view of social needs rather than mere academic study. He had gone to the Philippines early in the American occupation as a member of a committee sent to draw up an elementary school curriculum for the islands. Free to recommend almost anything to meet the needs of the population, the committee had the opportunity to create an original, constructive curriculum.

And what happened? The members assembled American textbooks for reading, arithmetic, geography, United States history, and other subjects with which they had been familiar in American schools. Without being conscious of it, they had organized a course of study for the traditional eight elementary school grades, on the basis of their American prejudices and preconceptions about what an elementary course ought to be.

Bobbitt was lucky. A director of education in the Philippines helped him and the committee to look at the social realities, and they then unceremoniously threw out time-hallowed content. Instead, they brought into the course a number of things to help the people gain health, make a living, and enjoy self-realization. The activities they introduced came from the culture of the Philippines and were quite different from those found in the American textbooks.

From this experience, Bobbitt saw his difficulty: his complete adherence to traditional curriculum beliefs had kept him from realizing the possibility of more useful solutions. He had needed something to shatter his complacency. As Bobbitt himself said,

> We needed principles of curriculum making. We did not know that we should first determine objectives from a study of social needs. We supposed education consisted only of teaching the familiar subjects.

[4] Franklin Bobbitt, *The Curriculum* (Boston: Houghton Mifflin, 1918).

We had not come to see that it is essentially a process of unfolding the potential abilities of a population and in particularized relation to the social conditions. We had not learned that studies are means, not ends. We did not realize that any instrument or experience which is effective in such unfoldment is the right instrument and right experience; and that anything which is not effective is wrong, however time-honored and widely used it may be.[5]

Bobbitt was little different from most people who are entering the field of curriculum for the first time today. They are unaware that what they have personally experienced in school may not be the final answer. They are very far from the idea of creating something different and more appropriate.

After his experience in the Philippines, Bobbitt stimulated other workers in the field. His book, *How To Make a Curriculum*, was the forerunner of others in the subject and had great influence on school practice.[6] Students of curriculum now see Bobbitt as the first to recognize the need for a new specialization, the study of curriculum making. It was Bobbitt who saw that professional agreement on a *method* of discovery is more important than agreement on the details of curriculum content. He offered the profession his method with the intention that others would try it, improve it, or suggest a better one. Bobbitt's method helps to define what is meant by curriculum making.

His method was guided by a fundamental assumption that would not be accepted by all curriculum makers today—namely, that education is to prepare us for the activities that ought to make up a well-rounded adult life. It is primarily for adult life, not childhood.

Analysis of Human Experience. The first step in curriculum making, according to Bobbitt, is to separate the broad range of human experience into major fields. One such classification includes language, health, citizenship, social, recreation, religious, home, vocation. The whole field of human experience should be reviewed in order that the portions belonging to the schools may be seen in relation to the whole.

Job Analysis. The second step is to break down the fields into their more specific activities. In this step, Bobbitt had to compromise with

[5]Ibid., p. 283.
[6]Franklin Bobbitt, *How To Make a Curriculum* (Boston: Houghton Mifflin, 1924).

his ideal. He recognized the desirability of using a scientific method of analysis, yet knew that thus far there was not adequate technique for the work. Hence, he tended to fall back on practical and personal experiences to prove that a given activity was crucial to one or more of the categories of human experience.

Bobbitt knew that only a few activity analyses had ever been made and that most of them were in the fields of spelling, language, arithmetic, history, geography, and vocation. He did, however, believe that activity analysis was a promising technique and turned to his colleague, W.W. Charters, for examples of how best to determine specific activities from larger units. Charters, in turn, drew from the idea of job analysis already common in industry. Business and industry at that time made an analysis for each job and prepared training programs for the tasks identified. For the position of application clerk the analysis would include these tasks: meets people who want to open accounts, asks them to fill out blanks, looks up rating in Dun's. A course of study was prepared to teach future clerks each of the identified duties.

It should be clear, however, that job analysis could result in either a list of duties or a list of methods for performing duties. The procedures for the analysis included introspection, interview, and investigation. In introspection, an expert related his or her duties and methods. Then, in an interview, a number of experts reviewed a list of duties to verify the tasks. Lastly, the investigator actually carried out the operations on the job. A problem in making a complete analysis occurred when trying to derive a description of mental operations where one cannot see the steps carried out with the material. The analyses indicated what the activities were if one were to learn the duties of a position.

Deriving Objectives. The third step is to derive the objectives of education. Objectives are statements of the abilities that are required to perform the activities. In *How To Make a Curriculum*, Bobbitt presented more than 800 major objectives in ten fields of human experience. Here, for example, is a partial list of the general objectives within a language field: (1) ability to pronounce words properly; (2) ability to use voice in agreeable ways; (3) use grammatically correct language; (4) effectively organize and express thought; (5) express thought to others in conversation, in recounting experiences, in serious or formal discussion, in an oral report, in giving directions, and before an audience; (6) command an adequate reading, speaking, and writing vocabulary; (7) ability to write legibly with ease and speed; (8) ability to spell the words of one's writing vocabulary; (9) ability to use good form and order in all written work (margins, spacing, alignment, paragraphing, capitalization, punctuation, syllabification, abbreviation). These objectives illustrate the level of generality needed to help curriculum makers decide what specific educational results were to be produced. Bobbitt also realized that each of the objectives could be broken down further into its component parts; indeed, he illustrated such detailed analysis.

Selecting Objectives. The fourth step is to select from the list of objectives those which are to serve as the basis for planning pupil activities. Guidelines for making this final selection of objectives include:

1. Eliminate objectives that can be accomplished through the normal process of living. Only the abilities that are not sufficiently developed by chance should be included among the objectives of systematic education. Possibly the more important portions of education are not accomplished in schools but through nonscholastic agencies.
2. Emphasize objectives that will overcome deficiencies in the adult world.
3. Avoid objectives opposed by the community. Specific objectives in religion, economics, and health are especially likely to be opposed.
4. Eliminate objectives when there are practical constraints against their being achieved.
5. Involve the community in the selection of objectives. Consult community members who are proficient in practical affairs and experts in their fields.
6. Differentiate between objectives that are for all learners and those which are practical for only a part of the population.
7. Sequence the objectives, indicating how far pupils should go each year in attaining the general goals.

Planning in Detail. The fifth step is to lay out the kinds of activities, experiences, and opportunities involved in attaining the objectives. Details for the day-to-day activities of children at each age or grade level must be laid out. These detailed activities make up the curriculum. As project activity and part-time work at home and in the community are introduced, there must be cooperative planning. Teachers, nurses, play activity directors, and parents together should plan the detailed procedures of the courses. Their plans should then be approved by the principal, superintendent, and school board.

W.W. Charters's Contribution

Although Charters enunciated a method of curriculum formulation that was very similar to Bobbitt's, he differed in the emphasis given to ideals and to systematized knowledge in determining the content of the curriculum. Charters saw ideals as objectives with observable consequences. He believed that honesty, loyalty, and generosity contributed to satisfaction. Ideals did not necessarily lead to one's own immediate satisfaction but to satisfaction in the long run or to satisfaction as defined by social consensus. However, he knew of no scientific measurement that would determine which ideals should operate in a school. There was no scientific way to determine whether open-mindedness or artistic taste should be the ideal of the school or student. Hence, Charters thought it defensible for a faculty to vote on the ideals it believed to be most valuable. Faculty selection of ideals was not to be arbitrary, however. The opinion of thoughtful men and women in public and private life needed to be carefully weighed and the needs of the student investigated.

Once ideals were selected they had to serve as standards for actions. They were not to be abstracted from activities. The teacher who wished to inculcate ideals in the lives of pupils needed to analyze activities to which an ideal applied and to see that the selected ideal was applied in the pupils' activities. For Charters, the curriculum consisted of both ideals and activities. Unlike Bobbitt, Charters gave explicit attention to knowledge in his method for making the curriculum.[7] He wanted subject matter useful for living and of motivational import to the learner. But he also wanted to reassure those who feared that organized information in such fields as chemistry, history, physics, and mathematics would have no place in a curriculum built around objectives derived from studies of life in the social setting. His answer showed how job analyses revealed the importance of both primary subjects (math and English in application) and derived subjects (subjects necessary for understanding the activity or the reason for the activity). Psychology, for example, was needed in order to explain methods of supervision.

On the one hand, Charters would determine subject material from

[7]W.W. Charters, *Curriculum Construction* (New York: Macmillan, 1923), pp. 103–06.

analysis of life projects in order that one would know which elements of the subjects are most important and require the most attention. On the other hand, he would select school projects that would give instruction in the subject items and allow the pupil to use the knowledge in a broader range of activities.

As representatives of the scientific movement in curriculum making, Bobbitt and Charters brought forth the following conceptions and dimensions of curriculum: It is a process which, if followed, will result in an evolving curriculum. The process of curriculum making is itself a field of study. The relation of goals (ideals), objectives, and activities is a curriculum concern. The selection of goals is a normative process. The selection of objectives and activities is empirical and scientific. Objectives and activities are subject to scientific analysis and verification. The relation of organized systematic fields of knowledge to the practical requirements of daily living is a central question for students of the curriculum.

IMPROVEMENT OF INSTRUCTION: HOLLIS CASWELL (1910–   )

Local Development of Curriculum

Until the end of World War I, major influences on curriculum came from outside the local school system. Academic scholars set the direction for purposes and content through national committees and textbook writing. Usually, local schools participated only to the extent of deciding what subjects to add and what textbooks to use. The high school curriculum was standardized on the basis of what college presidents wanted in the way of preparation for college. After 1920, the scientific movement directly influenced the curriculum through new types of school textbooks stressing skills related to the everyday needs of adults and children. College scholars found their power to determine the curriculum challenged by the scientific method of curriculum formulation. The first local systematic curriculum making also began around 1920 when several school systems tried to develop courses of study in single subjects and the study of particular problems, such as learning difficulties in spelling and how to overcome them through instruction.

The Course of Study Movement

By 1926, practically all schools were revising their curricula. They attacked the problem of curriculum development in a comprehensive way by defining the general objectives on which the entire curriculum was based and by which all subjects were correlated. It is true, however, that members of state education departments often chose the objectives and left the selection of activities to the teachers. Sometimes, the principals or representatives of teachers selected the objectives according to social needs. In these schools teachers worked in committees in order to list suitable activities to be tried out in practice. A director was provided to supervise the preparation of the course of study for an individual school district or an entire state, and a curriculum specialist served as general consultant.

Not all professional educators viewed the movement with favor:

> Too much of present-day curriculum making is amateurish, trifling, and a sheer waste of time—worse than that, an injection of pernicious confusion into what should be orderly progress. The let-everybody-pitch-in-and-help method is ludicrous when applied to curriculum building. It is too much like inviting a group of practical electricians to redesign a modern power plant.[8]

Hollis Leland Caswell extended our view of the curriculum field through his concern about the relationships between the course of study, teaching, and the learner's role. Caswell was one of the first to see the making of a course of study as too limiting in purpose. He shifted the emphasis from production of a course of study to the actual improvement of instruction. He saw curriculum development as a means to help teachers apply in their daily tasks of instruction the best of what is known about subject matter, the interests of children, and contemporary social needs. He involved 16,000 Virginia teachers and administrators in making a course of study for that state, for instance.[9] His involvement of all teachers instead of just a few selected representatives was a new thrust. Caswell considered the course of study as only one of several aids to the teacher and believed that when teachers made the course of study together they would learn the limits of its usefulness. He looked on the course of study as a means of providing source materials for teachers to use in planning their work rather than a prescription to be followed in detail.

Help for the Teacher in Curriculum Making

Caswell attempted to help teachers improve curricula by providing them with a syllabus of carefully chosen readings under seven topics.

[8]Guy M. Whipple, "What Price Curriculum Making," *School and Society* 31, (March 15, 1930): 368.

[9]Mary Louise Seguel, *The Curriculum Field: Its Formative Years* (New York: Teachers College Press, Teachers College, Columbia University, 1966), p. 148.

These topics or questions are important for what they tell us about the nature of curriculum and the task involved in making a curriculum.[10]

1. What is curriculum?
2. What are the developments that resulted in a need for curriculum revision?
3. What is the function of subject matter?
4. How do we determine educational objectives?
5. What is the best way to organize instruction?
6. How should we select subject matter?
7. How should we measure the outcomes of instruction?

The readings Caswell suggested to help teachers answer these questions included a range of sources, some of which gave conflicting opinions. Caswell himself believed that the curriculum is more than the experiences made available to the child. It consists of the experiences the child actually undergoes. Hence, the teacher's interaction with the pupil is a vital aspect of curriculum. Preparing a course of study is only the starting point for curriculum improvement.

Caswell also believed in curriculum revision. He said that curriculum revision is necessary in order for the school to meet more social and personal needs. Curriculum should help sensitize people to social problems and give pupils experience in social action. Caswell wanted the school to be an avenue of opportunity for all the people, contributing to interracial understanding and better intergroup relations, strengthening home life, stressing democratic ideals, and contributing to the conservation of resources.

Caswell thought that the demands for curriculum change must be evaluated. He recommended that any proposed change be screened, and that changes be accepted only if they are (1) consistent with democratic values, (2) consistent with the developmental needs of the learner, (3) something that other agencies cannot accomplish, (4) something that has or will gain the support of leaders in the community, (5) something that does not replace other existing curriculum areas of relatively higher value.

Caswell agreed that a curriculum design should synthesize the three basic elements of the curriculum—children's interests, social functions, and organized knowledge. In the tentative course of study for Virginia elementary schools, for example, he helped developers

[10]Sidney B. Hall, D.W. Peters, and Hollis L. Caswell, "Study Course for Virginia State Curriculum," *State Board of Education Bulletin* 14, no. 2 (January 1932).

provide scope and sequence. Social functions served as the scope. Some of these functions were protection and conservation of life, property, and natural resources; recreation; expression of aesthetic impulses; and distribution of rewards of production. These functions were worked on in some form in every grade. Sequenced experiences were arranged according to centers of interest; for example, home and school life were studied in the first grade, the effects of the machine on learning in the sixth. Specific activities were suggested to match both the social functions and the centers of interest using the most relevant subject matter.

Caswell saw the central task of curriculum development to be a synthesis of materials from subject matter fields, philosophy, psychology, and sociology. "Materials must be so selected and arranged as to become vital in the experience of the learner."[11] Thus, he saw curriculum as a field of study that represents no structurally limited body of content; rather, it represents a process or procedure.

RATIONAL CURRICULUM MAKING: RALPH W. TYLER (1902–)

In 1949, Ralph Tyler sent to the University of Chicago Press a manuscript, *Basic Principles of Curriculum and Instruction*,[12] a rationale for examining problems of curriculum and instruction. The rationale was based on his experiences as a teacher of curriculum and as a curriculum maker and evaluator. He had been especially active in designing ways to measure changes in learners in light of the schools' newly made efforts to help learners develop interests and perform more appropriately in society. Since then, nearly 90,000 copies of Tyler's rationale have been sold, and it is regarded as the capstone on one epoch of curriculum making.

Four Fundamental Questions in Curriculum Inquiry

Tyler assumed that anyone engaging in curriculum inquiry must try to answer these questions:

1. What educational purposes should the school seek to attain?

[11]Hollis L. Caswell and Doak S. Campbell, *Curriculum Development* (New York: American Book Company, 1935), p. 81.
[12]Ralph W. Tyler, *Basic Principles of Curriculum and Instruction* (Chicago: University of Chicago Press, 1949).

2. What educational experiences can be provided that are likely to attain these purposes?
3. How can these educational experiences be effectively organized?
4. How can we determine whether these purposes are being attained?

By purposes, Tyler meant educational objectives, and he proposed that school goals would have greater validity if they are selected in light of information about learners' psychological needs and interests, contemporary life, and aspects of subject matter that would be useful to everyone, not just specialists in disciplines. In order to select from the many objectives that would be inferred from such information, Tyler recommended that a school staff "screen" them according to the school's philosophy of education and beliefs about the psychology of learning.

Tyler realized that having purposes was only the first step. He used the phrase *learning experiences* to include a plan for providing learning situations that take into account both the previous experience and perceptions that the learner brings to the situation, and whether or not the learner is likely to respond to it, mentally, emotionally, and in action.

Tyler then turned his attention to how the learning situations or experiences could be ordered so that they would be focused on the same outcomes, that is, the significant changes in learning that the school seeks. He was preoccupied with how the curriculum could produce a maximum cumulative effect. He wanted a cumulative plan for organization that would help students learn more and learn more effectively.

His answer drew heavily from the early Herbartians' ideas of organization. Like Charles McMurry, he thought organizing elements or controlling ideas, concepts, values, and skills should be the threads, the warp and woof of the fabric of curriculum organization. Tyler approved using the concept of a place value numeration system, for example, which can be enlarged on from kindergarten through the twelfth grade. Such concepts were seen as useful elements for relating different learning experiences in science, social studies, and other fields. He described optional ways of structuring learning experiences both within schools and in the classroom. They could, for instance, be structured within special subject courses, like English and math, or as broad fields, like the language arts. Experience could also be structured within the format of lessons. He showed his own organization and curriculum preference by listing the advantages of relating content to real life through projects that allow for broader grouping of learning opportunities. He also saw merit in organizing courses that span several years rather than a single term.

Finally, Tyler regarded evaluation as an important operation in curriculum development. He saw it as the process for finding out whether the learning experiences as presented actually produced the desired results and for discovering the strengths and weaknesses of the plans. He made a real contribution by enlarging our concept of evaluation. Rather than focusing on only a few aspects of growth, tests should, he believed, indicate attainment of all the objectives of an educational program. Further, he did not believe that "tests" should mean only paper and pencil examinations. Observations of pupils, products made by learners, records of student participation, and other methods were included.

Criticisms of Tyler's rationale generally stem from Tyler's statement that the selection of objectives is a prerequisite for curriculum development. James MacDonald, for instance, thinks that statements of expected behavioral outcomes violate the integrity of learners by segmenting their behavior and manipulating them for an end that has no present worth for them.[13]

In prescribing three sources from which objectives can be derived, the student, the society, and the subject, Tyler attempted to reconcile the conflict between those who favored one or another as most important and to formulate a consensual basis that would allow individuals with divergent goals to work together in developing curricula. To effect a consistency among the resultant goals, he relied on the staff to apply their own philosophical and psychological criteria. On this point, critics contend, Tyler does not realize that information collected from the learner and society is biased and that, once that information has been gathered, there is no "scientific way" to infer what *should* follow from the facts reported. Further, Tyler's proposal for filtering educational objectives through a philosophical screen is regarded as vacuous and trivial.[14] It leaves to staff in individual schools the question of which objectives to keep and which to throw out. Tyler gives no criterion to use in making a choice among objectives.

Tyler's rationale for examining problems of curriculum and instruction summed up the best thought regarding curriculum during

---

[13]James B. MacDonald, "The Person in the Curriculum," in *Precedents and Promise in the Curriculum Field*, Helen F. Robinson, ed. (New York: Columbia University Press, Teachers College, 1966), p. 41.

[14]Herbert Kliebard, "The Tyler Rationale," in *Curriculum and Evaluation*, Arno Bellack and Herbert Kliebard, eds. (Berkeley, Calif.: McCutchan, 1977), pp. 56–67.

its first half-century as a field of study. His linkage to the McMurrys, Dewey, Bobbitt, and Charters is clear. The four questions he poses and the suggestions he gives for answering the questions pretty well define the field of curriculum as it was understood until very recently.

CONCLUDING COMMENTS

As indicated in Table 10, influential curriculum leaders have addressed themselves to significant questions about what should be taught and why. Their questions ranged from inquiries into purposes, such as whether morality can and should be taught, to questions about the selection of content, the relationship between content and method, and the way in which organization can have a cumulative effect on learning experiences.

Any new effort in curriculum thought and action must still treat the persistent questions of purpose, experiences, organization, and evaluation. The emphasis given to these matters and the way they are addressed, however, are changing. The last decade saw academic scholars and governmental agencies "usurping" the leadership in program development and turning toward specialized knowledge as opposed to concerns for real-life functions and personal interests. Presently there are signs of another change in leadership as local groups demand the right to participate in planning the programs for their children. Tyler's guidelines for continuity in experience and the integration of subject matters are not widely practiced. Currently, in the schools, bits and pieces of experience are coupled with academic specialization. The increased number of curriculum options such as alternative programs, short-term modules, electives, and the teaching of isolated skills are cases in point.

One should not be too hasty to condemn the present lack of attention to continuity and integration of experience and to providing common experience. Such considerations probably were more appropriate in an age represented by an industrial and economical model whereby a product was the outcome, and production a value. Curriculum thought and practice merely reflected this model, substantiating the learner's achievement of specific ends as the product and demanding a continuity of experiences which in some ways resembled an assembly line.

During the 1960s, the curriculum began to reflect the model of an affluent society in which people tended to be prized as *consumers*

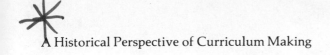

TABLE 10   A Summary of Early Curriculum Theorists' Ideas

Theorists	Purpose, Aims, and Objectives	Content	Method of Instruction	Organization
Charles and John McMurry	Moral development Good citizenship	Literature for relating aesthetics and the intellectual History and literature for citizenship Geography for correlating studies Later, acceptance of new branches of knowledge	Five formal steps in lesson plans Special methods in each subject field	Studies sequenced according to age and stage of learner development Information organized around problems and projects Activities related by topics and themes
John Dewey	Intellectual control over the forces of man and nature Social intelligence Trained capacities in the service of social interest Development as an aim	The intellectual method by which social life is enriched and improved Knowledge from organized fields as it functions in the life of the child	Survey of capacities and needs of learners Arrangement of conditions that provide the content to satisfy needs The plan for meeting needs to involve participation of all group members Intelligent activity, not aimless activity	Life experiences of learner used to carry learner on to more refined and better organized facts and ideas Curriculum organized around two concepts: that knowing is experimental and that knowledge is instrumental to individual and social purposes

continued

TABLE 10 (continued)

Theorists	Purpose, Aims, and Objectives	Content	Method of Instruction	Organization
Franklin Bobbitt	Meeting social needs Preparation of learner for adult life	Subject matter as a means, not an end	Deriving objectives from analysis of what is required in order to perform in broad categories of life Detailed activities to be planned by teachers, parents, and others	Specification of objectives to be attained each year Layout of activities involved in attaining objectives
Warrett W. Charters	Satisfaction through fulfillment of ideals (e.g., honesty) that sway socially efficient individuals	Organized knowledge that can be applied in activities needed for a socially efficient life	Projects and activities that are consistent with ideals	Experimentation to find the best way to order ideals, activities, and ideas
Hollis Caswell	Fulfillment of democratic ideals (improved intergroup relations, home life, and the conservation of resources)	No limiting body of content Key concepts most helpful in the solution of social problems	Teacher interaction with pupil Teacher applying the best of what is known about subject matter, children's interests, and social needs	Selected social functions (e.g., the conservation of life) to be worked on in some form in every grade Sequence of activities to be arranged according to centers of interest

TABLE 10 (continued)

Theorists	Purpose, Aims, and Objectives	Content	Method of Instruction	Organization
Hollis Caswell *continued*			Key ideas to be woven into the child's performance of social functions	
Ralph Tyler	No stated purposes Each curriculum person to evolve own purposes through a rational process, involving consideration of learner, social conditions, knowledge, and philosophical position Objectives to be behaviorally stated, but specificity to depend on one's theory of learning	Subject matter from subject specialists that could contribute to the broad functions of daily living	Opportunity to practice what the objectives of instruction call for Each opportunity to contribute to several objectives Activities that are within the learner's capacity and are satisfying	Provision for the reiteration of concepts, skills, or values Provision for the progressive development of the concept, skill, or attitude Relating of concepts from one field to content in other fields

rather than as *producers.* Just as society at large was characterized by the stimulation of consumerism and a range of offerings, the curriculum was characterized by a wide range of possible outcomes. Learners were given many more choices in what to learn and how. As affluent consumers, they expected to find curriculum offerings in "all colors," not, like Henry Ford's early expression, in "any color so long as it's black." How a new society responding to austerity and conservation, if indeed that is our future, will reflect itself in the schools remains to be seen. One can guess, however, that the old curriculum criteria of correlation and continuity of experiences may again be taken into account.

The very definition of the curriculum field has become fragmented. There are, for example, curriculum theorists who would restrict curriculum planning, to a preinstructional phase. Teaching or interaction with pupils would be another subject. Others now define curriculum as a structured series of intended learning outcomes. They regard the means of instruction—such as activities, materials, and instructional content—as the territory of instructional or product developers. Conceptualization and research in teaching and evaluation also are now proceeding independently from any single organized curriculum movement.

QUESTIONS

1. What are the continuing central concerns of curriculum specialists as revealed by the work of prominent historical figures in the field of curriculum?
2. What current curriculum doctrines and practices are carryovers from another historical period?
3. In what way is the present situation different from the past? How does this difference make some curriculum carryover irrelevant?
4. It is said that a history of curriculum thought and practice cannot be separated from the broader stream of cultural and intellectual history. What conditions, movements, or ideas had the greatest influence on curriculum making in the past century? What social and intellectual forces are likely to shape the curriculum field today?
5. What the McMurrys, Dewey, Charters, Bobbitt, Caswell, and Tyler thought about curriculum is less important than what they make *you* think about curriculum. What do they have to say to you today?

SELECTED REFERENCES

Bellack, Arno A. "History of Curriculum Thought and Practice," *Review of Educational Research* 39, no. 3 (1969): 283–92.
Bobbitt, Franklin. *The Curriculum*. New York: Houghton Mifflin, 1918.
———. *How To Make a Curriculum*. New York: Houghton Mifflin, 1924.

Caswell, Hollis L. and Campbell, Doak S. *Readings in Curriculum Development*. New York: American Book Company, 1937.

Charters, W.W. *Curriculum Construction*. New York: Macmillan, 1923.

Davis, O.L., Jr., ed. *Perspectives on Curriculum Development 1776-1976*. Washington, D.C.: ASCD, 1976.

Eisner, Elliot. "Franklin Bobbitt and the 'Science' of Curriculum Making," *School Review* 75, no. 1 (Spring 1967): 29-47.

Franklin, Barry M. "Curriculum History: Its Nature and Boundaries," *Curriculum Inquiry* 7, no. 1 (Spring 1977): 67-79.

Kliebard, Herbert M. "The Drive for Curriculum Change in the United States, 1890-1958—The Ideological Roots of Curriculum as a Field of Specialization," *Journal of Curriculum Studies* 11, no. 3 (September 1979): 191-202.

McMurry, Charles A. *How To Organize the Curriculum*. New York: Macmillan, 1923.

National Society for the Study of Education. *The First Yearbook of the Herbart Society for the Scientific Study of Teaching*. Chicago: University of Chicago Press, 1907.

———. *The Curriculum—Retrospect and Prospect*, Seventieth Yearbook, Part I. Chicago: University of Chicago Press, 1971.

Norton, John and Norton, Margaret. *Foundation of Curricula Building*. New York: Ginn and Company, 1936.

Seguel, Mary Louise. *The Curriculum Field: Its Formative Years*. New York: Columbia University, Teachers College Press, 1966.

Tyler, Ralph. *Basic Principles of Curriculum and Instruction*. Chicago: University of Chicago Press, 1949.

15 / THE PROMISE OF THEORY AND RESEARCH IN CURRICULUM

Six crucial areas of curriculum research and development are appraised in this chapter. Such appraisal is intended to help the reader to see where greater emphasis should be placed or to question whether some areas are as important as others and why. Future directions in curriculum inquiry are also spelled out by examining the current work of the most prominent curriculum scholars in two camps, those of the soft and hard curricularists. Finally, four frameworks for guiding curriculum research are presented. These frameworks and their specific questions should be of value to anyone wishing to engage in curriculum research.

Some curriculum workers do cognitive and empirical as well as practical research, adopting various methods for throwing light on what can and should be taught to whom under given circumstances. There are also theorists who try to stipulate what is meant by curriculum theory and how best to develop it. Many of these theorists are using forms of criticism as a research strategy.

Ideally, theorists and researchers should aid practitioners by providing principles for formulating desirable outcomes and designing instructional means. At the very least, they should provide practitioners with intellectual tools for conceptualizing their situations and raising questions that should be asked. At most, theorists should explain and predict relationships among a large number of variables such as life outcomes, school learning, and instructional plans. Attainment of the latter goal seems most unlikely, however.

It is the purpose of this chapter to examine representative samples of the work of curriculum researchers and theorists in order to illustrate curriculum as a field of inquiry and to suggest its future directions.

STATE OF THE FIELD

Both in 1960 and again in 1969, John Goodlad appraised the status of curriculum research and development.[1] These appraisals offer a good basis for measuring progress in the curriculum field. The appraisals were made with respect to six curriculum needs. They were the need for theoretical constructs, the need for concepts that identify the major questions in the curriculum field, the need to determine what subject matter can best be taught simultaneously, the need to arrange material for effective learning, the need for taxonomical analysis of objectives, and the need for studies indicating the relationships between specific instructional variables and the outcomes from instruction.

Let us look at each of Goodlad's 1960 concerns, and the status of research and development in each area in 1969 and in the present. We can then readily see where the field is progressing and where there is little improvement.

The Need for Curriculum Theory

Status of Curriculum Theory in 1969. Between 1960 and 1969, little was added to our knowledge of how to derive educational objectives. Elizabeth and George Macia and others attempted to adopt theories from outside the field of education to conceptualize phenomena related to curriculum.[2] One consequence was the differentiation of four different kinds of curriculum theory. *Formal curriculum theory* involves theorizing about the structure of the disciplines that will constitute the curriculum. Elizabeth Macia would leave this theorizing to the philosophers and members of the disciplines. *Valuational curriculum theory* involves speculation about appropriate means to attain the most valuable objectives and content to present in a curriculum. *Event theory* is very much like scientific theory in that it tries to predict what will occur when certain conditions are present. *Praxiological theory* is speculation about appropriate means to attain what is judged to be valuable. Prax-

---

[1]John Goodlad, "Curriculum: The State of the Field," *Review of Educational Research* 30, no. 3 (June 1960): 185–99; "Curriculum: The State of the Field," *Review of Educational Research* 39, no. 3 (June 1969): 367–75.

[2]Occasional papers by Elizabeth Macia, George Macia, Robert Jewett, and others treating educational theorizing through models (Columbus, Ohio: Center for the Construction of Theory in Education, Bureau of Educational Research and Service, Ohio State University, 1963–65.

iological theory forms the theoretical base for determining curriculum policy, the decision to adopt certain objectives and practices.[3] George Beauchamp described efforts at theory making in the field of curriculum during this period and concluded that little theoretical research had been done.[4] Joseph Schwab said that theoretical pursuits were not appropriate in the field of curriculum. He urged instead direct study of the curriculum: what it is, how it gets the way it is, and how it affects the people who partake of it.[5]

Status of Curriculum Theory in 1980. There have been several attempts to act on Schwab's recommendation. Decker Walker, for example, has proposed a model, based on practice, for guiding the study of deliberations, processes, and assumptions of curriculum developers. Walker has faulted those in the curriculum field for being so busy prescribing curriculum making that they have not paid sufficient attention to discovering how it is done.[6]

There is, however, opposition to Schwab's call for attention to the practical rather than the theoretical. Some theorists are trying to develop a more comprehensive and realistic philosophy of society and the individual instead of merely engaging in the practical problems of curriculum maintenance and incremental reform. They view curriculum theorizing as a way to demythologize curriculum, advancing two concerns of importance to modern revolutionaries: heightened consciousness about the consequences of technology, capitalism, and other institutional structures and exploration of the inner life to broaden our ways of knowing.[7]

Another important theoretical development is the usurping of curriculum theory by evaluators. As indicated in Chapter 8, theories of evaluation have been broadened to include frameworks for determining objectives, monitoring procedures for curriculum design and implementation, and guiding other curriculum decisions.[8]

Curriculum theorists, like Glenys Unruh, continue to resolve com-

[3]Elizabeth S. Macia, *Curriculum Theory and Policy.* Paper presented to American Educational Research Association, Chicago, Ill., February 10, 1965.
[4]George A. Beauchamp, *Curriculum Theory* (Wilmette, Ill.: The Kagg Press, 1968).
[5]Joseph J. Schwab, *The Practical: A Language for Curriculum* (Washington, D.C.: National Education Association, 1970).
[6]Decker Walker, "A Naturalistic Model for Curriculum Development," *School Review* 80, no. 1 (November 1971): 51–67.
[7]William Pinar, ed., *Heightened Consciousness, Cultural Revolution, and Curriculum Theory* (Berkeley, Calif.: McCutchan, 1974).
[8]Allan Ornstein, ed., "Evaluating Educational and Social Action Programs," *Journal of Research and Development in Education* 8, no. 3 (Spring 1975).

peting claims about what and how to teach by appealing to principles. Unruh sees democratic ideals as the theoretical base for curriculum development. Her plea for a theory of responsive curriculum development rests on John Dewey's concept of the democratic person and the democratic school in which administrators, students, parents, and community members cooperate and participate in curriculum planning and evaluation. She outlines seven propositions with hypotheses to support such a theory.

1. If planning for the freedom of individuals occurs, the curriculum will be more responsive to social, ethical, and moral values. Illustrative hypothesis: Racial attitudes will improve as curriculum developers from different races study the concerns of each race about the cultures of others.
2. If planners draw on the local culture, the curriculum will be more responsive to the needs and concerns of those served by the school. Illustrative hypothesis: If people from the school and from the community cooperatively design work experiences in the community for students and learning experiences in the school for laypersons, there will be greater consensus on means.
3. If means are used to exemplify and strengthen the nation's founding goals, curriculum development will embody the purposes of American democracy. Illustrative hypothesis: Increased dialog on values by state and local school boards will result in greater curriculum emphasis on decision-making skills.
4. If there is a commitment to planned change curriculum developers will consider new technological and social developments and respond to them in ways to enhance the freedom of individuals. Illustrative hypothesis: If students are given opportunities to confront value choices affecting the future, they will be able to judge whether legislative decisions harm or benefit the goals of a person-centered society.
5. If there is a more comprehensive assessment of needs, curriculum will be more responsive to both individual and group concerns. Illustrative hypothesis: Surveys of local needs as expressed by students, parents, teachers, and others will result in higher priority being given to humanistic and aesthetic developments.
6. If there is greater interaction and collaboration among groups, there will be more empathy for the needs of others. Illustrative hypothesis: If the purposes and needs of conflicting groups are presented in orderly discussion to all involved, then a mutually acceptable curriculum plan will be developed.

7. If there is a systems approach with procedures for setting goals, assessing needs, specifying objectives and priorities, and using evaluation to guide improvement, there will be more progress toward broad democratic goals. Illustrative hypothesis: The use of a systems approach will result in greater emphasis on formative evaluation, a wider variety of instructional methods, more positive expressions by teachers and students in the classrooms, and more positive attitudes toward school.[9]

There is great disenchantment with the notion that the curriculum field will amass empirical generalizations, put them into general laws, and weld these laws into a coherent theory. The idea that theory will tell us the necessary and sufficient conditions for a particular result in curriculum has given way to assessing local events and to developing concepts that will help people make their own decisions.[10]

The Need for Curriculum Conceptions in Curriculum

Status of Curriculum Conceptions in 1969. General theory and conceptualizations in curriculum had advanced very little in the decade before 1969. John Goodlad tried to bridge theory and practice with a conceptual scheme for rational curriculum planning. His categories and suggested processes, which build on the Tyler rationale of 1949, were intended to stimulate research and organize thinking in the curriculum field. However, he later saw no evidence that the intent was fulfilled. Also, Dwayne Huebner elaborated on a conception of curriculum as a field of study. He criticized the means-ends conception of curriculum and argued that curriculum should be conceived as a political process for effecting a just environment. One of the major questions he would have the curriculum workers ask was, Does the present educational activity reflect the best that humans are capable of?[11]

Status of Curriculum Conceptions in 1980. In 1979, John Goodlad revisited his 1966 conceptual system for curriculum, a rational

[9]Glenys G. Unruh, *Responsive Curriculum Development: Theory and Action* (Berkeley, Calif.: McCutchan, 1975).

[10]W.J. McKeachie, "The Decline and Fall of the Laws of Learning," *Educational Researcher* 3, no. 3 (March 1974): 7–11; Lee Cronbach, "Beyond the Two Disciplines of Scientific Psychology," *American Psychologist* 30, no. 2 (February 1975): 116–28.

[11]Dwayne Huebner, in *Precedents and Promise in the Curriculum Field*, Helen Robinson, ed. (New York: Teachers College Press, Teachers College, Columbia University, 1966), p. 107.

decision-making model for determining purposes and selecting and organizing learning opportunities. He found that the model or system provides a reasonably accurate identification of the elements of curriculum practice in complex settings such as the United States.[12] It does not, however, adequately reflect practices regarding levels of decision making. Consequently, Goodlad and his associates suggest three modifications:

1. More attention be given to the personal and experiential as a decision-making level in the conceptual system. (This is partly in response to the work of the curriculum reconceptualists who see learners as potential generators and not mere passive recipients of curriculum.)
2. Values be recognized as playing a part in all curriculum decisions, not just stated as a guiding educational philosophy at the beginning point in curriculum planning, as depicted in the original conceptional scheme.
3. The sociopolitical interests of special groups—the political milieu—be recognized as bearing on each level of decision making.

Incidentally, Goodlad sees a resurgence of interest in the classic curriculum questions, including organizational ones about scope, sequence, and integration.

There is a loss of faith in logical systems to solve curriculum problems. Many curriculum theorists are turning to aesthetic and personal dimensions. James MacDonald, for example, would have us ask such questions as these about curriculum: What kinds of activity open up perceptual experiences and sensitize people to others and to inner vibrations? What activities develop community relations, facilitate religious experiences, and enable one to create a personal sense of order? He believes that the major curriculum question should deal with the problem of facilitating the development of inner strength and power.[13]

Dwayne Huebner would change curriculum language that now reveals a concern for effectiveness, objectives, and principles of learning (a language he thinks reflects a dated institution) to a language that will focus on different concerns. He wants a language

[12]John I. Goodlad and associates, *Curriculum Inquiry: The Study of Curriculum Practice* (New York: McGraw-Hill, 1979).
[13]James B. MacDonald, "A Transcendental Development Ideology of Education," in *Heightened Consciousness, Cultural Revolution, and Curriculum Theory,* William Pinar, ed. (Berkeley, Calif.: McCutchan, 1974), pp. 85–116.

that will illuminate economics and technical policies that affect education. For example: How much of the richness of the world is made available to the learner? He wants a language that will also direct attention to the learner's choice in subject matter. For example: How can we best allow the learner to draw on the cultures of the world in creating possibilities for the future? Note that Huebner's use of culture is in contrast to selecting curriculum content for its potential to serve controlling social interests rather than the interests of the individual.[14]

Herbert Kliebard has proposed three possible ways of attacking the problem of conceptualizing the curriculum field. The first is to identify critical and persistent questions that have characterized the field. Chapter 14 in this book is consistent with this suggestion. Kliebard's second suggestion is to regard the field as a synoptic one in which the curriculum person brings perspectives from other fields to bear on school programs. This method means examining the more powerful concepts of the economists, anthropologists, sociologists, and other specialists to see whether they can guide program development. Kliebard's third suggestion is to create metaphors that might promise new directions and theoretical constructs. Instead of using the metaphors that now dominate thinking in curriculum (for example, "production" with its technological implications and "growth" with its agricultural implications), we should experiment with alternative "root metaphors."[15]

Currently, the field of curriculum is fragmented into several conceptual camps. In his 1978 map of the field, William Pinar discriminates among the following three groups, each holding a different view of what the field should be about.[16]

Traditionalists. Traditionalists, according to Pinar, value service to practitioners in the schools above all else. He names as visible traditionalists such persons as Ralph Tyler, John McNeil, Daniel and Laurel Tanner, and Robert Zais. According to Pinar, service, defined as a response to the practical concern for curriculum matters, is more important to traditionalists than research or the development of

[14]Dwayne Huebner, "Toward a Remaking of Curricular Language," in *Heightened Consciousness, Cultural Revolution, and Curriculum Theory*, William Pinar, ed. (Berkeley, Calif.: McCutchan, 1974), pp. 36–37.

[15]Herbert Kliebard, "The Development of Certain Key Curriculum Issues in the United States," in *Curriculum Development*, Mauritz Johnson and Philip Taylor, eds. (New York: Humanities Press, 1974).

[16]William F. Pinar, "Notes on the Curriculum Field 1978," *Educational Researcher* 7, no. 8 (September 1978): 5–12.

theory. The very closeness of the relationships between traditionalists and school teachers is said to prevent them from creating
new ways of talking about curriculum which may in the future be far
more fruitful than the present orientation.

Conceptual Empiricists. These persons tend to be trained in social
science and see service to practitioners as being subsequent to
research. Their basic premise is that a scientific knowledge of human
behavior, including curriculum, is possible. They argue that their
research functions serve school practitioners and that by the creation
of a science of curriculum the traditional aspirations of the field can
be realized. They differ from traditionalists by their allegiance to
social science, rather than to practitioners, and to "kids."

Decker Walker is named a conceptual empiricist and the following
also seem to fit the category: George J. Posner, who explores the application of cognitive science to curriculum research and development; Richard E. Schutz, who applies programmatic research and
development in the preparation of instructional materials; and
Jerome Bruner, who uses theories of cognition and learning to select
aspects of the world that are to be brought into classrooms. Pinar
criticizes conceptual empiricists for producing only technical recommendations and principles based on static regularities that imply a
subtle control of human behavior.

Reconceptualists. Their fundamental view is that an intellectual
and cultural distance from curriculum practice is required for the
present in order to develop more useful comprehensive critiques and
theoretical programs. Currently, reconceptualists are preoccupied
with a critique of the field—a field they believe is too much immersed
in practical, technical modes of understanding and action. The term
reconceptualist is credited to James MacDonald, who sensed a need
for reconceiving the fundamental concerns, questions, and priorities
that give direction to curriculum as a field of inquiry. This task is in
contrast to both the prevailing intents of traditionalists, who view
their task as giving guidance and prescriptive assistance to the practitioners, and the scientists, who pursue research on curriculum
variables.

Reconceptualists include Michael Apple, who engages in
ideological and social critique; Herbert Kliebard, who illuminates the
shortcomings of curriculum as science through historical critique;
and Dwayne Huebner, who exposes technological conceptions of

curriculum through aesthetic critique. Pinar criticizes the experience of schooling through a psychoanalytic-oriented critique and devises methods by which curriculum researchers can become conscious of their own participation in frozen social and psychological structures, and their complicity in the arrested intellectual development characteristic of American schooling. Pinar recommends a method of self-analysis, for example, by means of which learners can study their own responses to educational situations by (1) recalling and describing the past and then analyzing its psychic relation to the present; (2) describing one's imagined future and analyzing its relation to the present; and (3) placing this phenomenological psychic analytic understanding of one's education in its cultural and political context.

Daniel and Laurel Tanner have responded negatively to Pinar's map of the field.[17] They see the reconceptualists as radical critics rather than curriculum theorists. They also fault Pinar's notion of the need for an intellectual and cultural distance from school practitioners in order to develop a more comprehensive and theoretical program. Citing Dewey, the Tanners argue for "some kind of vital current between the field worker and the research worker." Without this flow, the latter is not able to judge the real scope of the problem that is being addressed. The Tanners also indicate how they think traditionalists and those representing empirical-analytical sciences have contributed to curriculum's body of concepts.

Replies to the Tanners, in turn, charge that they misunderstood what Pinar is saying. Reconstructionists, for example, are not repudiating research but do regard literary criticism, art history and criticism, philosophical inquiry, and historical analysis as research and as the forms from which reconceptualists' work is derived. Intellectual and cultural distancing only means "bracketing"—the suspension of judgments about things and events—a methodological tool to aid in judging the essence of the problem to be addressed.[18]

The Need for Studies of Correlation

Status of Correlation Studies in 1969. Goodlad omitted any mention of studies during the review period that treated the effects of "concurrent" offerings. He did, however, call attention to the interest

[17]Daniel Tanner and Laurel Tanner, "Emancipation from Research: The Reconceptualist Position," *Educational Research* 8, no. 6 (June 1977): 8–12.

[18]William F. Pinar, James H. Finkelstein, and C. Ray Williams, and Maxine Greene, "Letters to the Editor," *Educational Researcher* 8, no. 9 (October 1979): 6, 24–25.

in problems of sequencing subject matters. Thus we can assume that curriculum knowledge increased very little in the areas of integration and correlation of subject matters. Instead, the period was marked by the separation of subjects and linear organizational plans within fields.

Status of Correlation Studies in 1980. The effect of correlating subject matter is currently of interest but there has been little research. This is true especially in connection with bilingual education. There is, for example, the issue of whether non-English-speaking children should be taught to read first in their native language before learning to read English. Practice is ahead of knowledge. Although several bilingual programs are under way, few studies have explored the effect of learning two languages simultaneously or the best ways to make transitions from one language to another. A notable exception is work in linguistics which suggests the importance of beginning initial instruction in a child's first language, switching at a later stage to instruction in the school language whenever the home language tends to be denigrated; but whenever the home language is highly valued, the second language is appropriate for use in initial instruction.[19] Similarly, research on the interrelationships of literature, language, composition, and popular culture lacks any unifying theory.

With respect to administrative organizational planning, there is much discussion about the value of intensive or total immersion courses, which are taken one at a time, in place of traditional concurrent courses, which are taken three, four, or five at a time throughout the term. Hundreds of schools are experimenting with intensive courses during the one month of 4-1-4 plans. Yet, appallingly little research has been undertaken on the educational effects of either intensive or concurrent courses.[20]

The Need for Studies of Sequence

Status of Studies Treating Sequence in 1969. The quest for how best to arrange material in a field was very much alive in 1969. There were many experiments with different sequences in programmed and computer-based instruction. Robert Gagné's work stimulated several

[19]Merrill Swain and James Cummins, "Bilingualism, Cognitive Functioning and Education," *Language Teaching and Linguistics,* Abstract 12, no. 1 (January 1979): 4–18.

[20]Lon Hefferlin, "Intensive Courses—A Research Need," *The Research Reporter* 11, no. 3 (1972): 1–4.

investigations to assess the effects of scrambled versus hierarchical orderings of learning tasks. The findings were mixed, indicating that increasing complexity is not always the best criterion for ordering material.

Status of Studies Treating Sequence in 1980. Current research is directed at methods for conducting inquiry into learning hierarchies. Richard White has proposed a rigorous model to overcome such shortcomings as small sample size, imprecise specification of component elements, improper placement of tests, and omission of instruction.[21] A much simpler strategy for validating hierarchies has also been demonstrated,[22] and there is some indication that models for sequential ordering may be expanded to take into account the cognitive capacities of learners.[23] The expanded models would pay more attention to the learner's point of view than to a priori units based on subject matter analysis.

The Need for Analyzing Educational Objectives

Status of Taxonomical Analysis of Objectives in 1969. The pioneer taxonomy of objectives in the cognitive domain was completed in 1956, and. taxonomies in both psychomotor and affective realms were developed after 1960. Further, there was much research treating how best to refine educational objectives into precise behavioral subobjectives. Studies of the effects of behavioral objectives on learning were also common.

Status of Taxonomical Analysis of Objectives in 1980. A more complete and in-depth study relative to the development of a classification system of the behavior within the psychomotor domain was completed in 1972.[24] The structural analysis of feelings, attitudes, values, and the like has not kept up with similar research in the areas of mental abilities and personality. There still is interest in whether the levels of behavior given in taxonomies are cumulative or

---

[21]Richard T. White, "Research Into Learning Hierarchies," *Review of Educational Research* 43, no. 3 (Summer 1973): 361–75.

[22]John D. McNeil, "False Prerequisites in the Teaching of Reading," *Journal of Reading Behavior* 6, no. 4 (Winter 1975): 421–27.

[23]Robbie Case, "Gearing the Demands of Instruction to the Development Capacities of the Learner," *Review of Educational Research* 45, no. 1 (Winter 1975): 59–87.

[24]Anita Harrow, *A Taxonomy of the Psychomotor Domain: A Guide for Developing Behavioral Objectives* (New York: David McKay, 1972).

hierarchical. George Madaus and others, for example, found that with respect to the *Taxonomy of Educational Objectives—Cognitive Domains*, synthesis and evaluation of the categories did not depend on integration with lower-level behaviors per se.[25] In his critical review of taxonomies of education objectives, Robert M.W. Travers faults the Bloom taxonomy for being chiefly an inventory of test items and not a taxonomy of cognitive processes.[26] He views Piaget's system, by which knowledge is classified in terms of formal properties, as a better potential basis for developing a taxonomy of cognitive processes. Indeed, Piaget's framework has been used in a number of curriculum projects for analyzing learning activities in terms of the logical operations they involve (Project SOAR at Xavier University of Louisiana, the STAR Program of Metropolitan State College at Denver, Project ADAPT at the University of Nebraska, and an elementary science program developed at the University of California, Berkeley).

Interest in instructional objectives has taken three directions. First, much attention is given to the rationale for such objectives. There are attempts to state their functions, such as to organize subject matter, to help learners organize their time, and to provide directions for learning. Second, there is much argument regarding the nature of behavioral objectives. Cognitively oriented persons believe that covert behavior can be stated in objectives and that overt behavior may be more important as an indicator of the covert behavior than as a valued response in itself. Growing interest in the relations between subject matter and cognitive psychology has resulted in opposition to objectives that do not take into account changes in the student's cognitive processes as well as achievement in subject matter. Examples of cognitive processes are algorithms for division or problem-solving procedures.

Kenneth Strike and George Posner, for example, are trying to develop a new view concerning how educational objectives should be described. Their view calls for matching cognitive states and processes with the logical and conceptual features which characterize organized subject matter.[27] Posner has described in detail a number

[25]George Madaus et al., "A Causal Model Analysis of Bloom's Taxonomy," *American Educational Research Journal* 10, no. 4 (Fall 1973): 253–62.

[26]Robert M.W. Travers, "Taxonomies of Educational Objectives and Theories of Classification," *Educational Evaluation and Policy Analysis* 2, no. 2 (March-April 1980): 5–23.

[27]Kenneth A. Strike and George J. Posner, "Epistemological Perspectives on Conceptions of Curriculum Organization and Learning," in *Review of Research in Education*, vol. 4, Lee S. Schulman, ed. (Itasca, Ill.: F.E. Peacock Publishers, 1976), pp. 106–41.

of approaches to specifying the cognitive structures and processes required to perform tasks.[28] Once these structures and processes are represented, curriculum planners can more adequately specify intended learning outcomes.

Third, proponents of behavioral objectives are attempting to overcome criticisms about the triviality and proliferation of specific objectives. They are trying to define domains of objectives and to find formats for stating domains that will be more useful for purposes such as test construction and classroom management than the narrow and numerous objectives found in classrooms today.

The Need for Process–Product Research

Status of Process–Product Research in 1969. Process–product research aims to relate instructional variables to learner achievement and the curriculum planning process to improved instruction and learning. Much process–product research between 1960 and 1969 dealt with instructional objectives. Most curriculum materials investigations dwelt on specific treatment variables associated with the materials (for example, organizers, relevant practice, knowledge of results, and prompts). Goodlad realized, however, that there were two problems with this research. The first was methodological. It was not always clear, for instance, what constituted the process or treatment, nor was it always established that the treatment had been carried out as stipulated. The second problem was theoretical. It was often difficult to know the significance of a small manageable process–product equation within some large frame of explanation.

Status of Process–Product Research in 1980. The methodological and theoretical problems of 1969 have not been resolved. They are, however, more widely recognized now. Research into instructional effectiveness by means of the input-output approach has not yielded consistent results. Background factors tend to dominate the findings. No single resource or variable is consistently shown to exert a powerful influence on student outcomes. Perhaps one reason for this state of affairs is the emphasis on generalizations. Instead of making the search for generalizations the ruling priority, investigators should look for unique personal characteristics and uncontrolled events in given situations. We should try to use generalizations only as work-

[28]George J. Posner, "Tools for Curriculum Research and Development: Potential Contributions from Cognitive Science," *Curriculum Inquiry* 8, no. 4 (Winter 1978): 311–40.

ing hypotheses and then look for clues to particular factors that might cause departures from the predicted effects. These factors might be *learner variables*, such as a learner's perceptions of the curriculum event, or a learner's cognitive style; *teacher variables*, such as a teacher's attitude toward the curriculum and the learners, or teacher pressure for conformity rather than for learner independence; and *school or classroom ambient variables*, such as peer group interactions, morale, expectations, and consistency with home and community values.

Two current models of the ways in which various features of schooling, including the curriculum, exert their effect are those proposed by the Swedish scholar Urban Dahllöf[29] and A. Harnischfeger and Dave Wiley.[30] Dahllöf hypothesizes that group achievement is a function of (1) general intelligence and initial achievement level; (2) the level of the objective; and (3) the time actually spent in learning what is measured. He also draws attention to *frame factors*—the characteristics of the learning environment under the direct control of school authorities (other than the individual teacher). Frame factors include class size, organization and objectives of the curriculum, length of the school year, and location of school buildings in the community. Harnischfeger and Wiley believe that all influences on pupil achievement must be mediated through a pupil's pursuits—seeing, looking, watching, hearing, listening, feeling, and touching. These pursuits control what and how one learns. The curriculum and the teacher both control and condition these pursuits but not the student's ultimate achievement.

FUTURE DIRECTIONS IN CURRICULUM THEORY

The best predictor of the future is present activity. We can predict at least two directions for curriculum theory, because there are two kinds of theorists at work, the *soft* and *hard* curricularists. In the preface to *Curriculum Theorizing*, William Pinar says that 3 to 5 percent of curriculum workers are reconceptualists.[31]

---

[29]Urban Dahllöf, *Ability Grouping, Content Validity, and Curriculum Process Analysis* (New York: Teachers College, Columbia University, 1971).

[30]A. Harnischfeger and David Wiley, "Teaching Learning Processes in Elementary School: A Synoptic View," *Curriculum Inquiry* 6, no. 1 (Fall 1976): 5–43.

[31]William Pinar, ed., *Curriculum Theorizing* (Berkeley, Calif.: McCutchan, 1975).

Their stated purpose is not to guide practitioners but to understand the internal and existential nature of the educational experience. They are called soft curricularists because they model themselves after those in the humanities, in history, religion, philosophy, and literary criticism, not the hard sciences. They include intuition and existence as sources of knowledge, not only the senses and reason. The hard curricularists follow a rational means-ends approach, relying on empirical data to justify means, and a consistent philosophical position for validating ends proposed.

The Soft Curricularists

The reconceptualists, or soft curricularists, do not study change in behavior or decision making in the classroom, but the meaning of temporality, transcendence, consciousness, and politics. Dwayne Huebner, for example, writes of temporality—existence in time—and the need for an awareness of history. He would mesh an individual's biography with the history of the individual's society so that the individual could project his or her own potentiality for being.[32] Huebner challenges curriculum workers, for example, to present historical wisdom in a way that will be useful to particular individuals at different age levels.

For another example, we can look at Philip Phenix and his regard for transcendence as the going beyond any given state. As described in chapter 1, transcendence suggests a curriculum that has regard for the uniqueness of the human personality and that is characterized by an atmosphere of freedom. Politics is very much in the minds of the soft curricularists. They are concerned about the political implications that might follow reconceptualization of curriculum theory and, in turn, curriculum development. They realize that the political climate does not now favor radical activities as it did in the 1960s, and they are divided as to the best strategy for effecting social reconstruction. Donald Bateman represents one point of view regarding the politics of curriculum. He would present what is known about the content of curriculum, stressing that it is only racism, sexism, classism, and the like.[33] Dwayne Huebner, on the other hand,

---

[32]Dwayne Huebner, "Curriculum as Concern for Man's Temporality," in *Curriculum Theorizing*, William Pinar, ed. (Berkeley, Calif.: McCutchan, 1975), pp. 237–50.

[33]Donald R. Bateman, "The Politics of Curriculum," in *Heightened Consciousness, Cultural Revolution, and Curriculum Theory*, William Pinar, ed. (Berkeley, Calif.: McCutchan, 1974).

would be less negative and shift somewhat from harsh criticism to ways of working. He suggests building civil rights legislation for children, improving organizations for the governance of institutions, and becoming better acquainted with the knowledge from which new alternatives for schooling can come.[34]

The Hard Curricularists

The study of curriculum phenomena by hard curricularists is undertaken for the immediate purpose of accurate description and for future prediction and control. Decker Walker, for example, a member of this group, has prepared a naturalistic model for curriculum development in order to illuminate facets of the curriculum development process.[35] The model is meant to be descriptive rather than prescriptive. Walker's naturalistic model assumes that the curriculum is developed in accordance with an idea or vision of what ought to be (a platform), and that a curriculum design consists of a number of decisions made in producing curriculum materials. The process by which beliefs and information are used to make these design decisions is called *deliberation*. The heart of the deliberation process is the justification of choices. Walker, as a hard curricularist, defines deliberation by logical, not social or psychological criteria. Empirical confirmations (data) are seen as a most persuasive basis for justification. Good decisions are those consistent with given platforms and available information, although a platform may be changed by the curriculum designer as the work progresses. A defensible set of objectives is the output of deliberations based on a platform. The purposes of the hard curricularist can be inferred from the five intended uses of the naturalistic model:

1. *To test propositions.* For example: Do curriculum-making groups with similar platforms conduct similar deliberations and produce similar designs and objectives?
2. *To make descriptive studies.* For example: How do the platforms of those in one subject field differ from those in other fields?
3. *To establish connections between design elements (curriculum variables) and learning outcomes.* For example: What is the effect of a specific design element on a given outcome?

---

[34]Dwayne Huebner, "Poetry and Power—The Politics of Curricular Development," in *Curriculum Theorizing*, William Pinar, ed. (Berkeley, Calif.: McCutchan, 1975), pp. 271–80.
[35]Walker, "A Naturalistic Model."

4. *To formulate new curriculum questions.* For example: What kinds of grounds should be given greater weight in justifying decisions during deliberation?

5. *To identify questions in curriculum making that will be of interest to colleagues in other fields.* For example: Just as the curriculum practitioners' treatment of discovery learning led to renewed interest in this topic by psychologists, might not other matters of importance to noncurricularists come to light through study of platforms and deliberations?

Another hard curricularist is Mauritz Johnson.[36] Johnson sees the definition of curriculum and instruction as a directive force for the theory builder. He distinguishes among curriculum, the source of curriculum, and the relation of curriculum to instruction. According to Johnson, a curriculum is the output of a curriculum development system—a structured series of intended outcomes. A curriculum is the result of curriculum development which occurs as cultural content is selected and ordered. Johnson is interested in the best way of selecting cultural content within particular realms or domains (such as vocational and general education), but has not been very successful in clarifying the criteria or in devising procedures for using them.

Johnson's position on the issue of whether objectives should follow or precede instruction is clear. He believes that curriculum should guide instruction. The restrictions of curriculum should be minimal, however, in order to allow flexibility in instructional sequencing. Johnson believes that a definition of instruction must encompass all training and instructional situations and all domains of outcomes for all kinds of learners. There must also be an intent to bring about learning. He views learning experiences as the instructional route to intended outcomes and holds that such experiences must have both active (what the learner is to do) and substantive components (what content is to be involved).

For Johnson, the curriculum restricts but does not prescribe the content and form of instructional activity. It influences instruction primarily through the mediation of an instructional plan. A curriculum does not guide all aspects of instruction or control for the spontaneity and effectiveness of discourse in the instructional act.

---

[36]Mauritz Johnson, Jr., "Definitions and Models of Curriculum Theory," in *Curriculum and Evaluation*, Arno Bellack and Herbert Kliebard, eds. (Berkeley, Calif.: McCutchan, 1977), pp. 3–25.

Although curriculum does not specify the means of evaluation, it furnishes the criteria for evaluating instructional outcomes.

Presumably the purpose of Johnson's conceptualizing is to clarify the different components in a system. Improvement can then be enhanced by focusing on the components that are deficient, whether instructional techniques, materials, instructional plans, curriculum ordering, or curriculum selection. A soft critic of Johnson's hard line might look at the language Johnson uses: "system," "detailed control tactics," "well-established rules," "review by experts," "results." The critic would assume that this technological and military-like talk with its means-ends, cause-effect structure is unlikely to answer a people's need for liberating activities.

DIRECTIONS IN CURRICULUM RESEARCH

General frameworks and specific questions for guiding inquiry in the field of curriculum have been given in prior paragraphs describing the state of the field and the trends in theoretical curriculum research. There are, however, four specific kinds of inquiry likely to be pursued by productive scholars and practitioners.

Comprehensive Curriculum Inquiry

Decker Walker believes there are only five questions to be addressed by curricularists:

1. What are the significant features of a given curriculum?
2. What are the personal and social consequences of a given curriculum feature?
3. What accounts for stability and change in curriculum features?
4. What accounts for people's judgments of the merit or worth of various curriculum features?
5. What sorts of curriculum features ought to be included in a curriculum intended for a given purpose in a given situation?

The last question requires a normative rather than an empirical answer and is not necessarily generalizable.

Walker's questions reflect his assumption that the curriculum is a practical field of study. It is expected to make a difference in someone's learning. Also, the meaning of "curriculum feature" is vague in recognition of the field's lack of consensus on conceptions of curriculum. Hence, curriculum workers of different persuasions may define curriculum features in accordance with their own purposes.[37]

Synoptic Activity as Curriculum Inquiry

As we mentioned previously, Herbert Kliebard has speculated that one direction for the curriculum field is to bring together widely separated fields into a larger common area. The curriculum person's competence may lie, not in unearthing new knowledge, but in putting together many of the findings from other disciplines. The curriculum expert can take a number of narrow perspectives and unite them by applying them in the development of school programs. Ralph Tyler agrees that curriculum development is not a science. He believes its purpose is not to obtain new knowledge but to design programs that will help students learn things that will be helpful to them and to society.[38] Tyler faulted curriculum workers for not using research from disciplines. The kinds of research borrowings that might be useful in curriculum synoptic activity are:

1. *Concepts—the transfer of training and motivation.* Tyler believes there are more concepts than anything else that can be used, yet developers of many new courses ignore such concepts in their developmental efforts.
2. *Generalizations—principles or the relations among concepts.* Tyler shares the growing concern that there are few generalizations with broad applicability. Generalizations depend on conditions that may not be present in particular school settings.
3. *Facts.* General facts are often less useful than generalizations. Particular facts have to be collected for each situation.
4. *Methods.* Problem-solving procedures can be borrowed from disciplines and used in facing curriculum problems.
5. *Attitudes—skepticism.* A commitment to truth, to finding out the facts, even though they are unpopular, can be adopted for use in facing our real dilemmas.

Examples of synoptic activity in curriculum, illustrating the contributions of different subject matter fields to curriculum development, are found in: *the use of anthropology* in planning curriculum for an

---

[37]Decker Walker, "What Are the Problems Curricularists Ought to Study?" *Curriculum Theory Network* 4, nos. 2–3 (1974): 217–18.

[38]Ralph W. Tyler, "Utilizing Research in Curriculum Development," *Theory Into Practice* 13, no. 1 (February 1974): 5–11.

inner city ghetto when the concept of culture was taken from the research of anthropologists and put into use in guiding curriculum development in a different way; *the use of social psychology* with its concepts about peer group learning in the selection of learning opportunities; *the use of personality psychology* and its notion of human needs and the self in designing curriculum, particularly in the areas of moral and character education; *the use of sociology* and its concepts of social class, social mobility, and the descriptions of life in terms of these concepts to suggest new objectives for the schools; and *the use of learning* and its concepts and findings about the learning process for developing any curriculum and instructional program. Synoptic activity is predicated on our willingness to question what our curriculum is doing and what we know about the changes we propose. It means using research from many sources, including historical research, in guiding our efforts.

Conceptualization as Curriculum Inquiry

There are many signs that conceptualization in the curriculum field will continue. Louise Tyler, for instance, is adding to the view that curriculum decisions occur at societal, institutional, and classroom levels by specifying a *personal* level and spelling out in some detail the nature of personal decision making. She has, for example, contrasted an aspect of curriculum decision making at the four levels in terms of psychoanalytic constructs, such as *transference* (the projection upon another of the attitudes and responses attached to an emotionally significant person), indicating and explaining the dimensions of thought and feeling a student might experience in responding to learning situations and to the problem of revealing what has been learned.[39]

The opportunities for inquiry at the level of the personal domain are great. There is need to know, for instance, about the meaning of the various subjects as experienced by students at different developmental levels; what school means to children; what students fear in the school setting; and the functions of jokes and humor and the meaning of play.

Other curriculum persons are trying to conceptualize curriculum to take into account the *inward* experience of students reacting to

[39]Louise L. Tyler, "A Note on Evaluation from a Psychoanalytic Perspective: Loss of Innocence," *The Reiss Davis Clinic Bulletin* 11, no. 1 (Summer 1974): 49–59; Louise L. Tyler and John Goodlad, "The Personal Domain: Curricular Meaning," in *Curricular Inquiry* (New York: McGraw-Hill, 1979), pp. 191–209.

their educational environment. George Willis, for example, is grappling with all manner of speculative, analytic, and empirical studies in an effort to conceive how students develop meaning from their educational environment and how these environments can enhance the quality of experience for the individual.[40]

Action Research as Curriculum Inquiry

In action research practitioners put the findings of research into effect in order to resolve their own areas of need. Practitioners use action research in attempting to study their problems systematically. The value of such research is not determined by the discovery of scientific laws or generalizations but by whether or not the application leads to improvement in practice.

In the mid-1950s, teachers began using action research to improve their curricula. Gordon MacKenzie, Stephen Corey, and Hilda Taba were among those curriculum specialists who involved teachers in the research process. Teachers under their direction accumulated evidence to define their problems, drew on experience and knowledge to form action hypotheses to improve the situation of their daily work, tested promising procedures, and accumulated evidence of their effectiveness. The rationale and technical procedures for conducting such research is still available from several sources.[41]

Three forces aborted the growth of action research. First, the academic curriculum reform of the 1960s put little emphasis on local development of curriculum. Standardization was prized over uniqueness. Second, educational researchers in universities, who in the 1950s might have been willing to work with teachers in curriculum inquiry, found themselves in the 1960s attending instead to the interests of government agencies that were funding certain kinds of research. Third, many persons in the 1960s believed that problems of curriculum and instruction would best be resolved by the discovery and application of generalizations and laws of learning, not by individual teachers in unique situations.

[40]George Willis, "Curriculum Theory and the Context of Curriculum," in *Curriculum Theorizing*, William Pinar, ed. (Berkeley, Calif.: McCutchan, 1975), pp. 427–42.
[41]Association for Supervision and Curriculum Development, *Research for Curriculum Development* (Washington, D.C.: ASCD, 1957); Stephen M. Corey, *Action Research to Improve School Practice* (New York: Teachers College, Columbia University, 1953).

Currently, there is a return to recognizing teachers (as well as students and persons who are not directly involved in the school) as theorists and researchers in their own right. There are signs of a shift of responsibility for curriculum development from colleges and laboratories to classrooms and communities. We can expect again to see scholarly efforts aimed at helping teachers rather than at the production of research for fellow scholars.

The curriculum worker who is interested in trying to synthesize learner, subject matter, teacher, and total environment would find action research literature of the 1950s useful. Important, too, is John Dewey's advice about how knowledge can enter the heart, head, and hands of educators. In his *Sources of a Science of Education*, Dewey made these points among others:[42]

1. An inquirer can repeat the research of another, to confirm or discredit it. Moreover, by using this technique the inquirer discovers new problems and new investigations that refine old procedures and lead to new and better ones.
2. No conclusion of scientific research can be converted into an immediate rule for educators. Educational practice contains many conditions and factors that are not included in the scientific finding.
3. Although scientific findings should not be used as a rule of action, they can help teachers be alert to discover certain factors that would otherwise be unnoticed and to interpret something that would otherwise be misunderstood.
4. The practitioner who knows a science (a system) can see more possibilities and opportunities, and has a wide range of alternatives to select from in dealing with individual situations.
5. In education, practice should form the problems of inquiry. The worth of a scientific finding is only shown when it serves an educational purpose, and whether it really serves or not can only be found in practice.
6. Research persons connected with school systems may be too close to the practical problems and the university professor too far away from them to secure the best results.
7. Problems that require treatment arise in relations with students. Consequently, it is impossible to see how there can be an adequate investigation unless teachers actively participate.

[42]John Dewey, *The Sources of a Science of Education* (New York: Horace Liveright, 1929).

Perhaps the most eloquent argument for action research as a form of curriculum inquiry is found in John Dewey's answer to the question of how educational objectives are to be determined. He thought it false to say that social conditions, science, or the subject matter of any field could determine objectives. Indeed, he conceived of education as a process of discovering what values are worthwhile and to be pursued as objectives.

> To see what is going on and to observe the results of what goes on so as to see their future consequences in the process of growth, and so on indefinitely, is the only way in which the value of what takes place can be judged. To look at some outside source to provide aims is to fail to know what education is as an ongoing process. . . .
>
> Knowledge of the objectives which society actually strives for and the consequences actually attained may be had in some measure through a study of the social sciences. This knowledge may render educators more circumspect, more critical, as to what they are doing. It may inspire better insight into what is going on here and now in the home or school; it may enable teachers and parents to look farther ahead and judge on the basis of consequences in a longer course of development. But it must operate through their own ideas, plannings, observations, judgments. Otherwise it is not *educational* science at all, but merely so much sociological information.[43]

CONCLUDING COMMENTS

In this chapter, the state of the curriculum field was appraised by reviewing the status of curriculum research in six crucial areas. Appraisal of work in curriculum theory is characterized by divisiveness among traditionalists, scientists, and reconceptualists. There is concern about a lack of common ground of professional action and responsibility. The status of conceptual systems for identifying major curriculum questions is changing in the direction of giving more attention to the role of the learner as a decision maker in curriculum, the impact of social political forces in curriculum making, and curriculum criticism as a mode of inquiry in its own right. Although there has been little research in correlated studies, much activity is aimed at showing how best to arrange material for effective learning. Work in educational objectives, which has dominated much of curriculum thought and practice, is now being extended to how to construct tests that will reveal reasons for the learner's inabil-

[43]Ibid., pp. 74–76.

ity to utilize knowledge and the relation between the subject matter of objectives and the cognitive processes and structure that underlie competent performance.

With respect to the methodological and theoretical problems associated with process-product research, there are two apparently conflicting trends: (1) acceptance of opportunity to learn and time in instruction as the key variables in designing means to *minimal* ends and (2) recognition that no single variable will consistently exert a powerful or predictable influence on student outcomes.

Future directions in curriculum theory promise to be fruitful. The soft curricularists are drawing our attention to both the political and moral aspects of curriculum making. The hard curricularists have posed specific propositions to be tested that will greatly contribute to our understanding of curriculum making as a process. Anyone wishing to do research in the curriculum field should be greatly helped by the guidance of those advocating comprehensive curriculum inquiry, synoptic activity, conceptualization, and action research. All in all, there is plenty of evidence that the curriculum field is not moribund, but very much alive.

QUESTIONS

1. How are the categories of traditionalists, conceptual empiricists, and reconceptualists related to humanistic, academic, technological, and social reconstructionist conceptions of curriculum? Are reconstructionists contributing to both humanistic and social reconstructionist curriculum? In what way are conceptual empiricists advancing technological and academic curriculum?
2. In which of the six curriculum concerns used to appraise the status of curriculum research is there the least progress? What might account for the difference in progress? Are all the concerns or problems solvable?
3. Do you think the curriculum reconceptualists are sincere in saying that they are not interested now in guiding practitioners but are only trying to understand the meaning of the educational experience? Why or why not?
4. The classroom teacher in the early 1980s is likely to feel more pressure to be productive in curriculum and instruction. Which of the research directions given in this chapter do you think will be of greatest help to the teacher in responding to this pressure?
5. Try to give examples of the language used in your discussions of curriculum? In what way are conceptual empiricists advancing technological and academic curriculum?

ment, style, imagery). What consequences might the use of this language have in your treatment of problems in curriculum inquiry?

6. Do you regard synoptic activity, action research, and conceptualization as mutually exclusive areas of research? Why or why not?

7. Donald Chipley at Pennsylvania State University has identified three basic reasons for undertaking curriculum research. One of these purposes is to make an inventory of the content that is offered and the resources that are invested in particular educational developments. Another purpose is personal curiosity. An investigator has an interest in exploring new ideas and extending generalizable knowledge about curriculum relationships. The third purpose is decision making. One assesses various curriculum alternatives in order to make more rational decisions in particular situations. Which of these motives is closest to your own?

SELECTED REFERENCES

Goodlad, John I. and associates. *Curriculum Inquiry: The Study of Curriculum Practice*. New York: McGraw-Hill, 1979.

Herrick, Virgil and Tyler, Ralph, eds. *Toward Improved Curriculum Theory*. Chicago: University of Chicago Press, 1950.

McNeil, John D. "Curriculum—A Field Shaped by Different Faces," *Educational Researcher* 7, no. 8 (September 1978): 19–23.

Musgrave, P.W., ed. *Contemporary Studies in the Curriculum*. Sydney, Australia: Angus and Robertson, 1974.

Pinar, William, ed. *Curriculum Theorizing—The Reconceptualists*. Berkeley, Calif.: McCutchan, 1975.

——. "Notes on the Curriculum Field 1978," *Educational Researcher* 7, no. 8 (September 1978): 5–12.

Short, Edmund C. "Knowledge Production and Utilization in Curriculum: A Special Case of the General Phenomenon," *Review of Educational Research* 43, no. 3 (Summer 1973): 237–303.

Walker, Decker F. "Toward Comprehension of Curricular Realities," in *Review of Research in Education*, vol. 4, Lee S. Schulman, ed. Itasca, Ill.: F.E. Peacock Publishers, 1976, pp. 268–308.

INDEX